Shari'a-compliant Microfinance

In the recent past, Islamic finance has made an impressive case on the banking scene by becoming an alternative to the popular conventional financial systems, spurring a lively academic debate on how the Islamic finance industry can expand its services to cover the poor. Several propositions have been aired that suggest that the Islamic finance industry should consider developing an efficient *shari'a*-compliant microfinance model.

This book brings together original contributions from leading authorities on the subject of *shari'a*-compliant microfinance (Islamic microfinance) to propose innovative solutions and models by carefully studying experiments conducted in various countries. Where critiques of the current microfinance concepts, methods, regulatory measures and practices have often revolved around its practice of charging very high interest, this book discusses the several models that draw on both theory and case studies to provide a sustainable *shari'a*-compliant alternative. Arguing that while Islamic finance might have made a remarkable contribution in the financial markets, there remains a big question with regards to its social relevance; the book provides new perspectives and innovative solutions to issues facing the Islamic microfinance industry.

A comprehensive reference book for anyone wanting to learn more about *shari'a*-compliant microfinance, this book will also be of use to students and scholars of microfinance, Islamic finance and to anyone interested in learning about ethical and socially responsible businesses.

S. Nazim Ali is the Founding Director of the Islamic Finance Project and Acting Executive Director of the Islamic Legal Studies Program at Harvard Law School, Harvard University. For the last 25 years, his research and professional activities have concentrated on Islamic banking and finance.

Routledge Islamic Studies Series

This broad ranging series includes books on Islamic issues from all parts of the globe and is not simply confined to the Middle East.

Shari'a-compliant Microfinance

Edited by
S. Nazim Ali

LONDON AND NEW YORK

First published 2012
by Routledge
2 Park Square, Milton Park, Abingdon, Oxon OX14 4RN

Simultaneously published in the USA and Canada
by Routledge
711 Third Avenue, New York, NY 10017

Routledge is an imprint of the Taylor & Francis Group, an Informa business

British Library Cataloguing in Publication Data
A catalogue record for this book is available from the British Library

Library of Congress Cataloging in Publication Data
Shari'a complaint microfinance / edited by S. Nazim Ali.
  p. cm. — (Routledge Islamic studies : 16)
  Includes bibliographical references and index.
  1. Microfinance. 2. Finance (Islamic law) I. Ali, S. Nazim.
  HG178.3.S53 2011
  322—dc22
  2011003878

ISBN 978–0–415–78266–1 (hbk)
ISBN 978–0–203–80883–2 (ebk)

Typeset in Baskerville
by Swales & Willis Ltd, Exeter, Devon

Printed and bound in Great Britain by the MPG Books Group

Contents

   institutions: financially mainstreaming the microenterprise   81
   ALI ADNAN IBRAHIM

8 Re-thinking leasing from an interest-free perspective:
   exploring the prospects of Islamic microleasing for poverty
   alleviation   129
   ASAD KAMRAN GHALIB

PART III
Islamic microfinance case studies   145

9 Islamic microfinance in Indonesia: the challenge of
   institutional diversity, regulation and supervision   147
   HANS DIETER SEIBEL

10 Islamic microfinance in crisis countries: the unofficial
    developmental discourse   170
    M. SIRAJ SAIT

11 Minority funds in India: institutional mobilizing of
    micro savings   181
    SHARIQ NISAR AND SYED MIZANUR RAHMAN

12 Innovations in Islamic microfinance: lessons from
    Muslim Aid's Sri Lankan experiment   206
    MOHAMMED OBAIDULLAH AND AMJAD MOHAMED-SALEEM

PART IV
Resources on Islamic microfinance   217

13 Information sources on Islamic microfinance: a critical
    literature review   219
    ISLAMIC FINANCE PROJECT STAFF

    Annotated bibliography   232

    Appendix 1—Financing the poor: towards an Islamic
    microfinance—a short report   264

    Appendix 2—Microfinance: towards a sustainable Islamic
    finance model—a short report   268

    Glossary   272
    Bibliography   275
    Index   288

Illustrations

Figures

Tables

Contributors

Habib Ahmed

Sharjah Chair in Islamic Law and Finance, School of Government and International Affairs, Durham University, Durham, United Kingdom.

Prior to this he was with National Commercial Bank, Jeddah and an Economist, Islamic Research and Training Institute, Islamic Development Bank Group, Jeddah, Saudi Arabia.

Ahmed has studied in Bangladesh, Norway and the USA. He received his Ph.D. in Economics from the University of Connecticut. Before joining Islamic Research and Training Institute of the Islamic Development Bank Group as an Economist in 1999, he taught at University of Connecticut, National University of Singapore and University of Bahrain. He has more than 50 publications, which include articles in international refereed journals, research papers/monographs and books. His current research interests are Islamic economics and finance. His recent publications in Islamic economics and finance include the book *Product Development in Islamic Banks*; the journal article "Islamic Law, Adaptability, and Financial Development"; and the book chapter "The Islamic Financial System and Economic Development: An Assessment." He has also published the following research booklets: "Operational Structure of Islamic Equity Finance: Lessons from Venture Capital"; "Role of *Zakat* and *Awqaf* in Poverty Alleviation, A Microeconomic Model of an Islamic Bank"; "Exchange Rate Stability: Theory and Policies from an Islamic Perspective"; "Corporate Governance in Islamic Financial Institutions" (with Umer M. Chapra); and "Risk Management: An Analysis of Issues in Islamic Financial Industry" (with Tariqullah Khan).

S. Nazim Ali

Founding Director, Islamic Finance Project (IFP), and *Acting Executive Director*, Islamic Legal Studies Program, Harvard Law School, Harvard University, Cambridge, MA.

Ali is the founding director of the IFP, Harvard Law School, which was first established as the Harvard Islamic Finance Information Program in 1995 at the Center for Middle Eastern Studies, Harvard University. For the last 20 years, Ali's research and professional activities have concentrated on Islamic banking and finance. Most noteworthy among his contributions to the field are the IFP

DataBank (first launched as a CD-ROM in 1997, now available online) and the Harvard University Forum on Islamic Finance, with the proceedings compiled under his supervision. The most recently published title of this series is Integrating Islamic Finance into the Mainstream. As IFP director, Ali has been actively involved with several government agencies; most notably the US Treasury, the Federal Reserve Bank of New York and several central banks in various countries to create better understanding of Islamic finance and remove misconceptions about the Islamic finance industry. Ali received a Ph.D. from the University of Strathclyde, Glasgow, United Kingdom.

Samer Badawi

Formerly *Program Officer*, Consultative Group to Assist the Poor (CGAP), Washington, DC.

Samer Badawi is an international development consultant and communications advisor with regional expertise in the Arab world. He worked on several microfinance initiatives, including for the chapter in this book, with CGAP, a global resource center for microfinance whose members represent the bulk of public investment supporting financial services for the poor. He has served as a communications consultant for USAID programs in Egypt, Iraq and Afghanistan and as Washington correspondent for the London-based Middle East International, which named him one of its "most respected" contributors. He has appeared on CNN, MSNBC, Al Jazeera and Pacifica.

Asad Kamran Ghalib

Research Associate, Brooks World Poverty Institute, the University of Manchester, UK.

Asad Kamran Ghalib comes predominantly from a banking and financial services background and has been associated with a number of organizations around the world in the development, research, not-for-profit, financial and banking services industry for a period spanning over a decade. He has previously been associated with The Royal Bank of Scotland, National Westminster Bank, HSBC, Grameen Bank, United Nations Development Programme's International Policy Centre for Inclusive Growth, Brazil, United Nations University World Institute for Development Economics Research, Helsinki, and the Centre for Policy Studies, Central European University, Budapest. Asad earned his doctorate in Development Policy and Management from the Institute for Development Policy and Management, School of Environment and Development, University of Manchester, UK, and holds an M.Sc. in Management and Information Systems: Change and Development from the University of Manchester.

Wafik Grais

Chairman and Managing Director, Viveris Mashrek, Cairo.

Wafik Grais is co-founder and chairman of Viveris Mashrek, a Cairo-based financial advisory services company specialized in private equity investments in small and medium enterprises (SMEs), licensed by Egypt's Financial Services

Authority. He is special adviser to the president of Viveris Management, a long-established French private equity firm specialized in SMEs and Viveris Mashrek's co-founder. Previously, he spent 28 years in international finance notably with the World Bank in Washington, DC where he held several senior positions both at front office and corporate levels. He worked on the Middle East and North Africa (MENA), Europe and Central Asia, and East Asia. He was senior adviser in the Financial Sector group, head of the Financial Sector Assessment Program, lead resource on Islamic financial services, director of the private sector development and finance group for MENA, division chief of country operations for Ukraine, Belarus, Moldova, Georgia and Armenia after holding the same position on the Maghreb countries. Earlier, he managed the International Bank for Reconstruction and Development economic policy, dialogue and lending activities with the former Yugoslavia. In 1997 and 1998, he was part of the team setting up the Bank for Cooperation and Development in the Middle East and North Africa in Cairo, representing the government of Egypt. Wafik Grais holds a Ph.D. in economics, a Licence ès sciences économiques and a Licence ès science politique from the University of Geneva, Switzerland. He is fluent in English, French and Arabic.

Ali Adnan Ibrahim
Vice President, Al Baraka Banking Group, Manama, State of Bahrain.

Ali Adnan Ibrahim is an expert of Islamic finance and capital markets in the Muslim world. He is currently a Vice President at the Al Baraka Banking Group in Bahrain. Before joining Al Baraka, he was a Counsel at the law firm of Baker & McKenzie. He is also an Adjunct Professor of Law at Georgetown University Law Center and a Co-Chair of Islamic Finance Committee of the American Bar Association. Dr. Ibrahim holds a Doctor of Juridical Sciences degree from the Georgetown University Law Center, an LL.M. from Washington University in Saint Louis and an LL.B. (Hons) from International Islamic University, Islamabad. Dr. Ibrahim has a number of international publications to his credits on various issues of Islamic finance.

Amjad Mohamed-Saleem
Country Director, Muslim Aid Sri Lanka and Bangladesh Field Offices.

Amjad Mohamed-Saleem is a freelance writer and consultant on development issues. He is also the founder of Paths2People, an internet-based network of development professionals. He was formerly the country director of Muslim Aid in Sri Lanka where he was involved in post-tsunami and conflict reconstruction work from 2005–2009. He also ran the Bangladesh operations from 2006–2008.

Shariq Nisar
Director, Research and Operations, Taqwaa Advisory and Shariah Investment Solutions Pvt Ltd (TASIS), Bangalore, India.

Shariq Nisar earned his Ph.D. in Economics specializing in Islamic finance from Aligarh Muslim University. Today, he is among the senior most professionals of Islamic finance in India and is closely associated with both the academia as well as the industry in the country. He has pioneered *shari'a* screening of stocks in India and has been associated with some of the landmark *shari'a*-compliant deals here. He is also closely associated with academic activities wherein he focuses on Islamic finance education, research and training. He has structured Islamic finance courses for various universities and colleges and has been invited by various institutions to speak on Islamic finance in various countries including USA, Malaysia, Indonesia, Sri Lanka, Bangladesh, Iran and United Arab Emirates etc. Currently Dr. Shariq is working as Director of Research and Operations for India's premier *shari'a* advisory firm, TASIS. Shariq Nisar is a regular contributor in the planning of events and conferences at Harvard IFP. He was one of the speakers at its biennial Harvard University Forum on Islamic Finance.

Mohammed Obaidullah
Senior Economist, Islamic Research and Training Institute of the Islamic Development Bank (IDB).

Prior to joining IDB in November 2006, he served the Islamic Economics Research Center, King Abdulaziz University, Jeddah, Saudi Arabia and taught at the International Islamic University Malaysia as an Associate Professor. In 1999 he founded IBF Net: The Islamic Business and Finance Network and the International Institute of Islamic Business and Finance in India. He currently serves the International Association for Islamic Economics as its Secretary General. He has authored three books and over 30 research papers. His areas of interest include Islamic finance, security markets and development finance.

Syed Mizanur Rahman
Consultant, TASIS, Bangalore, India.

Syed Mizanur Rahman has a Postgraduate Diploma in Management from Indian Institute of Management, Ahmedabad. Prior to this, he finished his Bachelors in Computer Science from RV College, Bangalore. He is currently working with Dr. Shariq Nisar on a study covering Muslim funds operating in northern India and a few other interest-free financing projects. Interested in finding serious alternatives to conventional financing, Syed is involved in studying the challenges that institutions face in adopting alternative routes to generate financial resources while avoiding interest and the other namesake solutions available in the market. Syed has recently undertaken a very important work to revamp Harvard IFP website (http://ifp.law.harvard.edu) and the DataBank, which contains over 10,000 records on the field of Islamic finance and economics. He is coordinating this effort in Bangalore with a team of professionals to redesign its user interface.

M. Siraj Sait
Reader, University of Eastern London, London, United Kingdom.

M. Siraj Sait is a Reader in Law and co-director of the Centre for Innovative Land Rights at the University of East London, where he heads the Human Rights Programme and the Programme on Islamic and Middle Studies. He has been a consultant to United Nations High Commissioner for Refugees, UNICEF and recently served as the legal officer, Land and Tenure Section, Shelter Branch at the UN-HABITAT headquarters in Nairobi, Kenya, where he was also the gender officer for the Global Land Tool Network and the focal point for Women's Land Link Africa. Sait has been a consultant for Minority Rights Group International and a trustee of the Commonwealth Human Rights Initiative. A graduate of Madras University (India), London University, and Harvard Law School, he served as Supreme Court-appointed Commissioner on Forced Labour, State Prosecutor on Civil Rights, and Legal Advisor to Government in India. His recent publications include *Land, Law & Islam: Property and Human Rights in the Muslim World*; *Policy Makers Guide to Women's Land, Property and Housing Rights*; and *Mechanism for Gendering Land Tools*. He is currently working with H. Lim on developing the Islamic Tools Initiative in partnership with the Global Land Tool Network.

Hans Dieter Seibel

Professor of Sociology and Head of the Development Research Center at Cologne University, Germany.

Hans Dieter Seibel specializes on rural and micro-finance, agricultural development bank reform and small enterprise development. From 1999–2001, he was the Rural Finance Advisor at the International Fund for Agricultural Development in Rome and authored its Rural Finance Policy. From 1988–1991, Seibel was the GTZ team leader of Linking Banks and Self-Help Groups (SHGs) in Indonesia, which was adopted and adapted in various countries including India where 1.6 million savings-based SHGs have been credit linked to 36,000 banking units. Professor Seibel has published some 30 books and over 200 articles.

Saif I. Shah Mohammed

Law School, Columbia University, New York.

Saif I. Shah Mohammed spent 2005–2006 in Bangladesh, where he was one of the principal architects of the $180 million BRAC micro-credit securitization, the world's first securitization of micro-credit receivables. The transaction received International Financing Review Asia's Securitization of the Year 2006 award. Prior to his time in Bangladesh, Saif worked as an economic and litigation consultant in Boston. He graduated from Harvard University in 2002 with a degree in Economics, and completed his J.D. from Columbia University School of Law in 2009. He currently works at Cleary Gottlieb Steen & Hamilton LL.P. in New York. While at Harvard, he was a Research Assistant at the Harvard Islamic Finance Information Program.

Hussam Sultan

Manager, Fajr Capital Ltd, Dubai, United Arab Emirates.

Hussam Sultan works as a manager for Fajr Capital Ltd, an Islamic investment company based in Dubai. Prior to that he worked for HSBC Amanah as Business Development Manager, Product Development Manager and finally as a manager in the Central Shariah Group. While at HSBC Amanah, Hussam led the team that put together the first Islamic microfinance initiative to be launched by a global financial institution. Hussam is a graduate of Engineering from University College London, UK. He also holds a Postgraduate Diploma in Islamic Banking and Insurance from the Institute of Islamic Banking and Insurance and the Islamic Finance Qualification (IFQ) from the Securities and Investment Institute, UK. Hussam is an active participant in a number of Islamic finance and economics forums and is also an experienced writer, with over 100 published articles in various Arabic and English publications. Hussam is keen researcher in Islamic subjects and is fluent in both English and Arabic.

Rodney Wilson

Professor of Economics and Director, Center for Islamic Finance, Durham University, Durham, United Kingdom.

Rodney Wilson is Professor of Economics and Director of the Center for Islamic Finance at Durham University. He has served as a Visiting Professor at the Qatar Faculty of Islamic Studies, the Universities of Kuwait, Paris X and the International University of Japan. His research interests include Islamic economics and finance, Middle Eastern political economy and the political economy of oil and gas. He is the co-author of *Islamic Economics: A Short History* (2006) and *Economic Development in Saudi Arabia* (2004). His academic work has been published extensively in numerous journals including the *Thunderbird International Business Review*, *British Journal of Middle Eastern Studies*, *Middle Eastern Studies* and *Islamic Studies*. He obtained his B.Sc. and his Ph.D. from Queens University, Belfast.

Muhammad Anas Zarka

Senior Advisor, Shura Sharia Consultancy, Kuwait.

Muhammad Anas Zarka is currently a Senior Advisor at Shura for Sharia Consultation Group in Safat, Kuwait. Prior to that he was an advisor to The International Investor, Kuwait. He received his LL.B. (Hons) from Damascus University in 1960 and his M.A. and Ph.D. in Economics in 1963 and 1969 from the University of Pennsylvania. Zarka keeps in close touch with Islamic *fiqh* scholars and academics and had intensive tutoring in Islamic *fiqh* from his late father Sheikh Mustafa al-Zarka, a renowned *shari'a* scholar. After working for six years at the State Planning Commission, Syria, he joined King Abdul Aziz University, Jeddah, as a Professor at the Centre for Research in Islamic Economics in 1976. In 2000, he joined The International Investor, Kuwait, as a consultant and member of the Shari'a Group. His many papers in Arabic and English, published in scholarly journals and conference proceedings, focus on topics bordering economics, *fiqh* and finance. In 1990, he received the IDB Prize in Islamic Economics. Zarka is a member of the editorial advisory boards of *Islamic Economic Studies* and *Review of Islamic Economics*, and since 2002, of the Shari'a Criteria Committee of the Accounting and Auditing Organization for Islamic Financial Institutions, Bahrain.

Preface

After the two Harvard-sponsored conferences on Islamic microfinance, it occurred to me that a compilation of the papers that were presented could make a useful book. The purpose of those two conferences was to bring together talent from the microfinance industry and professionals from the Islamic finance industry to spur a discussion and the challenges surrounding the implementation of *shari'a*-compliant microfinance initiatives.

Islamic finance, though endowed with a core foundational goal of social justice and the eradication of interest, is seen by many as an option primarily for the rich and not for the common man. This belief has further been strengthened with Islamic finance institutions not actively participating in microfinance activities. Despite these beliefs, one can imagine an organic relationship between Islamic finance and microfinance given the fact that charitable work is embedded into Islamic ethics and doctrines.

Microfinance, especially Islamic microfinance, has not demonstrated successes as a financial tool in helping to reduce poverty and encouraging economic growth in often-neglected rural areas. However, most microfinance institutions have a high fee, some organizations have justified their fee structure through various models, e.g., charges for providing monitoring, supervision, advice and insurance services. It should be noted though that in principle both Islamic finance and microfinance have a noble goal of ensuring economic justice.

In order to provide a proper landscape of *shari'a*-compliant microfinance, a few more papers other than the conference papers were solicited. This was done in order to bring representatives from both the Islamic finance industry and the microfinance sector to discuss the role of the Islamic finance industry in expanding financial services access to the poor. This could be achieved through the existing microfinance organizations or the development of new *shari'a*-compliant microfinance organizations.

A partnership between the Islamic finance and microfinance industries to serve the poor, particularly in Muslim economies, can be mutually beneficial—and ultimately beneficial in the battle against poverty.

Though Islamic banking is starting to show a keen interest in microfinance, we still lack any major breakthroughs or initiatives that have created *shari'a*-compliant microfinance models. Part I of this monograph deals with this issue of microfinance and its compatibility with *shari'a* standards, and includes a discussion of organizational models for Islamic microfinance and suggestions for meeting the demand for sustainable *shari'a*-compliant microfinance. Developments in Islamic microfinance, such as leveraging philanthropy monetary *waqf* for microfinance are discussed in Part II.

From Indonesia to the Sudan, people are experimenting with microfinance initiatives as a means to alleviate poverty and encourage economic growth in a sustainable model. Though microfinance has been criticized for charging high interest rates to its rather poor clientele, it is a financial tool with proven successes that has encouraged economic growth in rural and oft-neglected areas. Part III investigates these case studies and plans that reveal both the problems and successes gained from microfinance programs in the Islamic world. Through this discussion, we hope to examine the manner in which microfinance products can become viable within the Islamic finance industry. Finally, Islamic microfinance resources are briefly discussed in Part IV of the monograph.

The initial assistance on the compilation of this monograph was provided by Yousra Fazili, A.M. '09 and Nadiah Wan, A.B. '07. Due to their relocation and their personal commitments they were not able to continue working on this project. However, the bulk of the initial work was performed with their assistance, for which I am very grateful. Later on, a number of individuals have assisted me with the project, most noteworthy being Mudiurasul Hassan, A.B. '12, who worked very hard with me in streamlining and editing the papers as well as in preparing the introduction.

The last part of the book resources on Islamic microfinance was initiated in 2007 and has continued until today. A number of individuals were involved in this compilation; a special mention goes to Arsalan Suleman, J.D. '07, Daniel Jou, A.B. '08, Hassaan Yousuf, A.B. '12, Sarah Akhtar, A.B. '12, Neha Tahir (Visiting Researcher from Stanford University), Nima Hassan, A.B. '14 and Nimra Karim (formerly with Consultative Group to Assist the Poor). Also, special thanks should go to Taha Abdul-Basser, A.B. '96; M.A. '02 for checking the Glossary and to all Islamic Finance Project researchers who have helped in the compilation of the annotated bibliography on Islamic microfinance that we hope that the readers will find it to be useful.

It is noteworthy to mention the support and encouragement that I received from Professor Baber Johansen, the former Director of Islamic Legal Studies Program (ILSP) at Harvard Law School and Dr. Peri Bearman, the former Associate Director of ILSP. Not to forget, my sincere thanks go to Samuel L. Hayes, Professor Emeritus at Harvard Business School and Mahmoud El-Gamal, Professor at Rice University, who moderated the conferences. Finally, I would like to thank the following individuals for their advice and assistance in organizing the conferences on microfinance: Professor M. Nejatullah Siddiqi, Shaykh Nizam Yaquby, Husam El-Khatib and to all those who were involved whom I have not mentioned in person.

S. Nazim Ali
Acting Executive Director, Islamic Legal Studies Program
Director, Islamic Finance Project
Harvard Law School

Introduction

S. Nazim Ali

Since the efforts of Muhammad Yunus and the Grameen Bank in Bangladesh, the world of microfinance has flourished. Today, microfinance is deemed to be an integral part of the global financial system, with over 1,400 microfinance institutions (MFIs) listed on the Microfinance Information Exchange (MIX) database. The Islamic finance industry, which shares with microfinance a commitment to the principles of social equality and justice, is also projected to experience high trajectory growth.

Although the fields of Islamic finance and microfinance largely overlap in their social objectives, Islamic finance institutions are yet to make significant forays into the sphere of microfinance. It is widely accepted that the main purpose of Islamic finance is to enable *shari'a*-compliant financial activity—and indeed, the field has shown great strides in its *shari'a* compliance. However, the field has also developed a reputation as a banking system for the rich that holds little relevance for the poorest segments of society. This contradicts what most consider to be the guiding principle of Islamic finance: reducing poverty and encouraging the equitable distribution of resources.

In this regard, microfinance may offer insights into improving the field of Islamic finance. Microfinance exists to provide resources for the extremely poor whilst stimulating local economies. Despite its general success, an argument against this type of financing is mainly directed at the exorbitant interest rates that are at times applied to "micro loans." While there are profitable considerations in applying such rates, conventional microfinance is, nonetheless, deemed non-compliant with *shari'a* for such usury.

Many have questioned whether it is possible, then, to merge the two industries so the benefits of each industry compensate for the weaknesses of the other. Proponents of Islamic microfinance argue that not having a *shari'a*-compliant option reduces opportunities for furthering the growth of microfinance in new markets. In other words, a synergy between microfinance and Islamic finance may enable the financing of segments of society that lean towards microfinancing based on *shari'a*. On the other hand, critics counter that the focus on making microfinance *shari'a*-compliant detracts from the main goal of providing resources to poor entrepreneurs—the real concern should be with helping the poor in the best way possible. The debate then becomes one that asks: is there an ethical dilemma in encouraging Islamic microfinancing or entrepreneurship that may have impermissible (*haram*) elements? Will borrowers prefer Islamic financing over conventional financing for the sake of complying with their religious beliefs or are we inventing a market of demand? Are these two models so vastly different that we must forge a new "Islamic" path?

The Islamic Finance Project (IFP) at Harvard University has proudly promoted academic inquiry in the field of Islamic microfinance and the discussion of such questions. Our first symposium on "Financing the Poor Towards an Islamic Microfinance" was held in 2007 while another symposium entitled "Microfinance Towards a Sustainable Islamic Finance Model" was held the following year. Several other events have provided a forum for academics, practitioners and *shari'a* scholars to discuss the role of Islamic finance for economic development, such as the special lecture held by Jaffrey Sachs on "Economic Development and the Muslim World." Appendix 1 provides a report of the events held at Harvard on Islamic microfinance. The goal of these events is to expand the scope of the discussion on Islamic finance, without endorsing any particular idea or opinion so as to provide an objective analysis of the field.

This book is a collection of selected papers from two symposia held at Harvard as well as contribution from leaders in the field to provide a balanced academic, economic and religious outlook on the topic. The articles in this book aim to discuss the real (or perceived) differences between Islamic finance and microfinance, analyze the issues surrounding a combined Islamic microfinance industry and offer innovative solutions to the challenges impeding their success and collaboration.

The first part of the book covers articles that analyze and discuss conventional microfinance in the context of Islamic finance principles. In their article, "Meeting the demand for sustainable, *shari'a*-compliant microfinance," Samer Badawi and Wafik Grais provide a factual overview of the traditional microfinance industry and discuss the core *shari'a* principles that dictate the workings of the Islamic finance industry. They conclude that traditional Islamic finance instruments are less suitable for providing consumption loans for the poor than asset-backed and risk-sharing Islamic finance models such as *ijara* and *musharaka* that may go a long way in improving conventional productive microfinance loans.

The tensions between traditional microfinance and Islamic finance are further explored in two chapters written by Hussam Sultan and Saif I. Shah Mohammed. In his chapter entitled "Islamic microfinance: between commercial viability and the higher objectives of the *shari'a*," Sultan highlights four key issues that confront the nascent Islamic microfinance industry, including the creation of debt amongst the poor, lack of product innovation, challenges in product development and a deepening suspicion towards the authenticity of the Islamic finance industry. Similarly, Shah Mohammed discusses "fundamental" differences in principle between traditional microfinance organizations and proponents of *shari'a*-compliant financing. His chapter, "Islamic finance and microfinance: an insurmountable gap?," discusses these conflicts, particularly those concerning the traditional focus of microfinance on assisting women in Bangladesh. In his view, ideological differences, not technical difficulties, are the main impediments to increasing collaboration between providers of traditional microfinance and Islamic finance organizations.

The use of *zakat* and charity funds to enhance the provision of Islamic microfinance services is central in the model proposed by Habib Ahmed in his chapter, "Organizational models of Islamic microfinance." He proposes that Islamic social welfare funds such as *waqf*, *zakat*, *sadaqah* and *qard hasan* be channeled effectively to complement microfinance loans. He argues that by providing means of addressing the consumption needs of the poor through Islamic social welfare instruments, there is a higher chance of retaining microfinance funds for more productive, income-generating purposes.

In the second part of this book, several authors discuss different technical and organizational models for implementing Islamic microfinance. Aware of the myriad challenges facing both Islamic finance institutions and microfinance organizations, these chapters present innovative models and solutions for consideration by stakeholders in the Islamic microfinance industry.

In his chapter, "Re-thinking leasing from an interest-free perspective: exploring the prospects of Islamic micro-leasing for poverty alleviation," Asad Kamran Ghalib explains the Islamic concept of leasing, or *ijara*, and outlines the structure of an Islamic micro-leasing product that enables collateral-free financing for productive microfinance loans. Through the Islamic micro-leasing model, Islamic microfinance providers may achieve their core goals of poverty alleviation and social justice by enhancing the ability of the poor to establish enterprises and break their way out of the vicious poverty cycle.

In his chapter, "Incentivizing microfinance for Islamic finance institutions: financially mainstreaming the microenterprise," Ali Adnan Ibrahim proposes a dual model in which two entities are established to undertake the profit and non-profit activities in microfinance. The profit-driven institution, "NewCo," would focus on providing microfinance services to borrowers while the non-profit "Microfinance Foundation" would offer research and development, technical expertise, governance and limited guarantees to "NewCo." Islamic finance institutions and social investors may fund "NewCo" while welfare contributions and philanthropic donations will cover the cost of the "Microfinance Foundation." In this way, incentives are provided to parties engaged in Islamic microfinance without undermining the overall competitiveness of Islamic finance institutions. This ensures that Islamic microfinance remains sustainable and profitable while fulfilling its aims of improving the economic wellbeing of its customers.

The separation of Islamic finance institutions from Islamic microfinance is further expounded in a chapter by Rodney Wilson entitled "Making development assistance sustainable through Islamic microfinance." In this chapter he proposes two models for Islamic microfinance organizations. The first model posits the establishment of a fund manager under the *wakala* principle, ensuring the proper management and disbursement of funds from *zakat*, non-governmental organizations and *tabarru'* donations of participants in exchange for a fixed management fee. In the second model, he proposes that the fund management company act as a financier under the *mudaraba* principle. In this way, the borrowers subscribe to the microfinance fund, making them eligible for funding as well as profits from the fund, while the management company earns profits instead of a fixed fee. However, in this model, *zakat* and charitable donations may not be used as a source of funding. Wilson concludes that in both models, the role of providing microfinance services should be carried out by specialized financial companies, rather than Islamic banking institutions.

The challenges of implementing Islamic microfinance are not limited to technical and ideological issues. Systemic and structural weaknesses may also present formidable obstacles to the development of a healthy Islamic microfinance industry.

In the third part of the book, Hans Dieter Seibel in his chapter entitled, "Islamic microfinance in Indonesia: the challenge of institutional diversity, regulation and supervision," specifically highlights poor supervision of rural banks and co-operatives as well as the lack of Islamic finance expertise in commercial banks as major concerns for the Indonesian Islamic microfinance industry. He concludes that without strong internal control, external supervision and self-regulation within the rural banking and Islamic finance sector, the outlook for Islamic microfinance in the most populous Muslim country in the world remains bleak. Similarly, M. Siraj Sait's chapter, "Islamic microfinance in crisis countries: the unofficial development discourse," uses a comparative study of Afghanistan and Indonesia to consider how the interplay of particular political, legal and economic factors creates opportunities for MFIs to deliver microfinance products. He studies how the improvised roles of various stakeholders that are driving the Islamic microfinance movement and creating new microfinance models in an environment where demand for Islamic microfinance is ever increasing.

In another chapter, Mohammed Obaidullah and Amjad Mohamed-Saleem further elaborate on a specific Islamic microfinance project by Muslim Aid to assist paddy farmers and rice millers in Sri Lanka. In this example, value-based *salam* and *mudaraba* contracts were used to offer productive loans to farmers and millers. Therefore, the microfinance project involved all stakeholders in the rice production process, ensuring that both farmers and millers would benefit in a fair manner. The authors conclude that the innovative structuring of Islamic microfinance products and targeting of the appropriate customer segment are essential to developing a sustainable and successful Islamic microfinance program. Shariq Nisar and Syed Mizanur Rahman study the role of minority funds in India in the general context of the microfinance movement. They discuss the underlying concept of these funds, their structure and their compliance to the *shari'a* standards of Islamic finance.

Despite these specific examples of successful Islamic microfinance products, it is generally conceded that a more comprehensive and collaborative approach to Islamic microfinance is required. This approach would involve Islamic finance and social welfare principles as well as the current models of conventional microfinance. Although Islamic finance is founded upon principles of social justice and fairness, the obligations of Islamic finance institutions to be profitable and *shari'a*-compliant often discourages them from entering the uncertain field of microfinance.

In order to provide a religious perspective, IFP has conducted personal interviews with *shari'a* scholars to solicit their opinions on *shari'a*-compliant microfinance. On the topic of social justice, there is unanimous consensus amongst scholars that one of the goals of Islamic finance is to reduce the widening gaps between the haves and the have-nots. Indeed, Shaykh Esam Ishaq sees this fundamental goal as the guiding principle of Islamic finance, which is based on reducing the unnaturally large gap between the wealthy and the poor. In light of these considerations, the goals of Islamic microfinance are part and parcel of those of Islamic finance. In fact, Shaykh Nizam Yaquby noted that the existence of Islamic finance is itself a form of social justice by avoiding riba. Although banks are not technically charitable organizations, providing general good to their community is one of their main goals. Providing *shari'a*-compliant banking services enables people who cannot afford homes or cars access to these assets that would otherwise be unavailable to them through the conventional banking system. A great achievement in and of itself for Islamic finance is that many under-privileged people have now, for the first time, learned to invest and save through Islamic banks. The philanthropy departments of these banks then channel excess funds to charitable purposes.

The question of whether Islamic finance has a duty to provide for the poor was also discussed. The consensus is that the onus is not on the Islamic financial institutions, as they have fiduciary duties to act in the best interests of their clients; rather it is on the clients themselves that must seek to channel their funds accordingly. Muhammad Anas Zarka, senior economist and *shari'a* advisor at the International Investor in Kuwait, noted that banks are not charities—they must act in the interests of their investors. The issue then really becomes: how do we make a financial agenda that seeks to help the poor and eradicate poverty in the best interests of a bank's principal investors? The banking industry is an intermediary that acts on behalf of its principles, its shareholders and its customers. Hence, a call to change cannot be levied against banking industries and systems without first rousing the moral consciousness of the people whom the bank owes a fiduciary duty to. How do we appeal to these people to devote some of their wealth and funds to helping the needy in a systemized manner that goes beyond simple charity?

Zarka also brought up another interesting point as he noted the regulatory bodies of Muslim countries are not doing enough to allow easy means for the market to distribute to the poor. In his words, "Since it is not on the agenda of those who have authority, and the industry is not authorized, then the poor get what we see: nothing." Zarka also opined in his chapter that Islamic finance is a young industry that has yet to focus on social justice. He discussed the viability of the Islamic instrument of monetary *waqf* (cash trust) to finance *shari'a*-compliant microfinance. In addition to initial donations, a monetary *waqf* further mobilizes temporary funds that can be extended to the productive poor as micro-credits. Moreover, Zarka asserted that there should be two tiers of philanthropic guarantors for a monetary *waqf* to strengthen its security standing: guarantors of liquidity and guarantors of losses. Not only would this help to increase the credit standing of a *waqf*, but it would also attract a large amount of temporary funds.

Problematizing and questioning the scope and feasibility of microfinance from Islamic banks, Daud Bakar, prominent *shari'a* supervisor from Malaysia, noted the difficulty of managing balance sheets between high-risk activity and lower-risk lending that predominates in Islamic banking. Ultimately, he concludes that what may be the most pragmatic response to incorporating microfinancing elements into Islamic banks are dual accounting methods that have separate balance sheets to better hedge for the risk associated with microfinance lending.

In due course, all scholars agreed that Islamic finance and microfinance are not fundamentally incompatible. On the contrary, the two are deemed as highly compatible financing systems linked by the moral imperative within Islam to help the poor and reduce income disparities. In advising how Islamic finance should cater to the poor, the scholars agree that a collaborative effort between financial, government and charitable institutions is crucial.

If Islamic microfinance attracts a customer base that would otherwise not have access to conventional microfinance, consensus holds that the additional efforts meant to ensure *shari'a* compliance is justified. An article by INSEAD shared a testimonial from an Afghani client of Foundation for International Community Assistance (FINCA), a Washington DC-based Islamic microfinance provider, who admitted: "Charging interest is against Islam and FINCA has offered us a way to take out loans without compromising our religious beliefs. If it wasn't Islamic I would have never taken these loans." Addressing the question of whether Islamic finance is doing enough to help the impoverished, the views accumulate to be a hybrid of affirmations and negations. While most proponents of Islamic finance see the need for Islamic finance to provide for the poor, most of them agree that this cannot be accomplished solely through the currently existing institutions. Thus, Islamic microfinance organizations are commonly agreed upon as the way forward, and the Islamic finance sector is now ready to handle this new market segment.

In general, the issues and innovative solutions proposed in this book provide only a glimpse into the universe of Islamic microfinance. Further research is necessary to generate new ideas and insights across the whole value chain of Islamic microfinance, from funding and product development to organizational models and service delivery. Indeed, one can argue that efforts to search for an Islamic path in the world of microfinance is a fine example of the constantly changing nature of Islamic finance as it seeks to be both innovative and relevant to society, affecting change in the moral understanding of economics as well as its practice on the ground.

The last part of this book is a collection of information sources on Islamic microfinance. This fits into one of the objectives of IFP, which has established a much-needed resource on Islamic finance and economics called the IFP DataBank. Established 15 years ago, this premier tool provides comprehensive information on Islamic finance, economics and other related areas free of cost. We hope that the DataBank complements this book in encouraging scholars, industry players, governments and other stakeholders to collaborate and work toward developing the Islamic microfinance industry. Failure to do so would only reflect our collective failure to live up to our obligations of alleviating poverty and promoting social justice.

Part I
Islamic microfinance and *shari‘a* compatibility

1 Meeting the demand for sustainable, *shari'a*-compliant microfinance[1]

Samer Badawi[2] *and Wafik Grais*[3]

Introduction

Despite its popularity in predominantly Muslim countries such as Bangladesh, microfinance has few champions in the burgeoning Islamic banking industry. Although some microfinance programs have attempted to introduce *shari'a*-compliant financial products, these have had only limited success. In many cases, the cost of maintaining an Islamic window at a microfinance institution has been much higher than expected. Moreover, the development and delivery of these products have generally been highly subsidized by donor or government funds. As such, current Islamic microfinance programs, even if they show limited success, do not appear capable of expanding to reach the tens of millions of unbanked Muslims. To do that, they would need to become profitable and represent a viable business proposition for Muslim and non-Muslim investors.

Islamic banks, with their wide range of well-developed and successful *shari'a*-compliant instruments and strong capital base, may be well-positioned to adapt these instruments for poorer customers. The prospect is exciting because such an effort could lead to the development of an Islamic microfinance industry that is profitable from the outset and potentially able to reach scale quickly. Although there may be no turn-key solutions for Islamic financial services directed to poorer customers, Islamic banks can draw upon the experience of a highly professionalized microfinance industry to reach the unbanked who demand *shari'a*-compliant financial services. Such an effort could ultimately strengthen the outreach of the entire microfinance industry and possibly contribute to innovations that would improve not only breadth and depth of outreach but also the overall transparency and efficiency of microfinance services.

The current microfinance landscape

Once a niche market centered on the single product of micro-enterprise credit, microfinance now signifies a wide range of financial services for the poor as well as diverse institutions and delivery channels. Sustained growth and stability have contributed to greater investment in microfinance, which in turn has helped further the professionalization of the industry's services and standards.

Diverse services and institutions

Safe places to save, old-age pensions, reliable money transfers, insurance—all are now recognized microfinance services that help people, heretofore excluded from access to financial services, build assets, plan for the future, and cope with the present. Along with diversification of products, the number of microfinance service providers and resources channeled through them has expanded. Commercial, postal, and agricultural banks are all part of the vision of "scaling up" microfinance by providing access to financial services for more and more poor people. Indeed, a recent CGAP (World Bank's Consultative Group to Assist the Poor) study suggests that poor people may have as many as 750 million credit and savings accounts in comparable alternative financial institutions.[4]

Diverse delivery channels

Some microfinance providers are overcoming the lack of infrastructure among poor sections of the populations by using technology to deliver financial services. South Africa's Wizzit has no branches of its own but instead it reaches the unbanked through their cell phones and a debit card.[5] Other banks have followed suit, and now 400,000 South Africans are making one million cell phone banking transactions every month. The Philippines' two biggest cell phone companies, Globe Telecom and SMART, both offer a service that allows customers to send money, pay for goods with their phones, and more. Some 4.5 million Filipinos have signed up in just four years. Even Vodafone, one of the world's largest mobile telecommunications firms, is piloting a link between cell phones and financial services for the poor in Kenya.

Growth

The microfinance industry is growing fast, adding nearly 15 percent more borrowers each year since 1999. The number of self-sustainable institutions is growing too. Today, there are at least 400 sustainable institutions reporting to the Microfinance Information eXchange, or MIX, the industry's most trusted source for market data. All told, these institutions have helped microfinance mature into one of the most successful and fastest-growing industries in the world; worldwide, the leading microfinance institutions are nearly twice as profitable as the leading commercial banks.

Stability

In the last decade in emerging markets, microfinance has been a more stable business than commercial banking. During Indonesia's 1997 financial crisis, for example, commercial bank portfolios imploded, but loan repayment among Bank Rakyat Indonesia's more than three million micro-borrowers barely declined at all. During the more recent Bolivian and Colombian banking crises, microfinance portfolios suffered slightly, but remained substantially healthier than commercial bank portfolios, and the microfinance institutions remained more profitable.

Investment

Microfinance funds' investment in microfinance institutions (MFIs) tripled in two years to $2 billion in 2006, and CGAP estimates that foreign capital investment in microfinance has reached $5 billion. Moreover, some of the world's largest commercial investors are putting millions into microfinance. Institutional investors such as pension fund TIAA CREF (Teachers Insurance and Annuity Association—College Retirement Equities Fund) have 17 percent of the market share in microfinance funds, up from 5 percent in 2004. In addition, equity fund Sequoia Capital—which provided venture capital funding to Google, Yahoo!, and YouTube—recently invested $11.5 million in India's SKS Microfinance, making SKS the largest for-profit MFI in the world.[6]

Professionalization

Microfinance is today widely understood and practiced as retail banking for low-income people, with standards and services that draw upon the professionalism of the larger banking sector. The services are the same: loans, deposit facilities, money transfers. Moreover, the standards are increasingly the same: more than 100 recipients of the CGAP Financial Transparency Award comply with International Financial Reporting Standards, for example, and core performance indicators for microfinance have been widely adopted.[7] Microfinance is serious business and, with its huge untapped market, may shape the future of retail banking.

Developing practical models for an Islamic microfinance

Islamic financial institutions have the potential to play an even greater role in the future of retail banking than they currently do by catering to a mostly overlooked segment of the poor—Muslims who demand *shari'a*-compliant products. With few donor-funded non-governmental organizations (NGOs) offering *shari'a*-compliant microfinance, there is an opportunity for well-capitalized Islamic banks to develop practical models that rely not on donor funds, but on well-known principles that emphasize profitability while offering the potential to be highly transparent as well as impact-driven. These principles, notably, are: the materiality of products, as represented in the *murabaha* and *ijara* instruments; and risk-sharing, as represented in the *musharaka* instrument. These instruments, and the principles that underlie them, can not only support the development of Islamic financial services for the poor, they can also potentially contribute to the development of the broader microfinance industry. The following discussion explores both opportunities, offering possible ways forward drawn from the broader microfinance industry.

The materiality model: *murabaha* and *ijara*

In a *murabaha* or *ijara* transaction, the provider of funds purchases a commodity and resells or leases it to the user with a mark-up against installments or delayed payment. In other words, the materiality of a *murabaha* or *ijara* transaction essentially objectifies transparency in the form of a commodity—a sewing machine sold or leased to a micro-entrepreneur, for example. In this case, the retail "price" of a microfinance transaction is actually set by a competitive market for sewing machines.

The client in such a transaction benefits from competition on the wholesale market, but the costs to a microfinance provider associated with purchasing, maintaining, selling, or leasing, and then tracking a commodity raise questions about the efficiency of a *murabaha* or *ijara* transaction. Will these added costs, though perhaps improving the transparency, actually result in higher prices for microfinance clients?

More practical experience is needed to address the question of efficiency. Still, the experience of conventional microfinance to date may be instructive. The average operating expense ratio (OER) of microfinance providers reporting to *The MicroBanking Bulletin*, published by the MIX, is approximately 30 percent. Although this figure probably represents considerable inefficiency (commercial banks typically report OERs of well below 5 percent), the higher cost is mostly a function of servicing many more—and much smaller—loans than larger lenders.

Islamic financial institutions must come to terms with the true cost of microfinance and the implications of serving poorer customers profitably and sustainably. One clear implication is around pricing. To cover their costs, conventional microfinance providers charge higher interest rates than those of larger commercial banks. These rates are usually significantly lower than those charged by informal moneylenders, however, boosting the demand for microfinance services where they are available.

This argument carries the assumption that demand for micro-credit and continuous external financing is highly inelastic around initial accessibility amounts. Still, the persistence of high interest rates, even in highly active and competitive markets such as Bangladesh, has led policymakers especially to question whether the price of financial services for the poor is too high. Although many in the microfinance field see this as political grandstanding—in some cases, a legitimate claim—there is little doubt that greater attention is being paid to the price of microfinance. In addition, questions are being raised about the accessibility of microfinance services for especially poor populations and, as a corollary, to whether MFIs are by necessity serving higher-income customers.

Islamic financial institutions would not be immune to these questions. To deal effectively with them, Islamic microfinance providers, regardless of the instruments they utilize, must: (1) be realistic about the cost of serving poorer customers, especially in remote rural areas; (2) engage policymakers and others to educate them about the true cost of microfinance; and (3) explore innovative ways to reduce the cost of microfinance transactions.

Much thinking has already been done and substantial investment has been channeled towards adapting existing technologies that can be used to provide banking services for the poor more cost-effectively. By accessing banking services through an automated teller machine, the Internet, or, increasingly, a mobile phone, clients of large commercial banks can assume much of the cost burden (i.e., maintaining bank branches) of delivering financial services. Recent efforts at extending these "branchless banking" services to poorer populations show great promise.[8]

However, the vast majority of microfinance programs still rely on loan officers to collect or disburse payments. The potential to avoid such costly activities is seen most clearly in the meteoric increase of mobile phone usage in the developing world. The number of mobile phone subscribers worldwide has doubled—to two billion—in just over two years, with more than 80 percent of that growth coming from developing countries, according to the GSM Association. This bodes well for the replication of successful models like those of Wizzit,[9] Globe Telecom, and SMART.

Besides mobile phones, technology may offer two other ways to further reduce the costs of *murabaha* or *ijara* transactions. The first, and more obvious, is by utilizing microchip technology to track assets. The second involves leveraging point-of-sale (POS) devices to extend outreach through banking agents.

Banking agents are retail vendors, lottery outlets, post offices—any trusted local establishment that can double as banking agents and act as a kind of bank branch for their customers, processing everything from bill and pension payments to deposits, withdrawals, and money transfers. In Brazil, for example, these agents are known as *correspondentes bancarios*, and their long track record of delivering reliable financial services to the previously unbanked points to an exciting opportunity for other microfinance markets.[10]

Banking agents process transactions with POS card readers, barcode scanners, and sometimes personal computers that connect with the bank's server using a dial-up or other data connection. The clerk at the retail or postal outlet collects and disburses cash and, in some cases, opens bank accounts for new clients and fills in credit applications. The retail outlets earn a portion of the transaction fee, and some generate so much business from handling these transactions that they dedicate an employee to operating the POS device.

Of course, the problems with this model revolve around the risk of fraud. The risk is so pronounced that some banks use management companies to not only identify, equip, train, and support banking agents, but to assume all liabilities for the cash they handle. The risk involved in a *murabaha* or *ijara* transaction, however, could be far less. In other words, an "Islamic banking agent" could be made to transact an actual commodity, not simply cash. Since these agents are typically local vendors, the link is a natural one and again leverages the competition of the wholesale market to offer lower, more transparent prices for poor clients.

By emphasizing materiality, *murabaha* and *ijara* instruments offer the potential to bank the poor through highly transparent transactions that leverage the economies of scale of wholesale markets. Still, many of the challenges of managing these transactions efficiently will mirror those of conventional microfinance. The prices associated with delivering financial services to the poor must not be underestimated by Islamic financial providers. Recognizing this, they must make efforts to educate policymakers and others about the value of their services to poor clients, even as they support the search for innovative solutions that can dramatically reduce the cost of these services. Many of the solutions today being explored in conventional microfinance can contribute to the more efficient and transparent delivery of *murabaha* and *ijara* transactions for the poor.

The risk-sharing model: *musharaka*

In a *musharaka* transaction, the financier enters into an equity participation agreement with other partners to jointly finance an investment project and participate in its management. Profits (and losses) are shared among partners based on their respective contributions to capital. A *musharaka* transaction gives the microfinance provider an equal stake in its clients' success and could potentially help address a critical development need in much of the Islamic world—creating jobs.

However, a *musharaka* transaction carries significant risks and associated costs for the microfinance provider. In practice, an Islamic microfinance provider would need to offer business development and capacity-building services through a separate window than that of the financial transaction. Some conventional microfinance providers do offer training and other services to their clients. In many cases, however, these services rely on donor funds or cross-subsidization from other segments of a microfinance provider's business. A similar approach could be taken by Islamic financial institutions offering microfinance—for example, these institutions could draw upon *zakat* contributions, or alms, to fund training opportunities through a *qard hasan* (or profit-free) model—but Islamic microfinance providers must take great care not to allow such activities to undermine the profitability of their financial services.

Addressing this challenge, some MFIs are finding ways to link with existing safety net programs to "graduate" the poorest from reliance on grants and into access to financial services. There are two basic models for linking grant-based programs with sustainable microfinance programs.

In the first model, safety net programs themselves develop basic financial services for their clients to help them better manage their livelihoods. The MFI's engagement with the safety net program is limited: the MFI simply coordinates with the safety net program to recruit successful "graduates" as customers. The advantage for the MFI is that the safety net program generates information about participants' behavior that can later help the MFI make better decisions about the likelihood these participants will repay loans. For example, an MFI would consider a safety net participant with a track record of showing up for work, saving regularly, or even repaying a loan offered by the safety net program to be a less risky borrower when s/he eventually approaches the MFI for regular microcredit. An MFI with access to such information can make safer loans to poorer clients than an MFI without this information. The relationship also benefits safety net participants, because it gives them a long-term path forward and motivates good performance while they are with the safety net program. This win–win situation creates little extra cost or risk for either the program or the MFI. Even a weak MFI can use this strategy to pursue its social mission to sign up promising clients without jeopardizing its ability to achieve sustainability.

The second model involves a more intense collaboration between an MFI and a safety net program. In this model, the MFI establishes a separate subsidiary or affiliate that works directly with safety net participants. In cooperation with the safety net program, the MFI subsidiary provides non-financial services and, perhaps, some subsidized savings or credit. Successful graduates gain access to the MFI's regular programs. The MFI subsidiary will need access to soft money to be able to offer its services to participants, until participants are able to join the mainstream microfinance program. This second model entails high costs and risks for the MFI, including the risk that handing out "grants" as part of the safety net program could undermine the culture of strict repayment discipline that is an essential part of the MFI's micro-credit operation. As such, there needs to be a clear distinction between the safety net and MFI components. This is typically accomplished by using separate staff working in a separate subsidiary. This direct engagement model would work well only for a mature, exceptionally strong MFI whose core business has such solid and sustainable operations that it can afford to have its management and staff resources diluted.[11]

Islamic banks, which boast strong systems and management capacity as well as a wide range of instruments—including, for example, *qard hasan*—have the potential to implement the second model above as part of a *musharaka* transaction. This would require the careful sequencing of grants, training programs, and financial services so as not to compromise the sustainability of the microfinance operation, on the one hand, and, on the other hand, to create the best conditions for the client's success.

Envisioning Islamic financial services for the poor

Islamic financial institutions can offer valuable products and services to microfinance clients. At the same time, the intent and design as well as the challenges of Islamic finance for the poor must be clear. With respect to intent and design, the asset-backed nature of Islamic finance (e.g., in a *murabaha* or *ijara* transaction) provides for an arguably different business relationship with clients than that of conventional microfinance, which views uncollateralized loans as essential to creating access to finance. This access can—and often does—support more than micro-entrepreneurship: for farmers and itinerant workers, it helps "smooth consumption" during months without income; and for victims of disasters, it can help rebuild homes or pay for emergency medical bills. The *musharaka* transaction also presupposes some sort of business activity for the microfinance client.

To the extent that microfinance is a development intervention, however, with the aim of lifting poor people out of poverty, Islamic financial services, while addressing the significant demand for *shari'a*-compliant products, may also offer practical models for conventional microfinance. In particular, models based on materiality and risk-sharing offer opportunities to build on current microfinance experience and to develop synergies around the development of new technology-driven delivery channels as well as "graduation" programs that can help develop and sustain the capacity of microfinance clients.

For any model of Islamic microfinance, if it is to attain the scale necessary to reach the tens of millions of unbanked, it must become profitable for micro-finance providers and affordable for microfinance clients. Getting there will take the investment, commitment, and bold leadership of Islamic financial institutions themselves. It will also take a practical approach that acknowledges the challenges of delivering affordable and profitable financial services to the poor and builds on the successes of the larger microfinance industry.

Notes

1 This chapter was presented at "Financing the Poor: Towards an Islamic Microfinance," at a symposium held at Harvard Law School, Cambridge, MA, April 14, 2007.
2 Formerly Program Officer, Consultative Group to Assist the Poor, Washington, D.C.
3 Formerly Senior Advisor, World Bank, Washington, D.C.
4 CGAP. "Financial Institutions with a Double Bottom Line: Implications for the Future of Microfinance." Occasional Papers No. 8. July 2004, 20pp. http://www.cgap.org/gm/document1.9.2701/OccasionalPaper_8.pdf.
5 Ivatury, Gautam and Pickens, Mark. "Mobile Phone Banking and Low-Income Customers: Evidence from South Africa." 2006, 14pp. http://www.globalproblems-globalsolutions-files.org/unf_website/PDF/mobile_phone_bank_low_income_customers.pdf.
6 Brennan, Margaret. "Sequoia Invests $11.5 Million in Microfinance Fund." CNBC.com. March 27, 2007. http://www.cnbc.com/id/17844093.
7 CGAP. "Core Performance Indicators for Microfinance." April 2006, 12pp. http://www.uncdf.org/english/microfinance/uploads/evaluations/Core%20Indicators--UNDP%20version.pdf.
8 CGAP. "Using Technology to Build Inclusive Financial Systems." *Focus Notes*, No. 32. January 2006, 16pp. www.ictregulationtoolkit.org/en/Document.3436.pdf.
9 See Ivatury and Pickens 2006.
10 Part of the excitement comes from the sheer scale of banking agents' services in Brazil. An estimated US$1 trillion in transactions were processed through Brazil's 58,000 agents in 2005, and about six million current accounts were opened across this network in the past three years, according to Banco Central do Brasil. Already, the model has spread to Mexico, Peru, Colombia, and Chile.
11 CGAP. "Graduating the Poorest into Microfinance: Linking Safety Nets and Financial Services." *Focus Notes*, No. 34. February 2006, 8pp. http://www.cgap.org/gm/document-1.9.2586/FocusNote_34.pdf.

2 Organizational models of Islamic microfinance

Habib Ahmed[1]

Introduction

With the failure of top-down (trickle down) development policies for a few decades to alleviate poverty in most developing countries, financing microenterprise is considered a "new paradigm" for bringing about development and eradicating absolute poverty. Growth in small and microenterprises can be an important means for employment generation and development in poor countries. High population growth rate and limited employment opportunities in the agricultural and modern manufacturing sectors leave a vast majority of the labor force without productive employment. Microenterprises can play an important role in employing the surplus labor force productively.[2] An important factor that determines the development of the microenterprises is the availability of finance for acquiring the necessary inputs and capital. Due to lack of collateral and asymmetric information problems, however, poor microentrepreneurs cannot obtain financing from conventional institutional sources. Before the advent of microfinance institutions (MFIs), most microenterprises were financed by non-institutional sources that charged exorbitant interest rates.

Though the importance of developing small-scale enterprises has been discussed for a long time, the innovative poverty focused group-based financing of microentrepreneurs is a relatively new concept. Pioneered by Professor Muhammed Yunus of Grameen Bank in Bangladesh, MFIs providing credit to the poor have burgeoned in both developing and industrialized countries. Specialized poverty focused MFIs are providing much-needed financing to a small segment of microentrepreneurs resulting in the increase of their income and wealth. MFIs innovative group-based format introduces social collateral minimizing the asymmetric information problems and ensuring higher recovery rates. The "Microcredit Summit 1997" envisaged that 100 million poor would have access to microfinance by 2005. Multilateral financial institutions and international donors have adopted microfinance as a powerful instrument for poverty alleviation and economic development.[3]

Most of the MFIs, however, have non-Islamic characteristics. Their financing is interest based. Furthermore, apart from the delivery of finance to the poor, many MFIs have social development programs that are mostly secular in nature.

This chapter studies the prospects of poverty focused microfinance from an Islamic perspective. I first outline the features of the conventional MFIs and critically examine their strengths and weaknesses. Drawing on the strengths of conventional MFIs, various organizational models of Islamic microfinancing are then outlined.

The chapter is organized as follows. In section two I first discuss the economics of financing microenterprises. Given the important role of development that microenterprises play in poverty alleviation, this section argues for social intermediation by specialized microfinance institutions. Section three presents the basic features and operations of conventional MFIs. In section four, the nature of Islamic MFIs are presented and compared with conventional ones. In doing so, the scope and constraints facing Islamic MFIs are discussed. Section five argues for Islamic banks' involvement in microfinancing. Unlike conventional banks, Islamic banks' objectives should include social dimensions. Given this social role, Islamic banks can provide much-needed financing to the poor for their economic advancement. In section six, the paper presents some specialized microfinance institutions based on the Islamic concepts of *zakat*, *waqf*, and *qard hasan* that can be effectively used to serve the poorer sections of the population. Specifically, models of cash *waqf*, *qard hasan* bank, and MFIs based on *zakat* and *waqf* are presented.

Financing microenterprises: need for social intermediation

Microenterprises can be defined differently, depending on the country's stage of development, policy objectives, and administration.[4] They constitute everything from small businesses and shops, to cottage industries and transport services.[5] Three broad categories of economic activities can be identified, namely: production, trading, and providing transport services. In production, the poor entrepreneur may be involved in agricultural or non-agricultural activities. Agricultural activities include farming, cattle rearing, poultry rearing, and fisheries. Non-agricultural production can cover a wide variety of activities ranging from food processing to producing different handicrafts and household items such as pots, mats, and cloth. Trading includes shop-keeping, small business, and selling specific items such as food. Providing transport services can be through rickshaws, boats, or motor vehicles used as taxis.

Smaller firms do not have any access to funds from traditional financial institutions. The underlying theoretical explanation for this phenomenon lies in the traditional problems of asymmetric information in financial intermediation. A financial institution raises funds and invests these in activities that yield returns in the future. In doing so, the financial institutions face a number of information-related problems inherent in financing. Before a financing decision is made, the adverse selection problem has to be resolved by identifying the right projects to ensure proper returns from investments. After funds are disbursed, the moral hazard problem has to be tackled to safeguard against the misuse of funds. This can be done, among other things, with the help of monitoring, which is costly. To minimize the credit risk, financial institutions require collateral that can be tapped into in case of default. To ensure profitability, the costs (both financial and operational) have to be kept to a minimum. Note that operational costs include those incurred for monitoring to avoid the moral hazard problem.

In the case of small firms with no prior history, asymmetric information is severe from the financiers' perspective. Bennett[6] points out some barriers that accentuate the asymmetric information problems when dealing with smaller enterprises in developing countries. Physical barriers of poor infrastructure, such as lack of markets, roads, power, communications, etc., can worsen both adverse selection and moral hazard problems. Physical constraints inhibit financial institutions from gathering information on their prospective clients and, once credit is advanced, it is difficult to monitor the use of the funds. Socioeconomic factors of clients such as low numerical skills due to illiteracy, coupled with caste/ethnicity/gender aspects preventing interaction also add to the adverse selection problem. Moral hazard problems are further exacerbated by a microentrepreneur's inability to bring forth sound financial collateral due to poverty. These barriers would make the assessment of projects and monitoring the use of loans very costly. Furthermore, as the size of the loan for microenterprise is small, the administrative cost per-unit of loan increases. These factors make it economically non-viable for traditional financial institutions to offer credit to microenterprises.

Given the problems in financing microenterprises and the fact that these small-scale enterprises are important means to increase employment and reduce poverty, there is a need for a social financial intermediation of funds for microentrepreneurs. Bennett[7] points out two approaches for financing microenterprises. First, the linking approach, under which conventional financial institutions are linked to the target group (i.e., the poor) through some intermediary. The second approach is to provide microcredit through specialized organizations, such as non-governmental organizations (NGOs), government agencies, cooperatives, and development finance institutions. Almost all of the financing for microenterprises in recent times have come from the latter institutions that cater to the needs of the poor. Whatever the type of the institution providing the finance, these institutions have to address the fundamental problems related to their operations and sustainability. To ensure income/revenue, these institutions have to mitigate the credit risk and reduce the moral hazard problem. To be viable, the costs of operations have to be kept to a minimum. Thus, the following questions related to the sustainability of institutions financing microenterprises have to be resolved:

- *Mitigating credit risk*: Ensure that the microentrepreneur repays the principal with returns in the absence of physical collateral.
- *Solving the moral hazard problem*: To decrease the probability of default, ensure that the funds taken are used for the planned productive activity without incurring large monitoring costs.
- *Economic viability*: Keep costs to a minimum for economic viability of the institution. Costs include both operating/administrative costs and financing costs.

MFIs: specialized financial institutions

Though the importance of financing small-scale enterprises has been felt for a long time, the concept of group-based poverty-focused microfinance is a relatively new concept.[8] Pioneered by the Grameen Bank in Bangladesh, group-based MFIs are banks for the poor and operate quite differently from conventional commercial banks. Whereas commercial banks are profit maximizing firms, MFIs are either government organizations or NGOs formed to provide the poor with much-needed financing. Given this nature, most MFIs have a social development program along with their credit facilities.

To get financing from these institutions, the client or beneficiary has to be "poor," as defined by specific bank-stipulated guidelines.[9] A person must form a group of five like-minded people with similar socioeconomic status to get credit. Male and female groups are formed separately and relatives cannot be in the same group. A group is usually trained for a couple of weeks to be familiar with the rules and procedures of the MFI. A number of groups are federated into a center with a center chief and deputy center chief elected from amongst them. Weekly meetings of the center are held at a convenient place in the locality. All members (i.e., beneficiaries) of the center are required to attend these meetings. An MFI official attends these weekly meetings to conduct the banking transactions and other business of the center.

MFIs extend credit of small amounts at a reasonable rate of interest. The loan is paid back in one year in (50) weekly installments. Credit is provided to the poor without any physical collateral. Instead, social collateral is introduced by forming groups. Loan repayment by an individual member of a group is the collective responsibility of all the members in the group and default by a member disqualifies all members to get new loans. As a result, members in the group monitor the activities of each other and peer pressure induces the repayment of the loan. This format of peer monitoring resolves the problem of asymmetric information and reduces the serious transaction costs involved with monitoring.[10] Most MFIs have various (forced) savings programs. For example, in case of Grameen Bank, 5 percent of the loans is deducted for group (risk) fund and a quarter of the total interest amount is collected as emergency (insurance) fund when the principal is handed over to a member. While the beneficiaries can borrow from the risk fund in case of major social event (such as a wedding ceremony), the emergency fund is given to members in times of distress. In addition, the members are required to put aside a small amount (Taka 1) every week in their personal savings account.[11]

Most MFIs have a social development program associated with financing. The objective of this program is to generate personal and social consciousness among the members. These programs include aspects that affect behavioral changes (such as personal hygiene, sanitation, drinking clean water, etc.), moral teachings (such as teaching honesty, discipline, and cooperation among themselves), and social customs (such as accepting family planning, not practicing the dowry system, etc.). Members know these principles and norms are prerequisites to obtaining loans from MFIs and these are continuously inducted into the members during the weekly meetings. At times, necessary inputs to implement these social programs (such as tube wells for water, oral re-hydration salt, etc.) are provided by the MFI on a subsidized basis.

The profitability of MFIs will depend on the revenues generated and the costs incurred. The revenue side can be managed by ensuring repayments of loans. This can be done by, among other things, minimizing the credit risk and the moral hazard problem. The total costs of providing microfinance include operating and financing costs. The former will include costs at the head office, the regional offices, and branches that cover the field-level work. The operating costs comprise a variable component (wages to employees at field and head-office levels) and a fixed component (rent, utilities, etc.). As the size of the loan for microenterprise is small, the administrative cost per-unit of loan is high.

The financing costs depend on the sources of funds. MFIs cannot attract deposits as commercial banks do. As the MFIs grow, the savings of beneficiaries accumulate, which can then be recycled into financing microenterprises. The time needed for an MFI to operate its activities based solely on beneficiaries' savings, however, may be very long. In the absence of deposits (other than savings of beneficiaries), the bulk of the funds of the MFIs is from external sources. Though sometimes external funds are provided at subsidized rates, certain conditionalities are attached to this.

MFIs and sustainability

While a large literature exists that shows the success of MFIs, some recent studies show failure of these institutions in reaching some of their objectives.[12] The problems relevant to sustainability are given here:

- *Mitigating credit risk*: As high default rates can make financial institutions vulnerable to bankruptcy, sustainability of these entities depend on how credit risk is mitigated. Banks mitigate credit risk in financing by requiring security in form of collateral, guarantee, etc. The credit risk is minimized by MFIs replacing physical collateral with social collateral. Group-based microlending acts as social collateral reducing the credit risk that exists in financial intermediation. The peer pressure from the group members and the center is a low cost and effective way of ensuring repayments. Furthermore, it is easier for the poor to pay small weekly installments instead of a large lump-sum amount when the loan is due. This also reduces the credit risk and ensures the MFI its returns.
- *Solving the moral hazard problem*: As money is given out to the poorer sections of the population, it has been observed that in some cases loans taken from MFI are often used for purposes other than those the loan is sanctioned for.[13] When loans are used for non-productive purposes, the chances of default increase. Buckley[14] reports that in 1993, 46 percent of the Malawi Mudzi Fund's (an MFI in Malawi) borrowers were in arrears (did not pay installments between one and four times) because they diverted the funds for consumption

purposes. Among the defaulters (those who did not pay more than four install-ments), the corresponding number was 33 percent.

- *Economic viability*: Ideally microfinancing would be a "win–win" situation, if the MFI operates at a profit and the poor benefit from the credit program. This, however, is not the case for most MFIs.[15] Due to lack of fund mobiliza-tion and the high administrative cost most MFIs are not economically viable. For example, Bennett[16] reports that administrative cost of five MFIs in South Asia is in the range of 24 percent to more than 400 percent of per dollar lent. Reed and Befus[17] study five MFIs and find average return on assets for three of these below 2 percent, one at 3.5 percent and the other at 14.6 percent. Hashemi[18] and Khandker[19] point out that Grameen Bank would operate at a loss without grants. A Subsidy Dependence Index (SDI) developed by Yaron[20] indicates that in 1996 Grameen Bank would have to increase its lending inter-est rate by an additional 21 percent in order to breakeven without subsidies.[21] Similarly, Hulme and Mosley[22] find that 12 out of 13 MFIs from six countries have positive SDI ranging from 32 percent to 1,884 percent.

We see from the above discussion that while conventional MFIs have been able to solve the problem of credit risk by introducing social collateral by forming groups and weekly repayments, it has not successfully resolved the problems of moral haz-ard and economic viability. Specifically, group-based microlending acts as social collateral and lessens the asymmetric information problem that exists in financial intermediation. Given these strengths and weaknesses of conventional MFIs, I next discuss the nature of microfinance organizations that operate under Islamic principles and values.

Islamic MFIs

Several Islamic MFIs have been initiated in various countries.[23] These institu-tions have adopted the group-based lending format of the conventional MFIs and adapted Islamic principles and values. The assets and liabilities of the Islamic MFIs are, therefore, different compared to their conventional counterparts. Inter-est (one form of *riba*) being prohibited in Islam, the composition of Islamic MFIs assets will comprise different types of non-interest bearing financial instruments. Important aspects of Islamic modes of finance are that financial capital cannot claim a return on itself and that the transaction must involve a real good or object. Principles of Islamic financing are many and varied. The type of financing instru-ment will depend on the type of activity for which funds are granted. As discussed earlier, the economic activities that microenterprises usually engage in are pro-duction, trading, and providing (transport) services. I point out the appropriate Islamic modes of financing for these activities below.

Other than interest-free loans (*qard hasan*), the principles of Islamic financing can be broadly classified as partnerships (*sharika*) and exchange contracts (*mu'awadat*).[24] Partnerships can be on the basis of profit sharing or output sharing. Profit sharing again can take two forms—*musharaka* and *mudaraba*. Whereas in *musharaka* more than one party finance and participate in a project and distribute the profit at an agreed ratio, in *mudaraba* one party supplies the funds and the other party carries out the project and shares the profit at agreed upon ratio.

Though there are different kinds of exchange contracts, the important among these is the deferred-trading principle. A deferred-trading contract can either be a price-deferred sale or an object-deferred sale. What is relevant for microfinancing is the price-deferred sale (*bay' al-mu'ajjal*) in which the object of sale is delivered at the time of the contract but the price is paid later. The price can also be paid in the future in installments. One type of financial transaction under this format is mark-up sale (*murabaha*), in which the Islamic MFI buys a good or asset and sells it to the client at a mark-up. The client pays for the good or asset at a future date or in installments. *Ijara* is a leasing contract in which the client uses an asset by paying rent. One form of this arrangement can be the hire-purchase scheme or lease-purchase scheme (*ijara wa iqtina'*), in which the installment includes rent and part of the capital. When the installments are fully paid the ownership of the asset is transferred to the client.

From the discussion above, we see that various kinds of financing arrangements can be used to finance different kinds of activities. *Musharaka* principles can be adopted in production (agricultural and non-agricultural). The Islamic MFI can provide part of the financial capital to produce an output and in return receive a share of the profit. In trading, the Islamic MFI and the client can jointly finance the purchase and selling of a certain good and distribute the profit. Production undertaken under *mudaraba* principle would imply that the Islamic MFI finances and the client manages the project. In agricultural production, output sharing can take the form of *muzara'a*. The Islamic MFI may fund the purchase of irrigation equipment, fertilizers, etc., which the landowner uses on his land to cultivate a certain crop. The harvested crop is then shared by the landowner and the Islamic MFI at an agreed ratio. Other than profit-sharing principle discussed above, *murabaha* and *ijara* forms of financing can also be used in production. For example, if a client is in need of initial physical capital (equipment, gadgets, etc.), the Islamic MFI can buy the items and sell these to the client at a mark-up. In agriculture, the item may be a cow or poultry that the Islamic MFI sells at a mark-up. The client pays back the price in agreed upon installments in the future. Similar transactions can take place under a leasing (*ijara*) contract.

In trading, profit-sharing schemes and deferred-trading contracts can be used. Under profit-sharing scheme, the Islamic MFI becomes a partner in the trading business and gets a share of the profit. The *murabaha* principle can also be applied where the items to be traded are first bought by Islamic MFI and then sold at a mark-up to the clients. The clients pay back the Islamic MFI once they sell the goods. In transport services, both mark-up principle and the leasing principle can be applied. For example, if a client wants to buy a rickshaw, the Islamic MFI can purchase it and sell it to the client at a mark-up. The client then pays the price on an agreed installment plan. Alternatively, a hire-purchase arrangement can be made in which the client pays rent plus a part of the capital in his installments. Once the installments are fully paid, the client becomes the owner of the rickshaw.[25]

Some traditional Islamic instruments meant for poverty alleviation are *zakat*, *waqf*, *qard hasan*, and other *sadaqat* (charities). These instruments can be integrated into microfinancing program to effectively alleviate absolute poverty.[26] Furthermore, the Islamic content of the Social Development Program can build the social capital needed for successful functioning of MFIs. Next, I discuss the status of Islamic MFIs with regard to the three fundamental problems related to sustainability of financing microenterprises:[27]

- *Mitigating credit risk*: As mentioned above, the innovative operational format of MFIs suits the poor, whose lack of physical collateral disqualifies them to borrow from traditional commercial banks. Islamic microfinance institutions (Islamic MFIs) have retained the innovative format of operation of conventional MFIs and oriented the program toward Islamic principles and values. Thus, like their conventional counterparts, Islamic MFIs have largely resolved the credit risks through social collateral of groups and weekly repayments.
- *Resolving the moral hazard problem*: Islamic MFIs have some inherent characteristics that can resolve the moral hazard problem faced by conventional MFIs pointed out above. The main mode of financing used by the Islamic MFIs is *murabaha/ bay' al-mu'ajjal* or *ijara* (leasing). These instruments involve real transaction and instead of cash being given out, an asset/good is exchanged. As a result, the opportunity of diverting funds for non-productive uses other than that requested for is reduced, if not eliminated. This increases the profitability of the MFI by decreasing the default rate.
- *Economic viability*: As Islamic MFIs operations are similar to their conventional counterparts, they face the problem of viability due to high operational and finance costs. Other than the initial start-up capital provided by a few volunteers, most of the funds for conventional MFIs come from external sources and beneficiary savings. Need for funds is the greatest during the initial stages of operations on the part of MFIs, when the beneficiaries' savings are nil or small. Islamic MFIs have not yet tapped the funds from Islamic institutional sources of *zakat*, charity, and *waqf*.

A survey by Ahmed[28] indicates that Islamic MFIs face certain problems in obtaining funds from external sources. First, the Islamic educational content of Islamic MFIs deters some external sources from funding these institutions. Second, though some funds are available from government agencies, they impose certain terms and conditions. Some of these terms and conditions are contrary to Islamic principles and limit the flexibility in the operations of Islamic MFIs. For example, the funds are given on interest and the MFIs are required to recover a certain fixed rate of return on their investments. As a result, funds from these sources cannot be employed in microfinancing with certain Islamic modes of financing such as *mudaraba* and *musharaka*. Islamic MFIs in Bangladesh identify lack of funds as one of the major constraints to growth and efficient operations.

Other than limiting the expansion of operations of MFIs, lack of funds has also other detrimental implications. They cannot hire sufficient workers at competitive wages. Lack of funds also means employing fewer field-level workers, lowering the employee–beneficiary ratio, and adversely affecting supervision and monitoring. Paying lower wages implies that they employ relatively low productivity workers. In the same survey, the officials of Islamic MFIs indicate that the benefits package given to employees is not as good as the established MFIs operating in the neighborhood. This sometimes induces employees with experience to move on to other MFIs paying better pay and benefits. These factors increase the probability of default and lowering the expected income of MFIs.

The above discussion shows that by adopting the group-based financing of the conventional MFIs, Islamic MFIs have resolved the problem of credit risk. Furthermore, the use of Islamic modes of financing linked to real transactions reduces the moral hazard problem by preventing diversion of funds for other purposes. The Islamic MFIs, however, have to tackle the economic viability problem faced by their conventional counterparts. Given this limitation of Islamic MFIs, I examine the prospects of Islamic banks to provide the much-needed funds to the poor microentrepreneurs next.

Financing microenterprises by Islamic banks

Most of the Islamic banks, like their conventional counterparts, have not ventured into microfinancing.[29] Whereas it is understandable why conventional banks are not involved in microfinancing, it is not befitting for Islamic banks to do the same. Islamic financial institutions have fundamentally different objectives compared to their conventional counterparts. Khan[30] points out that operations of Islamic banks have two aspects, namely the "mechanics of it" and the "spirit of it". While former relates to fulfilling the Islamic legal requirements in its operations, the latter relates to faith. Any institution (including non-Islamic ones) can fulfill the mechanics of Islamic banking by providing Islamic compatible financial contracts and transactions. The spirit of an Islamic enterprise, however, distinguishes an Islamic bank from a conventional bank. Khan[31] points out that different variants of conventional financial institutions (such as mutual funds, Rental Equity Participation Trusts, etc.) appear very close to Islamic modes of financing, but this doesn't make these institutions Islamic. He asserts that Islamic banking has to relate its activities to faith, if it is to distinguish itself from conventional financial institutions.

Khan[32] maintains that the philosophical basis of the faith component of Islamic banks lies in *adl* (social justice) and *ihsan* (benevolence). The implication of these concepts is "taking care of those who cannot be taken care of by the market, who cannot play with economic forces or do not have access to economic means to enable them to exploit the economic opportunities around them."[33] Given this characteristic, it is imperative on Islamic banks to include social dimensions in their operations along with the normal banking practices.

The question is how the social role of Islamic banks can be best exemplified.[34] One way of manifesting the social role of Islamic banks is to provide finance to the poor to increase their income and wealth. As mentioned above, most microfinance schemes have an integrated social development program. Islamic banks by adopting this approach of microfinancing can engage in a much broader program of wealth creation for the poor and bring about development. The innovative operational format used by the MFIs suits the poor and can be employed by the Islamic banks to provide such finance.

In addition to the social dimension, there are other arguments in favor of Islamic banks' involvement in microfinancing. Financing productive activities is the specialization of banks. Financing microentrepreneurs will be an extension of their client base. They already have the skilled manpower with the requisite know-how on which they can expand their microfinance operations. With its established network of branches, Islamic banks will be able to deliver services at a cost lower than that of MFIs.

With respect to the modus operandi of microfinance operations by an Islamic bank, the field-level operations can be conducted from its branches and a small department can coordinate these operations at the head-office (national) level.[35] At each branch, field workers will do the business under the supervision of field supervisors. An officer of the bank will oversee the microfinance operations of the branch. Microfinance operations will be focused among the poor in the vicinity of the branch. As in the case of MFIs, a small amount of credit is given to the poor without any physical collateral. In order to qualify for funds, beneficiaries have to be poor and form groups. Funds are provided under some Islamic mode of financing for three months to a year and repaid in weekly/monthly installments. An official from the Islamic bank conducts the microfinancing activities and collects installments at the weekly meetings at the center.

Given the above, we can compare the relative effectiveness of providing such finance by MFIs and by Islamic banks. We discuss the operations of Islamic banks in delivering microfinance in the light of the three fundamental problems discussed above. As pointed out, the Islamic banks will use the same format as the MFIs in microfinancing as this format suits the poor. Thus group-based financing will create the social collateral that will replace the physical collateral. This, along with the weekly installments will mitigate the credit risk and ensure the repayments to the Islamic banks. Islamic banks will use Islamic modes of financing and lessen the moral hazard problem faced by conventional MFIs. Details of costs and economic viability of the microfinance program of Islamic banks is discussed below.

Economic viability of microfinancing by Islamic banks

The operating costs of providing microfinance in case of Islamic banks will be much smaller than MFIs. As Islamic banks will provide microfinance from existing branches, it will not incur any extra fixed costs (rent, utilities, etc.). Furthermore, it will not require a whole range of professionals/employees, particularly at the top management level at the head office and regional offices. This will reduce the cost of operations at the head-office level. Note that the wages paid to the field workers and supervisors in case of Islamic banks are expected to be higher than their MFI counterparts. This will have two offsetting effects. On the one hand, higher wages will attract more productive field-level workers and on the other hand it will increase the wage bill. As the field-level workers are paid relatively low salaries as compared to professionals at the management level, the total wage bill for microfinance operations in Islamic banks is expected to be much lower than that of MFIs. Thus, we can conclude that the total operating costs of providing a certain amount of microfinance to a given number of beneficiaries will be lower in case of Islamic banks than those of MFIs.

As for the financing costs, Islamic banks' main sources of funds are deposits. The opportunity cost of using these funds is investment in alternative projects/investments. Most Islamic banks, however, have excess liquidity given the lack of Islamic compatible money-market instruments to park funds for shorter periods of time. Given this excess liquidity, the opportunity cost of using these funds is zero. Assuming that the Islamic banks offer its beneficiaries the same rate of return as MFIs on their savings, then we can conclude that the borrowing costs of funds will be lower in case of Islamic banks than MFIs. Furthermore, Islamic banks can employ adequate workers at competitive wages along with other benefits. This allows them to employ productive workers and maintain an appropriate employee–beneficiary ratio. These have a positive impact on the repayment rate and income of the bank. The above discussion shows that Islamic banks can finance microenterprises more efficiently (at a lower cost) than MFIs.

Islamic banks can devise a complementary program to finance the core poor. Extreme poverty leads to the diversion of funds from productive activities to consumption and asset purchases. This lowers the overall return on investment and makes it difficult for the poor to repay the loans. Most Islamic banks have a fund created from collections of penalties for late payments from overdue accounts. These funds, on principle, can only be spent on charitable activities. These funds can be integrated with the microfinancing either as outright grants or *qard hasan*. This will not only prevent diversion of funds from investment to consumption by the poor, but act as an added financial incentive to repay the funds taken for microentrepreneurs.

The discussion shows that implementing the social function by financing the poor will not be a burden to Islamic banks financially. Instead, Islamic banks are predisposed to provide microfinance in a "win–win" situation. That is, given the excess liquidity, Islamic banks can operate microfinance programs at no extra cost and improve the economic conditions of the poor. Experience from the Rural Development Scheme (RDS) of Islamic Bank Bangladesh Limited supports this assertion.[36]

Microfinancing using traditional Islamic instruments

In this section, I discuss how some traditional Islamic concepts/institutions of poverty alleviation and welfare enhancement can be used in microfinancing. These concepts include, among others, *zakat*, *waqf*, *qard hasan*, and *sadaqat*. *Zakat* is one of the fundamentals of Islam that has direct economic bearing upon others. It requires Muslims to distribute a part of their wealth among the specified heads in order to achieve economic emancipation of the poor. Similarly, *waqf* is a voluntary charitable act that has wide economic implications. These institutions were able to solve the problems of poverty and extend social services in the classical times.[37] *Sadaqat* (charities) and *qard hasan* (interest-free loan) are tools for supporting the poor and redistribution of income in their favor.

These traditional instruments of social welfare can be used in financing the poor entrepreneurs in two ways. First, these Islamic instruments can be integrated in the activities of the existing operations of Islamic MFIs/banks. Integrating *zakat* and income from *waqf* can be integrated into microfinancing can prevent fund diversions and benefit the poorest beneficiaries.[38] *Zakat* given to the poor can be used for consumption, asset building, and production purposes to complement funds of Islamic MFIs. These complementary funds can either be given as grants or interest-free loans (*qard hasan*) according to the needs of the beneficiary. As these complementary funds will reduce the need for diverting money for consumption and/or purchase of assets, it is expected the funds taken for productive activities will be invested accordingly. As a result, the overall return on invested funds is expected to be higher and the probability of default lower. Thus, integrating Islamic institutions of *zakat*, charities, and *waqf* with microfinancing will increase the probability of repayment of the funds to the Islamic MFI.

The second way in which the Islamic concepts can be used in microfinancing is to establish specialized institutions to cater for financing the poor microentrepreneurs. These organizations that can use group-based microfinancing are discussed below.

Cash *waqf*

Traditionally, the corpus of *waqf* has been in the form of land and real estate. One way in which the institution of *waqf* can be revitalized is by developing alternative ways that would enable people of all means to contribute to the creation of a *waqf*. In this respect, cash *waqf* is an old concept that needs to be revived. Cizakca[39] proposes the revival of cash *waqf* that flourished in Islamic empires starting from the medieval times and continued to the Ottoman period. *Waqf* were established in the form of cash for a charitable purpose. The cash was invested in the form of *mudaraba* or credit and the revenue generated from the investments were used for charitable purposes. The *waqf* funds were also given out as loans to underprivileged people and those of modest means. Cizakca suggests a model in which the concept of cash *waqf* can be used in contemporary times to serve the social objectives in the society. One use of cash *waqf* would be to provide microfinance to the poor. The *waqf* donated by individuals will serve as the capital of the microfinancing activity. The funds of the cash *waqf* can be used for microfinancing, provided guarantees are made to keep the amount of *waqf* intact through some mechanism. The loans given out can be at the market rates for commercial activities and *qard hasan* for urgent consumption needs of the poor.

Qard hasan banks

Qard hasan has an important position in Islam and was used widely in Islamic societies to give interest-free loans to the poor and the needy. Elgari[40] proposes establishing a non-profit financial intermediary, the *qard hasan* bank that gives interest-free loan (*qard hasan*) to finance consumer lending for the poor. The capital of the bank would come from monetary (cash) *waqf* donated by wealthy Muslims. Like any other bank, the institution will receive current deposits on which returns will be paid. The institution will advance short- and medium-term loans to individuals. The loans will only charge for actual administrative or service costs. The *qard hasan* bank can also get involved in group-based microfinancing to uplift the condition of the poor. The loans can be given both for consumption and investment purposes. A service charge to cover the costs of operations can be taken for the loans advanced.

MFI based on *waqf* and *zakat*

Kahf[41] proposes establishing an organization based on *zakat* and *waqf* to provide microfinancing to the poor. The returns from *waqf* and funds from *sadaqat* can be used to finance productive microenterprises at subsidized rates. In addition, *zakat* can be given out to the poor for consumption purposes to avoid diversion of funds from productive heads. The combination of microfinancing and *zakat* funds will make it easier for the poor to break out of the poverty cycle.

Ahmed[42] suggests a model of *waqf*-based Islamic MFI that can provide microfinancing and facilitate wealth creation of the poor. Cash *waqf* would form the capital of the MFI. The capital along with deposits will be used to finance the poor. The *waqf*-based MFI, however, has to create various reserves to cover various risks arising due to the nature of its assets and liabilities. A higher percentage of the *waqf* endowment can be used for microfinancing as these reserves held by the MFI increase. Ahmed's paper also suggests some other sources of funds that Islamic MFIs can tap into to expand their operations. Other than using *zakat* and *sadaqat* as additional resources, Islamic banks can also provide microfinancing efficiently without cutting into their profits.

The institutions described above have one common element. Being established as non-profit organizations, the funds of these institutions come from charitable sources. This implies that there are no financing costs of funds. By using the format of group-based financing and weekly installments, these institutions will mitigate the credit risk and ensure repayment. Similarly, the use of Islamic modes of financing mitigates the moral hazard problem. Finally, as the funds to be used will be based on charitable donations, the financing costs of funds will be non-existent. Furthermore, as the operating costs will be covered from the returns, these institutions can be economically viable entities.

Conclusion

Microfinance is widely acclaimed as a new approach to alleviate poverty and bring about development. This chapter provides the theoretical basis and operational framework for alternative institutions to provide microfinance-based lending according to Islamic principles. The chapter discusses the operations of conventional MFIs and examines their strengths and weaknesses. While conventional MFIs have successfully resolved the credit risk problem by instituting group-based lending and collecting weekly installments, the problems of moral hazard and economic viability still pose difficulties to them. As group-lending and weekly repayments effectively resolve the credit risk problem in financing the poor, these aspects can be adopted by the Islamic institutions providing microfinance. Given this as the basis, various alternatives of Islamic institutions that can provide microfinance are presented.

The Islamic institutions that can provide microfinance are MFIs, Islamic banks, and specialized institutions based on traditional Islamic instruments of *zakat, waqf, qard hasan*, etc. Use of Islamic modes of financing by these institutions can mitigate the problem of diversion of funds to non-productive uses as these transactions involve transfer of real assets/goods. Islamic MFIs, however, still have to deal with the viability problem due to high costs of operations. Islamic banks can finance poor mircoentrepreneurs as a manifestation of their social objectives. The chapter contends that Islamic banks can provide microfinancing more efficiently and effectively than MFIs mainly due to reduced operational costs. The institutions of *zakat, waqf, qard hasan*, and *sadaqat* can be integrated into microfinancing program to effectively alleviate absolute poverty. This can be done either by integrating these instruments in the operations of the Islamic MFIs/banks or by establishing new institutions. These institutions include the *cash waqf, qard hasan* bank, and MFIs based on *zakat* and *waqf*. These institutions can be viable as they do not have any financing costs of the funds they use in microfinancing.

As eradication of poverty is considered an important objective of an Islamic economic system, institutions providing microfinance can play an important role in reaching this goal. The chapter presents a strong case for alternative Islamic institutions to provide microfinancing and facilitate wealth creation for the poor. The institutional structures of contemporary MFIs, Islamic banks, and the traditional Islamic instruments (such as *zakat, waqf, qard hasan*, etc.) can be combined to finance poor microenterprises. These latter instruments, however, are not being employed in microfinancing to their full usable potentials. To make these various alternative models of Islamic microfinancing operational there is a need for more research on various aspects of these institutions.

Notes

1 Sharjah Chair in Islamic Law and Finance, Durham University, Durham, United Kingdom.
2 World Bank, *Employment and Development of Small Enterprises*, Sector Policy Paper, World Bank, Washington, DC. 1978.
3 For an extensive study on microfinance: Hulme, David and Paul Mosley, *Finance Against Poverty*, Volume 1, Routledge, London. 1996a; Hulme, David and Paul Mosley, *Finance Against Poverty*, Volume 2, Routledge, London. 1996b; Kimenyi, Mwangi S., Robert C. Wieland, and J.D.V. Pischke (Editors), *Strategic Issues in Microfinance*, Ashgate Publishing Ltd, Aldershot. 1998; Otero, Maria and Elisabeth Rhyne (Editors), *The New World of Microenterprise Finance*, Kumarian Press, West Hartford, CT. 1994; Schneider, Hartmut

(Editor), *Microfinance for the Poor, Development Centre of the Organization for Economic Cooperation and Development*, OECD, Paris. 1997.

4 Op. cit. World Bank, 1978, p. 18.

5 Though in some jurisdictions, a difference is made between microenterprises and enterprises financed by microfinance institutions, in this chapter I consider these two kinds of enterprises to be the same.

6 Bennett, Lynn, "Combining Social and Financial Intermediation to Reach the Poor: The Necessity and the Dangers", in Kimenyi, Mwangi S., Robert C. Wieland, and J.D.V. Pischke (Editors), *Strategic Issues in Microfinance*, Ashgate Publishing Ltd, Aldershot. 1998.

7 Ibid.

8 Though different approaches to microfinance have evolved, the format discussed here is that of Grameen Bank, which serves as the dominant model for most group-based microfinance institutions (Morduch, Jonathan, "The Microfinance Promise," *Journal of Economic Literature*. 1999b, 37, pp. 1569–1614).

9 Different MFIs define their target group in different ways. For example, to be eligible to get credit from Grameen Bank a household must own less than 0.4 acres of land and must not have assets exceeding the market value of one acre of cultivable land.

10 Huppi, M. and Gershon Feder, "The Role of Groups and Credit Co-operatives in Rural Lending," *World Bank Research Observer*. 1990, 5, pp. 187–204.

11 Ahmed, Habib, "Financing Microenterprises: An Analytical Study if Islamic Microfinance Institutions," *Islamic Economic Studies*. 2002, 9 (2), pp. 27–64.

12 For accomplishments of MFIs see Bornstein, David, *The Price of a Dream: The Story of Grameen Bank and the Idea that is Helping the Poor to Change their Lives*, University Press, Dhaka. 1996; Fuglesang, Andreas and Dale Chandler, *Participation as Process – Process as Growth: What We Can Learn from Grameen Bank*, Grameen Trust, Dhaka. 1993; Goetz, A. Marie and Rina S. Gupta, "Who Takes the Credit? Gender, Power, and Control over Loan Use in Rural Credit Programmes in Bangladesh," *World Development*. 1996. 24, pp. 45–63; Hashemi, Syed M., Sidney R. Schuler, and Ann P. Riley, "Rural Credit Programs and Women's Empowerment in Bangladesh," *World Development*. 1996. 24, pp. 635–653; Hossain, M., *Credit Programme for the Landless: The Experience of Grameen Bank Project*, Bangladesh Institute of Development Studies, Dhaka. 1983; Hossain, M., "Employment Generation Through Cottage Industries—Potentials and Constraints: The Case of Bangladesh." In Islam, Rizwanul (Editor) *Rural Industrialisation and Employment in Asia*, ILO, Asian Employment Programme, New Delhi. 1987.

13 Rahman, Aminur, "Micro-credit Initiatives for Equitable and Sustainable Development: Who Pays?" *World Development*, 27(1), 1999, p. 75.

14 Buckley, Graeme, "Rural and Agricultural Credit in Malawi, A Study of the Malawi Muzdi Fund and the Smallholder Agricultural Credit Administration," in Hulme, David and Paul Mosley, *Finance Against Poverty*, Volume 2, London: Routledge, 1996, pp. 333–407.

15 Op. cit. Morduch, Jonathan, 1999b.

16 Op. cit. Bennett, Lynn, 1998.

17 Reed, Larry R. and David R. Befus, "Transformation Lending: Helping Microenterprises Become Small Businesses," in Otero, Maria and Elisabeth Rhync (Editors), *The New World of Microenterprise Finance*, Kumarian Press, West Hartford, CT, 1994. pp. 185–204.

18 Hashemi, Syed M., "Building up Capacity for Banking with the Poor: The Grameen Bank in Bangladesh," in Schneider, Hartmut (Editor), *Microfinance for the Poor*, Development Centre of the Organization for Economic Cooperation and Development, OECD, Paris. 1997.

19 Khandker, Shahidur R., Baqui Khalily, and Zahed Khan, *Grameen Bank: Performance and Sustainability*, World Bank Discussion Papers, No. 306, The World Bank, Washington, DC. 1995.

20 Yaron, Jacob, "Performance of Development Finance Institutions: How to Access It?," in Schneider, Hartmut (Editor), *Microfinance for the Poor*, Development Centre of the Organization for Economic Cooperation and Development, OECD, Paris. 1997.

21 Op cit. Hashemi, Syed M., 1997.

22 Op. cit. Hulme, David and Paul Mosley, 1996a.

23 Op. cit. Ahmed, Habib, 2002.

24 Detailed expositions of the different principles of Islamic financing are found in Kahf, Monzer and Tariqullah Khan, *Principles of Islamic Financing, A Survey*, Islamic Research and Training Institute, Jeddah, Research Paper No. 16. 1992; Ahmad, Ausaf, *Contemporary Practice of Islamic Financing Techniques*, Islamic Research and Training Institute, Jeddah, Research Paper. 1993. 20pp.

25 Ahmad, Aka Firowz, "The Management System of NGOs Micro-Credit Program for Poverty Alleviation in Bangladesh," paper presented at the First International Conference on Islamic Development Management, Penang, December, 1998.

26 The use of these institutions are discussed in section five.

27 Op. cit. Ahmed, Habib, 2002.

28 Ibid.

29 Some state owned Islamic banks are providing microfinancing due to government policy. Examples are banks in banks in Sudan and Bank Nasr in Egypt.

30 Khan, M. Fahim, "Social Dimensions of Islamic Banks in Theory and Practice," Islamic Research and Training Institute and Islamic Development Bank, manuscript. 1997.

31 Ibid.

32 Ibid.

33 Ibid., pp. 12–13.

34 Ibid. Khan suggests a variety of activities like *qard hasan*, financing housing, meeting basic needs, and promoting and financing small entrepreneurs. All these aspects, however, can be covered in a comprehensive integrated program with focus of microfinancing.

35 Ahmed, Habib, "Frontiers of Islamic Banking: A Synthesis of Social Role and Microfinance," *The European Journal of Management and Public Policy*. 2004, 3, pp. 120–140.

36 Ibid.

37 For detailed discussions see El-Ashker, Ahmed Abdel-Fattah and Muhammad Sirajul Haq, *Institutional Framework of Zakah: Dimensions and Implications*, Islamic Research and Training Institute, Jeddah, Seminar Proceedings 1995. No. 23; Basar, Hasmet (Editor), Management and Development of Awqaf Properties, Islamic Research and Training Institute, Research–Seminar–Workshop Proceedings. 1987. No. 1; Cizakca, Murat, "The Relevance of the Ottoman Cash *Waqfs (Awqaf al Nuqud)* for Modern Islamic Economics", in Mannan, M.A. (Editor), *Financing Development is Islam*, Islamic Research and Training Institute, Jeddah, Seminar Proceedings Series. 1996. No. 30; Cizakca, Murat, "*Awqaf* in History and Implications for Modern Islamic Economics", paper presented at International Seminar on Awqaf and Economic Development, Kuala Lumpur. 1998.

38 Op. cit., Ahmed, Habib, 2002.

39 Cizakca, Murat, "Cash Waqf as Alternative to NBFIs Bank," paper presented in the International Seminar on Nonbank Financial Institutions: Islamic Alternatives, Kuala Lumpur, jointly organized by Islamic Research and Training Institute, Islamic Development Bank, and Islamic Banking and Finance Institute Malaysia. March 1–3, 2004.

40 Ibid.

41 Kahf, Monzer, "Shari'ah and Historical Aspects of Zakat and Awqaf," background paper prepared for Islamic Research and Training Institute and Islamic Development Bank. 2004.

42 Ahmed, Habib, "Waqf-Based Microfinance: Realizing the Social Role of Islamic Finance," paper presented at International Seminar on Integrating *Awqaf* in the Islamic Financial Sector, Singapore. March 6–7, 2007.

3   Islamic finance and microfinance

An insurmountable gap?[1]

Saif I. Shah Mohammed[2]

Introduction

Microfinance has been viewed as an important tool in poverty alleviation. However, Islamic finance, which has always envisioned a role for itself in development activity, has been strangely absent from the microfinance sector and microfinance debates.[3] This chapter examines the scope for cooperation between Islamic finance and microfinance.

Certain trends in the microfinance sector that have important implications for the involvement of Islamic finance are first discussed. I then ask if the technical challenges to the use of *shari'a*-compliant products in microfinance are insurmountable. I argue that while the standard micro-credit contract can easily be adjusted to fit the *murabaha* model, it is also worthwhile to re-conceptualize the standard micro-credit contract to recognize important insurance and service elements that are often embedded substantively in them. Formally recognizing some of these substantive elements in contractual forms may provide avenues for the involvement of Islamic finance in micro-credit activity that would add value to the clients of microfinance institutions and create scope for the involvement of Islamic finance in microfinance. Finally, I note that while the technical gap between Islamic finance and microfinance is not insurmountable, there is a perceptions gap between microfinance and Islamic finance that poses challenges.[4]

Microfinance institutions have been criticized for over-hyping their impact.[5] Critics have also pointed at incidents of abuse.[6] While being aware of such criticism of the sector, I must note as an initial matter that I do not address it here. It is not my objective here to discuss or defend the impact of microfinance in this chapter.

Implications of certain trends in microfinance

A recent empirical study of high-quality microfinance institutions found that nearly 20 percent of the funding for leading microfinance institutions that are committed to financial self-sustainability came from subsidized sources.[7] The study found that after accounting adjustments were made, over half of these institutions were profitable (though returns on assets were still negative overall), and the others in the survey were about to achieve profitability and financial sustainability. While it is true that the survey only included the leading microfinance institutions, it provides some support for the claim that microfinance institutions can operate profitably and sustainably. Microfinance has clearly come a long way from 1999, when Jonathan Morduch noted the bleak consensus view of a group of "sustainably-minded" panelists that only 5 percent of microfinance programs would ever be financially sustainable,[8] suggesting that there was no long-term escape from subsidies for microfinance.

The trend in microfinance towards financial sustainability and profitability has not gone unnoticed by the commercial financial sector. Even as far back as 2001, nearly 29 percent of funds used in microfinance activity in Latin America were provided by commercial banks.[9] In addition to the possibility of profit, the resilience of microfinance in weathering economic upheaval is being increasingly appreciated,[10] allowing microfinance institutions to advertise the benefits of their sector as a promising investment opportunity in emerging markets.[11] And by recent indicators, commercial sector interest in microfinance is growing rapidly. For example, one study that excluded non-governmental organizations (NGOs), cooperatives and government-controlled institutions to identify commercial microfinance institutions[12] found that total assets and loan portfolios of such institutions grew by around 200 percent between 2004 and 2006. Similarly, foreign investment in microfinance has also drastically increased recently. While government-owned development funding institutions (DFIs) account for nearly half of foreign investment into microfinance, private sector institutional investors have drastically increased their role in microfinance institutional vehicles (MIVs) that channel nearly half of foreign DFI, individual and institutional investor investments into microfinance. Investment levels in these MIVs doubled between 2005 and 2006. In fact, institutional investors such as pension funds account for nearly 20 percent of funds in 2006, up from only 2 percent in 2004. Lending by international banks to microfinance institutions grew by nearly $100 million—more than 20 percent—between 2005 and 2006.[13]

This increase commercial funding of microfinance is channeled in a number of ways. As noted, MIVs are often used to channel foreign capital to microfinance institutions. MIVs and domestic investors in microfinance can invest directly through equity, and a number of equity transactions—billed as private equity investments in microfinance—have been reported in recent years. And some microfinance institutions have made equity offerings to the public.[14]

Aside from equity investments, direct loans to microfinance institutions by international investors to microfinance institutions grew to nearly $550 million by 2006.[15] Similarly, domestic-currency loans to microfinance institutions—and syndication of these loans among domestic institutional investors—are increasingly common.

Increasingly, investors can also avail of a number of structured finance products to invest in microfinance. In 2002, Compartamos introduced the first microfinance investment bond, a $100 million offering, and the issue was arranged by Citigroup. That transaction has been followed by a number of innovative financial transactions in the sector. The first bond backed by loans to microfinance institutions was issued by Blue Orchard in 2004.[16] In July 2006, the world's first securitization of microfinance receivables was completed by BRAC in Bangladesh.[17] Bonds and collateralized loan obligations are now quite commonplace in the sector, and transactions involve many of the leading Wall Street investment banks as investors or arrangers.

But the involvement of commercial players in microfinance does not have to take place through financial instruments alone. Increasingly, the possibility of commercial banks "downstreaming" their operations to include microfinance lending is being noted.[18] More commonly, commercial banks are creating partnerships with existing microfinance institutions wherein microfinance institutions provide micro-credit loans on behalf of commercial banks. Many of the pioneering transactions of this nature have happened in India, where two methods have been used to link commercial banks to microfinance, bringing commercial funding to hundreds of thousands of microfinance borrowers. One method sees a self-help group (that is formed by groups of individuals independently with the help of a microfinance institution) borrowing directly from the bank, with the group responsible to the commercial bank for repayment. The second method, pioneered by ICICI in India, involves the sale of present and future microfinance loans by microfinance institutions to the commercial bank, effectively resulting in the microfinance institution making loans indirectly on behalf of the microfinance bank.[19]

Increasingly, retail players in developing countries are also noticing the potential of microfinance to increase both their customer base and their profits. Walmart in Mexico has embarked on expanding its operations to extend financial services to low-income borrowers, combining its retail operations with banking. Similarly, non-banking commercial enterprises can team up with microfinance institutions to reach their products to low-income groups, taking advantage of networks created by microfinance institutions and the ability of microfinance borrowers to fund and credibly pay for purchases through the methodology of microfinance institutions. Perhaps the most well-known example is the pioneering partnership between Grameen Phone (a commercial entity) and Grameen Bank (a microfinance institution) to reach and spread mobile phone technology to low-income and rural groups in Bangladesh.[20]

In addition to the commercialization of microfinance is the move towards better empirical measurement of the impact of microfinance activity. The work of institutions such as the Massachusetts Institute of Technology's (MIT) Poverty Action Lab[21] with randomized field experiments will likely have an impact upon the way microfinance institutions approach their work. Well-designed impact studies will play an increasing role in product design and delivery.

Successful microfinance institutions have created networks of clients. Existing relationships with these clients provide benefits in information and enforcement. Commercialization allows these institutions to scale up these networks to take advantage of economies of scale, and also address the growing needs of these clients, giving them incentives to continue participating in these networks.[22] Islamic finance institutions entering the industry may try to set up their own networks to compete with the established players, but this will be expensive. If the aim of involvement is to maximize access for the poor to *shari'a*-compliant funds, Islamic financial institutions would likely find that cooperating rather than competing with established microfinance institutions is most effective.

But commercialization also means that Islamic financial institutions are entering a sector in which established players are not without choices and existing partners. Because of the scale that many of the effective institutions have achieved, and because their ways of operating often reflect years of accumulated experience with operational constraints, microfinance institutions will be understandably reluctant to fundamentally change their products. The burden of persuasion will rest on the Islamic finance sector to prove a real difference in value as they push for change.

Additionally, the increased use of impact studies will mean that Islamic financial institutions will enter the sector at a time when microfinance institutions will have to be flexible in their design and delivery of products. Insofar as Islamic finance is viewed as a prohibition-driven industry, and the rationale and rules of Islamic finance jurisprudence are poorly understood, microfinance institutions may well be wary about cooperation.

Addressing the technical gap

The most common micro-credit contract is some variation of the Grameen model. Generally, these contracts have the following formal conditions:

- The loans are short term, usually payable within a year.
- A flat interest rate is usually cited, with interest calculated over the entire period and the entire principal amount initially borrowed. (The effective interest rates are thus higher than the cited rate.)
- Installments are periodic (weekly, bi-weekly or monthly), and usually of equal sizes, calculated by dividing the sum of the principal and total interest for the loan period at the cited flat rate by the total number of installments.

Additionally, many institutions include some element of group liability, though the general trend has been towards individualized lending.[23] Further, institutions may require (or strongly suggest) a compulsory building up of savings.[24] Some institutions allow for rebates on prepayments, and charge fees for missing installments.

Adjusting this contractual model to fit into the *murabaha* structure is somewhat trivial.[25] In fact, there are already *shari'a*-compliant microfinance institutions that have created *murabaha* products.[26] However, as I argue below, it may be helpful for the Islamic finance industry to think beyond the standard product.

Re-conceptualizing the micro-credit contract: more than loans

We are conditioned to think of micro-credit contracts as loans under the conventional sense of the term. This partially has to do with the use of language—it is, after all, micro-*credit* that we speak of, and a credit contract in our mind is a loan, and a loan has certain characteristics and features that we take for granted. This may also have to do with the way that micro-credit has been reported in the media. The classic anecdote is of a borrower (usually a woman) who goes to a micro-credit institution, takes a loan, invests the money in a micro-enterprise, which grows and allows her to repay the loan. Finally, microfinance institutions themselves have described their activities as lending. Depending on what the loan is used for, micro-credit contracts are analogized to short-term investment loans, or working capital loans, and sometimes (because of the size of the loan) to credit card loans.

Describing micro-credit contracts as loans of course leaves them open to the charge of being *ribawi*, or *interest bearing*. Certainly, given its formal terms, the standard Grameen-type contract (described above) would be *ribawi* under mainstream Islamic financial jurisprudence. Money is exchanged for money, with an increase for the lender when it is repaid. However, as already noted, it may be possible to adjust the contractual arrangements so that they fit into the *murabaha* category.

But viewing micro-credit contracts as simply *loans* may be misunderstanding and mischaracterizing their substance. Professor Robert Townsend tells us that the micro-credit contract should not be viewed as a simple fixed-debt obligation, and there are contingencies and processes that need to be taken into account.[27] In practice, microfinance institutions often delay collections, reduce interest rates and even cancel loans in times of distress, and thus the contract includes an insurance element as well. Additionally, microfinance institutions provide emergency aid and consumption loans to borrowers to help them get through disaster situations. During the disastrous floods in Bangladesh in 1998, the major microfinance institutions gave their local managers discretion to reschedule payments in flood-affected areas.[28] After the 2004 floods, which affected 39 out of 64 districts in Bangladesh, BRAC provided emergency food aid and soft-term consumption loans to its borrowers in flood-affected areas.[29] The expectations of such insurance services may be part and parcel of the contractual arrangement, even if not expressly provided for in the formal terms of the contract.

That these contracts are in substance loan-plus-insurance contracts rather than simple loan contracts may also explain the puzzling definitions of default rates that are common in the microfinance sector. At BRAC, for example, a loan is considered to have defaulted only if the borrower has not paid the amount collectible from her 52 weeks after the money was borrowed. A defaulting borrower finds it difficult to borrow again from BRAC. The number of weekly installments owed to BRAC is 46. However, a missed installment before the 52-week period is up does not count as a default. Further, no additional interest is calculated on a missed installment within the 52-week period. It is this kind of definition that is behind the high 97–99 percent repayment rates that are widely quoted. For a conventional loan with a fixed principal/interest repayment schedule, such a definition of default would seem strange. One can view such definition as slippery or delusional, but arguably, it is consistent with viewing these contracts as more than loans: BRAC builds into its enforcement of the contractual arrangement a six-week buffer and allowances for delays in payments from week to week.[30]

Recognizing that these contractual arrangements are something more than conventional loans does not automatically remove charges that there are *ribawi* elements in them; this is not the argument I am making here. But re-conceptualizing the micro-credit contract allows us to identify ways in which the Islamic finance sector can help microfinance institutions improve and enhance the value they deliver to prospective borrowers: Note that when substantive expectations are not formally noted in the contract, the uncertainty of the borrower is increased. Creating incentives for microfinance institutions to formalize some of insurance elements of the contract may enhance the value received by the borrowers.

A hypothetical example illustrates this dynamic. Let's say a *shari'a*-compliant micro-credit institution enters into a *murabaha* contract with a borrower with the purpose of helping her buy a cow. The cow would give milk, which in turn would generate income that would allow her to pay back the money received from the micro-credit institution, and help her climb out of poverty. But all else being constant, the borrower would still prefer a contract in which it was understood that the microfinance institution would reschedule payments and give her relief aid or consumption loans in the case of a natural disaster. The simple *murabaha* contract would simply not capture the benefits received from a loan contract offered by a conventional microfinance institution that informally includes an insurance component. Now let's say that a *waqf* fund guarantees that in case of a disaster, a certain amount of emergency aid and a *qard hasan* loan shall be provided to benefit an affected borrower if the rescheduling condition is pre-written into the contract. The *murabaha* micro-credit contract now not only includes the insurance element, but is also superior to the conventional micro-credit contract because of lower uncertainty in receiving the benefit of insurance.

The potential benefits of such formalization can be seen from the experience of BRAC during the 1998 floods. Zaman[31] reports that interviews with borrowers revealed that even during the floods, borrowers made it a high priority to not miss any installments as they viewed it as the only way to get a larger loan and thus increase their liquidity. For the same reason, borrowers were reluctant to reduce the savings that they had deposited at BRAC because they knew that under BRAC's rules, they would require a certain amount of savings to get a larger loan (and thus greater liquidity in the crisis). BRAC's discretionary rescheduling was inadequate. As discussed here, this is a natural avenue for greater, value-enhancing involvement by Islamic finance institutions.

Further re-conceptualizing the micro-credit contract: services

There is a dimension to the activities of many microfinance institutions that their critics often underplay or do not recognize. Microfinance institutions—particularly institutions such as BRAC taking a holistic approach to development—are heavily involved in the lives of their borrowers. Micro-credit lending often involves more than just disbursing and collecting money. Microfinance institutions often provide services to the borrowers as well.

Often these services are in the form of technical support and advice. For example, BRAC provides advice on seed selection, proper irrigation and fertilizer use to borrowers involved in activities such as horticulture. (Often borrowers have been the first to receive access to new seed varieties that BRAC has developed in its nurseries.) It also provides stock selection and basic veterinary care advice to borrowers involved in dairy and poultry farming. BRAC connects its borrowers producing handicrafts and garments to appropriate market outlets. Borrowers often also receive training on basic business skills, and are helped to identify and access new opportunities. Grameen introducing village telephones in Bangladesh is a notable example of a microfinance institution providing such opportunities.

Additionally, many microfinance institutions are involved in advocacy and dispute resolution, and access to such support is a valuable service provided to borrowers. The 16 Decisions in the Grameen system and BRAC's 18 Promises are well known. Many of these Decisions/Promises drilled into borrowers at group meetings involve education, nutrition, sanitation, healthcare, family planning and the shunning of female dowry and child marriage. While it is debatable how much these drills work to imbibe values into borrowers, there is some indication that micro-credit to women has an impact upon the nutritional and educational choices that borrowers can make for themselves and children.[32] It is reasonable to believe that support from microfinance institutions and peers who share the risk of the micro-credit contract enhance the negotiating power of female borrowers in family disputes, particular the knotty decisions involving family planning, child-rearing and the allocation of family spending on nutrition, education and healthcare.

Many microfinance institutions provide their borrowers with access to free or low-cost education and healthcare services (which are partially funded by profits from microfinance activities). For example, in addition to providing its borrowers with low-cost access to its hospitals and clinics, BRAC also uses the weekly group meetings of its borrowers to push vaccination and health education programs. Additionally microfinance institutions also provide borrowers with a powerful external discipline mechanism for the building up of productive assets and savings.

It must also be acknowledged that not all microfinance institutions provide such services. In Bangladesh, for example, BRAC and Grameen have taken the more holistic approach of providing services, while another large institution, ASA, confines its work to providing micro-credit loans and mobilizing savings. In the institutions that provide the additional services, arguably the expectation that such services will be provided is built into the contractual arrangement. These contracts then are not just exchanges of money for money, but exchanges of money for money *and* services.[33]

Formal inclusion of these services—particularly technical assistance—into micro-credit contracts may reduce the risk that they will be under-provided or neglected by microfinance institutions. It may also induce these institutions to better target and monitor the provision and the impact of these services. Again, Islamic finance can provide the impetus for such formalization.

Moving beyond the micro-credit contract: micro-equity products?

There may be a case for moving away from the standard micro-credit contract described above to more equity-based models. The weekly/monthly payment schedule that is seen in the standard micro-credit contracts may not fit the cash flows from the productive activities that borrowed funds are invested in. As a result, borrowers may be risk averse about the amounts that they borrow and invest. And they may choose to invest in activities with lower returns that provide continuous streams of incomes allowing them to meet their periodic installments instead of investing in activities with delayed but higher returns. For example, more than 50 percent of BRAC's borrowers invest in trading—a low-return activity, but one that provides a continuous (and fairly stable) stream of income. Further, borrowers who do invest in longer-term activities may be required to set aside liquid cash, earning no returns to meet periodic installments.

Professors Abhijit Bannerjee and Ester Duflo of MIT found evidence of under-lending to small firms in India, and that net returns (after interest) were nearly 73 percent.[34] Small firms were clearly credit-constrained, and were not operating near the point of diminishing marginal returns to additional investments. There may be economies of scale within reach of micro-entrepreneurs. By way of illustration, the average fixed costs for running a larger shop or raising two cows instead of one may be lower, for example, and the amount of labor required may not differ by much.

But in expanding their businesses, micro-entrepreneurs may face two constraints. First, microfinance institutions may themselves be capital constrained, and not be willing or able to provide them the additional funds. Second—and perhaps more importantly—the micro-entrepreneurs themselves may be wary of borrowing additional amounts to expand their businesses because of the risk of being stuck with loans too large to pay off in the case of disasters. Besides, larger loans also mean larger installments, which the liquidity available to the micro-entrepreneurs may not cover in the short term.

In assessing a profit-and-loss sharing "micro-equity" product, which would seemingly address such considerations, one has to keep in mind the kinds of constraints faced (and addressed) by the standard micro-credit contract. Particularly, administering and monitoring an equity product will be difficult. Entrepreneurs will typically be illiterate, and thus there will likely be little bookkeeping to keep track of income and costs.

Risk is sometimes reduced in the standard microfinance context by peer monitoring or group liability. Additionally, the promise of a larger loan in the future provides an incentive to repay (and often, prepay) the loan. But the standard micro-credit contract contains fewer moving parts to monitor. And even if mechanisms could be designed for effective monitoring, the cost of doing so would need to be considered.

Given economies of scale, making and servicing micro-equity investments would need to be scalable as well. For this, administrative processes of disbursement, monitoring and collection would have to be replicable across a wide range of activities and conditions. Personnel of these microfinance institutions would have to be able to respond and adapt to variety.

One way to overcome some of the operational constraints is to have specialized units for different kinds of activities (e.g., a specialized unit could disburse and monitor entrepreneurs involved in dairy production). But the cost-effectiveness of such specialized units—particularly in areas with spread-out populations or bad infrastructure—would need to be taken into account. An alternative approach would be to push the design of contracts and processes towards greater inflexibility by reducing the discretion of on-the-ground staff and micro-entrepreneurs. The number of moving parts to monitor and administer would thus be reduced. But such inflexibility may reduce the efficacy of having micro-equity contracts in the first place.

Monitoring cost and scalability constraints may not be insurmountable. Technology may soon provide solutions that the microfinance industry may use to good effect. Information and communications technology holds vast promise. Cellular telephony has taken off in many developing countries. In Bangladesh, all districts are now connected to cell-phone networks, and indeed, microfinance has had something to do with this. In the last decade, Grameen Phone was able to utilize the microfinance networks created by Grameen Bank as micro-entrepreneurs generating income through these cell-phones in rural areas were financed by micro-credit loans.

As cellular telephony penetrates deeper into developing markets, transactions will take place over cell-phones as well. Services in developing countries already match buyers to sellers over cell-phones. Microfinance institutions may find themselves able to track income and costs of their clients through the transactional information captured by cell-phone companies. Such technology may also allow on-the-ground staff performing monitoring activities to connect to specialists in centralized locations.

The large microfinance institutions—particularly the ones that take a holistic approach to development—already gather treasure troves of household information and personal information about their clients. These institutions do not always leverage these data very well, but improved data mining may allow institutions to track and monitor their clients and predict risks. Limited cooperation among microfinance institutions may help institutions keep track of transactions—sales of outputs as well as purchases of inputs—of micro-entrepreneurs.[35]

Additionally, microfinance institutions may act as bulk buyers of inputs that micro-entrepreneurs may use, thus providing access to cheaper inputs, or at least providing a benchmark for calculating profits and losses. Similarly, institutions may connect micro-entrepreneurs to outlets for their products. This too would allow benchmarking for profit calculations. For example, in Africa, the agriculture multinational Dunavant is involved in providing inputs, outputs as well as micro-credit facilities to its clients. In Bangladesh, BRAC provides producers of handicrafts with access to raw materials as well markets. Such approaches are conceivably adaptable to the micro-equity context.

One wonders, however, if the case for micro-equity products is overstated. An appropriately tailored micro-credit loan facility combined with an insurance product that protects against the downside risk of disaster would fulfill many of the same functions as a micro-equity product. A micro-credit borrower provided such a contract and wishing to expand her business would not have to fear the risk of not being able to meet large installments in the event of a disaster. The fact that installments would fit the cash flows generated by the investment would mean that liquidity concerns would not loom as threateningly for the borrower. On the insurance end of the contract, there is scope for both commercial and philanthropic involvement, varying with borrower circumstances and risk.

The pernicious perceptions gap

I have argued here that the technical gap between Islamic finance and microfinance is not insurmountable. The existing microfinance contract can easily be adapted to be *shari'a*-compliant. Further, there are openings for Islamic finance to make a case for value-enhancing involvement, by formalizing the insurance and service components of existing arrangements. Additionally micro-equity arrangements may be within reach as well. However, if Islamic finance is to involve itself in microfinance activity, there needs to be greater cooperation between the two sectors. There is a perception gap that separates Islamic finance and microfinance (at least in my experience in Bangladesh) that needs to be addressed for such cooperation.

Many Bangladeshi microfinance practitioners that I have spoken to speak of "antagonism" and "distrust" between themselves and the "Islamic sector." Some say that they avoid working with "Islamic" organizations where possible. They say that there is "little or no common ground" for cooperation. Such perceptions color their views of Islamic financial institutions as well, which are grouped with the "Islamic sector."

What explains this hostility? It may be such comments reflect the ideological biases of microfinance practitioners, and such biases may be unfair. On the other hand, microfinance institutions in Bangladesh faced local resistance early on from rural elites, including rural religious leaders, who claimed that their activities would "Christianize" the population.[36] Indeed, development practitioners in other contexts have faced similar resistance (e.g., the widely reported boycott by Nigerian clerics of a polio immunization campaign a few years back comes to mind[37]). Microfinance practitioners also point to ideological differences with the "Islamic sector," and here they feel that the gap may be unbridgeable. In particular, they point at ideological differences over microfinance institutions' work with women. But many microfinance practitioners view the empowerment of women as one of their central goals, and there is some support for the positive spillover effects of such work with women. But it is precisely this work that has been attacked by many religious leaders.

Islamic finance institutions must approach microfinance institutions keeping this backdrop in mind. It is perhaps unfair to burden Islamic finance institutions with such baggage. But these do play a role in forming perceptions. Suspicion is unavoidable—and needs to be recognized and addressed.

In my experience, many microfinance practitioners are able to recognize and applaud the work that many religious charities do in providing social safety nets. They are able to separate the political involvement of a few religious scholars from the rest. Some point proudly to the partnerships that they've been able to build in some areas with rural *imams*. They are able to recognize the potential of harnessing *zakat* funds for relief and rehabilitation. But many Bangladeshi microfinance practitioners I have spoken to view ideological differences over the goals of development, including the empowerment of women, will limit cooperation. As one microfinance practitioner told me: "The differences here seem to be *fundamental*."

One may claim that the history and politics of Bangladesh are *sui generis*. It is true that extrapolations from the Bangladesh experience to other parts of the Muslim world need to be made cautiously. However, there is good reason to think that the perceptions gap will exist elsewhere as well. It would be natural for microfinance institutions and development agencies to view the possibility of increased involvement of clerics in development activity with some suspicion.

Conclusion

Cooperation between microfinance and Islamic finance institutions will require more than the development of new *shari'a*-compliant microfinance products. The compatibility of Islamic finance and microfinance contractual forms may actually be the trivial part of the overall challenge. It is the perceptions gap between Islamic finance and microfinance that will require the painstaking work of reducing suspicion and building trust among religious scholars and microfinance institutions. The *ulema* must play a proactive role, reaching out and addressing the concerns of microfinance practitioners.

There is scope for cooperation between Islamic finance and microfinance. *Zakat* and *awqaf* funds have valuable roles to play in development activity. And funds from the Islamic finance products may help to bridge the tremendous gap between demand and supply of funds in the microfinance sector. But the gap in perceptions between the two sectors may hinder crucial cooperation, and delay reaching funding, services and assistance to the poor. Much work remains to be done, but the future can look promising if the Islamic finance sectors looks for creative ways to integrate microfinance and Islamic finance.

Notes

1 This chapter was presented at "Financing the Poor: Towards an Islamic Microfinance," at a symposium held at Harvard Law School, Cambridge, MA, April 14, 2007.
2 Law School, Columbia University, New York.
3 This is particularly surprising given the roots of modern Islamic finance in the Mit Ghamr experiment.
4 Many of the observations that I share in this chapter are based upon the Bangladeshi experience, with which I am most familiar. I realize while there are limitations to extrapolating too widely from the experiences of one country, with microfinance models developed in Bangladesh by organizations such as Grameen and BRAC being replicated around the world, microfinance institutions operating in Muslim societies

will naturally look closely at the experiences of these pioneering institutions and draw lessons from them.

5 Impact studies have found mixed results, but they have also been driven by problematic methodologies. See Karlan and Goldberg (2006).

6 See Porteous and Helms (2005).

7 Cull et al. (2007).

8 Morduch (1998).

9 Christensen (2001).

10 See, e.g., Patten et al. (2001). Jansson (2001) notes that Latin American microfinance institutions outperformed commercial banks during the economic crises of the late 1990s; Krause and Walter (2009) find that microfinance exposure can have useful diversification value to international investors, though not necessarily domestic investors.

11 Meehan (2004).

12 Rhyne and Busch (2006). There are, however, issues with defining commercial microfinance institutions in this way. Equity involvement may still come from non-commercial donor sources. And excluded institutions may and approach commercial markets through financial instruments. All the same, the trend noted in the Rhyne and Busch (2006) paper is consistent with other indicators of commercialization noted here.

13 Reille and Foster (2008).

14 News of various deals in the sector can be viewed at www.microcapital.org.

15 Reille and Foster (2008).

16 Meehan (2004).

17 For details on the transaction, see Rahman and Shah Mohammed (2008). The author was intimately involved in that transaction.

18 Meehan (2004); Chaudhuri (2004).

19 Basu and Srivastava (2005).

20 For the Grameen Phone story, see Sullivan (2007).

21 Abdul-Latif Jameel Poverty Action Lab, MIT, Cambridge, MA. http://www.povertyactionlab.org/.

22 Morduch (1999b) describes various contractual mechanisms that are used in microfinance to manage risk and incentivize performance, including progressive or step lending.

23 See ibid., for a survey of contractual mechanisms used in microfinance.

24 Ibid.

25 Dhumale and Sapcanin (1999).

26 Ahmed (2004).

27 Townsend (2003).

28 See Zaman (1999).

29 See Akhter (2004).

30 Indeed, during the structuring of the BRAC micro-credit securitization, one of the items that the investors asked for was a fixed collection schedule for each securitized loan. This was in line with their expectation for a conventional loan contract. But BRAC's system precluded a fixed collection schedule for a number of reasons. Weekly collection dates could change if the local collection officer was replaced. Repayments could be delayed based on local religious holidays and political disturbances. And as noted, BRAC has allowed local managers some discretion in rescheduling loans during natural disasters. This variability in collection dates had to be built into the model of cash flows from BRAC's securitized pool. It would simply not do to expect these contracts to work the same way as conventional loans.

31 Zaman (1999).

32 See Pronyck et al. (2007). On impact and issues with various impact studies, see Karlan and Goldberg (2006).

33 Such a conception of the micro-credit contract is consistent with some micro-credit institutions referring to the amount above the principal collected from borrowers as a "service fee."
34 See Banerjee and Duflo (2004).
35 No doubt concerns about abuse of such data will have to be addressed.
36 See Shehabuddin (1999).
37 Shehabuddin (1999) recounts similar anecdotes of clerical opposition to healthcare initiatives in rural Bangladesh.

4 Islamic microfinance

Between commercial viability and the higher objectives of *shari'a*

Hussam Sultan[1]

Introduction

Microfinance is the provision of small-scale financial services to the "unbanked" sector of society, largely in the developing world. When approached commercially, it is regarded as the only development activity that has the potential to be fully sustainable. The importance of microfinance and the vital role it plays in the fight against poverty was brought to the limelight in 2006 when Professor Muhammad Yunus of Bangladesh won the Nobel Peace Prize. Winning in this particular category highlighted the importance of developing poorer communities and giving impoverished people a chance to be self-sufficient. This is crucial for global peace, prosperity and meeting the millennium development goals, which included poverty reduction targets.

Development of communities and fighting poverty through entrepreneurship are fundamental elements of the Islamic economic system. It is reported that a man came to Prophet Muhammad (Peace be upon him) asking him for charity. The Prophet asked him: do you have anything in your house that can be sold? The man said: yes, some clothing and a container we use it for drinking water. The Prophet said: bring them to me. When the man brought his belongings to the Prophet, he auctioned the items and gave the proceeds to the man and asked him to buy food with half of it and an axe with the rest and asked him to go and gather wood and sell it and the Prophet asked him to come back after 15 days. When the man returned to the Prophet 15 days later he had made ten times more than what he had started with, the Prophet then said: this is better for you than "asking," as asking is only acceptable for one with extreme poverty, huge debts or blood money to pay.[2]

It is also narrated that the Prophet once said: "the best of food a man can eat is the one acquired by the earning of his hands, and Prophet Dawood used to eat from the earning of his hand."[3]

The above two reports from the Prophet clearly show that the Islamic way of dealing with poverty is by first encouraging a self-reliant approach, before dispensation of any charity. It also shows that an in-depth examination of the condition of the poor is important in the process of fulfilling any of their needs.

Purpose of Islamic Economics

The higher objectives of *shari'a* and the fight to reduce poverty

Imam Abu Hamid al-Ghazali[4] classified the higher objectives of *shari'a* (Maqasid al Shariah) into five major categories: The very objective of the *shari'a* is to promote the well-being of the people, which lies in safeguarding their faith (*deen*), their self (*nafs*), their intellect (*aql*), their posterity (*nasl*) and their wealth (*maal*). Whatever that ensures—he argues—the safeguarding of these five aspects serves the public interest and is desirable, and whatever hurts them is against public interest and doing away with it is desirable.[5]

Scholars that came after al-Ghazali more or less endorsed the five objectives of *shari'a*[6], although they differ in the sequence of priority regarding the five objectives. Al-Ghazali, in addition to other notable scholars, placed the safeguarding of wealth as the last but not necessarily the least important objective, as the protection of wealth was deemed to represent the outer boundary within which the other four objectives are protected. It is a known fact that poverty and the struggle for wealth can be the cause for the destruction and harm of the other four objectives. A well-known supplication of Prophet Muhammad was to seek refuge in God from disbelief and from poverty.[7] It is also needless to say that the number of times prayer and *zakat* are mentioned together in the *Qur'an*, is another accentuation on the tie between worship and financial stability. Poor or underdeveloped societies by implication, therefore, are less likely to be societies of stability and peace. This was the exact reason why the Nobel Prize committee awarded Professor Yunus his Nobel Peace Prize and not the Economic Prize.

Dr. Mohammad Umer Chapra emphasizes that wealth, as a trust from God, needs to be developed and used honestly and conscientiously for removing poverty, fulfilling the needs of all, making life as comfortable as possible for everyone, and promoting equitable distribution of income and wealth. Its acquisition as well as use needs to be primarily for the purpose of realizing the objectives of *shari'a*.[8]

Establishing the important link between the higher objectives of *shari'a* and the fight to reduce levels of extreme poverty—through the Islamic means of encouraging labour, entrepreneurship and partnership between those with wealth and those who need it—is an important factor in developing an understanding for the necessity to establish successful Islamic microfinance models that can take the challenge of alleviating poverty in developing societies across the globe as an objective of *shari'a*.

The need to develop Islamic microfinance as a tool to alleviate poverty

Establishing that the fight against poverty is an objective of *shari'a*, and seeing how the microfinance industry has made successful breakthroughs in the fight against poverty in many societies, it becomes imperative for an equivalent Islamic model to emerge that will not just achieve the economic objective of reducing poverty levels, but will also achieve it in a way that does not violate the *shari'a*.

According to CGAP,[9] empirical evidence shows that among the poor, those participating in microfinance programs who had access to financial services were able to improve their well-being both at the individual and household level much more so than those who did not have access to financial services.[10]

Bearing in mind the successes of the microfinance sector in fighting poverty and the dire economic status of the majority of the Muslim population of the world, the need for Islamic microfinance cannot be over-emphasized. The outreach of Islamic microfinance is still very small compared to conventional microfinance. In a 2007 global survey on Islamic microfinance, CGAP collected information on over 125 institutions and contacted experts from 19 Muslim countries. The survey and a synthesis of other available data revealed that Islamic microfinance has a total estimated global outreach of only 380,000 customers and accounts for only an estimated 0.5 percent of the total microfinance outreach.[11]

Historical background

It is a fascinating fact to note that the first Islamic bank on record in recent times according to popular consensus was an Islamic microfinance initiative, also known as the Mit Ghamr[12] Savings Bank (MGSB), founded in Egypt in 1963 by a pioneering Islamic economist, Ahmed al-Najjar. What follows is an extract from a paper by Ann Elizabeth Mayer[13] that discusses the social origins of Islamic banking in Egypt:

> The Islamic character of the bank was not advertised in its name, and the only Islamic principle embodied in the bank's operations was the elimination of interest. Deposits were of two kinds, either demand deposits or investment deposits.
>
> Investment deposits could be withdrawn only after a year and produced a return in proportion to the size of the deposit and in relation to the bank's profits. No interest was paid on deposits. Loans from the bank were interest-free. Loans made to the bank's depositors for pressing necessities, so-called "social loans", did not bring returns to the bank. Loans were also made on a profit sharing basis that was deemed to accord with Islamic principles. Loans made to investment depositors for investment purposes brought the bank a return that varied according to the conditions of the loan agreement and the profitability of the investment.
>
> In addition to providing banking services on an interest-free basis, the MGSB also had a social service fund for channelling the zakat, or Islamic alms tax, to the needy.
>
> Najjar's philosophy was that Islamic banks should provide small loans to the poorest of potential borrowers not served by existing institutions, these being small peasants, small artisans, and urban workers. In its first three years of operation the average amount of a non-investment loan made by the MGSB was LE50, and 80 per cent of the loans were in amounts of less than LE700. Since the bank's borrowers were unable to provide collateral, the bank was obliged to lend sums with no more security than the borrowers' promise to

repay. However, since the bank functioned as a resource for the local community; it could rely on strong community pressures to guarantee that money borrowed from it would be repaid. In fact, the bank seems to have had little trouble with defaulting borrowers.

The bank's investment loans went exclusively towards setting up or improving small business operations in the Mit Ghamr area. The purpose of the Mit Ghamr Savings Bank investment loans was to enable townspeople to become successfully self-employed and to increase their income. Some borrowers had an objective for which they wanted to take out a loan but lacked the requisite skill for putting their plan into operation. In such a case the bank, if it considered the plan sound, was prepared to offer its advice and technical services to facilitate the project. In one case in which a villager showed managerial capacity but lacked the initiative to borrow to finance the establishment of a small brick factory, the bank decided to construct the factory itself in order to set an example of what could be done with a small investment. The Mit Ghamr Savings Bank made the villager the manager and gradually transferred ownership to him as he acquired the funds to buy the factory. R K Ready, who observed the Mit Ghamr Savings Bank project, found the villagers eager to take advantage of the opportunity the bank offered to improve their lot and deeply grateful to it for offering them critical financing, which they were convinced would not have come to them from any other source.

There were persons in the government who insisted that the bank should be subjected to greater government control and supervision, and others who objected to interest-free banking and argued that the bank should be forced to revise its operations to conform to those of standard Egyptian commercial banks.

For reasons that remain in dispute, the government in 1967 began to evince serious misgivings about the management of the Mit Ghamr Savings Bank and moved to subject it to greater governmental supervision, a move that Najjar could not accept, he says, because of his conviction that to serve its mission effectively the bank had to operate separately from the government. In 1968 the government intervened and closed down the Mit Ghamr Savings Bank.

It can be clearly seen from the above extract that what is highly regarded as the first experiment in Islamic banking actually shared a lot of characteristics with modern-day microfinance institutions, such as:

- enabling rural people to become successfully self-employed;
- advising and assisting in technical and business matters when needed;
- providing small loans to the poorest who are normally not served by normal banks; and
- using community pressure to guarantee money borrowed.

Hence, it is fair to say that the first Islamic bank was actually a microfinance initiative. This fact is important when we look at the earlier points made regarding the need for any Islamic financial institution to take into account the higher objectives of *shari'a* when developing an economic solution and that fighting poverty is at the heart of these objectives.

While it can be argued, as Mayer has stated, that al-Najjar was influenced during his graduate years by West Germany's system of local savings banks, it can also be argued that he developed the basis for the modern-day Islamic banking by adapting a successful social banking experiment to the tenets of *shari'a* by eliminating interest from the banks operations and most importantly introducing the profit and loss sharing mechanism in a workable fashion.

Emergence of the microfinance business

Although most writings date the start of the microfinance movement to the early 1970s when small loans were extended to groups on poor women in places such as Bangladesh and Brazil, other researchers have contended West Germany to have had an example of a system of local savings banks, which played a major role in the economic recovery of West Germany post-World War II.

In any case, the correlation is clear between the objectives of any microfinance institution and those of the Islamic economic system—that is to say, the alleviation of poverty, treating people on the merit of their abilities and not their creditworthiness alone, and encouraging a culture of responsibility for the development of societies that one lives in.

It is also important to note that the microfinance movement did not start as a "charitable" movement, although perhaps mistaken by many to be so because of the evident human concern MFIs carry. The distinction between commercial and charitable operations poses a real challenge when it comes to putting together an Islam-compatible version of the microfinance institutions, as will be highlighted.

The most notable of institutions in the field of microfinance is without doubt the Nobel Peace Prize winner's institution, the Grameen Bank of Bangladesh. In his own words, Professor Yunus makes the distinction between what he calls "social business" and charity:

> A social business is not a charity. It is a business in every sense. It has to recover its full costs while achieving its social objective. When you are running a business, you think differently and work differently than when you are running a charity. And this makes all the difference in defining social business and its impact on society.[14]

The basis on which the conventional microfinance institutions operate is the provision of very small "loans" and "credit-lines," i.e. microcredit. A conventional institution is able to earn a "profit" margin on the basis of higher interest rates than what would normally have been charged by a commercial bank, for obvious commercial reasons due to the smaller transaction amounts and the cost of funding.

Islamic microfinance institutions on the other hand are required to find alternative ways to provide funding in order to be, if so desired, commercially viable.

A loan according to *shari‘a* stipulations cannot be recovered at any higher value than the original amount extended. The profit earned through money-for-money transactions (of the same currency) is interest, and hence prohibited. Therefore, unlike conventional financial institutions, financing in Islam is always based on real assets and inventories.[15]

Growth of the microfinance sector[16]

According to the 2006 Microcredit Summit held in Halifax, Canada, the number of institutions reporting involvement in microfinance have increased from 618 in 1997 to 3,164 in 2004. Microfinance institutions have expanded their client reach from 13.5 million in 1997 to nearly 92 million by 2004. The target is to reach 175 million clients by the end of 2015. At least eight institutions each individually reached one million clients. Microfinance is often specifically targeted towards female clientele, who make up 80 percent of the clients of the world's 34 largest micro-lenders.

No specific market research data is available or has been commissioned to accurately determine the size of the market for Islamic microfinance. However, figures on global poverty levels in general and poverty levels amongst Muslims are easily accessible. Globally, a high concentration of Muslims is often found in the poorest sections of society. Traditional microfinance with extremely high rates of interest goes against the principles of Islam. It is therefore necessary to develop a proposition that can help these people to emerge from poverty without violating their religious beliefs.

Challenges and obstacles facing Islamic microfinance institutions in developing a workable Islamic microfinance model

Islamic microfinance institutions will principally deal in providing direct financing for the funding of illiquid assets, as shown in a case study of Islamic microfinance in Yemen, or by engaging in partnership financing though the provision of liquid assets (cash) in return for profits to be earned from the small projects the cash is to be invested in. It is important to note the wider role and context microfinance plays in addressing poverty alleviation generally. Microfinance is not a catch-all solution by any measure, however, it has proven to be a very useful contributing tool that also has many challenges and difficulties that may make the provision of microfinance in certain areas less than ideal, to say the least. Therefore, it is crucial to address some of the challenges and obstacles that are associated with any microfinance project in general and Islamic microfinance more specifically.

The following is a list of key challenges that face the conventional microfinance industry and can also be faced by the Islamic microfinance sector:

> *The problem of debt creation*: While microcredit has been viewed as a poverty alleviation tool, the approach of "lending" to the poor is still a cause of concern to many. Traditionally in many societies the poor have always resorted to

other methods of raising cash, whether through aid, social nets and/or family support. The "democratization of credit" to the poor and ultra-poor with the view that microcredit is a "right" can be challenged from a moral point of view as a factor of weakening the social fabric of societies, particularly in the Muslim world where social support and charity have historically been to the cohesion of society. Commercializing the need of the needy is a delicate matter that needs to be treated carefully, especially when developing Islamic models for microfinance in light of the higher objectives of *shari'a*. Encouraging credit can help the poor, but it can also be a slippery slope, not just towards debt, but to a loss of certain values. One might argue that *shari'a* discourages the creation of debt and encourages the participation between parties and the sharing of profit and loss. However, some of the most widely used modes of Islamic financing are debt-creating instruments such as the *murabaha* and the commodity *murabaha* contracts.[17] This apparent conflict between solving the problem of poverty by creating the problem of debt needs further examination. Some of the conceptual solutions promoting equity-based financing appear to solve this dilemma but there are questions as to their commercial viability and operational practicality.

Lack of innovation in product offering: In assisting the needs of the poor, one realizes that their needs extend to far more than the immediate cash requirements for "business" or "entrepreneurial" needs. Research conducted has shown that the requirements of the poor are not necessarily for group-based micro enterprise loan products, but the development of the full range of services and products that poor people want and need: flexible savings, contractual savings, loans for education and health and micro-insurance/micro-*takaful* products.[18] The lack of product offering could viewed as short-sightedness in dealing with the problem of poverty and identifying the needs of the poor; however, it can also be argued that such a stereotypical view of the poor and their needs is a result of looking at the problem as one of a "market gap" and not a human issue that requires a holistic approach. The experience of Grameen Bank and its success story may be a proven example of looking beyond the "entrepreneurial" needs of the poor and making the difference in the standard of living of its clients. Treating the problem from a mere commercial point of view in looking at the return on investment, may provide the necessary funding from various interested investors in this new emerging "asset class," however, it should not be viewed as a poverty alleviation tool.

Product development challenges: The clients of any microfinance program have an immediate need for "cash," funding entrepreneurial activities, in addition to attending to other immediate family expenses needs (food, medicine, clothing etc.). Any Islamic microfinance model that is based entirely on financing assets, whether through *murabaha* or *ijara*, and ignoring the reality of the other immediate cash requirements will result in a less appealing model, especially when compared to their conventional counterparts. In a recent microfinance symposium,[19] field workers and microfinance practitioners were questioned on the prospect of providing Islamic microfinance solutions as opposed to conventional microfinance "loans." Their response was clear—while the demand for an Islamic model is most encouraging, there are no viable products that provide the "cash" lending demanded. Beneficiaries have been noted to prefer to receive the cash and dispense of it as they see fit, rather than having assets purchased and sold to them at a mark-up, as in the case of *murabaha*, or leased to them over a period of time, as in the case of *ijara*. This clearly identifies perhaps the most challenging factor in the development of a practical Islamic microfinance model, one that takes us back to the very first model, the MGSB: the dire need to introduce a model that provides liquid assets in the form of cash to the beneficiaries of any Islamic microfinance scheme.

Perceived lack of authenticity: Although not unique to Islamic microfinance programs in general, recent product innovation in the Islamic finance industry has led to a call to question the authenticity of "interest-free" products provided. The lack of regulation and consistency in the issuance of *shari'a* approvals has led to an increase in questioning of the validity of most products from a *shari'a*-compliance perspective by many communities. Such perceptions coupled with the added complexities of the Islamic financial products and contracts led to many potential beneficiaries opting for conventional microfinance products.

Current Islamic microfinance providers and their models

There are no official lists registering or compiling providers of Islamic microfinance, nor any regulatory or supervisory body that oversees and monitors the growth and performance of the Islamic microfinance sector. Nevertheless, the growing interest amongst Islamic charities and financial institutions is self-evident as a number of institutions have launched or have announced their intention to launch some sort of microfinance initiative.

Islamic microfinance is still in the experimental stage as many observers will say, therefore, it is worthwhile examining the existing models or "experiments" to see how the balance between commercial viability and the higher objectives of *shari'a* are achieved, if at all. It is worthy to note here that commercial viability is also an important factor even when a not-for-profit organization provides microfinance solutions, in order to make the scheme sustainable and self-funded.

The following is a list of some of the providers that have developed programs through which beneficiaries can avail themselves of microfinance schemes on a *shari'a*-compliant basis. Current providers can be classified under the following four main categories.

Islamic charities

Muslim Aid

Muslim Aid, a British non-governmental organization (NGO), is now in the process of piloting over the next three years, a variety of different microfinance models based on Islamic finance perspectives in an attempt to provide grass roots investments.

Since the early 1990s, Muslim Aid has been implementing a simple microcredit program, mainly in Bangladesh, to disburse loans and recover them without incurring service charges whilst being subsidized by the headquarters. However more recently, Muslim Aid has begun to take stock of its microcredit operations, and is trying to develop schemes for giving grants to the ultra-poor, microcredit with a service charge as well as investment for the small and medium enterprise (SME) sector. Muslim Aid has increasingly realized that what is needed is a better approach to help the poor with one that involves all aspects of the Islamic financial spectrum including *zakat* and *awqaf*.[20]

Muslim Aid's program is based in theory on the concept of *murabaha*, meaning that they disperse "cash" to beneficiaries in order to purchase assets that they will use for their small businesses. This may not always be compatible with the strict guidelines of a *murabaha* contract. Muslim Aid field workers admittedly recognize this weakness in the program or as they put it: "When the loan is given, the customers need to understand fully what their responsibilities are."

In addition to this, in giving out the loan for buying business assets, there were no clear guidelines of whether this loan fell under *murabaha*, *ijara*, *musharaka* or *mudaraba* category. There is very little documentation on this and hence it is one of the weaknesses of the program.[21]

Islamic Relief

Islamic Relief is an international relief and development charity that aims to alleviate the suffering of the world's poorest people. It is an independent NGO founded in the UK in 1984. As well as responding to disasters and emergencies, Islamic Relief promotes sustainable economic and social development by working with local communities. In July 2008, the charity partnered with HSBC Bank Middle East Limited in the launch of a microfinance initiative (see HSBC Bank Middle East, p. 000).

Government initiatives

Hodeidah Microfinance Programme (HMFP)—Yemen[22]

Hodeidah, a port city with a population of nearly half a million, is characterized by an active economy based on trading, fishing, food production, small industries, handicrafts and transportation. The HMFP was implemented in 1997, with a view to serving the thriving and diverse local micro enterprise landscape.

In the early 1990s, during and after the Gulf War, many families returned to this city from Saudi Arabia and other Gulf States. Today, roughly 30 percent of the total population in Hodeidah is made up of returnees, a key market segment for HMFP. A majority of the population holds a conservative Islamic belief and a strict disapproval of interest-related transactions. As a result, the population studied showed a clear preference for the methodologies of Islamic banking in terms of receiving credit.

HMFP is the first microfinance project of its kind in Yemen and consequently has had to develop its human resources organically. Publications indicate the program as having had 1,770 active clients as of June 2000, 23 percent of whom were women and US$350,000 in outstanding loans, with the average loan size being 38,000 Yemeni rial (YR) (equivalent to $240).

Following the Grameen lending model, there is a cycle of loans the clients go through before reaching entitlement to a higher loan disbursement. The first loan can be up to 50,000 YR ($300), and the maximum loan for the final level is 250,000 YR ($1,500). HMFP uses a group-based methodology. Group members are not confined to the same loan amounts or the same activities, although loan amounts need to be within the range of the cycle set by HMFP. There is also a small percentage of individual loans (10 percent).

The procedure is as follows: upon receipt of the loan application, the credit officer investigates the group and conducts a feasibility study for their activities. From this study, the officer can estimate the precise loan amount. If the feasibility study is positive, the client should identify items (commodities/equipment) needed from the wholesaler and negotiate a price.

The credit officer then purchases items from that source and resells them immediately at that price to the client. HMFP has two elements of accounting/finance, which differ from most microfinance organizations, both of which have implications for the content of financial statements. The first is capitalization of the service charge expected upon disbursement, which affects the balance sheet. The second is the absence of the "principle of interest" on outstanding loan balances affecting yield on the portfolio and thus income earned.

International NGOs

The Foundation for International Community Assistance (FINCA International)

FINCA International is a non-profit, microfinance organization founded by John Hatch in 1984 and headquartered in Washington D.C. In 2006, FINCA became the first microfinance institution in Afghanistan to offer non-interest bearing *murabaha*[23] Islamic financing. FINCA began its operations in Afghanistan in 2004. Two years later, following market demand, it switched its products to the *murabaha* practice. Paul Robinson, FINCA's country director in Afghanistan, says not only are the products better received than conventional forms of lending, but also the *murabaha* practice is also better for business.[24]

The experience of FINCA with Islamic microfinance provision in Afghanistan faced the problem of sustainable funding for the program as there are no Islamic microfinance investors in the market yet. It also faced other challenges that a typical *murabaha* contract leads to, namely:

- Cost of implementing the scheme: Other examples such as the HMFP in Yemen described above show that a *murabaha*-based microfinance scheme will require a dedicated *murabaha* officer to go out and purchase the goods required by the beneficiaries of the scheme.

• Cash-free financing: As discussed earlier, beneficiaries of any microfinance program do use part of the money raised through conventional loans to fulfill other needs (health, education etc.). A *murabaha* transaction does not provide any cash.

• Complexity: *Murabaha* contracts tend to be more paper-intensive and may require a number of contracts to be signed by the beneficiary.

As we can see above, the need for cash-based commercial funding is a fundamental requirement for any successful Islamic microfinance scheme.

Banks and financial institutions

Islamic Development Bank (IDB)

The IDB is an international financial institution established in pursuance of the Declaration of Intent issued by the Conference of Finance Ministers of Muslim Countries held in Jeddah in December 1973. The purpose of the Bank is to foster the economic development and social progress of member countries and Muslim communities individually as well as jointly in accordance with the principles of *shari'a*.

The IDB is actively engaged in exploring the development of *qard hasan*[25] tools for financing, as an alternative to the high interest rates charged by traditional microfinancing. In addition to exploring microfinancing funds to serve the poor, financing schemes for trade and leasing companies and other financial institutions suited to the infrastructure and needs of low-income countries are being investigated.[26]

The IDB is looking to promote grass roots initiatives to target grants directly at serving local social issues. In promoting private sector development, the SME sector is highlighted as a key focus for funding, with priority financing provided to basic infrastructure and *shari'a*-compliant microfinancing.[27]

HSBC Bank Middle East—through its HSBC Amanah division

HSBC Bank Middle East Limited announced in July 2008 through its Islamic banking window HSBC Amanah, the launch of an Islamic microfinance pilot scheme.[28] The scheme runs in partnership with Islamic Relief (see p. 000), a major international relief and development charity.

As per the partnership arrangement, HSBC Amanah will be providing funding towards Islamic Relief's microfinance projects in Rawalpindi, Pakistan. HSBC Amanah will also assist Islamic Relief as required in developing the *shari'a* structure for financing models and contracts and providing Islamic finance training to Islamic Relief staff.

Islamic Relief will, in turn, manage microfinance projects, identify and screen beneficiaries, set out eligibility criteria, encourage entrepreneurs to come forward with business ideas for investment and provide financial and social reports to HSBC Amanah.

The above initiative by HSBC Bank, while commendable, also highlights the limitations through which Islamic banking windows can offer a practical Islamic microfinance model. Commercial banks are bound by strict risk management guidelines that aim to limit their exposure to "higher risk" customers as defined by traditional credit scoring methods. The typical credit profile of a microfinance beneficiary does not fit with the typical profile of a commercial bank customer; hence direct microfinance provision by commercial banks will be a very remote possibility and can only be accomplished through two means:

- Corporate social responsibility (CSR) schemes: commercial banks will normally have a set budget for philanthropic spending through which funding will be channeled to the microfinance beneficiaries through approved and recognized charitable organizations in order to minimize cost and achieve efficient results.
- Provision of funding to commercial and non-commercial microfinance institutions: This may also include facilitating services such as remittances and cross-border transfers. To date there are no reports on any Islamic commercial bank providing "Islamic" funding to any Islamic microfinance institution as most of the funding provided is similar to either the one provided by HSBC Bank on a philanthropic basis or direct funding done by large financial institutions such as the IDB.

Conclusion

The development of a commercially viable Islamic microfinance model is vital not just for the fight against poverty but for the advancement of the Islamic banking and finance industry. Therefore, the need to implement, innovative and workable Islamic microfinance models that conform to the higher objectives of Islamic *shari'a* rather than responding to market demand or replication of conventional CSR initiatives, becomes more relevant now than ever before.

The Islamic microfinance sector has key challenges to overcome, namely aligning product authenticity to customer needs in a viable, innovative and simplified fashion. The Islamic banking and finance industry has a significant role to play in leading and driving the development and funding channels available to the micro enterprise and SME level of local economies, though the task should also be shared with other financial institutions, government departments and international NGOs, as collaboration is key, in addressing client needs with suitable funding structures, in addition to welfare assistance for the "poorest of the poor."

Although the Islamic banking and finance industry has developed at the outset as a natural response to the needs of poor Muslims, the industry seems to have concentrated on growing in banking areas such as retail and investment banking, hence, there is still much room to develop this market of Muslims in need of microcredit who also care about acquiring funding without violating the principles of *shari'a*.

The growth of microfinance enterprises that are available to Muslim clients in Muslim countries is a step in the right direction, however, more innovative solutions need to be developed in order to make the provision of such micro-credits accessible and commercially viable. The challenge here will always be distinguishing between the needs of the poor and the needs of the poor entre-preneurs. Therefore, a paradigm shift is needed on how Islamic microfinance is perceived and implemented as we need move away from a framework of charity towards one that empowers the poor without compromising both the objectives of *shari'a* or the commercial viability of the Islamic microfinance propositions.

Notes

1 Manager, Fajr Capital, Brunei Darussalam. The views expressed in this chapter are solely those of the author in his personal capacity.
2 Narrated by Abu Dawood, Sunan Abi Dawood, The Book of Zakah, number 1642.
3 Narrated by Al-Bukhari, Sahih Al Bukhari, The Book of Buyu (Sales), number 1967.
4 A leading Islamic jurist and theologian, died AD 1111.
5 Al Mustasfa, by Imam Abu Hamid Muhammad bin Muhammad al-Ghazali, published by Dar Al Kutub Al Ilmiah, 1993.
6 See Al Muafaqat by Abu Ishaaq Al Shatibi, published by Dar Ibn Al Qaim, 2003.
7 اللهم إني أعوذ بك من الكفر والفقر
8 Chapra, M.U. "The Islamic Vision of Development in the Light of Maqasid Al-Shariah," published by the *International Institute of Islamic Thoughts*, Washington, 2008.
9 Consultative Group to Assist the Poor (CGAP), http://www.cgap.org.
10 Bangladesh Rural Advancement Committee (BRAC) clients increased household expenditures by 28 percent and assets by 112 percent. After more than eight years of borrowing, 57.5 percent of Grameen borrower households were "no longer poor" as compared to 18 percent of non-borrower households.
   In Lombok, Indonesia, the average income of Bank Rakyat Indonesia (BRI) borrow-ers increased by 112 percent, and 90 percent of households graduated out of poverty.
   In Vietnam, Save the Children clients reduced food deficits from three months to one month.
   At Kafo Jiginew in Mali, clients who had been with program for as little as one year were significantly less likely to have experienced a period of acute food insecurity; and those that had, experienced a shorter period.
11 Nimrah, K. et al. "Islamic Microfinance: An Emerging Market Niche." CGAP: *Focus Notes*, No. 49, 2008. 8pp.
12 Mit Ghamr is a town in Egyptian Delta.
13 Mayer, A.E. "Islamic Banking and Credit Policies in the Sadat Era: The Social Origins of Islamic Banking in Egypt." *Arab Law Quarterly*, 1 (1985), 50pp.
14 Yunus, M. "Each of You has the Power to Change the World," Boston: Lecture at MIT, June 6, 2008.
15 Usmani, M.T. *An Introduction to Islamic Finance*. The Hague: Kluwer Law International, 2000a, 248pp.
16 No figures are available on the Islamic microfinance sector; there are however, a number of projects running in Sudan, Bangladesh, Sri Lanka, Yemen and Indonesia.
17 Commodity *murabaha*, as it is generally known, is sale of certain specified commodities, through a metal exchange, on a cost plus profit basis.

18 Rutherford, S. "Raising the Curtain on the Microfinancial Services Era." CGAP: *Focus Notes*, No 49. May 2000. http://www.cgap.org/p/site/c/template.rc/1.9.2560/.
19 The Arab Microfinance Symposium, Dubai 30 November 2008.
20 Ifthikar, H. and Saleem, A.M. "Challenges for Practical Shari'ah: Experiences from Muslim Aid," Sri Lanka Field Office: August 2008.
21 Ibid. p. 15.
22 Source (for detailed information also): United Nations Capital Development Fund (UNCDF) web site. www.uncdf.org.
23 A sale contract in which the seller has to declare their cost and profit.
24 http://knowledge.insead.edu/islamicmicrofinance080205.cfm.
25 A virtuous loan. A loan with the stipulation to return the principal sum in the future without any increase.
26 Report of "IDB 1440H VISION" BRAINSTORMING SESSION held on Tuesday, 5 Safar 1426H (15 March 2005) At IDB Headquarters, Jeddah.
27 Ibid.
28 http://www.ameinfo.com/163835.html.

Part II

Developments in Islamic microfinance

5 Making development assistance sustainable through Islamic microfinance

Rodney Wilson[1]

Microfinance involves the provision of financial services for those too poor to have access to banks.[2] Although microfinance schemes have been operational since the 1960s, they mostly involve conventional finance whereas many low-income Muslims would prefer to have *shari'a*-compliant finance. The aim of this chapter is to explore how microfinance could be provided on a *shari'a*-compliant basis and what instruments and structures could be used. The literature in this area has been very limited, but there have been a number of recent notable contributions indicating the increasing interest in the topic.[3] Two key issues have already been addressed but not resolved. First, would Islamic microfinance best be provided by specialist *shari'a*-compliant financial institutions or by existing Islamic and conventional banks?[4] Second, are credit unions organized through co-operatives the way forward, or are commercial institutions such as banks or investment companies preferable?[5]

The theme of this book concerns the bridge between ideals and realities. Islamic microfinance is often approached idealistically as it is designed to help the poor—a commendable objective but one that is difficult to achieve given the complexities of poverty alleviation. In reality, not only financial, but also social factors determine poverty. Often the problem is not primarily a finance gap but rather the lack of knowledge and ambition amongst much of the poor as well as social discrimination that persists from generation to generation. In other words, the problem is not solely with the supply side of finance, but often with the demand side as well. However, making *shari'a*-compliant finance that is perceived as *halal* available for legitimate business activity, together with technical assistance, may encourage poor Muslims to think about how they can make better use of their God-given talents.[6] The core concept to impart is that of *khalifa*, or vicegerency—the righteous management of resources through being aware of responsibly to the Creator. The aim should be to reach a state of *mutamainna*, a righteous state achieved through the pleasure of Allah by, among other things, serving fellow believers and being economically productive.[7]

Microfinance model

The history of microfinance predates modern banking. In the past, it involved informal financing through moneylenders, pawnshops, loans from friends and relatives and supplier credits from merchants and landlords. Most of this involved debt-based credit, often priced very expensively, possibly to account for the risks with unsecured lending and the high administrative charges of arranging and managing many small loans. Often there was also an element of exploitation. Sometimes borrowers were desperate to secure funding to meet immediate needs and as such, were made victims of unscrupulous lenders, to whom the poor were often indebted from generation to generation in a vicious cycle of poverty. Such unfair conditions exist even today, as those too poor to secure bank funding and with no collateral to offer continue to use informal sources of finance, despite the increasing presence and impact of modern banking even in the least developed of countries.

The socialist critique of such alleged exploitative practices from the mid-twentieth century onward did not result in their abolition, even in countries with left-leaning or communist governments. Indeed, with the failure of state organizations to meet the credit needs of the poor, informal microfinance often flourished in these societies, as the commercial banking sector was typically weak and seldom innovative. Consequently, many put their faith in non-governmental organizations (NGOs) as alternative providers of microfinance. These organizations often were funded through international development assistance aimed at encouraging, among other things, the emergence of institutions serving civil society, an objective that could be seen as a way of bypassing corrupt national governments. Many development activists saw microfinance as an important tool in empowering the poor, contributing to the growth of civil society and decentralizing decision-making.

The Grameen Bank

The Grameen Bank is an outstanding example of a successful microfinance institution. The award of the Nobel Peace Prize in 2006 to the founder of the Grameen Bank, Muhammad Yunus, brought microfinance to international attention. With 6.91 million borrowers and 2,319 branches throughout Bangladesh, Grameen Bank has enjoyed remarkable success. By keeping down operating expenses to less than 10 percent of the value of its loans, it has been able to make small loans of less than $100 viable, and has a mere 2.5 percent of its loan portfolio classified as impaired or at risk. Rather than demanding collateral and legally enforceable contracts, the Grameen Bank has developed a system based on, in its own words, "mutual trust, accountability, participation and creativity."[8]

The key to the Grameen Bank's early success in the late 1970s and 1980s was believed to have been its organization of borrowers into small homogeneous, five-member groups. The Bank issued group loans, which were repaid through weekly installments, while group peer pressure encouraged timely payment. Although this system worked for a time, there were operational problems. It was unable to cope with major economic shocks, notably the floods of 1998. Half of Bangladesh was submerged for a ten-week period, destroying much of the country's infrastructure as well as crops and livestock. Subsequently, the Grameen Bank II model was launched introducing three simple products: a basic general purposes loan, a

housing loan and a higher education loan. Borrowers do not qualify for the housing or higher education loans unless they meet all their basic loan obligations. If
borrowers fail to meet their basic loan obligations, they are provided with a flexi-
loan as a rescheduling facility affording a longer repayment period. But there is a
penalty, as the increments to the basic loan ceiling builds up over the years with
timely repayments get wiped out. Bank assets are written down by 50 percent for
the amount of basic loans outstanding, with 100 percent provisions where borrowers refuse to move to a flexi-loan. Although there is not a formal system of credit
scoring, borrowers must have a personal savings and a special savings account
with the bank as well as a pension's savings account if they wish to qualify for a
larger loan. They must also take out deposit insurance, which repays outstanding
loans if a borrower dies.[9]

Shari'a-*compliant microfinance*

Although Bangladesh is a predominately Muslim country, the Grameen Bank is
not a *shari'a*-compliant financial institution as it charges interest on its loans and
pays interest to depositors. Interest for income-generating basic loans is 20 percent, whole housing loans are charged at 8 percent and higher education loans at
5 percent, implying a degree of cross subsidy. Savings rates vary from 8.5 to 12
percent depending on the category and size of deposit. From an Islamic perspective this amounts to *riba*, and the fact that the Grameen Bank calculates its rates in
simple rather than compound terms does not mitigate the *riba* transactions.

There are also wider concerns with conventional microfinance from a Muslim perspective. Although the provision of alternatives to exploitative lending is
applauded, the sustainability of such alternatives when they conflict with the values
and beliefs of local Muslim communities is at issue. Simply extending materialism
and consumerism into poor rural communities and urban shanty town settlements
could actually undermine social cohesion by raising false expectations, resulting
in long-term frustration and possible social discontent or even economic crime.
Insofar as microfinance contributes to the growth of civil society rather than social
fragmentation, it is seen as desirable, although there is a worry that such institutions of civil society are secular. Considering that supporters of Islamic alternatives
to conventional microfinance aim to enhance Muslim society, it is unlikely that
they would promote values that might be contrary to the *shari'a*.

Comprehensive microfinance involves not only credit through debt finance
but also the provision of equity, savings schemes, money transfers and insurance.
The *shari'a*-compliant equivalents of conventional debt facilities might include
qard hasan (interest-free loans), the only type of permissible loan under *shari'a* law,
murabaha (mark-up trade finance), *salam* (forward purchase credit) and *istisna'*
(project financing), as well as *ijara* (the facilitation of operational leases), which
eliminates the need for micro enterprises to tie up their scarce capital resources in
equipment or buildings.[10] Muslim-run micro enterprises could choose one of these
financing methods or obtain an assistance package, with a retailer for example,
combining *murabaha* for the purchase of stock with *ijara* for the rental of premises.

The role of Islamic microfinance agencies, however, will not be simply to react to client requests, but to be proactive in advising what methods and combinations of financing are appropriate for particular purposes, which will necessitate detailed knowledge of the micro enterprise being financed.

Potential Islamic microfinance instruments

Islamic finance is usually provided through *shari'a*-compliant instruments that have their origins in *fiqh* (Islamic jurisprudence), but which have been adapted to be viable in the modern world, and in particular, competitive with conventional products. Often these instruments are designed to serve a similar function as their conventional equivalents, as the financing needs of Muslim clients are no different than anyone else's. The main difference between *shari'a*-compliant financing facilities and their conventional counterparts is in terms of legal contracts, especially with respect to the rights and responsibilities of the parties under national law and their substance, in the sense that they are usually linked to the trading in, or the production of, underlying real assets, although this can involve services as well as commodities. The responsibility of the *shari'a* board members of Islamic financial institutions is to scrutinize the contracts for *shari'a* compliance, but the contracts themselves are drafted by conventional law firms, not the *shari'a* scholars.[11]

Traditional informal microfinance can be regarded as inappropriate, as there is contractual uncertainty, and therefore the potential for misunderstanding and exploitation or, in other words, an element of *gharar*. The teaching of the Qur'an applies:

> When you deal with each other, in transactions involving future obligations in a fixed period of time, reduce them to writing [. . .] It is more just in the sight of God, more suitable as evidence and more convenient to prevent doubts amongst yourselves.
>
> *(Sura* 2:282)

Historically, many of the recipients of informal microfinance were illiterate, but today, with universal literacy in many Muslim countries and communities even amongst the poor, it is increasingly untenable to use this as an argument against formalizing contracts. Of course, drawing up legal contracts brings additional costs, but this can be reduced substantially once contracts become standardized, as is increasingly the case with *shari'a*-compliant financial contracts. The purpose of written contracts is not to impose formalization for its own sake but rather to ensure the contracts are just and free of ambiguity, which could result in disputes that are likely to be costly in both financial and emotional terms for those involved.

As they are linked to real transactions, Islamic financial contracts are usually designed for specific purposes. *Murabaha*, for example, is used for the purchase and resale of commodities, while *ijara* applies to operational leases involving property or equipment, and *istisna'* covers the manufacture or supply of specific items and is increasingly used for project finance. Of course, all of these can be structured for microfinance operations, but often clients want cash, which they can use at their discretion rather than being tied to a particular commodity or transaction. *Shari'a*-compliant microfinance cannot include the offer of overdraft facilities, as these usually involve *riba*. An alternative is *tawarruq*, whereby the acquisition of a commodity is financed through *murabaha*, but the client then sells the commodity for cash to the bank or its agent. The provision of *tawarruq* has proved controversial as some *shari'a* scholars stress its Islamic legitimacy according to *fiqh* while others assert that it is a mere loophole device with little financial substance. There are unresolved arguments about whether *tawarruq* should be offered to everyone, only the affluent, as they are less likely to face debt repayment problems and may be more able at managing discretionary cash, or the poor, whose cash needs should be given priority. The latter consideration might lend support for microfinance institutions offering *tawarruq*.[12]

Arguably, *qard hasan* is a better instrument than *tawarruq* for the provision of liquidity, but the problem with this type of interest-free loan is that there is no profit for the financial institution providing the funding. The attraction of *tawarruq* is that a mark-up is charged as well as transaction fees relating to the re-sale of the commodity. Of course, with *qard hasan* an arrangement fee can be charged to cover set-up costs as well as a management fee to cover the cost of the loan administration, but any charges that exceed costs would amount to *riba*, especially if they are related to the size and duration of the loan. Having flat arrangement and management fees, however, potentially penalizes those who take loans of lesser amounts, typically the less affluent, as the fees will be proportionately higher the smaller the loan amount.

It has been suggested that *tawarruq* should be confined to business cash advances while *qard hasan* should be restricted to personal lending because businesses can generate profits to cover the *tawarruq* mark-ups, while personal lending, especially to those in need, should be on a "not for profit" basis. With microfinance, however, the distinction between business and personal lending often becomes blurred, making it difficult to have a clear demarcation between where *tawarruq* should end and *qard hasan* begins. The fact that *qard hasan* in classical Islamic jurisprudence was designed for those in need may provide a better criteria for demarcation as it involves morality, unlike the often arbitrary distinction between what is business and what is personal. Nevertheless, we still need to know how to define need; indeed all that can be said is that microfinance was geared to serve those in need.

A wakala *(agency) model for microfinance*

As Islamic microfinance involves charitable assistance such as *qard hasan* (interest-free loans)—which requires subsidies or cross subsidies—could grant aid be harnessed? And could *zakat* funding be used for this purpose given its remit? Structures that might be appropriate for the inclusion of *zakat* or NGO donor funding as the grant element of a financial package are a possible way forward. One potential structure investigated is based on the *wakala* model (see Figure 5.1) that is widely

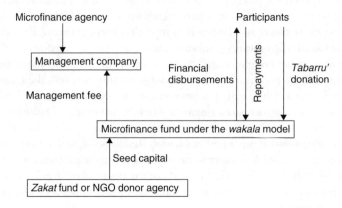

Figure 5.1 The *wakala* model

used for Islamic *takaful* insurance. Such a scheme could ensure that *zakat* promotes self-sustaining development that helps those on low incomes rather than creating a dependency culture.

An advantage of the *wakala* model is that it combines some of the features of a credit union with professional financial management but ensures the protection of the participants' interests. The concern would be the possible exploitation of participants by the management as there is the potential for a conflict of interest—with participants losing out—if management remuneration is excessive or not transparent. Hence, with the *wakala* model the management is remunerated by a fixed fee; they do not share in the *wakala* fund whose sole beneficiaries are the participants. The latter make a donation to the fund, which can be regarded as a *tabarru'*, a term that implies solidarity and stewardship.[13]

Like a credit union, participants are entitled to draw disbursements from the fund, which can exceed their contributions at any given date. Obviously, not all participants can withdraw funds in excess of their contributions at the same time, as there would be insufficient funds to meet the demand. This implies the necessity of a rationing mechanism. With conventional lending, this is implemented through the pricing of the funds, or in other words, the interest rate, which determines the equilibrium between the demand for and the supply of funds. Of course, with *shari'a*-compliant microfinance there cannot be any interest or *riba*; hence the supply of funds is classified as *tabarru'*. The motivation for *tabarru'* is not a price incentive such as an interest payment but rather to help fellow participants meet their financial requirements while at the same time building up entitlements to similar help.

Disbursement criteria

To prevent a sudden exodus of capital and the depletion of the *wakala* funds, the rationing mechanism involves prioritizing who can draw their entitlements first.

Those that can put together viable business schemes that demonstrate how the funds to cover repayments can be generated will receive priority, while those whose projects are less credible will be rejected in the first instance until they improve their plans sufficiently to justify resubmission.

The management company will be responsible for deciding which applications are supported and which are rejected, but in the case of the latter, the aim should be to educate the participant as to how they can improve their proposal and resubmit, or draw up a new proposal that is a more viable business proposition. The objective of the management company is to appraise and reduce risk, but not to price for risk, as there is no interest charge for any funding. Islamic finance concerns justice in financial dealings, and in the case of microfinance this implies transparency by the management company in demonstrating how funds are rationed and consistency in decision-making so that none of the participants are penalized unfairly.

Sources of revenue

Revenue coming into the *wakala* fund originates from five sources. First, there are the donations, *tabarru'*, from the participants. As these are donations, they do not necessarily have to be repaid, but rather they give *wakala* membership privileges, notably the right to apply for financial assistance. Whether they give any right to the assets in the fund beyond this, such as a benefit from any income earned on fund assets is debatable. Indeed, it can be argued that there should not be any financial return from *tabarru'*; rather the return is the knowledge that fellow participants are being helped.

Second, when participants apply for financial support, there is a modest fee. If they are successful in obtaining funding, there is a management fee for the duration of the financing. Such fees are referred to as *ji'ala*, the return for the provision of legitimate fee-based services. These fees do not represent *riba* or interest as they merely cover costs, namely the arrangement costs, the administrative costs of maintaining and sending out balance statements to each of the participants and the processing repayments from those in receipt of funding.

The third source of funding is from the repayments by those participants who have obtained funds, which of course get recycled back into the fund with no addition to the principal advanced. These repayments help ensure the fund does not diminish in nominal value, although it will be negatively affected in real terms by inflation and payment defaults.

A fourth source of funding is the subsidy, either from a NGO donor agency, in which case it may be simply a one-off contribution, or from a *zakat* fund that may involve recurrent payments. For *zakat* funds to be utilized, it must be shown that the funds are providing assistance for the poor and those in need rather than simply aiding business ventures. *Zakat*, of course, is not a loan but a form of almsgiving, one of the five pillars of Islam that demonstrates religious devotion and recognition of obligations to Allah. It should therefore not be abused by those who administer the funds, who should be guided by the principle of *khilafah*, accountability to the

Almighty for actions undertaken including those involving finance. Participants in the fund will of course be liable for *zakat* themselves, although their liability will be modest as microfinance is designed for the poor. They would not, however, have to pay *zakat* on the assets in the fund as these are donated and held in trust under the *wakala* model, and hence there is no personal liability. *Tabarru'* should not be treated as a substitute for *zakat* however, as the latter, as a religious obligation, brings a spiritual benefit. *Tabarru'* is not a religious obligation but rather is socially motivated and brings some individual benefits for those funded and is, therefore, very different to *zakat*.

The fifth source of funding is any income made on the financial assets held in the fund. These are the responsibility of the management company as its remit extends beyond the credit appraisal and the administration of disbursements. As there will always be a time lag between the receipt and disbursement of funds, and as it is a sensible precaution to maintain reserves, there are financial assets that can be actively managed to yield a return rather than merely being held as idle cash balances. These should not be regarded as long-term asset holdings however but rather as treasury holdings, which should be relatively liquid and subject to minimal risk. Consequently, although it might be justifiable to hold equities, as they are liquid, the capital risk rules out holding such instruments. Bonds and floating rate notes are a preferable alternative, but a *shari'a*-compliant microfinance fund cannot hold securities paying interest. Hence the choice becomes limited to *sukuk* securities, with *salam sukuk* paying a fixed rate and *ijara* and *musharaka sukuk* paying a variable rate.[14]

Treasury management

With treasury, as with any form of asset management, portfolios should be diversified, and therefore *sukuk* should not make up the entire portfolio. Even within the *sukuk* category there should be diversity between fixed and variable return *sukuk* and sovereign and corporate *sukuk*. For immediate transactions purposes the microfinance institution will need to keep bank accounts, and in the case of a *shari'a*-compliant microfinance institution, these can be either with an Islamic bank or an Islamic window of a conventional bank.

Some deposits will be held in current accounts, which should be *shari'a*-compliant. Although current accounts with conventional banks pay no or minimal interest, the funding is used to finance loans involving *riba*. Clients with *shari'a*-compliant deposits with conventional banks offering these facilities have the assurance from the *shari'a* boards of these banks that their funds are segregated from the other liabilities and assets of the bank and will only be used for financing through *shari'a*-compliant structures for purposes that are *halal*.

Deposits may also be placed in *murabaha* treasury accounts or *mudaraba* investment accounts. Both these type of accounts pay returns; the *murabaha* account is a mark-up related to the underling commodity transaction that the bank funds, either directly or through an agent or broker. With *mudaraba* the return will be related to the bank's profitability, or in the case of a specified *mudaraba* deposit, the profit generated by the project for which that the funding is used. These deposits can be indefinite in duration but subject to a period of notice, with the longer period bringing a higher proportion of the declared profit rate or time deposits with returns also related to the duration of the deposit. Usually with treasury management the aim is to have time deposits maturing to cover anticipated liquidity needs, a methodology that should also help Islamic microfinance organizations maximize treasury income. At present there are no *shari'a*-compliant certificates of deposit, but these could also be developed to facilitate profitable treasury management.

Regulation, financial reporting and shari'a compliance

As the microfinance institution itself will not usually be a bank, it will have to rely on banks to provide transactions facilities. A microfinance institution can, of course, apply for a banking license, but this would imply it was regulated as a bank, which would mean reduced flexibility over disbursements, less discretion over asset holdings and additional costs of developing robust systems for regulatory compliance, including possibly paying to be rated. Most credit unions are not subject to central bank regulation, but there may be regulation by other government ministries such as those responsible for social affairs. A case could be argued for making the *shari'a*-compliant microfinance institution accountable to the *waqf* authorities or the institution responsible for the administration of *zakat*, especially if *zakat* is a source of funding. Of course, the effectiveness of such regulation will depend on the capacity and capability of the *waqf* or *zakat* authorities and their professional competence in the field of financial management. The acquisition of such skills may be a necessary part of the institutional building process.

Part of the regulatory skill will relate to accounting knowledge, as any microfinance institution should be obliged to keep accurate records of all transactions so that they can produce an annual report containing income and expenditure statements as well as tables providing details of all assets and liabilities. An interim, less detailed six monthly statement is also desirable. In jurisdictions where an application process is appropriate to make *wakala* trusts registered charities, the provision of detailed financial reports will be a legal requirement. There are specific accounting standards for *shari'a*-compliant institutions issued by the Accounting and Auditing Organization for Islamic Financial Institutions (AAOIFI) covering issues such as the valuation of *murabaha* and *ijara* assets and the reporting of revenues from such assets. It would seem sensible for *shari'a*-compliant microfinance institutions to adhere to these standards.

Islamic microfinance organizations could either have their own board of *shari'a* scholars or rely on scholars who are associated with the *waqf* or *zakat* authorities. The remit of the *shari'a* scholars would be first to ensure that all contracts issued by the microfinance organization were *shari'a*-compliant, and second, that all asset holdings were also compliant. As in the case of Islamic bank reports, there should be a formal statement of *shari'a* compliance in the financial reports issued by Islamic microfinance organizations, with the statements endorsed by named scholars. Information should also be provided on the *shari'a* scholars' qualifications and experience.

Screening of fund usage

The disbursements by *shari'a*-compliant microfinance institutions should be only for *halal* activities. Responsibility for ensuring this will also rest with the *shari'a* scholars. The sector and financial screens used by the Dow Jones Islamic Indices are potentially of relevance as these restrict the uses of *shari'a*-compliant funds to ensure no activities are *haram*.[15] Sector screens exclude the finance of alcohol production or sales, pork product manufacturing and distribution, media output deemed obscene and *riba*-based financing. In practice these exclusions make little difference to microfinance institutions, as their members are unlikely to be involved in production of *haram* items; the only concern is with distribution where the finance is for small retail establishments. While *shari'a* scholars agree on the excluded activities, there has been some debate about whether retailers can be funded if their primary business activities are *halal* but if a minor proportion of their business involves *haram* products or services. Not surprisingly there is unease about the latter even if it is merely secondary to the business. Most would prefer to see microfinance used to purify business activity, rather than perpetuate what is *haram*, however insignificant.

Financial screening is less of an issue with *shari'a*-compliant microfinance than it is for Islamic banks, *shari'a*-compliant investment companies and fund managers. Companies are excluded if their outstanding debt exceeds one-third of their capitalization or if interest accounts for more than one-third of income because of extensive holdings of conventional savings deposits or bonds.[16] As most of those who approach microfinance institutions lack the collateral and the income to secure a bank loan, they are not involved with conventional interest-based institutions.

The only problem that can arise is when small retailers extend significant supplier credits to their clients and have receivables worth more than the cash value of the items sold. With supplier credits it is normal to charge an additional sum for the deferred payments, but the difficulty with this from a *shari'a* perspective is that the retailer or distributor involved extensively in offering such credit is acting like a conventional bank. Under the Dow Jones Islamic Index criteria, businesses are excluded if conventional receivables exceed 50 percent of total income. If the receivables were with respect to *murabaha* or *ijara* contracts, this would not present a problem as such instruments are *shari'a*-compliant—although on financial grounds there might be concern that the business was acting like an unregulated Islamic bank, which would increase risk.

Mudaraba *as an alternative structure*

Although a *wakala* structure for *shari'a*-compliant microfinance has many advantages, there is scope for experimentation with alternatives. As with *takaful* insurance, one obvious alternative is to adopt a *mudaraba* structure (see Figure 5.2).

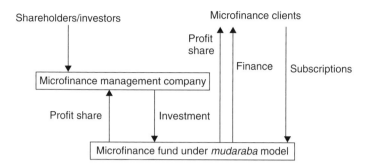

Figure 5.2 The *mudaraba* model

This has three notable differences from the *wakala* model, as *mudaraba* is a profit and loss sharing contract, not simply an agency agreement. First, with a *mudaraba* structure the microfinance management company acts as a financier—the *rabb-al-mal*—and invests directly in the microfinance fund and earns a share of any profits generated by the fund.[17] This contrasts with the management fee earned under the *wakala* model as, arguably, earning a profit share acts as an incentive for the management company to ensure the microfinance fund is efficiently run.

The second difference is that the microfinance clients subscribe to the microfinance fund rather than making a donation or *tabarru'* contribution. This not only qualifies them as potential applicants for funding but also earns them a share in any profits generated by the microfinance fund. The shares of the profit that accrue to the microfinance management and the clients are pre-determined and could be equal on a fifty–fifty or a sixty–forty basis in favor of either of the parties. In other words, there is a joint venture arrangement, but any profit split between the parties is acceptable as long as they are in agreement and it is not changed during the life of the microfinance undertaking. Although the shares are pre-determined, the profits of course are not, and hence the actual amount earned by each of the parties will fluctuate from year to year depending on the profitability of the fund and the projects being supported.

Under *mudaraba*, unlike *musharaka*, the parties to the contract are treated differently, and therefore, it is important to identify who serves as *rabb-al-mal* and who serves as *mudarib*. As the structure discussed here is based on *mudaraba* rather than *musharaka*, only the *rabb-al-mal* and not the clients, who are regarded as *mudaribs*, are responsible for any losses. This creates a further incentive for the management company—as the *rabb-al-mal*—to ensure the fund performs. It is arguably justifiable to designate the microfinance clients as *mudaribs* rather than *rabb-al-mal* as their purpose in seeking funding is to embark on, or further develop, their entrepreneurial activity. By eliminating any possible burden of financial losses from the *mudaribs*, however, this reduces their risks and encourages enterprise.

The third difference between the *mudaraba* and the *wakala* model is that with the latter some of the funding comes from *zakat* or NGOs. But with the former this is not the case. This exclusion in the case of *mudaraba* is based on the rationale that because the venture is more commercial than social in nature, and it would be inappropriate to assign *zakat* disbursements to an undertaking that is designed to produce profits for commercial investors. Indeed, the shareholders may hope to exit and realize capital gains if they sell their shares to other investors, and although there is nothing inherently wrong with this, it would be dubious if the value of their shares had been boosted through *zakat* disbursements designed to help the poor and needy, not relatively affluent investors.

Conclusions

Although this chapter is largely conceptual and theoretical, there are a number of existing *shari'a*-compliant microfinance schemes, notably those operated by Bank Simpanan Nasional in Malaysia,[18] the Aceh relief aid schemes in Indonesia,[19] the Hodeidah microfinance program in Yemen[20] and the United Nations Development Programme *murabaha*-based microfinance initiatives at Jabal Al Hoss in Syria.[21] Examination of these schemes could be the basis for further empirical study.

The State Bank of Pakistan has drafted guidelines for the provision of Islamic microfinance, but these focus on how conventional banks can provide such services rather than the creation of new institutions.[22] The implication of this chapter is that *shari'a*-compliant microfinance is best provided by non-banking institutions, which in the case of the *wakala* model may have links to the *waqf* and *zakat* authorities.[23] With *mudaraba* profit-sharing microfinance there is scope for commercial undertakings, but arguably, specialized finance companies rather than banks, even Islamic banks, may be more appropriate institutions to get involved.

Notes

1 Professor, Durham University, United Kingdom.
2 Access to the most up to date microfinance articles is available through the Microfinance Gateway of the World Bank, www.microfinancegateway.org.
3 Recent papers include Sait, S. and Lim, H., 2007: 174–201; Segrado, C., 2005; El-Hawary, D. and Grais, W., 2005a, 2005b: 1–4; Ferro, N., 2005; Khan, Atif R., 2005.
4 Nelson, Stephanie. "Microfinance: The Opportunity for Islamic Banks." *Islamic Finance News*, Kuala Lumpur, 3 (43), December 1, 2006, 19pp.
5 Chowdhry, Sajjad. "Creating an Islamic Microfinance Model—The Missing Dimension." *Dinar Standard*, November 2006. http://www.dinarstandard.com/finance/MicroFinance111806.htm.
6 Djojosugito, Reza Adirahman. "Legal Framework to Induce Paradigm Shift in Islamic Alternatives to Poverty Alleviation." Paper presented at the *International Seminar on Islamic Alternatives to Poverty Alleviation: Zakat, Awqaf and Microfinance*, Dhaka, Bangladesh, April 21–23, 2007.
7 Ali, Abbas J. *Islamic Perspectives on Management and Organisation*. Cheltenham: Edward Elgar, 2005.
8 www.grameen-info.org/bank/index.html.
9 www.grameen-info.org/bank/bank2.html.

10 Mirakhor, Abbas and Iqbal, Zamir. "*Qard Hasan* Microfinance (QHMF)." *New Horizon*, April/June 2007, pp. 18–20.

11 El-Gamal, M.A. *Islamic Finance: Law Economics, and Practice*. Cambridge: Cambridge University Press, 2006.

12 Issues regarding *tawarruq* were explored in depth at a workshop in London on February 1, 2007 hosted by the Harvard Law School Islamic Legal Studies Program and the London School of Economics.

13 Lewis, Mervyn K. "Wealth Creation through *Takaful*," in Munnawar Iqbal and Rodney Wilson (eds), *Islamic Perspectives on Wealth Creation*. Edinburgh: Edinburgh University Press, 2005, 187pp.

14 Wilson, Rodney. "Making Development Assistance Sustainable Through Islamic Microfinance." IIUM *International Conference on Islamic Banking & Finance*, Kuala Lumpur, Malaysia, April 2007.

15 Dow Jones, *Guide to the Dow Jones Islamic Market Index*. New York, June 2005.

16 Wilson, Rodney, "Screening Criteria for Islamic Equity Funds," in Sohail Jaffer (ed.), *Islamic Asset Management: Forming the Future for Shariah Compliant Investment Strategies*. London: Euromoney Books, 2004, 45pp.

17 Dhumale, Rahul and Sapcanin, Amela. "An Application of Islamic Banking Principles to Microfinance." A study by the Region Bureau for Arab States, World Bank Group, Washington D.C., December 1999, 14pp. http://www.ruralfinance.org/fileadmin/templates/rflc/documents/1114499916629_WB_Islamic_MF_edited.pdf.

18 National SME Development Council Secretariat. "Strengthening Enabling Infrastructure to Support SME Development." *Bank Negara Press Release*, Kuala Lumpur, August 8, 2006.

19 Seibel, Hans D. *Islamic Microfinance in Indonesia*. Sector Project Financial Systems Development, Deutsche Gesellschaft für Technische Zusammenarbeit (GTZ), Easchborn, January 2005, 124pp.

20 Clark, Heather. "Islamic Banking Principles Applied to Microfinance: Case Study—Hodeidah Microfinance Programme, Yemen." United Nations Capital Development Fund, New York, January 2002.

21 Imady, Omar and Seibel, Hans Dieter. "Sanduq: A Microfinance Innovation in Jabal Al-Hoss, Syria." *NENARACA Newsletter*, Amman, September 2003, pp. 1–12.

22 Said, Pervez, Shafqat, Mahmood and Ur-Rehman, Zahid. *Draft Guidelines for Provision of Islamic Microfinance Services and Products by Financial Institutions*. Karachi: State Bank of Pakistan, 2006.

23 The involvement of *waqf* and *zakat* institutions in the provision of Islamic microfinance will be considered at the Islamic Financial Services Sector Development (IFSD) Forum held in Dakar, Senegal in May 2007.

6 Leveraging philanthropy

Monetary *waqf* for microfinance[1]

Muhammad Anas Zarka[2]

Introduction

Shari'a's emphasis on distributive justice, surprisingly evident from the earliest Meccan *surahs*, is a culmination of earlier divine revelations, only more comprehensive, practical and unambiguous. Distribution ranks quite high in the *shari'a* hierarchy of values, and is an explicit Quranic criterion for evaluating a society, as evident in verses 69:34 and 89:18 of the Holy Qur'an. Refusal to share with the needy is considered transgression " طغيان."[3] Combating poverty, or need fulfillment, is the primary goal of re-distribution in Islam and is one expression of the divine verdict to honor the children of Adam.[4] *Shari'a* made it mandatory for an individual to earn a living for himself and his dependants. If unable, *shari'a* installed four major safety nets, in a specific order, to relieve the poverty of those who cannot fully support themselves: (1) intra-family maintenance; (2) *zakat*; (3) public treasury (*bayt al-mal*); and (4) ad hoc taxation. A lower-level safety net such as public treasury is activated only when a higher-level one, such as intra-family maintenance or *zakat* is insufficient or inapplicable. If a person's poverty can be relieved by providing microfinance, this becomes a high-priority method because we are helping the individual to do what is mandatory on him/her, and helping him/her to avoid being a burden on others. Thus, monetary *waqf*[5] as a way to combat poverty fulfils a major economic goal in Islam.

Why does the Islamic finance industry not do much about social justice?

Initially there was a pragmatic response to the frequent complaint that the Islamic finance industry failed to deal with issues of social justice: this was an industry in its infancy. Viability was much in doubt, and the first order of business was to survive commercially while maintaining *shari'a* compatibility. Later on, the focus of the industry's captains and perhaps clients shifted to achieving good returns. Unremarkably, the industry gave clients what they wanted and did not bind itself to the lofty goals advocated earlier by the pioneers of Islamic finance. But there are indeed more durable *fiqh* reasons for the lack of an Islamic finance voice in matters of social justice: the modus operandi of the relationship between the industry and its depositors has been the *mudaraba* contract. This contract, jurists are unanimous, explicitly and for good reason, prevents the *mudarib* from engaging in non-profit-seeking activities. Woe to the *mudarib* who goes further astray and employs the funds received for charitable purposes!

The conclusion we can draw from this is that if we want the Islamic financial industry to work for social justice (part time of course, because it must first provide all of the important usual services expected of such an industry), we must appeal to its clients. Only they have the power to mandate philanthropic activities. The present chapter is a modest appeal in this direction.

The goal of monetary *waqf* and its *fiqh* structure[6]

The goal of monetary *waqf* is to provide microfinance to the productive poor in various *shari'a*-compliant modes that is sustainable in the modern institutional setting. The terms of financing must sustain the *waqf*, but should otherwise be most favorable to recipients. *Qard hasan* (interest-free loans) cannot be the only mode because survival of the monetary *waqf* requires the generation of some income. The proposed monetary *waqf* is an exception from the *fiqh* point of view in two aspects: (1) it is monetary rather than real; and (2) it employs temporary funds.

Though monetary *waqf* was discussed and permitted by some early jurists, it was usually deemed an exception with limited applicability, and for well-known, sensible reasons—most notably the high risk of misappropriation and squandering of sums of money. The emergence of modern banks and financial institutions and their Islamic counterparts, as well as auditing and accounting professions and institutions has made control and monitoring of sources and uses of money over extended periods of time quite feasible. Hence, monetary *waqf* has become both possible and more desirable, as attested by the widespread appreciation of the great potential of microfinance in poverty alleviation.

Permanence is a prime requirement of *waqf* to most jurists. But temporary *waqf* has been explicitly approved by some. Note that microfinance cannot be funded directly from *zakat* collections, as *zakat* must be given to the poor and not loaned to them. There is, however, an important exception that is put to good use by the monetary *waqf* and this is discussed in detail below.

The basic concept

Most people have a great reserve of goodwill towards the poor and needy, and like to help them to some extent. Islam and all known religions nurture and strengthen this moral sentiment. Financing is one form of aid that many would love to partake in but cannot because of two hurdles: the cost of administering and collecting the funds, and the risk of loss (default by recipients for any reason). The proposed monetary *waqf* employs "philanthropic resources" to overcome these two hurdles, thus facilitating for many people of average means the ability to participate in helping the poor through microfinance. Monetary *waqf* assures lenders to the *waqf* of instant liquidity for their withdrawals while insulating them from any risk of default.

Beneficiaries of the proposed *waqf*

Eligible recipients of microfinance include poor people who can be expected to pay back from future income what they receive now as a loan. We may call them the "productive poor."

Would collateral be among the conditions for eligibility to receive financing from the *waqf*? Definitely not, and for good reason: such a condition would exclude the weakest and very needy, who have little or no collateral to offer. They are the very people who are denied financing under current banking practices. We must substitute the need for typical collateral by using group, social and moral collateral, as well as benefit from earlier experiences in this regard by Grameen Bank and other micro-lending initiatives.

Can the productive poor receive *zakat*? Yes, for sure. But helping them by microfinance, if possible, is more sensible from both *shari'a* and economic points of view. For example, it spares more *zakat* funds to the unproductive poor, such as the sick or very old, who may not be able to repay a loan but are in need of poverty alleviation methods.

Providers of funds to the proposed *waqf*

There are four main groups of providers for monetary *waqf*:

Donors

Permanent donations of money and real resources may be accepted by the *waqf*, no matter how small. This flexibility opens the door for wide public participation.

Lenders of qard hasan

An innovative feature of this *waqf* is that it also employs some of the temporary financial resources that it receives as *qard hasan* from lenders in microfinancing activities. This opens a large untapped source for microfinance from demand deposits. For simplicity, suppose that monetary *waqf* keeps an account at each major bank to facilitate the following scenario: A bank client willing to become a lender to the *waqf* may issue his bank a standing order such as:

> Whenever my current account (saving account) exceeds a certain level, I hereby authorize you, the Bank, to loan the excess on my behalf to the monetary *waqf* account with you. If my account falls short of that level, please replenish it from what the monetary *waqf* owes me.

Lenders to the *waqf* may do this either for a fixed term (say a month to a year) or may provide funds they can recall on demand.

Just as banks discovered that not all demand deposits are withdrawn at the same time and that some new deposits come as others go, the monetary *waqf* can prudently extend microfinance from the total accumulated loans it received. Loan withdrawals may give rise to occasional liquidity shortages. To guard against this the monetary *waqf*, like good bankers, would keep some idle funds as reserves. The *waqf* should also have guarantors of liquidity.

Guarantors of liquidity

Each guarantor promises to lend the *waqf* a certain sum of money as *qard hasan* if and when the *waqf* needs liquidity to honor withdrawals by lenders. Such loans will be for a given term, say three months, and will not be used to provide microfinance directly.

Guarantors of losses

Some of the microfinancing extended will not be paid back for a variety of reasons. Monetary *waqf* may or may not be able to cover such losses from the income generated from successful financing deals. The *waqf* should have guarantors of losses who stand ready to donate specific sums of money to cover such losses.

Note that in many cases, a beneficiary who becomes unable to pay back the microfinance s/he had received also becomes *gharim* (one burdened with debt) according to *zakat* rules in the Holy Quran (9:60). S/he thus becomes a legitimate recipient of *zakat* in order to pay back what s/he owes the *waqf*. Hence, guarantors of losses can pay the sums they pledge from their *zakat* obligation.[7]

This gives strong incentives to many persons to become guarantors and is likely to have a commendable multiplier effect on potential lenders to the *waqf*. Suppose the rate of losses on microfinance extended is 5 percent. A guarantor of 5 dinars to cover losses will protect 100 dinars loaned to the *waqf*, hence inducing many people to become riskless lenders. Thus, we see strong complimentarity between *zakat*, which must be given as one-way transfers to the poor and cannot be advanced to them as a loan, and monetary *waqf*, which is designed to provide charitable finance.

Prospects

The availability of resources to fund monetary *waqf* is a lesser and transitional hurdle in my view. Once a small monetary *waqf* establishes its integrity, effectiveness and financial soundness in any community, many people will come forward as providers of funds. There are, however, two enduring constrains.

First, the availability of quality managerial talent to impartially screen potential beneficiaries, dispense financing efficiently and recoup funds (i.e. achieve very low rate of defaults). Second, innovative business and engineering talent to assess the soundness of projects the poor may propose, and to generate (for those lacking a proposal) a large number of promising micro-projects (both productive and skill building) that are well tailored to the abilities and local economic environment of the poor.

Analytic postscript

Philanthropy is a very scarce resource. A well-known economist suggested we should use it sparingly in any proposed policy or institution. Institutional economics teaches us the importance of transaction costs (in our case, the costs and risk to lenders to monetary *waqf*). The present chapter takes these two pieces of conventional wisdom to heart by structuring a monetary *waqf* that leverages as far as possible its three "philanthropic resources," namely *waqf* donations, the moral sentiments of guarantors of liquidity, and the share of *gharimun* (those burdened with debt) in *zakat* provided by guarantors of losses. By employing all three to eliminate the transaction costs to lenders to the *waqf*, such a system would thus increase the flow of funds to microfinance.

Notes

1 This chapter was presented at "Financing the Poor: Towards an Islamic Microfinance," at a symposium held at Harvard Law School, Cambridge, MA, April 14, 2007.
2 Senior Advisor, Shura Sharia Consultancy, Safat, Kuwait.
3 Qur'an: 68:16–31.
4 Qur'an: 17:70.
5 Funding monetary *waqf* from demand deposits is one novel idea that came up in an extended discussion I had in the mid-1990s with my friend and colleague at the Islamic Economics Research Center, Jeddah, Dr. Mohammed El-Gary. Some other ideas stated here have certainly arisen since then, but I cannot sort out mine from his. It is fair to say that it is a joint idea to which I am adding more elements.
6 For *fiqh* details on monetary and temporary *waqf*, see *Al-Mawsu'a al-fiqhiyyah*, Vol. 44, pp. 123–124, 166–167.
7 I am grateful to Sheikh Dr. Ahmad Al-Hajji Al-Kurdi, member of Fatwa Committee of Ministry of Awqaf, Kuwait, for this important idea.

7 Incentivizing microfinance for Islamic financial institutions

Financially mainstreaming the microenterprise[1]

Ali Adnan Ibrahim[2]

Introduction

The Islamic finance institutions (IFIs) operate within a special incentive structure that prevents them from investing in microfinance initiatives beyond a certain limit, which is often criticized as being nominal or unsatisfactory. Critics of such limited engagement by the IFIs contend that the IFIs could play a more desirable and far-reaching role in microfinance. As argued herein, the IFIs could be incentivized to invest in microfinance while simultaneously adhering to their aims and goals that are consistent with the existing incentive structure.

As for the existing incentive structure, the IFIs not only compete with their conventional counterparts but are also striving for integration of Islamic finance with the international financial markets. Both competition and the pressure for integration create a special legal, regulatory and financial environment for the IFIs. On the legal and regulatory side, IFIs must conform to the conventional corporate form, which introduces the first tier of constraints on the IFIs activities. The corporate form almost invariably insists on maximizing the shareholders' wealth. Financial competitiveness introduces the second tier of constraints. The IFIs compete with their conventional counterparts in offering financial services while attempting to stay financially sustainable. The third tier of constraints comes from the obligation to remain *shari'a*-compliant. That is to say, while maintaining the corporate form and offering competitive financial services, the IFIs must conduct themselves in a manner that is consistent with the Islamic law, as interpreted by the relevant Islamic-law supervisory board.[3] Put differently, the three-tiered pressures force the IFIs to (1) keep maximizing the shareholders' value within the applicable legal and regulatory framework; (2) stay profitable; and (3) remain *shari'a*-compliant. Guarding these imperatives, market forces and the relevant constituencies punish IFIs for any deviant behavior.

Seeking to improve the existing incentive structure, this chapter proposes a new transaction form, which is developed on a hybrid model that encourages a partnership between the IFIs and the philanthropic organizations, as generally preferred by some scholars.[4] The hybrid model appears quite attractive, but is susceptible to a number of challenges unless structured in a manner that is consistent with the above incentive structure. These considerations include retaining the IFIs' profit motives, compliance with international legal and regulatory framework and, importantly, compliance with *shari'a*.

The chapter, accordingly, proposes a unique microfinance model that will not only be attractive for the IFIs but also for their conventional counterparts. It is hoped that the adoption of the proposed model will eventually lead to the availability of more financial resources for microfinance. As discussed below, the proposed model seeks to empower microentrepreneurs, and a limited number of small and medium enterprises (SMEs).

This chapter is organized in four sections. Section 1 explains internal (i.e., doctrinal) and external (i.e., consumers and scholars) pressures on Islamic finance industry to demonstrate further interest toward contributing to the social services including providing Islamic microfinance. Section 2 deals with the landmark issues in the conventional microfinance industry and the recent innovations/trends that seek to help further growth of microfinance. Section 3 sets out the challenges faced by the Islamic microfinance industry, outlines experiences of some Muslim countries and discusses future strategies. Finally, section 4 explores a new model for Islamic microfinance, viewing Islamic microfinance in an innovative perspective for future growth.

The expansion prospects of Islamic finance toward microfinance

This section examines the scope of Islamic microfinance, and the principles of its development and growth. Before embarking upon this analysis, it is important to raise some basic but important questions: Whether Islamic finance is more focused on for-profit ventures, and, if so, whether it should continue doing the same? Why should Islamic finance be expected to walk the extra mile to make the social contributions? Whether Islamic finance is more synonymous with for-profit activities or providing non-profit social services? The discussion on these questions follows below.

Islamic microfinance: understanding the institutional framework

Islamic law commands behavior that is respectful of other human beings, their honor, property and their wellbeing. Helping the needy, relaxing the due timelines for the payment of debt and honoring contracts are not only considered as model behavior but also constitute acts of worship under Islam.

The Quran and the Prophetic Traditions spell out the strictest disapproval of poverty. Both the primary and the secondary sources, as described elsewhere,[5] set out a number of injunctive instances where the fight against poverty is glorified. Those who help the poor out of poverty have been praised with the highest compliments. This is the general Islamic position on poverty.[6] In sum, Islam imposes an obligation on the believers to take "care of those who cannot be taken care of by the market, who cannot play with economic forces or do not have access to economic means to enable them to exploit the economic opportunities around them."[7]

Recent scholarship has identified that the modern Islamic microfinance techniques could be learnt from a Prophetic Tradition.[8] For understanding the deduction that follows, it may be pertinent to summarize the Prophetic Tradition here.

As reported, a poor man came to the Prophet, while he was sitting in the company of other men. The poor man requested financial help. The Prophet paused and then asked him whether he had any assets. The poor man counted a piece of cloth and a utensil at home. The Prophet asked him to bring those and, upon their being present, inquired from the other men present of an expression of interest in buying the two articles that the poor man brought. Upon receiving the best offer, the articles were sold for two dirhams. The Prophet asked him to take one dirham to his family and buy an axe from the remaining one. When he brought the axe, the Prophet himself fixed the handle on it, and asked him to cut firewood and sell it. He then asked the poor man to come back in a fortnight, after advising him of the circumstances under which soliciting for financial help may be justified. As agreed, the poor man returned, with a modest gift to the Prophet, and informed the Prophet that he had earned ten dirhams.

In the context of developing Islamic microfinance programs, the following fundamental elements were deducted from the above Prophetic Tradition:

1. Access of the poorest of the poor to the program . . .;
2. Careful assessment of the financial health of the poor; enquiry blended with empathy; insistence on contribution and beneficiary stake . . .;
3. Transformation of unproductive assets of the beneficiary into income-generating ones through rigorous valuation (on the basis of price discovery through auction method);
4. Meeting of basic needs on a priority basis and investment of the surplus in a productive asset;
5. Direct involvement of the program in capacity building in the run-up to income generation and technical assistance to the beneficiary . . .;
6. Technical assistance in the form of imparting requisite training to the beneficiary for carrying out the business plan/income-generating project; monitoring through a time-bound schedule and impact assessment through a feed-back mechanism; and
7. Transparent accounting of operational results and liberty to use part of income to meet higher needs.[9]

Commenting on the above deduction, it was contented that "the Islamic approach to poverty alleviation is more inclusive than the conventional one. It provides for the basic conditions of sustainable and successful microfinance, blending wealth creation with empathy for the poorest of the poor."[10] This contention apparently refers to the doctrinal emphasis on individual as well as collective actions to alleviate poverty. However, as discussed in section 2, conventional microfinance has been making much progress on developing new techniques and strategies to increase efficiencies and effectiveness. Indeed, most of the conventional techniques have been considered relevant for the growth of Islamic microfinance. In this regard, a discussion on the prospects of convergence to the conventional form appears below.[11]

Furthermore, the macro features of the microfinance institution (MFI)

> arising from [the] Islamic root would reflect the features of justice, equity, and social peace. [A scholar] . . . points out that there are various . . . institutions and structures that Islam has instilled to redistribute income and wealth . . . in the society. The institutions include, among others [*zakat* or the religious tax, Islamic trust and benevolent loan.][12]

Further discussion on the role of these institutions is outlined below.

Internal and external pressures on Islamic finance industry: understanding social, religious and market perspectives

Islamic scholars and the Islamic finance consumers often call upon the Islamic finance industry to devote more resources toward social welfare, including contributing to poverty alleviation.

The doctrinal injunctions for social welfare, as discussed above, constitute the internal pressures for the Islamic finance industry, whose appeal to its customers clearly suggests its claim for a devout compliance with Islamic law, or *shari'a*. It may be relatively easier for the Islamic finance industry to address the internal pressure according to its organizational priorities set by the management. However, the internal pressure continues to represent itself externally through scholarly criticism and customer demand. To date, most of the external pressure has been through the scholarly works where scholars generally remind the industry of what is expected of it and/or criticize it for ignoring the social objectives.[13]

Social-economic role of Islamic finance industry

It may be pertinent to provide a representative account of the scholarly or external pressure reminding the Islamic finance industry of the doctrinal principles. In general, however, scholars have also urged Islamic finance industry to expand toward "social goals."[14] It has been proposed that "[a] network of mutual financial institutions with close ties to religious establishments can perform the necessary intermediation between those institutions' world of high finance and those required social functions."[15] More specific scholarly suggestions are set out below.

Islamic microfinance is considered a form of Islamic finance that is close to ideal. It was argued:

> Using Islamic principles of equal opportunity, entrepreneurship, risk sharing, charitable obligation and participation by the poor will strengthen microfinance principles. As . . . argued, "many elements of microfinance could be considered consistent with the broader goals of Islamic banking. Both

systems advocate entrepreneurship and risk sharing and believe that the poor should take part in such activities." In its ideal form, an Islamic bank is much more than just an institution guided by Islamic principles and avoiding interest payments; it seeks to achieve a just and equitable society. With their distinctive values, Islamic financial schemes can reach out to groups excluded by conventional banks and "catalyze economic development and reduce poverty."[16]

Islamic law emphasizes the achievements of social and economic justice, and encourages circulation of money in the community as charity but also, complementarily, as risk capital.[17] To this end Islamic law requires compliance with a series of mandates, which are summarized below:

> Islamic [*shari'a's*] emphasis on distributive justice, surprisingly evident from the earliest [parts of the Quran], is a culmination of earlier . . . revelations, only more comprehensive, practical and unambiguous. Distribution ranks quite high in the Shari'a hierarchy of values, and is an explicit Qur'anic criterion for evaluating a society, as evident in Holy Qur'an. . . . Refusal to share with the needy is considered transgression. . . . Combating poverty, or need fulfillment, is the primary goal of re-distribution in Islam and is one expression of the Divine verdict to honor the children of Adam. Shari'a made it mandatory on the person to earn a living for himself and his dependents. If unable, Shari'a installed four major safety nets to relieve poverty of those who cannot fully support themselves: (a) intra-family maintenance, (b) Zakat [i.e., a religious obligation to pay 2.5 percent of the surplus to the needy, or religious tax], (c) public treasury (baitul-maal), and (d) ad hoc taxation, in that order. A lower level safety net such as (c) public treasury is activated only when a higher-level one, such as (a) intra-family maintenance or (b) Zakat is insufficient or inapplicable. If a person's poverty can be relieved by providing micro-finance, this becomes a high-priority method because we are helping him/her to do what is mandatory on him, and helping him not to be a burden on others.[18]

More recently, the challenges to Islamic microfinance were analyzed in the following manner:

> It is agreed that there is at present no established model of Islamic Microfinance which has led to a patchwork of initiatives. Pragmatic and innovative approaches serve a short-term purpose of growth. But as the . . . reports shows, in many countries, while there has been a significant expansion, microfinance sectors have tended to stagnate. The lack of a coherent and reliable framework has implications for replicability, sustainability, and ability for outreach, which are of course already issues for many [microfinance] institutions. It is true that the relative infancy of Islamic financial institutions, in comparison to longer established conventional interest-based banking, face both "internal"

and "external" problems, but these will have to be addressed in order for them to work out. The challenge is not merely the absence of appropriate regulatory frameworks for Islamic microfinance, but the lack of necessary methodologies that reflect application of Islamic principles.[19]

However, the criticism on the inability of IFIs seems to acknowledge the inherent limitations of the IFIs for conducting microfinance:

> In all three areas of environmental, social and corporate governance, Islamic finance has golden opportunities *to redefine the brand name* in a manner that enhances its providers' profitability and market value, increases access to the fast-growing potential market segment of middle-class Muslims, and enhances its ability to recruit top-drawer talent from that same market segment for its products. In what follows, we shall review some of the possible features of Islamic finance that are currently underutilized or unutilized in defining the industry's brand name. However, *multinational as well as large indigenous Islamic finance institutions are not directly capable of engaging in the poverty alleviation, microfinance, and other socially beneficial activities that are necessary for establishing this new identity and brand name.*[20]

In view of the pressures on IFIs, participating in social welfare initiatives is a big challenge. On this issue, it was noted that

> the industry has not focused on poverty alleviation because it needed to meet both world-class banking standards and Shari'a [i.e., Islamic law] require-ments to serve its customers, in addition to providing profits to investors. While the social goals of the Shari'a are noble, Islamic finance has been work-ing to meet commercial standards first as a sign of the sector's viability before trying to meet its social responsibilities.[21]

As discussed above, Islamic finance is considered almost synonymous with socially responsible finance. Its risk-sharing focus, as against the "debt-based approach,"[22] is seen as counterbalance to the disparity between lender and borrower. More spe-cifically, while examining contemporary Islamic finance, it was noted that Islamic finance must transform itself from "*Shari'a*-compliant" to "*Shari'a*-based" focus.[23] Put differently, "Islamic finance stresses interest-free methods of providing capital, including joint venture methods where risk and reward are shared by the insti-tution and the borrower."[24] Fighting against poverty is important in Islam, and microfinance is an important means for achieving victory. However, the conven-tional practices of charging high interest rates run counter to the spirit of Islamic finance.[25] In this respect, Islamic finance is expected to be more poor-friendly that the conventional microfinance that charges high interest rates to the poor to offset the high operating costs.[26] As for innovation in developing newer products and services for Islamic microfinance, the Islamic finance industry has not achieved any significant milestone.

Understanding market pressures

Islamic microfinance faces challenges similar to what Islamic finance faces in integrating with the international financial markets. The absence of integratable features is a critical obstacle to scaling Islamic microfinance—a precursor for attaining financial sustainability and profitability. So the products, services and the transaction models, which may be developed for Islamic microfinance, should have the requisite flexibility to accommodate participation from conventional microfinance.

The IFIs not only compete with their conventional counterparts but are also striving for integration of Islamic finance with the international financial markets. Both the competition and the pressure for integration force a special legal, regulatory and financial environment for the IFIs that presents itself in the form of peculiar constraints. On the legal and regulatory side, IFIs must conform to the conventional corporate form, which introduces the first tier of constraints on the IFIs activities. The corporate form almost invariably insists on maximizing the shareholders' wealth. Financial competitiveness introduces the second tier of constraints. The IFIs compete with their conventional counterparts in offering financial services while attempting to stay financially sustainable. The third tier of constraints comes from the obligation to remain *shari'a*-compliant. That is to say that, while maintaining the corporate form and offering competitive financial services, the IFIs must conduct themselves in a manner that is consistent with the Islamic law, as interpreted by the relevant Islamic-law supervisory board.[27] Put differently, the three-tiered pressures force the IFIs to (1) keep maximizing the shareholders' value within the applicable legal and regulatory framework; (2) stay profitable; and (3) remain *Shari'a*-compliant. As a result, market forces and the relevant constituencies punish behavior that deviates from these norms.

Therefore, Islamic finance industry appears to be at an impasse to resolve, what may be termed as the apparent conflict between the market realities and the doctrinal commitments. These challenges are heightened when the IFIs contemplate conducting a microfinance program. In general, a significant number of microfinance initiatives end up imposing predatory returns on the poor customers (whether by way of charging high interest rate or *shari'a*-compliant returns that are priced equally high). Here, the IFIs face the fourth challenge: How to make microfinance less expensive for the poor? Section 4 herein seeks to address this challenge by, *inter alia*, (1) developing an incentive structure that would ensure availability of more funds for microfinance while the IFIs remain within the existing three-tiered pressures; (2) allowing the public sector funds to complement the private investments by lowering the costs of lending to the poor.

Understanding innovations in the Islamic finance industry and their impact

The Islamic finance industry has been receiving a significant supply of funds from Middle East, where the financial markets have been liquid as a result of increased oil prices. The industry has been susceptible to pressures from the supply side including investing in opportunities that allow higher returns in relatively shorter time. The returns available in some sectors have been quite lucrative. The bulk of Islamic finance investments in recent years have been diverted to the real estate and other sectors that promised quicker returns. As a trend, investments for 3–5 years have become more popular. Investments entailing longer positions such as project financing remained limited. As a result, the investments made by the Islamic finance industry have become more concentrated on short-term sectors and have shied away from longer-term investments. The project-hungry trend in the market forced the IFIs to compete with their conventional counterparts aggressively. Triggered by the competition, the IFIs innovated only along the business opportunities that offered higher returns in the shortest possible time. In other words, the financial priorities of innovation in Islamic finance were largely set by the market where institutional and sophisticated investors dominated. Consistent with this trend, the bulk of innovation concentrated on developing *shari'a*-compliant techniques for debt-financing, or *sukuks*.

Taking an aerial view of the recent growth in Islamic finance, one notices three main consequences of this innovation trend. First, the innovation helped grow and develop the Islamic capital markets, which continue to be in the developing phase. Here, it would be pertinent to provide an overview of Islamic capital market and its international growth.

Independent of its growth in the Middle East, Islamic finance has become a big success in Malaysia and Singapore.[28] Outside the Islamic world, the UK has already established its mark in facilitating Islamic investments and is now preparing to become the first western jurisdiction to issue Islamic debt.[29] Other competitors attracting the Islamic capital include Hong Kong[30] and Japan. Japan is in the process of issuing its first-ever Islamic bonds.[31] In 2006, a Texas-based US firm had issued Islamic bonds ($165.67 million), although the issuer defaulted and is currently undergoing bankruptcy proceedings.[32] The increasing growth of Islamic finance in the international markets suggests that Islamic finance is most likely to increase in the US as well.[33] The current international issuance of *sukuk* is over $170 billion,[34] including those deals in the pipeline. The global *sukuk* saw positive development after its drop in 2008. The market is dominated by corporate *sukuk* issues, which totaled $98.6 billion,[35] opposed to the sovereign and quasi-sovereign *sukuk*, which totaled $71 billion.[36] Before the recent financial crisis, the Islamic bonds market was projected to grow to $225 by year 2010.[37] Islamic indexes of US firms have received unprecedented welcome by the Muslims in the US and abroad and remain popular. However, US-specific statistics for Islamic finance are not available in the public domain.[38]

Second, the trend discouraged development of a variety of long-term products. Such products are generally considered desirable for a stable portfolio.[39] Long-term products may exist in the Muslim countries, where Islamic finance retains a larger market share, independent of any specific focus on Islamic finance. To explain the lack of long-term products, the industry professionals consider that the lack of specialized expertise needed for financing the long-term project (such as financing infrastructure projects) is one of the primary reasons for low growth in long-term products.[40] However, no adverse effects of the absence of long-term products have been noted for IFIs thus far.

At a macro level, however, long-term products in the economy are encouraged by monetary policy for liquidity control. Since the main supply side of the funds available for Islamic finance is from Middle Eastern countries,[41] the monetary policy for such countries is equally relevant for the Islamic finance. That is to say that the central banks of the Middle Eastern countries may require the IFIs to develop and grow long-term products. No such policy directive has appeared as yet, but now this scenario appears quite likely, particularly in view of the soaring inflation in some of the Middle Eastern countries.[42]

Third, the short-term growth trend could not address the dire need of developing products that could have filled the vacuum for investments in the social service and the development sector. These products could have included entrepreneurial finance, microfinance and others to encourage financially sustainable participation in social welfare. As a result, "Islamic financial sector . . . has not been forthcoming in performing its social role."[43] Lack of innovation in the social services apparently had an opportunity cost. It was noted that, if the Islamic finance industry could integrate with microfinance, it could reach a three-billion-person market.[44]

Islamic trust

BACKGROUND

Islamic trust or *waqf* has been one of the most discussed topics with regard to institutionalizing the Islamic charitable initiatives. Islamic trust has been used to organize projects of public and social welfare, such as creation and running the affairs of the mosques, establishment of free hospitals and educational institutions and, now, MFIs.

The history of Islamic trust goes as far back as the early centuries of Islam. Some recent scholarly works have also argued that the introduction of the institution of trust in the common law was heavily inspired by the concepts of Islamic trust.[45] On the other hand, a number of Muslim countries did away with the institution. It was argued that the reasons for discontinuing of the Islamic trust in various Muslim countries included the pressures from the colonial powers of civil law origin, which abolished the intermediate actors between the state and the public from their own system—a trend that has now been discontinued.[46]

THE SCOPE

As for the legal character of the Islamic trust, it is generally treated as a distinct personality, although there is some level of divergence of views within the Islamic schools on this issue. In this respect, the Islamic trust resembles a corporation. However, the issues such as shielding of liability of the managers and the limits of exposure of the authors/settlers remain popular points of inquiry among the scholars.[47]

For the purposes herein, it would be pertinent to note that Islamic trust closely resembles non-profit cooperatives. However, the issues pertaining to juristic personality and some aspects of corporate governance remain subject to further jurisprudential development.

Further discussion on the modern Islamic trust, and whether it could be an appropriate vehicle for Islamic microfinance, is set out in section 3.

Guarantee mechanism in Islamic microfinance

Group-lending and mutual guarantee within the group are the best approaches to ensure a guarantee mechanism in an Islamic version of microfinance.[48] This is the model that the Grameen Bank has successfully implemented in Bangladesh. However, some scholars are of the view that the social collateral of group-lending, despite being successful, has not resolved the problems of moral hazard, asymmetric information and economic viability.[49]

Similar to its development in conventional microfinance, a third-party guarantee has been considered relevant for Islamic microfinance. It has been observed that the structure of Islamic surety (or *kafalah*) and Islamic insurance (or *takaful*) would be appropriate.[50]

Scholars have also discussed significance of hedging products for the Islamic trusts. In this respect, it was argued that the Islamic trust could protect itself from withdrawal risks by subscribing to Islamic insurance (or *takaful*[51]) and "profit-equalization reserves."[52]

Microfinance: contemporary lessons and trends

In general, microfinance refers to loans transactions with the poor with a view to help them help themselves out of poverty. With no collateral secured for the transactions, the most popular amount for a single microfinance loan is up to $200.

This section outlines the current trends in the conventional microfinance and offers brief insight as to the most recent developments on conducting financially sustainable microfinance. This section focuses on only such issues that have been considered relevant for developing Islamic microfinance, or those that would otherwise be significant to understand the Islamic microfinance for the purposes herein.

Microfinance

Background

By way of a historical introduction to modern microfinance, many specialized financial institutions emerged in the developing countries during the 1950s and 1960s with the objective of providing access of financial resources to the poor, living in conditions of severe destitution and vulnerability.[53] These financial institutions generally faced the dual challenges of outreaching to the poor and, at the same time, ensuring financial sustainability. Newer microfinance initiatives combined financial and social intermediation both in urban and rural areas. The challenges in reaching the poor mainly include (1) transaction costs and (2) institutional development sustainability.[54]

Microfinance has become much more popular and understood than it was, say, a few decades ago. Institutions that specialize in providing micro-credit have grown and developed almost in every country. Realizing the need to combat poverty through empowering the poor has also led to the establishment of various initiatives that have sought to provide comprehensive research capabilities. New perspectives for conducting microfinance have triggered innovation at a wide scale. As a result, microfinancing is no longer viewed as an activity that is a high-risk and no-return. Rather, it is now a for-profit industry and "most [MFIs] report repayment rates approaching 100 percent among their clients."[55] Recognizing its profitability, microfinance has attracted participation from a number of conventional banks.[56] Such participation has also helped reducing the transaction costs by introducing the technological capabilities that are otherwise only available to the conventional banking industry.[57]

General principles

Based on the experiences of various successful microfinance providers, scholars have derived the following general principles: (1) supply-side (or donor-driven) approaches are often less advantageous than demand-driven strategies; (2) lending with low interest rates (or subsidized finance) is inappropriate way of reaching a large number while simultaneously being financially sustainable in doing so; and (3) client-oriented participatory approaches should complement institutional developments, rather than by mere technical and financial assistance.[58]

Strategies

As for strategies for reaching the poor, the evidence suggests that "informal financial arrangements benefit many people and that formal financial institutions can also expand their outreach greatly."[59] Other suggestions by scholars include: developing greater risk mitigation strategies;[60] targeting the economically productive; increasing client–staff ratios within the given institutional service structures; achieving sustainability to attract potential lenders; inducing market competition that forces the financial intermediaries to lower their costs while simultaneously expanding their outreach and increasing their services; innovation for new and cheaper services; and increasing outreach facilitated by demographic trends.[61] Furthermore, internal financial control mechanisms throughout the institutional structure are crucial for high-quality information flow, transparency and efficiency.[62] Scholars agree that (1) meeting challenges of sustainability and outreach are not easy; (2) demand-driven operations, rather than donor-driven, facilitate local participation; and (3) financial innovation is a key to empowering success.[63]

As noted, learning from the experiences of the others, following the best practices models and implementing the technical tolls have been regarded as equally important.[64] This will result in a proper assessment of demand for loans, operating costs and market risks and, ultimately, it will ensure project's viability.[65]

In order to lower the transaction costs, it was noted that using non-governmental agencies (NGOs) and self-help groups (SHGs) as financial intermediaries helped significantly reduce the transaction costs.[66] The same study found that NGOs and SHGs, funded from the grants, proved beneficial for training and participation purposes.[67]

As for a credit delivery model, it would be pertinent to briefly discuss the model developed by the Grameen Bank of Bangladesh, the pioneer in microfinance. The Bank reaches out to the poor groups in rural areas, especially those with modest land assets. Without using their assets as collateral, the bank relies on the group mechanism for ensuring repayment, by transferring the risk from the Bank to the group. By imposing joint liability on the group, the Bank screens out the high-risk borrower. In case of default, the group receives sanctions. Loans are approved only with the approval of the group. This process of peer monitoring helps reduce transaction costs.[68] As for the institutional structure, the Bank operates with a network of "branches" that are supervised by "area offices" and then by the "zonal offices." The zonal offices develop strategies and set out policies for their respective zones.[69] The Bank assessed that a network of 1,500–2,000 branches could achieve viability within 4–6 years.[70]

Recent trends: social business, profitability and supporting microfinance with guarantees

It would be pertinent to note the transformation toward a greater model that could help the alleviation of poverty more effectively. Most recently, the concepts of social business and third-party guarantee for securing commercial loans have emerged with a view to expanding the means for fighting poverty.

Social businesses

While discussing the success of the free market and the profit maximization assumption about the individuals, Dr. Muhammad Yunus introduced his concept of "social business."[71] He maintained:

> We have remained so impressed by the success of the free-market that we never dared to express any doubt about our basic assumption. To make it worse, we worked extra hard to transform ourselves, as closely as possible, into the one-dimensional human beings as conceptualized in the theory, to allow smooth functioning of free market mechanism.
>
> By defining "entrepreneur" in a broader way we can change the character of capitalism radically, and solve many of the unresolved social and economic problems within the scope of the free market. Let us suppose an entrepreneur, instead of having a single source of motivation (such as, maximizing profit), now has two sources of motivation, which are mutually exclusive, but equally compelling – a) maximization of profit and b) doing good to people and the world.

Each type of motivation will lead to a separate kind of business. Let us call the first type of business a profit-maximizing business, and the second type of business as social business.[72]

In the above background, Dr. Muhammad Yunus went on to note that:

Social business will be a new kind of business introduced in the market place with the objective of making a difference in the world. Investors in the social business could get back their investment, but will not take any dividend from the company. Profit would be ploughed back into the company to expand its outreach and improve the quality of its product or service. A social business will be a non-loss, non-dividend company.

Once social business is recognized in law, many existing companies will come forward to create social businesses in addition to their foundation activities. Many activists from the non-profit sector will also find this an attractive option. Unlike the non-profit sector where one needs to collect donations to keep activities going, a social business will be self-sustaining and create surplus for expansion since it is a non-loss enterprise. Social business will go into a new type of capital market of its own, to raise capital.[73]

With the help of social businesses, as Dr. Muhammad Yunus concluded, "[al]most all social and economic problems of the world will be addressed through social businesses. The challenge is to innovate business models and apply them to produce desired social results cost-effectively and efficiently."[74]

Undoubtedly, the idea of social business is quite profound in its reach and objectives. Being a leader in microfinance industry, the vision of Dr. Muhammad Yunus provides a clear insight into what microfinance may become in the coming years. Microfinance and social business are important means to achieving the end, the alleviation of poverty.

Although Dr. Muhammad Yunus envisioned separate category of business as "social business," the same end-result could also be achieved by businesses that proportionally serve profits and social considerations. As discussed in section 4, investors can cap their returns at a certain percentage and allow the business to keep the residue for, say, social objectives of the business. A number of corporate finance strategies and instruments can certainly help in dealing with the modalities of such transactions.

Bankability of microfinance

Collateralization is not only a challenge for the poor to arrange for but also for the MFIs, which have to establish bankability while negotiating loan with the financial institutions. Since the nature of microfinance remains high-risk for the mainstream financial institutions, a significant number of MFIs face the challenge of arranging the supply of funds for their microfinance operations. Lack of funds stalls the whole idea of lending to the poor. To overcome the challenge, the Grameen Foundation came up with an innovative solution by introducing the Grameen Foundation Growth Guarantee Program.

GRAMEEN FOUNDATION GROWTH GUARANTEE PROGRAM

The Grameen Foundation established a $60 million Growth Guarantee Program, implemented in two phases of $31 million and $29 million respectively. The program is organized in collaboration with Citibank. In general, the program provides 25 percent financial commitment to Citibank, which, in turn, issues a letter of credit to the financial institution or any syndicate that is looking to loan funds to a MFI.[75] In this way, the program serves as credit enhancement tool for the approved MFIs.

The Grameen Foundation describes the mechanics of the Growth Guarantee Program and its financial impact as follows:

> Donor-guarantors, individuals or institutions who share [Grameen Foundation's] vision that microfinance is a scalable solution to poverty, provide a guarantee to Citibank. The donor-guarantors do not give up their money, but enable their assets to be put to valuable use as guarantees. Citibank in turn issues letters of credit to local banks to support financing for [MFIs] selected by [the Grameen Foundation]. An important feature of this program is its multiplier effect. Each dollar provided as a guarantee is leveraged several times for the [MFIs] in their own currency through a variety of transaction structures such as term loans, credit lines, and bond issues. The Growth Guarantees is a uniquely flexible model that makes local financial markets work on behalf of the world's poor.[76]

However, it is only a selected number of MFIs around the world that have been able to secure the guarantee or would be eligible to apply for it. The Growth Guarantee Program seeks out "high-performing poverty-focused [MFIs] aspiring to expand rapidly and capable of managing large amounts of commercial financing. Such organizations are [expected to be] recognized as industry leaders in financial performance, management, and growth."[77] To date, there have been four successful MFIs representing India, Nigeria, Pakistan and Peru.[78]

Figure 7.1 is a graphical representation of the Growth Guarantee structure.

Key points of the Grameen Foundation Growth Guarantee Progam are:

- The Grameen Foundation provides a letter of credit support to the lending financial institution.
- The lending financial institution provides the requested loan facility to the microfinance provider

GRAMEEN–JAMEEL GUARANTEE PROGRAM FOR THE ARAB WORLD

The Grameen Foundation and the Abdul Latif Jameel Group jointly developed the Grameen–Jameel Guarantee Program in 2003. The program is similar to Grameen Foundation's Growth Guarantee Program except for the geographic restriction—the program supports MFIs in the Arab world. The other distinctive feature

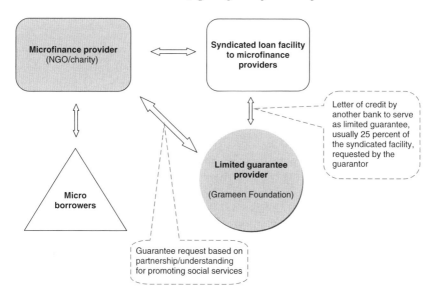

Figure 7.1 The Grameen Foundation Growth Guarantee Program

of the program is that the guarantee issued pursuant to this program is generally issued by the Mohammad Jameel Guarantee Fund.[79]

The Grameen–Jameel program plans to deploy up to $50 million, in various phases, for the Arab region.[80]

Figure 7.2 provides a graphical representation of the Grameen–Jameel Growth Guarantee structure.

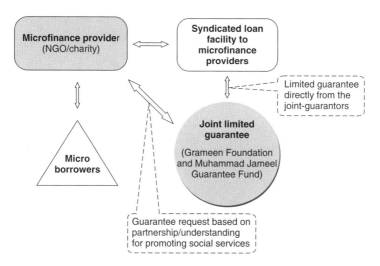

Figure 7.2 The Grameen–Jameel Guarantee Program

Key points of the Grameen Foundation Growth Guarantee Progam are:

- The Grameen Foundation provides a limited guarantee to the lending financial institution.
- The lending financial institution provides the requested loan facility to the microfinance provider.

PUBLIC AND PRIVATE SECURED DEBT

In 2004, the Grameen Foundation issued the first and the largest microfinance bonds of $40 million in the US. The bonds were to mature in seven years. The funds collected by the issue supported MFIs in nine developing countries.[81]

The transaction was quite innovative. While JP Morgan serviced the bonds, the Overseas Private Investment Corporation (OPIC) issued a $30 million guarantee. The bonds were broken down into senior and junior notes. The senior notes were guaranteed by the OPIC guarantee unlike the junior notes that were not backed by the guarantee, but yielded higher returns.[82]

As for the private placement of debt, the Kashf Foundation of Pakistan issued private debt to a syndicate of financial institutions. It is, however, not clear if the Grameen Foundation Growth Guarantee Program was invoked in the private placement, which provided a $2 million guarantee to the Foundation's commercial loan through a letter of credit by Citibank Pakistan.[83]

Some observations on the recent trends

As discussed above, innovation in microfinance has not only introduced newer products and services but it has also expanded its horizon to international financial markets for raising the microfinance funds. Microfinance has recently witnessed its transformation into a profitable industry, it has also became more international in terms of the chain of supply of funds. The recent innovations, based on sophisticated research and development, have greatly contributed in minimizing the operating costs and by emphasizing on increasing the efficiencies. From improved lending strategies to programs for capacity building, the milestones for doing a sustainable microfinance have contributed significantly to the growth of this unique market.

On the other hand, microfinance remains a high-risk sector in terms of the conventional risk assessments evaluations. The very nature of the microfinance, that is, financing the poor and the poorest of the poor, is not likely to meet the standards of bankability used by the conventional investors and financial institutions.

Recently introduced guarantee programs, as discussed above, have tried to significantly fill the vacuum between the poor and the commercial lending. However, the guarantee programs and the issuance of international bonds remain restricted to a limited number of qualifying MFIs, and therefore a fewer number of the poor benefit from the supply of funds available through the innovative transaction models. Furthermore, commercial lending, however arranged, has not solved the problem of charging high interest rates from the poor. This aspect of microfinance convinced the pioneer of modern microfinance, Dr. Muhammad Yunus, to explore alternative avenues of supplying the funds, such as developing social businesses.

In view of the above, it appears that existing market structure remains wanting in making a sustained commitment to fight poverty, especially through microfinance. If this is the case, we hope that the profound scholars and professionals from the microfinance industry will continue to provide financial innovations to overcome the challenge.

As for the Islamic microfinance model proposed herein, other parts of this chapter examine if providing an incentive structure that combines the prudence of (1) for-profit and social business, on one hand, and (2) private and public financial support, on the other, might assist in carrying out microfinance activities more efficiently.

Islamic microfinance challenges: experiences and strategies

The recent interest in Islamic microfinance has followed the growth of the mainstream Islamic finance industry. However, the traditions of Islamic charities date back many centuries.

While Islamic microfinance initiatives are emerging everywhere in the Muslim world, three main trends are apparent. First, the Islamic microfinance initiatives are functionally converging to the practices of conventional microfinance. Second, the more successful of the Islamic MFIs have been noted to have better strategy to attain sustainability and profitability. Such strategies were generally based on the conventional experiences. Third, a significant number of Islamic scholars have been arguing in favor of running Islamic microfinance through a traditional vehicle, the Islamic trust. Discussion of these trends continues below.

An overview of market growth

The concept

Islamic microfinance continues to face challenges of scale and lack of funds. Other challenges include lack of more attractive products to the micro-customers.

Various international initiatives seek to promote Islamic microfinance and offer a number of services, which include direct and indirect financing, financial intermediation, information analysis, credit support and enhancement, guarantees etc. The most notable initiative has been from the Islamic Development Bank (IDB). The IDB has developed a microfinance-specific Islamic Solidarity Fund for Development (ISFD) and committed US$500 million for microfinance development through its Microfinance Support Program (MSFP).[84]

Similar services have also been available to the conventional MFIs, which have quite successfully leveraged them. Research, analysis and intermediation services have sought to strengthen the self-sustaining business model of the MFIs.

Financial intermediation, credit support and guarantees have allowed MFIs to tap funding through syndications and various capital market products including centralized debt obligations and bonds.

Despite the availability of the above institutional support to the Islamic MFIs, the Islamic MFIs have not been able to leverage the available support, however. There is, therefore, a dire need for products and services for Islamic MFIs to allow them to achieve scale and a self-sustaining business model.

In addition to being a for-profit initiative, to strengthen the business model of Islamic microfinance would fill the above vacuum by providing the much needed liquidity and the related support to the Islamic MFIs.

The market

Over 44 percent microfinance clients reside in the Muslim countries.[85] An exceeding number within various Muslim countries have expressed preference for Islamic microfinance products.

The microfinance loan portfolio only in the Middle East and North Africa (MENA) region has grown beyond US$ 1.175 billion and is currently the second fastest (after Asia) growing segment of global microfinance in terms of outreach.[86] Some 79 percent of the sources of fund come from the financial institutions (i.e., public and private commercial banks and cooperatives) and 15 percent from the development finance institutions.[87]

Grouped with other Muslim countries, the portfolio and growth size could be even larger and more optimistic.[88] However, the global Islamic microfinance portfolio growth does not appear to be consistent with the growth of microfinance portfolio in the Arab world in general. One of the main reasons for such slower growth (despite high demand) has been lack of funds. Other challenges are set out below.

Recent optimism

Recent studies have shown that the Arab microfinance sector has not only become sustainable in 2008 but also has been one of the most efficient and profitable. Following are some achievements of the Arab microfinance:[89]

- The highest return on assets (ROA) in the world (2.4 percent).
- The lowest financial revenue ratio (i.e., lowest interest rate) (22.8 percent).
- The lowest total expense to assets ratio (1.9 percent).
- A low portfolio at risk[90] (PAR) ratio (2 percent).

One of the important conclusions from the above is that an MFI can be profitable despite charging a lower financing cost. This could be an important lesson for Islamic MFIs seeking to provide cheaper microfinance than their conventional counterparts.

The challenges

Apart for some exceptions, Islamic microfinance faces certain challenges that have affected its self-sustainable model. Such challenges include:

- higher transaction costs;
- higher operational costs;
- less product diversity (over 70 percent *murabaha*);
- lower ROA; and
- elevated PAR ratio.[91]

While some of the above and other challenges are related to scale and may improve over time when the scale increases, it appears that some of the above challenges are also attributable to the business model. That is to say, as a considerable portion of funds for Islamic microfinance may have historically been generated out of charitable donations (carrying no pressures for higher returns), there are limited pressures for being and staying profitable. Some 22 percent funding for microfinance in the MENA region is reported to have come from grants.[92]

The prospects and challenges

The prospects

In contrast with the recent practical experience where Islamic microfinance initiatives use the conventional microfinancing techniques, a comparative analysis has found that Islamic microfinance could be more successful than its conventional counterpart in a number of areas.[93] It was argued that[94]

> Islamic microfinance institutions could tap into financial resources that are not available to microfinance institutions. These resources include religiously-enjoined tax and charity; evidence suggests that Islamic microfinance institutions "benefit from the social capital derived from the Islamic values and principles. Islamic teachings make the microentrepreneurs better debtors."

The Islamic approach of targeting the family for group lending (through women) mitigates the problem of adverse selection, asymmetric information and agency problem; and some of the techniques used by Islamic MFIs, such as not giving away cash loans, have been profitable.

The challenges

There could be several challenges facing Islamic microfinance, but any list of challenges to Islamic microfinance is not likely to include the lack of financial resources, but will most likely include financial disintermediation.[95] It was hoped that

> with large capital inflows entering the Islamic banking [and finance] industry and the possibility of securitizing microfinance contracts . . ., we stand at the

beginning of a second microfinance revolution, in which Islamic microfinanciers alleviate poverty with sustainable, replicable, and inexpensive transactions, without the risks and costs associated with conventional microfinance.[96]

The availability of religiously motivated funds certainly gives an edge to Islamic MFIs in terms of a more diverse pool of funds that they can tap into. Since the religiously motivated funds are largely based on voluntarism of the individuals, the supply of such funds will remain fluctuating; and, therefore, may not be dependable.[97]

Furthermore, it has been argued that the

> charity-based approach should be restricted to either providing temporary start-up support . . . or devoted to capacity building to take care of the shortage of strong institutions and managers. A charity-based approach is also needed for providing social safety net to the extremely poor and the destitute. . . .[98]

It was also emphasized that the "donor funds should complement private capital, not compete with it."[99]

With reference to charitable funds, it has been noted that while practicing Islamic microfinance, the providers tend to rely on subsidized funds to provide capacity building and business development services. Such funds may be available in the form of benevolent (or interest-free) loans or religious tax income. Scholars have proposed that such services should be provided by a separate window.[100] However, there is a tendency for using these funds as a subsidy, which threatens the financial sustainability and its for-profit characteristics. The subsidy is generally perceived as creating a disparity in the market where the subsidized actors gain advantage over the unsubsidized ones, which restricts equal market access. The question whether Islamic charitable funds create the affects of subsidy is further discussed in below.

ISLAMIC LAW COMPLIANCE

It was also noted that, despite its promise, microfinance has not been reaching the poorest of the poor. Islamic finance has been expected to address this defect.[101] In fact, the existing Islamic microfinance products are almost similar to those of the mainstream Islamic finance; with the exception a few, however.[102] Evidence suggested that the *shari'a* compliance of microfinance instruments remains subject to the flexibility that the customers may demand or demonstrate.[103] The available evidence also suggests that the Islamic microfinance instruments charge high interest rates by using the prevalent transaction models. As reported, the "mark-up rate ranges between 12–12.5% with a compounding annualized implicit interest rate of 24–25%."[104]

It is argued that absence of the underlying assets would make it difficult to apply principles of Islamic finance to microfinance.[105] This observation seeks to point out the credit-based deferred payment, cost-plus or similar sale transactions that are regularly used in the Islamic finance industry.[106] In practice, however, the loans to the poor are almost invariably used for the capital investment and purchasing raw material, for which the Islamic finance transactions are available.

The discussion regarding the analysis of challenges faced by the Islamic microfinance continues in the text below.

Recent experiences

The experience of Islamic microfinance in the Muslim world offers a mixed account of optimism. In general, Islamic finance initiatives only had a limited success.[107] In this respect, the scholars noted that:

> In many cases, the cost of maintaining an Islamic window at a microfinance institution has been much higher than expected. Moreover, the development and delivery of these products have generally been highly subsidized by donor or government funds. As such, current Islamic microfinance programs, even if they show limited success, do not appear capable of expanding to reach the tens of millions of unbanked Muslims. To do that, they would need to become profitable and represent a viable business proposition for Muslim and non-Muslim investors.[108]

For instance, Indonesia, the largest Muslim populated country, was examined recently in this context. The work noted failure of Islamic rural banks in proving that they could efficiently and dynamically provide microfinance services.[109] Another example is post-9/11 Afghanistan, where one might expect Islamic microfinance to be more pervasive but Islamic microfinance is almost absent.[110] It was also noted that a number of conventional microfinance providers were embarking upon offering Islamic finance products and services.[111] A comparison of Islamic microfinance between Indonesia and Afghanistan was offered as follows:

> Both Afghanistan and Indonesia face opportunities for strengthening Islamic microfinance protocols – where the roles of stakeholders are generally fluid, negotiable and overlapping. The dynamics of creating an inclusive microfinance industry in post-conflict or post-disaster societies present particular challenges but they also offer stark choices not unlike in other "normal" situations. The alternatives include pragmatic responses that are *Shari'a* conversant or justifiable, on the one hand, and those rigorously conjured through Islamic jurisprudential enquiry as being *Shari'a*-compatible. Equally, there are attempts at adaptation and fusion of conventional and Islamic microfinance. Whether Islamic microfinance is being designed by the believer, agnostic or secular for faith, development or empowerment, legal methodologies matter as much as politics and economics. How can Islamic microfinance be gendered, made affordable and upscaled while upholding the fundamental

Islamic principles? It appears that the approaches adopted in Afghanistan have not fully and holistically addressed this challenge.[112]

Islamic microfinance experience in Syria reported 100 percent repayment. Evidence from Yemen also reports increasing optimism on repayment. It was also reported that the transaction costs were negligible, but the interest rates that were charged were quite high.[113] Charging of high interest rate despite success appears self-contradictory because the only reason to justify higher interest rate for micro-entrepreneurs was offsetting the high "operating costs."[114] Keeping in view the doctrinal position in this respect, it may be pertinent to note that charging of high interest rate to the poor may appear as their exploitation.

The prospects of convergence to the conventional form

The scope

In view of the above, it appears that the Islamic finance scholars overwhelmingly suggest that the modern practices of microfinance may be adopted by the Islamic microfinance initiatives. However, the Islamic content of the transactions may be preserved and advanced by constant innovation.[115] In sum, the Islamic microfinance industry is not only advised to keep up to date on the practices and strategies of the conventional microfinance but also to keep innovating toward the Islamic content of the microfinance transactions.

In this context, it may be pertinent to note that more approximation or convergence of conventional finance transactions, which impose charging of higher interest rates to microfinance customers, will defy the Islamic content. That is to say, whether it is the interest charged by the conventional microfinance, one the one hand, or the deferred payment or the lease-ending-with-sale, on the other hand, the payment streams from the microentrepreneurs is likely to be equally expensive to the poor. For staying competitive and cost-efficient, the Islamic microfinance initiatives are likely to follow cost-plus or similar transactions, which are standardized in the mainstream Islamic finance and predominantly use the benchmarking of the market interest rate. This practice achieves transactional convergence by approximating the conventional transactions. Continuation of approximation strategy is likely to make the task of doing Islamic microfinance more challenging.

Tools, practices and strategies

In recent scholarship on Islamic microfinance, there appears an implied consensus in using modern conventional tools in establishing and operating Islamic microfinance.[116] It was observed that the "best practices" developed by the conventional microfinance do not contradict the principles of Islamic law; it is the transactions that are not likely to converge, rather there should be transactional divergence.[117] In this context, convergence to the conventional transactions, by approximation or otherwise, will run counter to the spirit of doing Islamic microfinance—helping the poor and fighting poverty—and it may seem exploitative—by way of charging higher contract prices when the operating costs are lower.

Like many other conventional strategies, the modern techniques of microfinance are not inconsistent with the principles of Islamic law, and could be used for Islamic microfinance. Since microfinance has become quite a profitable industry, modern techniques that include group lending and securitization are now seen as regular features of microfinance.[118]

It was noted that the conventional MFIs

> have successfully resolved the credit risk problem by instituting group-based lending and collecting weekly installments, the problems of moral hazard and economic viability need to be resolved. As group-lending and weekly repayments effectively mitigate the credit risk problem in financing the poor, these aspects can be adopted by the Islamic institutions providing microfinance.[119]

In sum, financial sustainability, profitability and potential to reach a scale have been considered the most important starting points for Islamic microfinance on the way of its success. Other aspects include sharing the most advanced and sophisticated experiences and insights of the conventional microfinance.[120] Further suggestions for ensuring the success of Islamic microfinance include using conventional techniques to capture diverse services and institutions for providing financial services; technology-based delivery channels; adopting and implementing growth and stability strategies; conforming to modern financial reporting standards; ensuring accessible financial services to the poor; employing rigorous innovative models for cost reduction; capacity building; training; and developing graduation programs for the microentrepreneurs.[121]

Recent (Islamic trust-based) models of Islamic microfinance

The monetary waqf

As noted above, Islamic scholars have always given considerable attention to Islamic trust for the social welfare project. Recent Islamic scholars continue this tradition.

An eminent Islamic finance scholar has proposed a trust-based Islamic microfinance model. The model, named as the monetary *waqf*, is based on a one-time permanent donation and the subsequent supply of benevolent loans made to the trust. The trust delivers microfinance through the modes that are consistent with Islamic law. The trust then becomes a guarantor to the suppliers of benevolent funds. On its guarantee side, the trust has two sets of philanthropic guarantors, one guaranteeing the liquidity and the other providing guarantee against the losses. The philanthropic guarantors provide their guarantee through issuing standing instructions to their banks for releasing funds to and withdrawing from the trust within specified time and in the specified financial conditions.[122]

Undoubtedly, it is a profound proposal. However, this proposed model faces some serious implementation challenges with regard to scaling and integrating the Islamic trust with conventional microfinance and financial markets. First, the supply of benevolent funds will create a perverse incentive for the trust management to efficiently maximize the utility of the use of funds.

Second, the supply of benevolent funds offers an arbitrage opportunity to the management, which is an incentive to breach their fiduciary duty. One of the instances of this arbitrage could be to invest the proceeds in interest-bearing accounts and withdraw the interest plus principal, and return only the principal. Since the model has a virtually consistent supply for benevolent funds, the arbitrage could also go on indefinitely. Furthermore, it is certainly possible to effectively counter this agency problem but that will increase the operational costs. Since the sources of funds is one-time donation for administrative costs and the others funds are time-bound guaranteed benevolent loans, this model is likely to respond inefficiently to the increased costs needed to reduce the agency problem.

Third, the benevolent funds represent subsidized capital, which could potentially harm the market for Islamic microfinance initiatives and conventional microfinance providers. The subsidy is likely to affect the market adversely, by discouraging unsubsidized actors from entering the market and by potentially forcing out the existing unsubsidized actors. Even if, *in arguendo*, all the Islamic microfinance providers were to be converted to and reorganized as the proposed trust model, doing so will single out the conventional microfinance providers, and the adverse affects of the subsidy will become more apparent on the microfinance market.

Other advantages of waqf

The structure of an Islamic trust has been considered appropriate to ensure sustainability for it has permanent income-generating physical assets, and it has served this purpose for centuries in the Muslim societies. On the other hand, however, "the restrictions on development and use of assets under [the Islamic trust] for pre-specified purposes introduce rigidity into the system."[123]

As argued, the structure of Islamic trust was found more efficient than the conventional MFIs. The balance sheets of the Islamic microfinance trust and a conventional microfinance institute were compared to highlight more liquidity and diversity of income in the Islamic trust (see Tables 7.1 and 7.2).[124]

Since the Islamic trust is presented to attract religiously motivated charitable income, structuring Islamic MFIs in this way would not only reduce the financing costs but also improve its viability.[125]

Table 7.1 Balance sheet of a typical MFI

Assets	Liabilities
Cash	Deposits
Loans	Funds from external sources
	Equity

Table 7.2 Balance sheet of *waqf*-based Islamic MFI

Assets	Liabilities
Cash	Savings deposits
Assets	*Qard hasan* deposits
	Waqf certificates
• Low-risk assets	*Takaful* reserves
• Microfinancing	Profit equalizing Reserves
	Reserves/economic capital
loans	Capital *waqf*
• *Qard*	
investments	
(*murabaha, ijara,*	
salam, istinsa', mudaraba,	
musharaka)	

The shortcomings in the waqf structure

The above benefits of Islamic trust, as compared to the conventional MFIs, for microfinance certainly enrich our understanding about the institutional comparisons and their competitive advantages.

However, there is nothing inherent in the concept of Islamic trust that by itself attracts a diverse supply of funds. The competitive advantage that Islamic microfinance initiatives are argued to posses includes their ability to draw financial support from a wider array of supply sources. These sources include the religious tax and other charitable donations that Muslims are under a strong religious obligation to fulfill. The institution of Islamic trust is just a vehicle, in this context, that happens to be a recipient of the diverse supply of fund. Therefore, it simply could have been any other institution or vehicle too, say, any incorporated entity that is eligible to receive such donations or funds.

Indeed, having a conventional entity, as opposed or in addition to the Islamic trust, may offer more efficient way of conducting Islamic microfinance. First, the conventional corporate form (or its more tax-efficient likes) provides a greater certainty as to its chartered functions and offers more clearly defined corporate governance issues. Although such corporate entities and their treatment in various international and local jurisdictions may differ, one could almost invariably be certain about a number of aspects of the corporate entity such as incorporation, dissolution, acquisition etc. On the other hand, there is no consensus about dissolution and acquisition of an Islamic trust, which alone may disqualify *waqf* as a preferred vehicle to be part of a structure that is expected to be financially sustainable and profitable.

Second, it is more efficient to use a corporate vehicle for Islamic microfinance from the perspective of integration with the conventional market institutions. That is to say, market pressures such as the possibility of acquisitions and takeovers forces greater profit maximization and better financial discipline in the firm. Since there is no consensus within the Islamic school that the Islamic trust is susceptible to market pressures, the Islamic trust, in a worst-case scenario, is likely to be perceived as being shielded from the disciplining pressure of the market.

Third, as long as the Islamic trust is undergoing a jurisprudential transformation for improving its operational efficacies, providing Islamic microfinance through a conventional vehicle might be a more prudent way of proceeding further. Such conventional vehicle may be incorporated as closely to the substance of Islamic trust as possible. An important benefit of this strategy would be that Islamic microfinance will not face any structural handicap from its counterparts while maneuvering through the financial markets.

Furthermore, as soon as the transformed Islamic trust is available, it could be adopted instead of the conventional vehicle for conducting Islamic microfinance, if needed. In such a case, the conventional corporate vehicles used to describe a transaction model in section 4 below could be substituted with an Islamic trust that is capable of offering the needed structural capability and capacity. However, it may be argued that more insistence on doing Islamic microfinance through Islamic trust could be perceived as insistence merely on form, especially if the substance of Islamic trust could be achieved otherwise.

Exploring a new model: investing with the poor[126]

The above discussion indicates that Islamic microfinance faces peculiar challenges, which may appear hard to overcome. There appears to be no advisable single structure in conventional microfinance that could help Islamic microfinance overcome these challenges. It also not likely that the conventional microfinance may have any structural help to offer to the Islamic microfinance, keeping in view the special incentive structure (discussed in section 1) within which Islamic finance and Islamic microfinance operate. With regards to any structural proposals by the Islamic finance scholars, other than the modern Islamic-trust structures, there appears to be no other specific structure proposal.

Against this backdrop, a new microfinance business model is needed to address the challenges that face the sustainable, profitable and poor-friendly Islamic microfinance. This section explores such a model that incorporates not only the sophisticated features of conventional microfinance but also efficiently retains the salient features of Islamic microfinance. The proposed model also takes into consideration the market pressures that the Islamic finance industry faces today in the international financial markets, which may often be viewed as disincentivizing investing in Islamic microfinance. The model, however, incentivizes microfinance for the IFIs.

Islamic microfinance: a fresh perspective

Based on the recent literature on the conventional and Islamic microfinance, the proposed model offers the following capabilities that are properly incentivized for the relevant actors. Importantly, the model offers appropriate flexibility that is needed to accommodate both conventional and *shari'a*-compliant microfinance. The model and its salient features are discussed below.

Pursuing efficiencies of scale in Islamic microfinance: need for a diverse R&D

The research and development (R&D) capabilities for developing risk mitigation strategies and achieving efficiencies of scale have always been primordial to the growth of Islamic finance, and this is also true of developing Islamic microfinance. One may expect the supply of funds may in part be used to absorb the R&D costs associated with Islamic microfinance. On a comparative note, however, R&D significantly contributed in making the mainstream Islamic finance pricier than the products and services offered by its conventional counterpart. On the flip side, Islamic microfinance represents the smaller portion of the microfinance industry, which by itself is not a sizable industry. Here, it would be pertinent to note the global microfinance assets were estimated to be at $60 billion with asset growth of 39 percent.[127]

Since the size of Islamic microfinance market is smaller than conventional microfinance, it appears that incurring R&D costs, which are often substantial, may either not be possible for the Islamic microfinance industry or, assuming that it would be possible, cost overruns would impact on sustainability and competitiveness of the Islamic microfinance initiatives. This situation poses an impasse: The survival of Islamic microfinance is clearly threatened without promoting R&D, and the attempts to afford R&D perils the financial viability—Islamic microfinance gets challenged either way. As discussed below, the R&D cost may be shifted to an incentivized actor.

Monitoring and related services

The current microfinance literature suggests that a better success rate of microfinance operations could be expected through capacity building and business planning help. It is also pertinent to note that economic analyses of the market that assess the right demand for the products and services to be provided by the microentrepreneur, technical assistance and monitoring (guidance and monitoring) would also be greatly beneficial. Furthermore, the scholars have also focused on the need for social intermediation for financing microentrepreneurs.[128] The social intermediation may also include connecting the microentrepreneur with the market, say, with the domestic and international buyers that prefer to deal with small and local business. This kind of intermediation will not only provide microentrepreneurs a ready market but also another source of R&D that comes, say, in the form of compliance manuals with the purchase orders. For instance, Starbucks and Whole Foods Market have been known for promoting small local farmers, and similar buyers could be matched with microentrepreneurs. This form of social intermediation may also be included in guidance and monitoring for the discussion below.

In addition to R&D, business prudence will suggest that the costs associated with guidance and monitoring need to be eliminated, or minimized. However, guidance and monitoring appears critical for the success of the microfinance in general. In sum,

R&D for designing products and services and guidance and monitoring could help bring about a state of the art facility with the most sophisticated capabilities to ensure customization of the cutting-edge strategies in microfinance. As discussed below, the guidance and monitoring cost may also be shifted to an incentivized actor.

Social businesses

Working toward the establishment of social businesses, as contemplated by Dr. Muhammad Yunus, a hybrid of social and conventional business may be worth exploring. To this end, the investors may be asked to consider lowering their rates of return to the extent that their investment stays generally profitable. The incentive to lower the returns may come mainly from the social considerations and partially from minimizing the risk. Shifting some of the risk to an incentivized actor may help a social investor in agreeing to lower the rate of return.

Guarantee

After its recent availability, third-party guarantees have been successful in arranging commercial loans for microfinance. As discussed above, the restrictive nature of the guarantee makes it hard for a greater number of microfinance providers to benefit from the facility.[129]

Despite that the role of social intermediation has been emphasized and the significance of a third-party guarantee has been acknowledged, there appears to be no model that incorporates these features to provide the needed depth and breadth in the microfinance market. The proposed model below incorporates this feature and offers it through an incentivized actor.

Tax exemption

Islamic microfinance scholars have almost unanimously argued that the charitable and other religiously motivated funds may be tapped into Islamic microfinance. Invariably, such funds may be treated as donations. However, it is expected that the tax treatment of such funds would vary keeping in view the applicable tax regime, based on the donor, the donated amount and the donee.

It is also expected that, in the relevant jurisdictions, some of for-profit Islamic MFIs may not be able to offer tax exemption to the donated funds. In such case, there would a perverse incentive for making donations to Islamic microfinance initiatives. As discussed below, the issue of tax-exempt donations could also be solved by separating the for-profit features of microfinance from the non-profit ones.

Transparency

Islamic charitable institutions have not only been criticized for lack of transparency but some of them were also investigated for criminal and terrorist activities.[130] It is, therefore, important to emphasize that the proposed model has inherent incentives to comply with the applicable disclosure, and accounting and auditing regimes. In addition, voluntary adoption of any additional measures would significantly improve the transparency standards and would accordingly be helpful to mitigate any concerns of impropriety.

Making microfinance less expensive for the microentrepreneurs

Sharing the risk between the social and conventional investors, on the one hand, and the incentivized actor, on the other, is likely to reduce the inherent high-risk dynamics of microfinance. Accordingly, it will lower the cost of microfinance; a benefit that may be transferred to the microentrepreneurs by way of charging reduced interest rate, or the reduced contract price—for the Islamic microfinance.

Separation of for-profit and non-profit for a sustainable Islamic microfinance

Most of the above features could increase the operating cost significantly, and will ultimately impact on the sustainability of the initiative. The cost-intensive nature of the above considerations will also directly impact on whether microfinance operation could be profitable. In the interest of achieving economic efficiency, the for-profit and non-profit activities may be separated in one model.

The separation of for-profit activities from the non-profit activities is likely to resolve the tension between the high costs of microfinance operations and achieving sustainability and profitability. The majority of cost-intensive considerations could be moved to the non-profit side where, as discussed below, there is a built-in incentive for its aggressive compliance and implementation.

Exploring a new transaction model: financially mainstreaming the microenterprise

The new transaction model presented here ("the Model") separates for-profit side of microfinance ("NewCo") and its non-profit side ("Microfinance Foundation") in the Model. The Model also incorporates the following considerations, some of which have been established in the scholarship on conventional and Islamic microfinance:

1 achieving efficiency, scale, sustainability and profitability;
2 providing capacity building, training and intermediation to microentrepreneurs;
3 doing and promoting social business;
4 continued reliance upon advanced research;
5 more efficient handling of the donations;
6 devising strategies to make more funds available for microfinance such as risk-sharing and leveraging with the guarantees;
7 reaching the poorest of the poor; and
8 making microfinance inexpensive.

The Model: a summary

The Model seeks to bring together for-profit and non-profit funds to organize a for-profit microfinance entity (NewCo) and non-profit corporate entity (Microfinance Foundation) to complement each other. This is mainly achieved in the following stages:

1   NewCo issues preferred stock to investors with control rights. Microfinance Foundation acquired the non-voting preferred stock in NewCo. The common, in relevant cases, may be retained by the sponsoring professionals who also incorporate Microfinance Foundation.
2   Microfinance Foundation is set up to allow participation of public and private donors for developing microfinance.
3   NewCo and Microfinance Foundation set up their specialized subsidiaries that mirror the sectoral and geographic specializations. NewCo provides microfinancing through its specialized subsidiaries and the relevant subsidiaries of Microfinance Foundation provides R&D and guidance and monitoring to the microentrepreneurs, and the agreed repayment guarantee/surety to NewCo subsidiaries.
4   The microentrepreneurs graduate after repayment, and any profit generated by the NewCo subsidiaries flows to pay the preferred. If declared, the common receive dividend, and the residue stays with NewCo. Microfinance Foundation may be compensated by contract, but not necessarily for providing the guarantee.
5   Microfinance Foundation supports multiple structures of NewCo that include the NewCos that provide conventional microfinance.
6   Based on a totally different structure, which is not within the scope of this work and therefore not discussed herein, NewCo and its investors take an equity position in small and medium businesses of the graduating microentrepreneurs. At all stages, all the transactions summarized above remain *shari'a*-compliant.

The Model: the stages

STAGE ONE: NEWCO AS A FOR-PROFIT "SOCIAL BUSINESS"

The Model brings together the IFIs and the Islamic and other philanthropic investors to take equity positions in NewCo.[131] Both IFIs and philanthropic investors take preferred stock,[132] of the negotiated class, and with the negotiated control rights. The redemption rights of the preferred are negotiated in a *shari'a*-compliant manner.

Microfinance Foundation takes a non-voting preferred position in NewCo and avoids any control rights. There are three reasons for doing this. First, Microfinance Foundation should have a financial incentive in providing the services, which are discussed below, and should also have an interest in the success of NewCo. Second, if the financial interest of Microfinance Foundation is coupled with control rights in NewCo, Microfinance Foundation will not only be inevitably conflicted but will also be able to influence the strategic decision-making by the management in favor of its interests. Since Microfinance Foundation is expected to provide services to the multiples of conventional and *shari'a*-complaint NewCos (discussed in stage five below), the risk-averse appetite and representing competing interests may be avoided by restricting Microfinance Foundation to non-voting commons. Third, Microfinance Foundation's equity position would be helpful in resolving the challenge of asymmetric information that it may encounter in regards its repayment guarantee. This issue is discussed in greater detail below.

NewCo's basic structured could be described as follows (Figure 7.3).

Key points of the Grameen Foundation Growth Guarantee Progam are:

• Various stakeholders take short-term and/or long-term positions in NewCo.
• Following *shari'a*-compliant incorporation and capitalization, the activities of NewCo are supervised by a *Shari'a* Supervisory Board.

As for the social business considerations, some or all of the investors may cap their returns on the preferred on any agreed proportion. This way, the investors will be considered social investors to the extent of the residue returns are left in NewCo, and, by doing so, allowing NewCo to have its own permanent capital base. Since the rate of return is generally high in microfinance, the IFIs may cap their returns, for instance, consistent with or lower than their average investments. The IFIs may find the opportunity to cap the returns helpful in carrying out microfinance, while avoiding any unnecessary exposure and challenge to their overall business competitiveness.

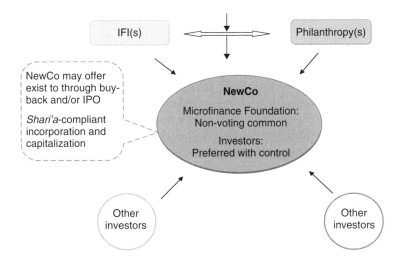

Figure 7.3 Incorporating an incentivized actor to conduct "social business"

In some cases, the common stock may belong to the sponsoring individuals and/ or entities, who are most likely to be microfinance professionals and may have also incorporated Microfinance Foundation. Since some investors are expected to cap their returns in the interest of NewCo developing its independent pool of funds, it would be important that the investors negotiate a funds retention and dividend policy. In the absence of such policy, the common stockholders may become eligible to dividends that may comprise some of the residuary amount left by the preferred holders. The funds retention and dividend policy will ensure that: (1) the residuary funds in NewCo are appropriately used; (2) there is no disadvantage to the preferred whenever a dividend is declared; and (3) there is no windfall to the common stockholders but the common stockholders remain adequately incentivized nevertheless. This policy could be agreed to by way of a shareholders' agreement or, for added security, could be incorporated in NewCo's charter.

As for the *shari'a*-compliant structure, NewCo may be organized on the *musharaka* model because of the control rights and the managerial role performed by the investors. However, the appropriate *shari'a* structure shall remain subject to the approval of all the parties.

NewCo's management may develop an exit strategy for the investors including the buy-back of the preferred and the initial public offering.

STAGE TWO: MICROFINANCE FOUNDATION AND ITS STRUCTURE

Microfinance Foundation, an incentivized actor, as a non-profit entity, should be incorporated by a set of sponsoring individuals and/or entities and should be run by highly skilled professionals with significant experience in microfinance. Microfinance Foundation may receive international and public donations, and tax-deductible private philanthropic donations. Microfinance Foundation may provide a range of services through its sector-specific subsidiaries, as discussed below.

Microfinance Foundation must have sophisticated in-house expertise on both conventional and Islamic microfinance, in addition to its sophisticated expertise in economic and market overview and analysis in relation to microfinance.

An important function that Microfinance Foundation would perform, through its subsidiaries or on its own, is development and implementation of various risk mitigation strategies for the financing guaranteed by it. Since Microfinance Foundation has sophisticated in-house expertise, it develops comprehensive economic overviews for a given market and for given sectors. Based upon such overviews, Microfinance Foundation develops business plans and implements by assisting the borrowers in organizing their business models. The microentrepreneurs also receive adequate training for their business activities.

STAGE THREE: THE SUBSIDIARIES AND THEIR FUNCTIONS

NewCo's subsidiaries, and securitization   Working toward commencement of its operations, NewCo incorporates bankruptcy-remote special purpose vehicles as its subsidiaries for certain geographic and sector-specific microfinancing, unless the tax or financial considerations suggest otherwise. The subsidiaries, also called subs, could be the single-person limited liability partnerships or the acquired affiliates as may be deemed appropriate under the relevant regime.

For maximum utilization of the NewCo funds and to ensure that more funds always remain available, NewCo may issue Islamic bonds (or *sukuk*) structuring the microfinance contracts and their flow of proceeds to serve as the underlying assets. Such bonds could be *mudaraba* or *wakala sukuk*. Another strategy could be developed as a more permanent feature of the Model. That is to say, securitization of microfinance contracts and selling them to entities that remain available to buy such loans (the closest example could be the likes of Fannie Mae and Freddie Mac for microfinance).

The issuance of Islamic bonds and the securitized sale of microfinance contracts will also serve as another layer of supervision on the NewCo and its subsidiaries, minimizing any incentives for bad credit decisions.

The incorporation and capitalization subsidiaries should be *shari'a*-compliant. The same may be true for any acquired affiliates.

A relevant graphical representation of the Model is given in Figure 7.4.

Key points of the Grameen Foundation Growth Guarantee Progam are:

* NewCo creates its subsidiaries, which may have varying shareholding structures and any sector-specific specialization.

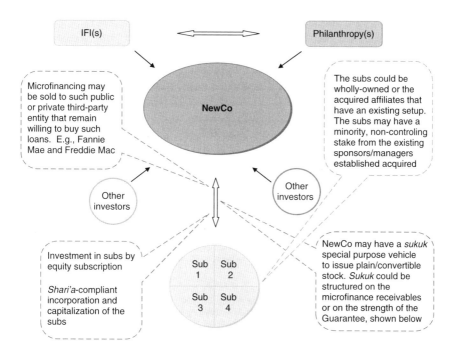

Figure 7.4 Expansion of NewCo's structure

- NewCo subsequently issues *sukuk* through any relevant subsidiary for making *shari'a*-compliant microfinance funds available.
- NewCo possibly shares/disposes of the microfinance portfolio with/to any public or privet third-party in a *shari'a*-compliant manner.

The microfinance contracts by each subsidiary could include micro-*musharaka*, micro-*ijara*, micro-*murabaha* etc. Such contracts could be with various classes of microentrepreneurs. Different strategies for different classes of microentrepreneurs will be efficient for the guidance and monitoring to be provided by Microfinance Foundation. The classes of microentrepreneurs could include village and urban housewives, small shopkeepers in rural and urban areas, individuals looking for work or the poorest of the poor.

A relevant graphical representation of the Model is given in Figure 7.5.

Key points of the Grameen Foundation Growth Guarantee Progam are:

- This delivers microfinance to microenterprise in compliance with *shari'a*.

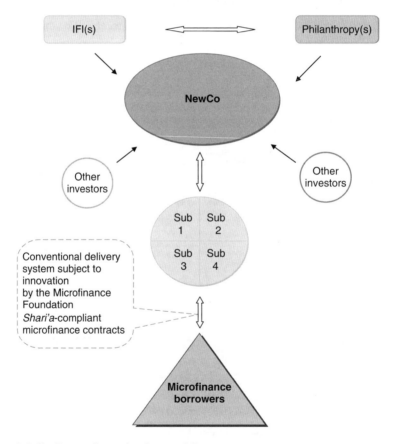

Figure 7.5 Shari'a-compliant microfinance delivery system

Microfinance Foundation, its subsidiaries, their guarantee and services Microfinance Foundation develops R&D, which includes designing products and services, technical services and risk mitigation strategies for NewCo's microfinance portfolio. To NewCo and microentrepreneurs, Microfinance Foundation also provides guidance and monitoring, which includes (1) developing economic overviews and comprehensive market analysis of various sectors in which the NewCo supports microentrepreneurs; (2) developing and dispensing business planning and operations guidance; (3) performing social and business intermediation, and, most importantly; (4) offering repayment guarantees through its subsidiaries.[133] A relevant graphical representation of the Model is given in Figure 7.6.

Key points of the Grameen Foundation Growth Guarantee Progam are:

- Microfinance Foundation's subsidiary mirrors NewCo's subsidiaries for efficient integration and coordination.
- Microfinance Foundation develops sophisticated microfinancing techniques, conducts markets surveys, provides capacity building to assist the microentrepreneurs and supervises the microfinancing portfolios.
- Microfinance Foundation provides guarantees to the relevant subsidiaries of NewCo on behalf of the microentrepreneurs.

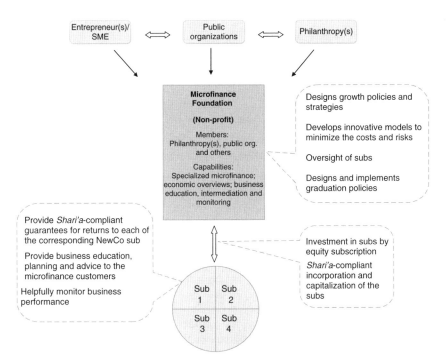

Figure 7.6 Incorporating the R&D and credit-enhancement organization, Microfinance Foundation

The guarantee As for the guarantee in general, Microfinance Foundation provides, limited or total, guarantees for NewCo's returns on its positions through its subsidiaries.[134] Based on its assessment, Microfinance Foundation also guarantees repayment of the principal owed to NewCo in part or in whole. Specifically, the guarantee could be in the form of Islamic surety contract (or *kafalah*).[135] The guarantee could cover range of exposures depending on the surrounding legal and regulatory structure and the overall market conditions. For instance, in some scenarios the guarantee may only cover portfolio losses on the microfinance contracts in excess of a certain percentage of the expected returns during the currency of the microfinance contracts. In other circumstances, it may cover full contract price. Any agreed act of default may trigger the call on the guarantee.

A full guarantee may result in two problems. It may provide an incentive for bad credit decisions by NewCo, and it may have the effect of subsidy. Bad credit decisions will gradually destroy the financial sustainability of both NewCo and Microfinance Foundation. The subsidy may have the effect of gradually reducing competition in the microfinance market—discouraging the unsubsidized actors from entering the market.

The issue of bad credit decisions could be handled by making the guarantee specific and limited. For instance, a full elimination of the microfinance contracts' losses may not be necessary everywhere and every time. As long as the Microfinance Foundation insulates NewCo from default on microfinance contracts in excess of any agreed proportion (i.e., a limited guarantee), NewCo's incentive for bad credit decisions may be minimized. This form of guarantee could be the standard or the most preferred model. However, keeping in view the conditions of some markets or while ensuring reaching the poorest of the poor, the limited guarantee model may be dispensed with for a certain time or until some positive indicators suggest reverting to the standard model.

As for the subsidy issue, since the services offered by Microfinance Foundation would also be available to conventional MFIs, no adverse affects of the guarantee are likely.

The guarantee from Microfinance Foundation would allow the NewCo to have microfinance contracts with even those who may otherwise not qualify for the microfinance, that is, the poorest of the poor. This way the guarantee certainly expands NewCo's portfolio as well as the availability of microfinance to those who may not be qualified for microfinance customarily—the poorest of the poor.

A relevant graphical representation of the Model is given in Figure 7.7.

Key points of the Grameen Foundation Growth Guarantee Progam are:

- Microfinance Foundation provides guarantees for the microfinancing to be issued by the relevant subsidiary of NewCo.
- Microfinance Foundation provides contract supervision and *shari'a*-compliance support to the relevant subsidiary of NewCo.
- Microfinance Foundation provides capacity building, technical assistance and the appropriate market surveys to the microentrepreneurs aiming at enhancing their profits and success.

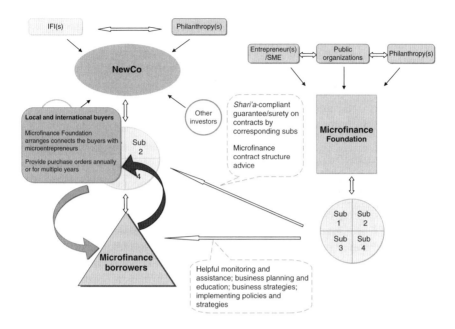

Figure 7.7 Microfinance Foundation supporting NewCo and microentrepreneurs

- Microfinance Foundation connects the microentrepreneurs to the local and international buyers and arranging buyers' credit.

Monitoring, intermediation, moral hazard etc. As for monitoring services, Microfinance Foundation monitors NewCo's microfinance customers by keeping close coordination with them in the process of educating them. Microfinance Foundation helps the microentrepreneurs in developing a business plan and shares with them insights of its economic overview to see what business activities or services may be pursued within a given market. This way, Microfinance Foundation will be able to guide the microentrepreneurs toward sectors that are not already saturated and have more growth opportunities. Microfinance Foundation will also be able to match the local and international business to deal with the microentrepreneurs as the buyers of their products.

As for the asymmetric information, this is taken care of by having the guarantor on the NewCo's board, and may also be worked out by agreements for information sharing on specific matters.

Moral hazard in the Model may boil down to two phenomena: (1) incentive for NewCo to take bad credit decisions; and (2) asymmetric information in which the guarantor relies upon NewCo and may have informational disadvantage. Since Microfinance Foundation (the guarantor) is on the NewCo's board and may otherwise insist upon procedures for the efficient and better credit decisions. To minimize asymmetric information, the Model is flexible enough to accommodate Microfinance Foundation's access to information.

Compensation to Microfinance Foundation   As for the compensation of services to Microfinance Foundation, NewCo subsidiaries can negotiate the financial model with the subsidiaries of Microfinance Foundation. However, this payment cannot be for the guarantee, because Islamic law treats the guarantee generally as a gratuitous act and any charge beyond the permitted threshold for this would invalidate *shari'a*-recognition of the transactions. This payment may be coupled with penalties if the credit guidelines provided by Microfinance Foundation were not followed. Such penalties will reduce the moral hazard at the subsidiaries.

STAGE FOUR: GRADUATING MICROENTERPRISE

After the successful coordination of NewCo and Microfinance Foundation, the microentrepreneurs will hopefully repay the microfinance contracts. At this stage, the microentrepreneurs may either become eligible for another round of microfinance contracts or graduate out of the microfinance network of the Model.

However, it may not be realistic to expect that the graduation would make them eligible to seek commercial loans on the strength of their personal collateral. But Microfinance Foundation may introduce different tiers toward which each graduating microentrepreneur keeps progressing. The graduation in this sense may reflect the relative betterment in the financial profile of a microentrepreneur and it may offer him/her the microfinance contracts in higher amounts. Put differently, Microfinance Foundation could develop and present a growth incentive plan to the microentrepreneurs. In such an incentive plan, Microfinance Foundation could set graduation thresholds, the realization of which would trigger the relevant incentive plan. The series of incentives could continue until the NewCo customers achieve a certain personal net worth threshold and finally graduate out of the growth incentive plan. Such incentives could include eligibility for health-care plan for the microentrepreneurs and his/her family.

A relevant graphical representation of the Model is given in Figure 7.8.

Key points of the Grameen Foundation Growth Guarantee Progam are:

• Microentrepreneurs graduate from the microfinance program successfully.
• The willing graduates may continue with the existing program or work toward becoming a SME individually or as a group.

STAGE FIVE: TOWARD A NEW STRUCTURE—INVESTING IN THE GRADUATING MICROENTERPRISE

As discussed above, an important feature of the Model is to help the microentrepreneurs upgrade their financial profile and gradually work toward sustaining their financial independence. In this regard, Microfinance Foundation and NewCo may work out a new model in which NewCo and other investors could invest in the SMEs composed of any number of microentrepreneurs that had a successful completion of their microfinance contracts.

In this respect, it may be pertinent to mention that the intermediations services

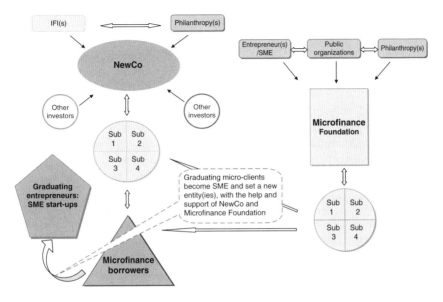

Figure 7.8 Graduating microentrepreneurs become SMEs

provided by Microfinance Foundation in the form of matching the local and/ or international buyers with the microentrepreneurs are likely to maximize the chances for the emergence of sound SMEs.

A relevant graphical representation of the Model is given in Figure 7.9.

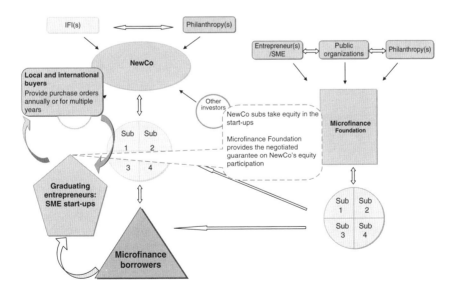

Figure 7.9 The SME connected with local and international market

Key points of the Grameen Foundation Growth Guarantee Progam are:

- The SME connects with the local and international market.
- The SME continues to be supported by the Microfinance Foundation.

STAGE SIX: MICROFINANCE FOUNDATION ACHIEVING EFFICIENCIES OF SCALE

The role of Microfinance Foundation is almost central to developing microfinance within the Model. However, the actual potential of its contribution could only be achieved if Microfinance Foundation starts supporting multiple NewCo structures, by letting them grow around it within one region or a country.

A graphical representation of such efficiency is given in Figure 7.10.

Key points of the Grameen Foundation Growth Guarantee Progam are:

- Microfinance Foundation achieves efficiency and scale and looks to provide support to multiple structures of NewCos for *shari'a*-compliant microfinancing.
- Ideally, at least one Microfinance Foundation supports multiple NewCos in one country/region.

Taking Microfinance Foundation's potential further ahead, it could start offering support to such other new or existing structures that conduct the conventional microfinance in a manner that is similar to IFI-based NewCo structures. Support to the conventional structures could be in a variety of forms keeping in view the market conditions in a particular geographic region or a legal jurisdiction. For instance, support to the conventional NewCo structures may include training programs, market analysis and intermediation and any outsourced entrepreneur development services for smaller MFIs.

A graphical representation of such efficiency is given in Figure 7.11.

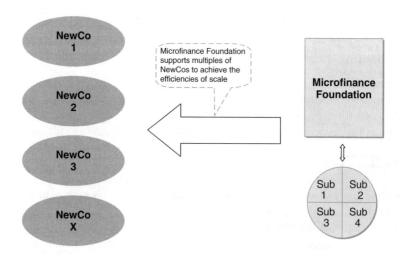

Figure 7.10 Microfinance Foundation supporting multiple NewCo structures

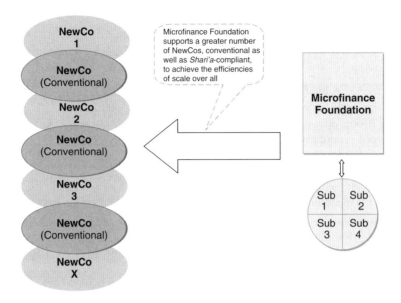

Figure 7.11 Microfinance Foundation supporting multiple structures comprising Islamic and conventional NewCos

Key points of the Grameen Foundation Growth Guarantee Progam are:

- Microfinance Foundation achieves even greater efficiency and scale and looks to provide support to multiple structures of NewCos that comprise *shari'a*-compliant as well as conventional NewCos.
- Ideally, at least one Microfinance Foundation supports multiple structures comprising Islamic and conventional NewCos in one country/region.

Conclusion

Islamic finance continues to compete with conventional finance. Although it has performed well within its nascent history, newer challenges keep Islamic finance under pressure to innovate, but most of the innovations have resulted in approximation of conventional finance, or have resulted in a form-oriented transactional convergence. As the approximation or convergence strategies represent a pressure on the IFIs to assimilate growth strategies of their conventional counterparts, they also create a perverse incentive for the IFIs for, among others, expanding toward providing financial services to the poor primarily because of the very nature of the pressures created by the prevalent corporate model.

The existing scholarship on "social business" encourages a business model that accommodates the contemporary, free-market business strategies to be adopted for achieving objectives of the "social business." One of the main features of the "social business" is that it singles out the individualistic profit maximization—

emphasizing that the profits of the social business can be invested back in the business and may be used for equity redemption of the social investors.[136] While the "social business" offers a refreshing perspective on the goals to be achieved within the contemporary settings of international financial markets, its realization, as hoped, may entail moving with a slower pace before it is widely prevalent. In such case, microfinance needs to work with the existing market-model that is heavily driven by the individualistic profit maximization considerations.

The Model discussed herein offers this flexibility: It does not single out investors with profit maximization objectives; it rather encourages them to invest along with the "social investors." In this way, the model minimizes the risk of unavailability of the capital to be allocated for microfinance.

It was not within the scope of this chapter to discuss business details on which various financial institutions, Islamic or their conventional counterparts, could invest with the NewCo—it will be discussed in a future work. The Model proposed herein is flexible enough to facilitate investments by any incentivized actor including banks, financial institutions, insurance companies, private equity and other funds.

As for Islamic financial services to the poor, the proposal made herein provides an incentive structure that enables innovation beyond approximation. It is hoped that the Model will not only generate further scholarly treatment of the subject but also, most importantly, help the poor, who expect Islamic finance to play a meaningful role in their lives too. It is also hoped that the model assists the Islamic finance industry to live up to those expectations without compromising its financial competitiveness.

Notes

1 This chapter was presented at the "Pre-Forum Workshop on Microfinance: Towards a Sustainable Islamic Finance Model," Eighth Harvard University Forum on Islamic Finance, Harvard Law School, Cambridge, MA, April 18, 2008.
2 Vice President, Al Baraka Banking Group, Manama, State of Bahrain.
3 In some Muslim countries, such as Pakistan and Malaysia, there are central supervisory boards to confirm or veto the supervisory boards of each IFI within their jurisdiction. Other countries insist that the IFIs self-regulate their Islamic law issues by referring to their supervisory boards.
4 Ali, S. Nazim 2007: 3–4.
5 Ibrahim, A.A. 2008: 9–12.
6 Various materials discuss this position in greater detail. See generally Chapra, M.U. 1985; Iqbal, M. 2002; Roberts, R. 1925.
7 Ahmed, H. 2007.
8 Obaidullah, M. 2007: 2–3.
9 Ibid.
10 Ibid.
11 The discussion is in sub-part "C" of part entitled "Islamic Microfinance Challenges: Experiences and Strategies."
12 Ahmed, H. 2007: 2 (discussing also that other scholars have also proposed establishing non-profit financial intermediaries that are based on the religious tax, Islamic trust and benevolent loan.)
13 El-Gamal, M.A. 2006.

14 Ibid.: 191.
15 Ibid.: 185.
16 Sait, S. and Lim, H. 2007: 5–6 (footnotes omitted).
17 Khan, A.R. 2005.
18 Zarka, M.A. 2007.
19 Sait, S. and Lim, H. 2007: 6 (footnotes omitted).
20 El-Gamal, M.A. 2006: 185 (emphasis added).
21 Ali, S. Nazim 2007: 2.
22 Ibid.
23 Ibid. *Shari'a*-compliant in this context refers to the commercial transaction that is made compliant with Islamic law whereas the expression *shari'a*-based means promoting all those financial activities that are consistent with and represent the spirit of Islamic law.
24 Ibid.: 1–2.
25 See generally Ali, S. Nazim 2007: 5; El-Gamal, M.A. 2006: 187 noting two different criticism on conventional microfinance: "[W]hile the success of Grameen Bank's microfinance operations in Bangladesh has given many Westerners cause to celebrate, Islamist groups and Islamic finance providers alike have generally criticized Grameen for its social agenda (especially as it pertains to empowerment of women) as well as the relatively high interest rates that it charges on its conventional loans."
26 Ali, S. Nazim 2007: 1. See also Badwi and Grais 2007 arguing that "Islamic financial institutions must come to terms with the true cost of microfinance and the implications of serving poorer customers profitably and sustainably. One clear implication is around pricing. To cover their costs, conventional microfinance providers charge higher interest rates than those of larger commercial banks. These rates are usually significantly lower than those charged by informal moneylenders, however, boosting the demand for microfinance services where they are available. Indeed, most MFIs report repayment rates approaching 100 percent among their clients." Ibid.: 2.
27 In some Muslim countries, such as Pakistan and Malaysia, there are central supervisory boards to confirm or veto the supervisory boards of each IFI within their jurisdiction. Other countries insist that the IFIs self-regulate their Islamic law issues by referring to their supervisory boards.
28 Trofimov, Y. 2007: A1.
29 The UK government is preparing for an Islamic bond issue of "a few hundred million pounds," which is expected by the end of this year. See IFLR 2008a.
30 Kwok, V.W. 2007; IFLR 2008b.
31 Pilling, D. et al. 2006.
32 This was the first-ever securitization originating out of the US. The issue was based on sub-sea gas reserves and underwritten by Merrill Lynch.
33 IFLR 2008c. On a related note, US-specific statistics for Islamic finance are not fully available publicly. For instance, the Islamic banking component of Islamic finance in the US was estimated at $2 billion recently. The capital markets' share is estimated to be much higher but remains unknown primarily due to the fact that most of the Islamic finance transactions are concluded privately. The increased interest could be in the US capital and securities markets, real estate, Islamic mutual funds etc. Consistent with this trend, Islamic indexes of US firms, which have been quite successful within the US and abroad, are also likely to further progress.
34 IIFM 2010.
35 Ibid.
36 Ibid.
37 Alvi, I.A. 2007.
38 The Islamic banking component of Islamic finance in the US was estimated at $2 billion recently. The capital markets' share is estimated to be much higher but remains unknown primarily due to the fact that most of the Islamic finance transactions are concluded privately.

39 Long-terms products guarantee a steady flow of funds for a longer period of time and help manage the portfolio risk better.

40 The author received feedback from the participants of the IDB's Islamic Capital Market Conference, Jakarta, Indonesia, August 2007.

41 Ibrahim, A.A. 2008: 4–5.

42 Worth, R.F. 2008 (noting that "[e]ven as it enriches Arab rulers, the recent oil-price boom is helping to fuel an extraordinary rise in the cost of food and other basic goods that is squeezing this region's middle class and setting off strikes, demonstrations and occasional riots from Morocco to the Persian Gulf."). El-Gamal, M.A. 2006: 187 (noting that "banks in the GCC region, as well as in other majority-Muslim countries, have suffered from excessive liquidity, which has generally led to massive increases in all asset prices in the region").

43 Ahmed, H. 2007: 19.

44 Ali, S. Nazim 2007: 2. Assumingly, the market segment represents combination of the Muslim population (which alone is one billion) and the poor of the world.

45 Cizakca, M. 2002: 273 (arguing that there "is substantial evidence that the formation of the Trust law in England was strongly influenced by Islamic *waqfs*," relying upon Gaudiosi, M. 1988).

46 See Ibid.: 271.

47 Ibid.: 273–275.

48 Obaidullah, M. 2007: 2–3.

49 Ahmed, H. 2007: 9.

50 Yasni, M.G. and Winarni, E.S. 2008.

51 Ibrahim, A.A. 2008: 31 (maintaining that the "development of the Islamic insurance industry has followed a non-conventional structure wherein the insurance company participates on a profit-loss sharing basis with a pool of participant (or policy holders) that mutually agree to cover each other in case of loss. In this structure the Islamic insurance company does not provide assurance/insurance to the policy holder, but acts on behalf of the policy holders to manage the business. The contributions or premia are pooled into a fund and invested into Islamic law-compliant investment opportunities. Profits are calculated after paying any claims, and surplus is shared between the company and the policy holders at a pre-agreed proportion. In this regard, the relationship of company vis-à-vis the policy holders is in the form of contract one above" (footnote omitted). Ibid.).

52 Ahmed, H. 2007: 19.

53 Bonvin, J. and Al-Sultan, F. 1997: 7–8.

54 Ibid.

55 Badwi, S. and Grais, W. 2007: 2.

56 See generally Fischer, S. 2003: 3.

57 See generally Ibid. (noting, among others, that it is possible for the loan officers who travel to the far-flung target communities to enter the transactions in to the system in the real time with the help of latest technologies). See also IT against Poverty, http://knowledge.allianz.com/microfinance/microcredit/?90/microfinance-technology-grameen.

58 Bonvin, J. and Al-Sultan, F. 1997: 7–8.

59 Pischke, J.D. et al. 1997: 9–39.

60 Ibid. (noting further that "[a]dvances in financial intermediation and infrastructure, stimulated by deregulation of financial sectors and facilitated by modern technology, have also put the spotlight on participatory mechanisms for integrating the poor into the economic mainstream. The advances in financial intermediation include recent efforts to design and deliver very small loans to poor borrowers, often women organized into small groups, providing more accessible deposit facilities, and much greater attention to management").

61 Ibid.

62 Ibid.
63 Ibid. (noting also that even the most successful microfinance providers do not reach the "truly destitute" or the "hard core poor").
64 Zander, R. 1997: 43–55 (providing also a set of best practices and technical modules).
65 Ibid.
66 McGuire, P.B. and Conroy, J.D. 1997: 82.
67 Ibid.
68 Hashemi, S.M. 1997: 110–111.
69 Ibid.: 111.
70 Ibid.: 122.
71 Yunus, M. 2006: 5–6.
72 Ibid.
73 Ibid.: 6.
74 Ibid.: 7.
75 Grameen Foundation 2008a; Grameen Foundation 2007a.
76 Grameen Foundation 2008a.
77 Ibid.
78 Ibid.
79 Grameen Foundation 2006.
80 Grameen Foundation 2008b.
81 Baue, W. 2004.
82 Ibid.
83 Grameen Foundation 2007b.
84 "Islamic Microfinance: Emerging Market Niche," CGAP Focus Note No. 49 (August 2008) available at www.cgap.org/gm/document-1.9.5029/FN49.pdf (last viewed on 26 September 2010) (hereafter "CGAP 2008").
85 CGAP 2008.
86 2009 Arab Microfinance Analysis & Benchmarking Report, a report by Microfinance Information Exchange (MIX), Sanabel and CGAP (May 2010) available at http://www.themix.org/sites/default/files/2009%20Arab%20 Microfinance%20Analysis %20and%20Benchmarking% %20Report_0.pdf (last viewed on 29 September 2010) (hereafter "2009 Arab Microfinance Report").
87 2009 Arab Microfinance Report.
88 This can be more precisely calculated based on a comprehensive market study of Muslim countries' specific data in response to the questions that include: (1) What is the portfolio size of microfinance loans in the Muslim countries? (2) What is the portfolio growth rate in the Muslim countries? (3) What are the positive indicators in the Muslim countries? and (4) What are other positive indicators for the Islamic microfinance?
89 2009 Arab Microfinance Report.
90 "Portfolio at Risk [PAR] is a standard international measure of portfolio quality that measures the portion of a portfolio, which is deemed at risk because payments are overdue. PAR 30 means the portion of the portfolio whose payments are more than 30 days past due. PAR 30 above 5 or 10% is a sign of trouble in microfinance. High delinquency makes financial sustainable impossible for an institution." Definition by CGAP, available at http://www.cgap.org/p/site/c/template.rc/1.26.3803/#par (last viewed on 29 September 2010).
91 CGAP 2008.
92 2009 Arab Microfinance Report.
93 Ahmed, H. 2002: 38.
94 Ibid.: 33–34.
95 El-Gamal, M.A. 2006: 186–187 (noting that "[d]isappointment at the low levels of economic and social development of Muslims worldwide was highlighted in a recent report by the Organization of Islamic Conference and discussed at the opening session

of the Conference's meeting in Turkey in November 2004. The problem in the Islamic world is not lack of funds. In fact, banks in the GCC region, as well as in other majority-Muslim countries, have suffered from excessive liquidity, which has generally led to massive increases in all asset prices in the region. Neither is the problem one of lack of desire on the part of wealthy Muslims (and the world community at large) to help poorer Muslims around the world. Indeed, Muslim charities have been faulted mainly for their means of collection and disbursement of funds, but never for lack of resources. The problem, in fact, is one of financial disintermediation in the Islamic world, in which perception about Islamic permissibility of various credit extension schemes may be to blame").

96 Khan, A.R. 2005.
97 Obaidullah, M. 2007: 1.
98 Ibid.
99 Ibid.
100 Badwi, S. and Grais, W. 2007: 4–5.
101 Ali, S Nazim 2007: 3.
102 See generally El-Gamal, M.A. 2006 (explaining that "[s]ome attempts have been made to provide Islamic alternatives, with assistance of institutions such as cash trusts (*waqf*). Such initiatives would be particularly useful, since trusts (*awqaf*) can serve as ideal vehicles for channeling Muslim charitable contributions to subsidize Microfinance operations to some of the poorest Muslims around the world. However, those initiatives, as well as socially focused ones that utilize more traditional "Islamic financing" tools such as *murabaha*, remain very few, and they are largely viewed as being on the fringe of Islamic finance").
103 Sait, S. and Lim, H. 2007: 3 (referring to another work on Yemen, noting that "the extent to which a microfinance product is altered depends on how strongly these beliefs regarding interest are held . . . . where these beliefs are not as pervasive, institutions may make cosmetic changes to their operations and products, such as changing the term 'interest' to 'service charge.' In other cases where these beliefs are fundamental and widespread, more extensive adaptations have had to take place, which affect the core of an institution's systems, operations and beliefs").
104 El-Hawary, D.A. and Grais, W. 2005a.
105 Ali, S. Nazim 2007: 4.
106 Ibrahim, A.A. 2008: 27–32 (explaining Islamic finance contracts including cost-plus and leased-based transactions).
107 Badwi, S. and Grais, W. 2007: 1.
108 Ibid.
109 Seibel, H.D. 2008: 1 (noting further that "[t]here are two options of promoting Islamic microfinance [in Indonesia]: (1) assisting Islamic commercial banks to establish units with Islamic micro-finance products, or (2) reassessing in a participatory process the challenges and realistic opportunities of Islamic rural banks and cooperatives, with a focus on effective internal control, external supervision, and the establishment of associations with apex services to their member institutions").
110 Sait, S. and Lim, H. 2007: 3.
111 Ibid. (explaining that "[w]hile Islamic Microfinance was not part of the official development discourse or general microfinance planning, realities on the ground forced a rethink. The potential high demand for small loans was accompanied by end-user skepticism over their compatibility with Islam. For example, Ariana Financial Services Group (AFSG), established by Mercycorps, narrated its hard work to convince people that its services were not un-Islamic. Making a virtue out of necessity, a number of MFIs in Afghanistan have since packaged themselves as Islamic. The Danish MADRAC (Microfinance Agency for Development and Rehabilitation of Afghan Communities) in November 2006 launched new Islamic credit services for needy people in rural areas. The US-based FINCA International also announced that as

of September, 2006 all FINCA Afghanistan credit products are *Shari'a* compliant. Likewise, the French-based Oxus Development Network (ODN) now provides loans following the principles of Islamic banking").

112 Ibid.

113 El-Hawary, D.A. and Grais, W 2005a: 5.

114 Ali, S. Nazim 2007: 1; Badwi and Grais 2007: 1 (arguing that "Islamic financial institutions must come to terms with the true cost of microfinance and the implications of serving poorer customers profitably and sustainably. One clear implication is around pricing. To cover their costs, conventional microfinance providers charge higher interest rates than those of larger commercial banks. These rates are usually significantly lower than those charged by informal moneylenders, however, boosting the demand for microfinance services where they are available. Indeed, most MFIs report repayment rates approaching 100 percent among their clients" Ibid.: 2).

115 Ibrahim, A.A. 2007 (analyzing the difference between procedural and transactional convergence, and that the latter may not be consistent with Islamic law).

116 Seibel, H.D. 2008: 20; Sait, S. and Lim, H. 2007: 7; Zarka, M.A. 2007: 3; Badwi and Grais 2007: 5; Ahmed, H. 2002: 38; Obaidullah, M. 2007: 2–3; Khan, A.R. 2005; and El-Hawary, D.A. and Grais, W. 2005a.

117 Obaidullah, M. 2007: 2–3. A similar argument was made in the context of corporate governance that the modern practices are indeed consistent with Islamic law; it is the modern transactions that tend to have inconsistent features. See Ibrahim, A.A. 2007 (analyzing the difference between procedural and transactional convergence, and that the latter may not be consistent with Islamic law).

118 El-Gamal, M.A. 2006, p. 212 (describing, in footnote 10, that "[e]xtensive economic literature on micro financing has shown that repayment rates on micro loans are incredibly high, especially when supported by group-lending technologies such as those pioneered and popularized by Grameen. This makes such lending profitable. Especially given new securitization technologies that have allowed microfunds to emerge, again pioneered in Bangladesh through Grameen Foundation USA's first bond issuance of $40 million to support Microfinance institutions in nine developing countries").

119 Ahmed, H. 2007: 19.

120 Badwi and Grais 2007: 1; see also Obaidullah, M. 2007: 1 (discussing the relevance of modern practices for Islamic microfinance (MF) that the modern "principles broaden the definition of MF from micro-credit to provision of an array of financial services, such as, savings, insurance and remittance as a panacea for the poor and the underprivileged to move out of poverty into a state of increasingly better standard of living. The principles advocate free pricing of the services. They emphasize that access to MF and not cost of MF should be under focus in designing and implementing a poverty alleviation strategy. The strategy should aim at sustainability through a shift from a charity-based donor-dependent approach to a market-based for-profits approach emphasizing systemic efficiency and transparency and restricting use of donor funds to temporary support in the initial stage of an MFI and capacity building. Recent writings advocate use of charity for providing social safety nets for the extremely poor who are unbankable and, therefore, unserved by the for-profit MFIs. The principles also underscore inclusiveness and integration of MF with the formal financial system").

121 Ibid.: 3–5 (concluding that "Islamic microfinance providers, regardless of the instruments they utilize, must: (1) be realistic about the cost of serving poorer customers, especially in remote rural areas; (2) engage policymakers and others to educate them about the true cost of microfinance; and (3) explore innovative ways to reduce the cost of microfinance transactions").

122 Zarka, M.A. 2007.

123 Obaidullah, M. 2007: 2–3.

124 Ahmed, H. 2007: 7–11 (comparing the balance sheets in the following manner: Furthermore, the author developed the financial model in support of the argument).

125 Ibid.: 19.
126 The expression "Investing with the Poor" is an improvisation of expression "bankers to the poor" referred to by Mr. Robert A. Annibale, Global Director of Microfinance, Citigroup. See Ali, Nazim 2007.
127 Chen, Greg et al. 2010. Interestingly, although Islamic finance's size is much bigger but the growth rate of Islamic finance and the conventional microfinance is almost the same.
128 Ahmed, H. 2007: 5–6.
129 See the discussion in this chapter on p. 000.
130 Crimm, N.J. 2005; Keyes, D. 2006.
131 NewCo should be authorized to conduct activities of microfinance and should have all the applicable regulatory approvals before the commencement of its operations. NewCo's structure should always allow the flexibility to welcome incoming investors in any numbers.
132 The subscription price paid by the investors will constitute the pool of funds for the NewCo's microfinance business. Against the subscription amount, the NewCo will issue its preferred stock to IFIs and the philanthropic investors.
133 The functions of Microfinance Foundation would generally include: Designing microfinance growth policies and strategies; developing innovative models to mini-mize the costs and risks; oversight of the subsidiaries; designing and implements graduation policies; providing *shari'a*-compliant guarantees for returns to each of the corresponding NewCo subsidiaries; providing business education, planning and advice to the microentrepreneurs; helpfully monitoring business performance; providing microfinance contracts structure advice; providing helpful monitoring and assistance; business planning and education; developing and analyzing business strategies; and implementing policies and strategies.
134 The incorporation and capitalization subsidiaries should be *shari'a*-compliant. The same may be true for any acquired affiliates.
135 If the scale permits, Microfinance Foundation could organize the insurance model based on *takaful* for the Islamic microfinance industry.
136 See generally Yunus, M. 2007: 3–21.

8 Re-thinking leasing from an interest-free perspective

Exploring the prospects of Islamic microleasing for poverty alleviation[1]

Asad Kamran Ghalib[2]

Introduction

The world of Islamic banking has grown phenomenally particularly over the past decade. Though existing literature contains anecdotal figures and reliable data are onerous to get hold of, the expansion of the sector has been exceptional, given current statistics that originate from a wide variety of sources. The *Halal Journal* refers to the International Monetary Fund's (IMF) estimates of the total worldwide assets of Islamic financial institutions to exceed USD 250 billion while it predicts the growth rate to be around 15 percent annually.[3] Eagle refers to the Islamic financial world as one of the fastest growing segments of the financial sector and the "$180 billion/day industry."[4] Aaron MacLean quotes Hussein A. Hassan of Deutsche Bank who envisages Islamic finance to be the world's fastest-growing banking sector for years, based on what he calls "a modest estimate of 20 percent annual increase in deposits."[5]

In terms of the number of institutions providing facilities under the Islamic banner, figures in literature vary anywhere from over 300 to 450. According to Eagle "in 1975 there was one Islamic bank; today there are over 300 in more than 75 countries." Such institutions may range anywhere from pure and dedicated large Islamic banking corporate, large investment houses to conventional, high street banks (with *shari'a*-compliant banking units), and small microfinance institutions (MFIs) offering financing options under Islamic guidelines.

What is astounding for both Muslims and non-Muslims alike is how a financial system could become so successful and widespread when it prohibits interest, which is, on the contrary, the mainstay of, and a powerful decisive and controlling element in, the non-Islamic financing mechanisms.

Financing in Islam: the fundamental doctrines and underlying principles

Islamic law, known as the *shari'a*, lays down the guidelines and principles for financing within the religion's realm. The most significant feature of a truly Islamic economic system is that it ought to be fair, and the Quran has condemned interest because it jeopardizes that ideal.[6] The system can be fully understood only in the context of Islamic attitudes towards ethics, wealth distribution, social and economic justice, and the role of the state. Principles encouraging risk sharing, individual rights and duties, property rights and the sanctity of contracts are all part of the Islamic code underlying the banking system.[7]

Apart from prohibiting interest, Islamic banking finances only *real* transactions, with underlying assets; speculative investments such as margin trading and derivatives transactions are excluded. Lending, or financing, is backed by collateral since collateral-free lending would normally be considered as containing a speculative element, or moral hazard.[8] The principle deduced from the above discussion concludes that the *shari'a* prohibits those transactions that involve interest, gambling, unethical investments, contractual terms of a transaction involving uncertainty, deception, ambiguity or lack of clarity and give rise to speculation (*gharar*). Hence, Islamic financial transactions are structured using contracts or combination of contracts that satisfy the requirements of *shari'a*.[9]

The rationale behind the entire concept of Islamic financing transactions rests "on the concept of a social order of brotherhood and solidarity."[10] The parties to an Islamic financial and banking transaction are considered business partners who bear the risks, gains and losses on a joint basis. Based on the concept of joint risk sharing, Islamic financial instruments and products are therefore equity-oriented.

In summary, Edwardes analyses Islamic banking along the following six key features:[11]

1 It is free of interest.
2 It is trade-related and there is a perceived "genuine" need for the funds.
3 In its purest form, it is equity related.
4 It is meant to avoid exploitation—no usury.
5 It invests ethically.
6 There are retail and wholesale applications.

The basic forms of Islamic financing

Literature on Islamic financing emanates various classifications of a range of different models devised by the *shari'a* and authors have categorized these modes according to an assortment of methods. Kazarian,[12] Iqbal and Mirakhor[13] and Dhumale and Sapcanin[14] have classed all Islamic banking contracts under three groups: concessionary modes, participatory mechanisms and trade financing. Participatory mechanisms are further divided into profit-and-loss sharing (*mudaraba*, *musharaka*, etc.) and non-profit-and-loss-sharing (*ijara* and *murabaha* etc.). Whereas, according to Eagle, the main *shari'a*-compliant banking products include *mudaraba* (profit sharing), *wadi'a* (safekeeping), *musharaka* (joint venture), *murabaha* (cost plus) and *ijara* (leasing). Tarek and Kabir[15] and Usmani[16] define the following as the five basic Islamic financing contracts:

1 *Mudaraba* (participation financing).
2 *Musharaka*.
3 *Murabaha* (financing resale of goods).

4   *Salam and istinsa'.*
5   *Ijara and ijara wa iqtina'* (lease financing).

Gafoor, on the other hand, categorizes them across only three broad areas: investment financing, trade financing and lending.[17] As shown in Figure 8.1, he classes *musharaka* and *mudaraba* under investment and mark-up, leasing and hire purchase under trade financing.

While *musharaka* is understood as a joint enterprise in which partners share in both profit and loss, *mudaraba* is a special kind of partnership where one partner gives money to another for investing it in a commercial enterprise. The investment comes from the first partner who is called *rabb-al-mal*, while the management and work is an exclusive responsibility of the other, who is called *mudarib*.

Though perceived to be somewhat similar, both *musharaka* and *mudaraba* have some fundamental differences between them. The foremost of these being the party providing the capital for investment, which in *musharaka* comes from all the partners (in an agreed ratio), while in *mudaraba*, investment is the sole responsibility of *rabb-al-mal* (the financial institution). The other major difference lies in the participation of the management of the business. In *musharaka*, all the partners can participate in the management of the business while working for it, while in *mudaraba* the *rabb-al-mal* has no right to participate in the management, which is carried out by the *mudarib* only.[18]

The third most common type of Islamic finance is the *murabaha* model. Instead of lending money to the borrower, the financial institution providing this type of service purchases the goods on behalf of the customer (at a freely disclosed price) and re-sells them to the entrepreneur at a higher, mutually agreed price. This price consists of the cost of the goods plus an agreed profit margin. This margin comes in the shape of a fixed mark-up intended to cover the administration costs. Payments are made on a deferred basis and the *shari'a*-compliant financial product provider retains title and ownership of the goods until all agreed installments have been paid.

In *musharaka* and *mudaraba*, the lending body assumes the role of an investor and resultantly assumes a certain portion of the business risk of the enterprise that comes along, while in the *murabaha* model, the extent of the risk and return of the financing institution are restricted due to its predominantly lending role.

Lastly, *salam* is a sale whereby the seller undertakes to supply some specific goods to the buyer at a future date in exchange of an advanced price fully paid on the spot. Here the price is cash, but the supply of the purchased goods is deferred, while *istisna'* is the second kind of sale where a commodity is transacted *before* it comes into existence. According to Usmani, it means to order a manufacturer to manufacture a specific commodity for the purchaser.

Understanding leasing as a financing mechanism

Leasing in its simplest sense means a contract whereby the owner of an asset grants a person the right of its use in return for an arranged fee over an agreed period of

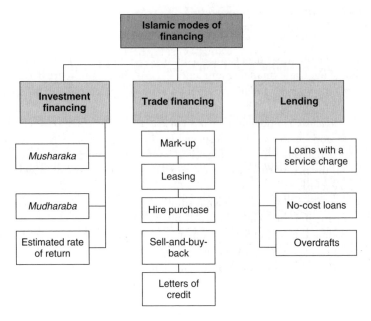

Figure 8.1 The basic forms of Islamic financing

time in an agreed manner. Leasing contracts come in three forms: hire purchase, finance lease and contract hire.

There are a few distinct types of leases that lend themselves easily for synthesis and replication within an Islamic finance model. Hire purchase, also sometimes referred to as "lease purchase," form of leasing allows the lessee or leaseholder (the client) to pay off the full, agreed amount of the asset over a defined period to the lessor (the owner), at the end of which s/he owns the asset. A finance lease is a long-term lease over the expected life of the equipment, usually three years or more, after which the lessee pays a nominal rent to own the leased asset outright. In this leasing model, although the ownership of the asset lies with the lessor during the lease period, the lessee is responsible for its maintenance and insurance. The lease payments are designed are in such a manner that the lessor recovers the full cost of the equipment, plus charges, over the period of the lease. A contract hire lease is quite similar to a finance lease with the exception that the residual value of the asset is pre-determined and the payments are calculated in light of this value.

The fundamental difference between an operating lease and a finance lease lies in the ownership of the leased asset at the end of the stipulated time period. As opposed to the finance lease, the ownership does not transfer to the lessee at the end of the contract, due to which the leasing company is responsible for its maintenance and insurance during the lease period. The lessor therefore retains ownership at all times, even at the end of the stipulated length of contract. The agreement is structured in such a manner that the user of the asset pays off its whole value, along with the charges.

Leasing from an Islamic perspective

The four major forms of business transactions permitted by the *shari'a* are discussed above. The fifth, *ijara*, is analogous to the English term of leasing. Taqi Usmani defines *ijara* broadly as a transaction "to transfer the usufruct (the right of use and enjoy the benefits) of a particular property to another person in exchange for a rent claimed from him."[19]

Ijara comes in two basic forms: *ijara*—operating lease, and *ijara wa iqtina'*—finance lease. In a simple *ijara* transaction, the financial institution purchases the goods on behalf of the client, acquires the title and passes its possession to the customer for use against a pre-determined rent (which comprises the cost plus mark-up). As per the agreement, the title of the goods does not at any stage pass on to the customer. If, at a later stage, the customer wishes to purchase the goods, a separate agreement must be arranged clearly stating the terms of the purchase. An *ijara wa iqtina'*, or finance lease, is the same as the *ijara* described above except that title to the asset is expected to pass to the customer at some time, usually at the end of the contract period. It can be used to purchase both goods and property.[20]

Basic rules of leasing

Various religious scholars have come with a number of principles that act as guidelines for transacting business on the *ijara* model according to the *shari'a*. Given below are some of such guidelines proposed by Usmani:

1 Leasing is a contract whereby the owner of something transfers its possession to another person for an agreed period, at an agreed consideration.
2 It is necessary for a valid contract of lease that the ownership of the leased property remains with the seller, and only its possession is transferred to the lessee. Thus, anything that cannot be used without consuming cannot be leased out. Therefore, the lease cannot be affected in respect of money, "eatables," fuel and ammunition etc. because their use is not possible unless they are consumed.
3 As the ownership of the leased property remains with the lessor, all the liabilities emerging from the ownership shall be borne by the lessor, but the liabilities referable to the use of the property shall be borne by the lessee.
4 The lessee cannot use the leased asset for any purpose other than the purpose specified in the lease agreement. If no such purpose is specified in the agreement, the lessee can use it for whatever purpose it is used in the normal course. However if s/he wishes to use it for an abnormal purpose, s/he cannot do so unless the lessor allows her/him to in express terms.
5 The lessee is liable to compensate the lessor for any harm to the leased asset caused by any misuse or negligence on the part of the lessee.
6 The leased asset shall remain in the risk of the lessor throughout the lease period in the sense that any harm or loss caused by the factors beyond the control of the lessee shall be borne by the lessor.

7 A property jointly owned by two or more persons can be leased out, and the rental shall be distributed between all the joint owners according to the pro-portion of their respective shares in the property.

8 The rental must be determined at the time of contract for the whole period of lease. It is permissible that different amounts of rent are fixed for different phases during the lease period, provided that the amount of rent for each phase is specifically agreed upon at the time of affecting a lease.

9 The lease period shall commence from the date on which the leased asset has been delivered to the lessee, no matter whether the lessee has started using it or not.

10 If the leased asset has totally lost the function for which it was leased, and no repair is possible, the lease shall terminate on the day on which such loss has been caused. However, if the loss is caused by the misuse or by the negligence of the lessee, s/he will be liable to compensate the lessor for the depreciated value of the asset as; it was immediately before the loss.

As compared to other *shari'a*-compliant products, the *ijara* model can be seen to be a more suitable financial product that can adapt to the needs of the typical microfinance client. The following characteristics of a leasing transaction warrant its suitability:

• It does away with conventional collateral for credit, since the commodity or asset being financed serves as collateral itself.
• Under an *ijara* contract, there is no requirement for maintaining accounting records, something not readily available from microentrepreneurs in areas where the literacy rate is low.

Poverty, the rationale of microfinance and its best-practice guiding principles

Out of a global population of around 6.5 billion people, approximately half— nearly three billion people—live below the poverty line.[21] If an average household is taken to consist of five members, the total number of households living below the poverty line amounts to 600 million. Rising inflation, disease, war, environmental issues, unemployment, health constraints, demographic features and "inherited poverty" are some of the many factors that lead to such state. Amongst the afore-mentioned and other factors that contribute towards poverty, lack of financial and material resources is the most apparent of its manifestations. A deficiency in such resources implies an absence in the availability of collateral, which results in the formal financial and banking sector's denial in advancing credit, thereby contrib-uting to their exclusion from the conventional financial lending sector. Ironically, such exclusion is more extensive in the lesser-developed countries, where poverty is more common.

Various governments and international agencies have been devising and implementing a range of models and programs to combat the growing problem.

Providing low-cost, subsidized, collateral-free finance to enable people to kick-start microenterprises of their own, in order to make them self-reliant is one such approach. The most common vehicles for this form of financing, amongst others, are non-governmental organizations (NGOs) and MFIs.[22]

Microfinance explained

Despite the abundant research and literature on microfinance, there is still no universally agreed definition of this term. Various researchers and organizations have come up with a wide array of definitions and descriptions that correspond to their individual perspectives and viewpoints.

The Microcredit Summit in February 1997, for instance, described microcredit as "programs that extend small loans to very poor people for self-employment projects that generate income, allowing them to care for themselves and their families." Professor Yunus looks at the concept from Grameen's standpoint and uses a more lender-oriented approach: "Microcredit is the extension of small loans to entrepreneurs too poor to qualify for traditional bank loans."[23] Delgado sums it up as being the practice of extending small loans to the poor (also known as micro-loans) for income-generating activities often coupled with other financial services such as savings and insurance.[24] Latortue describes it as "a credit methodology that employs effective collateral substitutes to deliver and recover short-term, working capital loans to microentrepreneurs (or potential microentrepreneurs)."[25]

Regardless of the way it is defined, we can conclude microcredit to be a system, whereby loans are advanced to the destitute, without a need for collateral for the purpose of setting up their own microenterprises, with the ultimate objective of enabling them to become self-sufficient. The most prominent feature of advancing loans through this mechanism is that it helps in creating a more self-reliant population, rather than distributing charity and aid to people, which are consumed without creating sustainable businesses. This process helps in building human capacities and creating sustainable livelihoods.

The rationale behind microfinance is primarily to provide credit access to the poor, who had always been perceived to be "unbankable" by formal financial intermediaries such as commercial banks. Consequently, the poor were usually refused credit primarily due to the lack of collateral. Small amounts of collateral-free loans are advanced to the rural poor to start up microenterprises of their own, pay back installments and eventually help themselves out of poverty. This helps not only to combat poverty, but also to provide a means to improve and maintain quality of life in the face of uncertainty.

Microfinance provides a solution to help people out of poverty and make them increasingly self-reliant. As self-dependency grows amongst individuals and households, so does output, employment, per capita income, production and growth: all those factors that compose an idyllic formula for the overall progress of a nation to a gradual route towards development, independence and prosperity.

Microfinance is not all about lending and borrowing small amounts for a profit, the practice entails a whole process that involves and impacts individual lives,

entire households and communities. It brings prosperity, empowerment, independence and awareness. The economic advantages may be the foremost and primary
intention, but the consequential social benefits, though intangible, may prove even
more long-lasting and far-reaching, having such an effect on those concerned that
it may surpass the tangible financial gains.

In order to make the most of this model and to ensure that it does indeed assist
the poor, there are certain principles that, if adhered to, will make the lending
program generally effective.

Microfinance best practices

Brandsma and Chaouali have provided certain guiding principles underlying best-
practice microfinance.[26] These can be summarized as:

1   *Covering cost*: To become sustainable, MFIs, regardless of their institutional set-
    up must cover their costs of lending. If costs are not covered, the institution's
    capital will be depleted and continued access of microenterprises to financial
    services and even the existence of the MFI will be in jeopardy.
2   *Achieving a certain scale*: Successful MFIs have reached a certain scale, as mea-
    sured by the number of active loans. This number depends on local settings,
    lending methodology used and loan sizes and terms offered.
3   *Avoiding subsidies*: Microentrepreneurs do not require subsidies or grants but
    they do need rapid and continued access to financial services. Besides, micro-
    lenders cannot afford to subsidize their borrowers. Subsidies send a signal to
    borrowers, that the government or donor funds are a form of charity, which
    discourages borrowers from repaying. Moreover, MFIs have learned that they
    cannot depend on governments and donors as reliable, long-term sources of
    subsidized funding.
4   *Promoting outreach and demand-driven service delivery*: Successful MFIs increase
    access to financial services for growing numbers of low-income clients, offer-
    ing them quick and simple savings and loan services. Loans are often short
    term, and new loans are based on timely repayments. Loans are based on bor-
    rowers' cash flow and character rather than their assets and documents, and
    alternative forms of collateral (such as peer the pressure) are used to motivate
    repayment.
5   *Maintaining a clear focus*: It takes time and commitment to build a sustainable
    microfinance program. Thus mixing the delivery of microfinance services
    with, for example, the provision of social services is inadvisable because it
    sends conflicting signals to clients and program staff.

The nexus between Islamic financing and microfinance

In light of the observations, the underlying principles and best practices of microfinance noted above, it is clear that the microfinance model is consistent with
the broader goals of Islamic banking. Said et al., while attempting to establish the

analogies between *shari'a*-compliant lending models and microfinance, state that there are many similarities in the nature of Islamic banking and microfinance as both forms of finance represent unconventional solutions to financial needs starting from egalitarian, classless and democratic approaches being open to all customers without setting any apparent restrictions to the different categories of clients.[27] Similarly, both systems advocate financial inclusion, entrepreneurship and risk sharing through partnership finance. Moreover, both have their focus on developmental and social goals to be accomplished in society.

Dhumale and Sapcanin concur that "both systems advocate entrepreneurship and risk taking and believe that the poor should take part in such activities."[28] They quote the disbursement of collateral-free loans in certain instances as an example of how Islamic banking and microfinance share common aims. Hawairy and Grais, on the other hand, are of the opinion that microfinance facilities can expand their outreach by offering Islamic financial services in communities reluctant to deal with conventional financial instruments.[29] Microfinance emphasizes the concern with increased penetration of financial services, support to poor entrepreneurs and service to the community. It relies on small repeatable short-term financing instruments as well as group responsibility.

Even-handedness, egalitarianism, classlessness and equity, as noted in the basic Islamic doctrines above, are some of the cornerstones of the Islamic ideology of entering into any business transaction. As microloans are disbursed amongst the millions of individuals in rural areas, borrowers start to become progressively independent as they start to reap the benefits of the microenterprises, which resultantly promulgate equity within households across villages. Consequently, the poor start to rely less and less on hand-outs, aid, charity and alms—something the religion discourages for those people who are able-bodied and capable of earning a living themselves. Writing about beggary, Obaidullah quotes a saying of the Holy Prophet (Peace Be Upon Him): "Begging is right only for three people: one who is in grinding poverty, one who is seriously in debt, or one who is responsible for compensation and finds it difficult to pay."[30] The components of this *hadith*, as analyzed by Obaidullah, can be seen to emphasize the following fundamental conditions of a successful microfinance program:

- Access of the poorest of the poor to the program.
- Careful assessment of the financial health of the poor; enquiry blended with empathy; insistence on contribution and beneficiary stake.
- Transformation of unproductive assets of the beneficiary into income-generating ones through rigorous valuation (on the basis of price discovery through auction method); involvement of the larger community in the process.
- Meeting of basic needs on a priority basis and investment of surpluses in productive assets.
- Direct involvement of the program in capacity building in the run-up to income generation and technical assistance to the beneficiary.
- Technical assistance in the form of imparting requisite training to the beneficiary for carrying out the business plan/income-generating project;

monitoring through a time-bound schedule and impact assessment through a feed-back mechanism.

- Transparent accounting of operational results and liberty to use part of the income to meet higher needs.

Obaidullah concludes that the Islamic approach to poverty alleviation is more inclusive than the conventional one. It provides for the basic conditions of sustainable and successful microfinance, blending wealth creation with empathy for the poorest of the poor.

Consequently, Islamic banking and microcredit programs can be seen to complement one another in both practical and ideological terms of promoting equity, discouraging beggary and mendicancy, encouraging helping fellow beings and assisting those poor potential entrepreneurs who are capable of running a business but lack capital, and face the danger of being left out if not provided timely support and opportunity.

As its ultimate goal is the maximization of social benefits as opposed to profit, through the creation of healthier financial institutions that can provide effective financial services also at a grass roots levels, some authors argue that Islamic finance,[31] if inserted in a new paradigm, could be a viable alternative to the socio-economic crisis lived by the Western paradigm.[32]

Islamic microleasing—the model and the practicalities

Small enterprises and businesses owned by microentrepreneurs need improved access to finance especially for acquiring capital equipment and applications of new technology for operations. However, their access to finance is restricted because such set-ups do not usually have reliable credit history, adequate capitalization and additional assets for collateral. Thus, informal markets where loans are costlier and maturities shorter provide most of their financing needs.[33]

Relatively new, if compared with other modes of microlending by NGOs or MFIs, microleasing has gained rapid popularity and expansion worldwide. Promoted by Grameen Bank over a decade ago in 1992, it quickly gained enormous recognition, owing to a number of characteristics that make it especially feasible to small businesses.[34]

As discussed in the section above, many MFIs today, especially those operating in the Muslim world, have initiated Islam-based lending and financing programs to cater to the needs of those who are averse to *riba*. *Murabaha* and leasing, or *ijara*, in various capacities and forms have been found to be fairly prevalent among MFIs offering *shari'a*-compliant microlending substitutes.

The procedure of setting up an *ijara* is fairly straightforward. As shown in Figure 8.2, the client approaches a *shari'a*-compliant MFI to purchase an asset on *ijara* basis [1]. The MFI, in the capacity of a lessor, purchases the asset on the client's behalf on full payment [2] to the equipment supplier [3]. The possession of the equipment is transferred to the lessee (the microentrepreneur) [4], who utilizes it according to the agreed terms and conditions for a fee payable in installments over

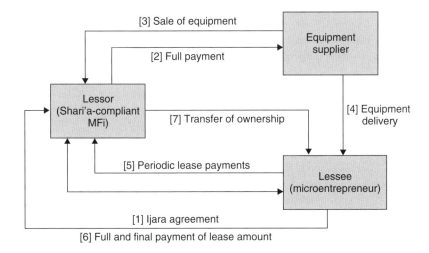

Figure 8.2 The life cycle of a typical *ijara* contract

an agreed period of time [5]. The fee includes the cost price of the asset, along with an agreed and pre-determined mark-up. The title of the asset is, however retained by the lessor so that it cannot be sold or pledged in any way. Depending on the nature of the *ijara* contract, the full and final payment of the asset is made to the lessor at the end of the lease term [6] and the ownership thus passes on to the lessee, who owns a free and clear title to the equipment [7].

The term of the lease is spread over the estimated useful life of the asset and its value is depreciated at an agreed rate that corresponds to the prevailing market practice relevant to the nature and type of the asset. Depending on whether the original agreement was a simple *ijara* or an *ijara wa iqtina'*, the asset is valued at the end of the lease term as being equal to the residual value. The lessee then has the option of buying the asset from the lessor, either at the residual value, or pursuant to a previously agreed price. As such, the title eventually passes to the client.

The advantages of leasing an asset as opposed to its outright purchase

As evident from the process outlined above, one of the greatest benefits of the lease agreement is the absence of any form of tangible collateral. This notion falls in line with the fundamental objective of any model of financing by MFIs and NGOs. A feasible business plan and a steady cash flow projection are all that clients need for obtaining assets via this model, along with a promissory note undertaking regular payments and an acceptance note evidencing receipt of the asset.

The asset itself acts as collateral, and the legal owner (in this case, the MFI or NGO) does not have to rely on the credit history, asset or capital base of the microentrepreneur, but just her/his ability to use the leased asset appropriately and generate enough funds to honor the lease payments regularly. This idea is based on the underlying proposition that *profits are earned through the proper use of an asset, rather than from its ownership.*

Microleasing is characterized by low transaction costs resulting from the simple and quick procedures involved. These procedures compare very favorably both with the often time-consuming attendance at group meetings required by most MFIs and with the accessibility (transport to town, etc.) and corruption costs characteristic of trying to borrow from a commercial bank.[35]

Gallardo[36] has identified a number of advantages that accrue to lessors. These include:

- The increased security, which results from the lessor buying the asset, thus removing the possibility of funds diversion.
- Reduced appraisal and documentation costs compared to standard commercial bank lending.
- The increased profit, which results from the lessor being able to claim tax relief on the depreciation of the asset, provided they do not take deposits.
- As already mentioned, repossession should be simpler than with a bank loan.

From the microentrepreneurs' perspective, leasing is definitely a beneficial and cost-effective option in comparison to borrowing from the conventional commercial banking environment. One significant aspect that has been observed to have a significant and widespread occurrence in literature on microleasing is the debate on interest rates. Havers argues that although leasing interest rates are higher than those which are (in theory) available from commercial banks, they tend to be rather lower than those that are (genuinely) available from MFIs.

Dowla makes extensive use of data from a variety of sources[37] (though the cases Dowla quotes are not strictly operating in terms of the *shari'a* rulings, yet the figures are equally applicable to *ijara* transactions[38] because MFIs offering *shari'a*-compliant products often make references to traditional interest rates as a benchmark) that reveal that interest rates being charged by the informal sector[39] were simply exorbitant. Depending on the source, the cost of capital to the borrowers varies from 10 to 120 percent per annum simple interest rate for initial investment, and up to 240 percent for working capital financing. The interest rate charged by moneylenders is in the range of 60 to 120 percent per annum. The studies further show that even friends and relatives may charge interest on informal loans (30 to 96 percent interest per annum). In contrast, Grameen charges an average leasing interest rate of 20 percent, which is both realistic as well as affordable given the rates charged by the informal sector, as seen above.

Despite the rapid popularity of the concept, the future of microleasing lies in a number of factors that have to be taken into consideration. Havers points out that building technical expertise on leasing is significant for both the lessors and the lessees, as this removes various obstacles in the entire process and builds confidence. Another possible option for creating sustainable leasing programs is the availability of wholesale funds to microleasing organizations by mainstream commercial financial organizations and donors. Establishing links between MFIs, NGOs and conventional leasing companies interested in microleasing is another vital step that can be taken to introduce the model to a wider audience.

Islamic microleasing and its role in poverty alleviation

As explained above, one of the most pronounced benefits of leasing equipment to the microentrepreneur by an MFI is that no initial capital outlay is required and neither is any collateral. The lessor invests the capital for the asset purchase, while the leased asset acts as collateral itself (since the ownership and title remains with the lessor during the period which payments are being made).

By taking out an *ijara* contract, individuals have improved chances of combating poverty and breaking out of the vicious cycle which, as exhibited in Figure 8.3, makes it very difficult for the poor to better their situations, unless they are provided with the right opportunities to initiate small businesses of their own. This leads to improved incomes and enhanced savings. Resultantly, their credibility increases and this enables them to qualify for more credit and larger lease contracts, which, *ceteris paribus*, will lead to more income, more investment and, ultimately, more savings.

This unique *cyclical function* has been referred to as the *virtuous cycle* by Mohammad Yunus, which runs as follows: "low-income → credit → investment → more income → more credit → more investment → more income."[40] In stark contrast to the age-old vicious cycle of poverty (see Figure 8.3), this proposition enables people to move out of poverty, rather than going round and round in the poverty cycle for the rest of their lives.

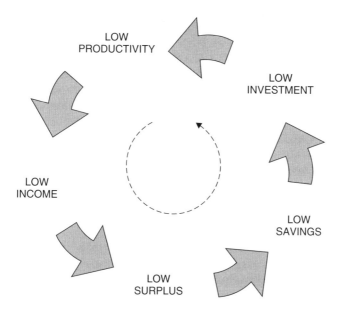

Figure 8.3 The vicious cycle of poverty

Conclusion

Poverty today is so rampant and so widespread that sometimes it seems there is no end to it. Destitution leads to desperation; desperation turns to crime and corruption, and consequently takes the form of a seemingly never-ending process. The beauty of the doctrines of financing in Islam is that social equity and fairness lie at its heart, which means that the notion is based on the conception of removing poverty and social inequality, which are at the root of many evils. In Islam, any economic system that results in the rich getting richer because of its peculiar nature, and conversely that allows the poor to remain poor cannot be deemed acceptable within the religion, "in fact, Islam believes in striking at the roots of inequality rather than merely alleviating some of the symptoms."[41]

Addressing the Make Poverty History campaign in 2005, Nelson Mandela said:

> [L]ike slavery and apartheid, poverty is not natural, it is man-made and it can be overcome and eradicated by the actions of human beings. And overcoming poverty is not a gesture of charity. It is an act of justice. It is the protection of a fundamental human right, the right to dignity and a decent life.[42]

According to Dr. Martin Luther King Jr., the American civil rights leader, Victor Hugo once said that

> progress is the mode of man: when it is blocked, just as an obstacle in a river makes the water foam, so an obstacle to progress makes humanity seethe. Any plans for the future, therefore, which seeks to calm the troubled waters will have to sweep barriers away, rather than pour oil over turbulent tides.[43]

Islam teaches, propagates and advocates peace and equality in society. An equal and just society leads to peace and harmony. Such peace and fairness can exist only if, as Hugo has stated above, there are no barriers and obstacles. The basics of Islamic finance rest on eliminating any such impediments for ordinary people. The Islamic microleasing model discussed above does just that: making collateral-free financing available to entrepreneurs in order to start-up their enterprises and eventually help themselves out of poverty. As explained earlier, such methods of financing convert the vicious cycles of poverty into virtuous cycles, thus creating a fairer social set up and ultimately achieving the ultimate Islamic goals of social equity, fairness, justice and brotherhood.

Notes

1 This chapter was presented at the "Pre-Forum Workshop on Microfinance: Towards a Sustainable Islamic Finance Model," Eighth Harvard University Forum on Islamic Finance, Harvard Law School, Cambridge, MA, April 18, 2008.
2 Doctoral Candidate, University of Manchester, Manchester, United Kingdom.
3 The *Halal Journal* (2006). "Malaysian Islamic Banks Profits Lag behind Gulf

Counterparts," by TodayOnline July 7, 2006, 11:44. Islamic Finance: Islamic Banking. Retrieved December 3, 2007, from http://www.halaljournal.com/artman/publish/article_832.shtml#top.

4 Eagle, L. (2009). "Banking on Sharia Principles: Islamic Banking and the Financial Industry." Retrieved April 26, 2011, fromhttp://www.bankersacademy.com/pdf/Islamic_Banking.pdf.

5 MacLean, A. (2007). "Islamic Banking: Is It Really Kosher?" *The American*.

6 Zaheer, K. (1996). "A Critical Look at the Alternatives to the Popular Models of Interest Free (IF) Banking." *Renaissance* (May–June).

7 Dhumale, Rahul and Amela Sapcanin (1999). "An Application of Islamic Banking Principles to Microfinance," a study by the Region Bureau for Arab States, World Bank Group, Washington, DC, December 1999, 14pp. Retrieved April 26, 2011, from http://www.ruralfinance.org/fileadmin/templates/rflc/documents/1114499916629_WB_Islamic_MF_edited.pdf.

8 Seibel, H.D. and W.D. Agung (2006). "Islamic Microfinance in Indonesia." Cologne: University of Cologne, Development Research Center.

9 Ashraf, M. (2007). "Shariah-compliant Financial Products." *Accountancy*.

10 Imady, O. and H.D. Seibel (2006). "Principles and Products of Islamic Finance." Cologne: University of Cologne, Development Research Center.

11 Edwardes, W. (1999). "Islamic Banking." *Princeton Economics Journal*. Princeton Economics International, Princeton, NJ.

12 Kazarian, E. (1993). *Islamic versus Traditional Banking. Financial Innovations in Egypt*. Boulder, CO: Westview Press.

13 Iqbal, Z. and M. Abbas (1987). "Islamic Banking." IMF Occasional Paper 49. Washington, DC: IMF.

14 Dhumale, Rahul and Amela Sapcanin (1999). "An Application of Islamic Banking Principles to Microfinance," a study by the Region Bureau for Arab States, World Bank Group, Washington, DC, December 1999, 14pp. Retrieved April 26, 2011, from http://www.ruralfinance.org/fileadmin/templates/rflc/documents/1114499916629_WB_Islamic_MF_edited.pdf.

15 Tarek, Z.S. and H.M. Kabir (2001). "A Comparative Literature Survey of Islamic Finance and Banking." *Financial Markets, Institutions & Instruments. New York University Salomon Center* 10(4): 155.

16 Usmani, M.T. (2001). "Musharakah & Mudarabah." In *An Introduction to Islamic Finance*. Retrieved April 26, 2011, from http://www.muftitaqiusmani.com/images/stories/downloads/pdf/an%20introduction%20to%20islamic%20finance.pdf.

17 Gafoor, A.L.M.A. (1995). *Interest-free Commercial Banking*. Groningen, The Netherlands: APPTEC Publications.

18 Usmani, M.T. (2001). "Musharakah & Mudarabah." In *An Introduction to Islamic Finance*. Retrieved April 26, 2011, from http://www.muftitaqiusmani.com/images/stories/downloads/pdf/an%20introduction%20to%20islamic%20finance.pdf.

19 Ibid.

20 Ashraf, M. (2007). «Shariah-compliant Financial Products.» *Accountancy*.

21 Shah, A. (2006). "Poverty Facts and Causes: Causes of Poverty." Retrieved January 3, 2007, from http://www.globalissues.org/TradeRelated/Facts.asp#fact1.

22 There is no standardized definition of microenterprises and it seems that the context varies across countries. The European Union legislation defines these as those that have ten or fewer employees, while in America and Australia, any business that employs five or fewer workers falls in this category.

23 Yunus, M. (2006b). "What is Microcredit?" Retrieved January 15, 2008, from http://www.grameen-info.org/index.html.

24 Delgado, E. (2005). *Group Lending: Learning from the International Experience. Urban & Regional Planning Economic Development Handbook*. Ann Arbor, MI: Taubman College of Architecture and Urban Planning, University of Michigan.

25 Latortue, A. (2003). "Tackling Aid Effectiveness from the Top: Donor Peer Reviews Synthesis Report. CGAP III Strategy, 2003–2008." Washington, DC: CGAP, January.

26 Brandsma, J. and R. Chaouali (1998). *Making Microfinance Work in the Middle East and North Africa*. Washington, DC: The World Bank, Middle East and North Africa Region, Private and Financial Sector Development Group and Human Development Group.

27 Said, P. et al. (2006). "Draft Guidelines for Provision of Islamic Microfinance Services and Products by Financial Institutions." Karachi: State Bank of Pakistan, Islamic Banking Department.

28 Dhumale, Rahul and Amela Sapcanin (1999). "An Application of Islamic Banking Principles to Microfinance," a study by the Region Bureau for Arab States, World Bank Group, Washington, DC, December 1999, 14pp. Retrieved April 26, 2011, from http://www.ruralfinance.org/fileadmin/templates/rflc/documents/1114499916629_WB_Islamic_MF_edited.pdf.

29 El-Hawary, D. and W. Grais (2005b). "The Compatibility of Islamic Financial Services and Microfinance: A Little-Explored Avenue for Expanding Outreach. Microfinance Matters." United Nations Capital Development Fund.

30 Obaidullah, M. (2007). "Islam, Poverty and Micro Finance 'Best Practices'." Retrieved April 26, 2011, from http://instituteofhalalinvesting.org/content/Islam_and_poverty.pdf.

31 Al-Harran, S. (1996). "Islamic Finance Needs a New Paradigm." Retrieved April 26, 2011, from http://www.kantakji.com/fiqh/Files/Finance/ISLAMIC%20FINANCE%20NEEDS%20A%20NEW%20PARADIGM.htm.

32 Segrado, C. (2005). "Islamic Microfinance and Socially Responsible Investments." MEDA Project. Microfinance at the University. Torino: University of Torino.

33 Gallardo, J. (2003). "Leasing to Support Micro and Small Enterprises." Policy Research Working Paper. Washington, DC: The World Bank, 1857.

34 The publications to which he refers include those that have conducted extensive surveys of interest rates in the microleasing environment in Bangladesh. The first one is the Rural Industrialization Survey Project (RISP) by Bangladesh Institute of Development Studies (BIDS) and the other one is a book, *Small Firms Informally Financed* edited by Rizwanul Islam, Von Pischke and de Waard.

35 Havers, M. (1999). "Microenterprise and Small Business Leasing-Lessons from Pakistan." *Small Enterprise Development Journal* 10(3).

36 Gallardo, J. (2003). "Leasing to Support Micro and Small Enterprises." Policy Research Working Paper. Washington, DC: The World Bank, 1857.

37 Dowla, A. (1998). "Micro Leasing: The Grameen Bank Experience." St. Mary's City, MD: St. Mary's College of Maryland.

38 Ibid.

39 These may include friends and relatives or the moneylenders.

40 Hulme, D. and K. Moore (2006). "Why Has Microfinance Been a Policy Success in Bangladesh (and Beyond)?" Manchester: Institute for Development Policy and Management, University of Manchester.

41 Zaheer, K. (2001). "Condemnation of Concentration of Wealth." *Renaissance* (October).

42 Mandela, N. (2005). "Make Poverty History." Retrieved February 11, 2008, from http://www.makepovertyhistory.org/extras/mandela.shtml.

43 Kamoche, K. (2005). "Kenya's Naked Constitution." Retrieved January 03, 2008, from http://generator21.net/g21archive/africa108.html.

Part III

Islamic microfinance case studies

9 Islamic microfinance in Indonesia

The challenge of institutional diversity, regulation and supervision[1]

Hans Dieter Seibel[2]

Origins and evolution of Islamic finance in Indonesia[3]

Indonesia is probably the country with the greatest diversity of both conventional and Islamic microfinance. The former has evolved for a period of over one hundred years, preceded by a prehistory of informal finance, whereas the latter has evolved since 1990. Indonesia possesses one of the most differentiated microfinance infrastructures in the developing world, comprising some 6,000 formal and 48,000 semiformal registered microfinance units serving about 45 million depositors and 32 million borrowers, 800,000 channeling groups and millions of informal financial institutions and self-help groups (SHGs). There is hardly an institutional type of microfinance not found in Indonesia. One of the most successful microfinance models worldwide, the reformed village units of Bank Rakyat Indonesia (BRI), was designed by the Harvard Institute for International Development (HIID) in the early 1980s (Annex 1).

Islamic finance in Indonesia, the country with the largest Muslim population, has evolved in response to political demands from Muslim scholars and organizations. The first Islamic cooperatives were established in 1990, followed by Islamic rural banks in 1991 and the first Islamic commercial bank (ICB) in 1992. In 1998, Bank Indonesia (BI), the central bank, gave official recognition to the existence of a dual banking system—conventional and Islamic, or *shari'a*-based—as part of a new banking act. This led to the establishment of a second ICB and, until December 2003, the establishment of eight Islamic commercial banking units (ICBUs), out of a total of 138 commercial banks. As of December 2006, their number had reached 3 ICBs and 22 ICBUs (see Table 9.1).[4] The growth pattern of Islamic rural banks has been quite different. After an initial period of growth until 1996 when they reached a total of 71, their number almost stagnated during and after the Asian financial crisis, reaching 78 by 1998 and 84 by 2003 out of a total of 2,134 rural banks. By December 2006, their number had reached 105.[5] Rapid expansion of Islamic cooperatives started in 1996, six years after inception, as a result of promotion by PINBUK, an Islamic non-governmental organization (NGO), and continued throughout the Asian financial crisis; it stagnated after 1999 at around 3,000 and declined to less than 2,900 as of 2003, out of a total of some 40,000 financial cooperatives.

Table 9.1 Growth of Islamic banking, 1991–2006

Type of Islamic bank	1991	1992	1999	2000	2001	2002	2003	2004	2005	2006
Commercial banks (CBs)	0	1	2	2	2	2	2	3	3	3
CB units	0	0	1	3	3	6	8	15	19	22
Total CB offices	0	1	40	62	96	127	299	401	504	636
Rural banks	4	9	78	78	81	83	84	86	92	105
Total number of banks	*4*	*10*	*81*	*83*	*86*	*91*	*94*	*104*	*114*	*130*
Total number of offices	*4*	*10*	*118*	*140*	*177*	*210*	*383*	*487*	*596*	*741*

Source: Seibel (2005a: 30).

Highlights of the *evolution of Islamic finance* (as of Dec. 2003) include the following:

- Origins due to initiatives by Muslim scholars around 1990.
- Recognition of a dual—conventional and Islamic—banking system by the central bank in 1998.
- *ICBs*: continuing upward trend since 1992; 2 ICBs and 8 ICBUs out of 138 commercial banks.
- *Islamic microbanks* (Bank Perkreditan Rakyat, BPR, referred to in English as rural banks or people's credit banks) : Initial growth since 1991 until 1996 followed by stagnation; 84 out of a total of 2,134 rural banks.
- *Islamic cooperatives*: Start in 1990, rapid expansion after 1996, stagnation in 1999, followed by decline; 2900 Islamic financial cooperatives out of some 40,000 (Annex 2).

ICBs

The market leaders in Islamic finance in Indonesia are the commercial banks. During the reporting period, 1991–2003, they focused on medium- and large-scale finance. We are now observing the beginnings of a slow expansion into microfinance. Since BI gave official recognition in 1998 to a dual banking system—conventional and Islamic—interest in Islamic meso- and macro-finance has spread among commercial banks, inspired by religious concerns and fuelled by low rates of non-performing loans. As of 2003, ICBs accounted for a mere 0.74 percent of total assets of the banking sector. During 2001–2003, however, the share of ICBs has increased from 0.17 percent to 0.74 percent and stood at 2.19 percent in Dec 2005 (Table 9.2).

Most remarkable is the difference in performance between conventional and ICBs. In relative terms, (1) the Islamic banks lend more of the funds deposited, with a loan- or financings-to-deposit ratio (LDR/FDR) of 97 percent compared to 54 percent of the total commercial banking sector; (2) their gross non-performing

Table 9.2 Islamic vs. conventional commercial banks, Dec. 2003

	Islamic	Conventional	Total
Date of origin of first bank	1992	1895	
Total number of banks/banking units	10	136	138 + 8 units
Total number of banking offices	255	7,475	7,730
Including BRI microbanking units		11,524	11,779
Total banking assets	0.74%	99.36%	100.0%
Total loans outstanding	1.16%	88.84%	100.0%
Total deposits	0.64%	99.36%	100.0%
LDR/FDR	97%	53%	54%
Improvement in NPL ratio 2000–2003	13.0% to 2.3%	26.8% to 8.2%	26.8% to 8.2%
Return on assets	0.65%	2.1%	2.1%

Source: Seibel (2005a: 50).

loans (NPL) ratio is consistently lower, and the improvement of their performance is faster than that of conventional banks after the Asian financial crisis of
1997/1998. Non-performing loans of ICBs amount to 2.3 percent of financings
outstanding, which is far below the 8.2 percent of the total commercial banking
sector. NPL ratios fell as follows:

- Conventional banks: From 26.8 percent in 2000 to 14.1 percent in 2001 and
  8.2 percent in 2003.
- Islamic banks: From 13.0 percent in 2000 to 4.0 percent in 2001 and 2.3
  percent in 2003.

Yet, despite the Islamic banks' better performance in terms of portfolio quality,
their return on average assets (ROAAs) of 0.65 percent is less than a third of that
of the total commercial banking sector at 2.12 percent. This difference is partially
attributed to the rapid increase in the number of ICBUs, which have only recently
started to lend.

Note should be taken, however, that in Indonesia the establishment of Islamic
banks was not preceded by a broad popular demand for *shari'a*-based services.
According to surveys carried out around 2000 on behalf of BI, in provinces with an
average Muslim population of 97 percent, only 11 percent were found to understand products and benefits of *shari'a* banking. BI (2002:10) thus concluded that:

> There is still a gap between needs and knowledge of *shari'a* financial products
> and services. The gap could delay the success to mobilise potential public fund
> to investment because of low switching rate from potential demand to real
> demand. Furthermore, the gap will also make marketing and selling effort for
> *shari'a* banking products and services more difficult.

Islamic microbanks/rural banks (BPRS)

During the 15-year period of 1989–2003, the total BPR sector had grown to 2,134,
comprising 2,050 conventional BPR and 84 BPR-*Shari'a* (BPRS). After a promising

start in the early 1990s, the development of Islamic microbanks has almost come to a standstill. During the six-year period, 1991–1996, when their number had reached 71, the BPRS grew at an overall average of 12 per year. During the two years when the Asian financial crisis hit Indonesia in 1997 and 1998, their growth slowed down to less than four per year. During the following five years, 1999–2003, their net growth almost stagnated, averaging one per year: seven were newly established; two were closed at the beginning of 2004. Their total number was 84 in December 2003.

Despite the fact that BPRS had only two years less to evolve than conventional BPR, they have attained a mere 4 percent of the number and 1.5 percent of the assets of the rural banking sector. The average annual growth of the conventional BPR during the 15-year period was 137 institutions on a yearly basis compared to only 6.5 BPRS over a 13-year period. Conventional rural banks have thus grown more than 20 times faster than Islamic rural banks on a yearly basis. Moreover, BPRS are much smaller than conventional BPR; their average assets amount to only 38 percent of the assets of conventional BPR. During 2001–2003, total assets of the BPRS grew (nominally) by 70 percent, compared to a growth rate of 173 percent of the total BPR sector (Table 9.3).

There are several reasons for the poor performance of Islamic microbanks in Indonesia:

- governance and management problems: Many were established by absentee owners for moral reasons, with an emphasis on social banking, and are managed by retired conventional bankers, who lack dynamism and Islamic banking expertise;
- inadequate internal control (by absentee commissioners) and a lack of external auditing (due to small size below the limit where auditing is required);

Table 9.3 Islamic (BPRS) vs. conventional rural banks (BPR), Dec. 2003

	Islamic	*Conventional*	*Total*
Date of origin of first rural bank	1991	1989	
Total number of rural banks as of Dec. 2003	84	2,050	2,134
Percent of BPR sector	*4%*	*96%*	*100%*
Of these newly established:	83	1283	1365
Percent	*6%*	*94%*	*100%*
Av. number of rural banks p.a. since origin	6.5	136.7	
Total rural banking assets	1.5%	98.5%	100%
Size of BPRS in % of average BPR	38%		
Asset growth during 2000–2003	70%	175%	173%
Total loans outstanding	1.5%	98.5%	100.0%
Total deposits	1.2%	98.8%	100.0%
LDR/FDR	126%	103%	103%
Total outreach: Rural banking sector	1.5%	98.5%	100.0%
Total outreach: Microfinance sector	0.14%	99.86%	100.0%

Source: Seibel (2005a: 37).

- lack of popular demand for Islamic banking services;
- emphasis on the informal sector to the neglect of more profitable market segments;
- lack of mastery of overly complex Islamic banking practices (Annex 3).

Islamic financial cooperatives

The development of Islamic banking has been paralleled by that of Islamic financial cooperatives (BMT, BTM, Baitul Qirad in Aceh), which evolved in several stages as shown in the Table 9.4. The first Islamic cooperative was established in 1990. After 1995, the NGO PINBUK started promoting Islamic cooperatives. There were big jumps in numbers during the crisis years 1997/1998, followed by a slowing-down, stagnation and eventually by a decline.

Islamic financial cooperatives suffer from the same regulatory and supervisory neglect as the rest of the sector (Table 9.5). There does not seem to be much difference in that respect between Islamic and conventional cooperatives. At most one-fifth of Islamic cooperatives are in reasonably good health. The majority are dormant or non-performing; most of the remaining ones exist for the purpose of receiving funds from the government. The Ministry of Cooperatives does not register cooperatives as Islamic or conventional and provides no information on, or special assistance to, Islamic cooperatives.

Table 9.4 The evolution of Islamic cooperatives

No.	Phase	Period	Number
1	Initial growth	1990–1995	300
2	Rapid growth promoted by PINBUK	1996	700
		1997	1,501
		June 1998	2,470
3	Slowing-down of growth	2000	2,938
4	Stagnation and decline	2001	3,037
		2003	2,856

Source: Seibel (2005a: 33).

Table 9.5 Islamic vs. conventional cooperatives

	Islamic	Conventional	Total
Total number of financial cooperatives	2,900	37,627	40,527
Percent	7.2%	92.8%	100.0%
Total assets	n.a.	n.a.	n.a.
Total loans outstanding	1.1%	98.9%	100.0%
Total deposits	2.9%	97.1	100.0%
LDR/FDR	90%	34%	35%
NPL ratio	n.a.	n.a.	n.a.
Return on assets	n.a.	n.a.	n.a.
Total borrower outreach (loan accounts)	0.7%	99.3%	100.0%

Source: Seibel (2005a: 37, 50).

In sum, the outreach of Islamic cooperatives is negligible, and their overall per-formance poor:

- There is a lack of regulation, supervision and reliable reporting.
- A large majority of Islamic cooperatives are dormant or technically bank-rupt.
- Their outreach is negligible, accounting for 7.2 percent of all financial coop-eratives, but less than 1 percent of borrower outreach of the sector.
- Their loan portfolio (much of it overdue) accounts for 1.1 percent of the finan-cial cooperative sector and 0.19 percent of the microfinance sector.
- The savings of the depositors are at great risk.
- Overall there is little difference in performance between conventional and Islamic cooperatives, the latter having inherited most of their problems from the former.
- No remedy is in sight except in the framework of a total overhaul of the coop-erative system.
- Fresh money pumped into the sector by donor or government agencies with-out effective regulation and supervision will further aggravate their downfall, as has been historically the case of the state-supported cooperative sector.

Islamic financial products

Islamic financial products are complicated, unfamiliar to most and poorly under-stood by many banking staff. Most of the lending is trade financing at a fixed margin (*murabaha*), which is felt to be little different from conventional banking except that it requires two contracts by the bank: one with the seller and one with the borrower to whom the bank sells the commodity. Some statistical details are given in Annex 5.

The strength of Islamic finance lies in its conservative character: only real trans-actions with sufficient collateral, but no speculative investments, are financed. This, however, has substantially reduced financing of start-ups and micro-entrepreneurs without collateral; a major section of a potential microfinance market (Table 9.6).

Assessment

Islamic microfinance, lacking broad popular demand and Islamic banking exper-tise, so far has been more a political than an economic project in Indonesia. Experience differs substantially by sub-sector:

- Only commercial banks appear to be capable of quickly acquiring the art of Islamic banking by training young and dynamic people, but most of the commercial banks lack experience in microfinance as a specialized field. This may change with the recent entry of BRI and some other banks into Islamic banking.

Table 9.6 Financial products of Islamic commercial and rural banks, in percent, 2000 and 2005

	2000	*2005*
Financings:		
Musharaka	2.6	12.5
Mudaraba	30.5	20.5
Murabaha	62.6	62.3
Istisna'	6.0	1.8
Qard hasan	0.0	0.8
Other	0.8	2.1
Total financings in %	100.0	100.0
Amount in million rupiah	1,239,423	15,231,942
Deposits:		
Wadi'a	21.5	13.1
Mudaraba savings	32.7	28.0
Mudaraba fixed deposits	45.8	58.8
Total deposits in %	100.0	100.0
Amount in million rupiah	1,028,923	15,582,329
FDR, %	123.5	97.8

Source: Seibel (2005a: 97).

- Islamic, unlike conventional rural banks, have failed to prove themselves as efficient and dynamic providers of microfinance services.
- Unsupervised Islamic, like conventional, cooperatives are an outright menace to their member-shareholders and depositors, who risk losing their money.

No information on recent developments in an increasingly differentiated Islamic microfinance sector during the last three years (except in Aceh) is available. On the basis of the existing experience with Islamic finance in Indonesia, decision-makers in favor of promoting Islamic financial services are now confronted with two major options, which are not necessarily alternatives:

1 Focusing on ICBs in Indonesia and assisting them to establish branches and units with Islamic microfinance products.
2 Reassessing in a participatory process the challenges and realistic opportunities of Islamic rural banks and cooperatives with a focus on effective internal control, external supervision (direct, delegated or auxiliary), and the establishment of associations of respective microbanks and cooperatives with apex services to their member institutions.

Recommendations

I recommend that decision-makers in Islamic organizations, government agencies and donor organizations cautiously examine the following opportunities for the development of a healthy Islamic financial sector in Indonesia:

- *Commercial banks*, in setting up branch networks of Islamic microfinance institutions (MFIs), may learn from the rich experience of successful microfinance strategies and institutions within Indonesia, particularly the BRI Microbanking Division, one of the most successful microfinance programs in the developing world, which has recently started to set up Islamic units.
- *Islamic rural banks* need to be revamped if they are to play a more than marginal role in Indonesia. This will require an overall development plan for the BPRS sector mutually agreed upon by all stakeholders and a strong banking association to provide a full range of fee-based support services to their members. Some of the more successful Islamic rural banks may serve as exposure training sites to future managers. Auditing should be mandatory regardless of size.
- *Islamic cooperatives* suffer from much the same set of problems as the whole cooperative sector. There is little chance for any intervention to be successful in the short run except in limited areas (such as Aceh). They need a system of prudential regulation, mandatory auditing and effective supervision by an appropriate financial authority, which is definitely not the Ministry of Cooperatives & SMEs. They should be fully financed through equity and savings deposits of members; only healthy and well-supervised cooperatives should be permitted to collect deposits from non-members. They need strong associations and federations to provide a full range of support services to their members.
- *Permodalan Nasional Madani (PNM)* is a government-owned corporation (TÜV-certified) with independent management, carved out of the central bank after the financial crisis of 1997/1998 with the mandate of restructuring and strengthening rural banks and cooperatives serving micro and small enterprises, including a strong focus on Islamic microfinance. It has recapitalized a number of Islamic rural banks and cooperatives; it has also provided them with Islamic banking software and training. PNM is now facing the challenge of fully commercializing its services with national outreach after the government withdrew its regular budgetary allocations and turned PNM into a profit-making company. Its central bank origin may be instrumental in promoting mandatory auditing and setting up a financial authority for cooperative supervision. PNM needs financial and institutional strengthening.
- *In the reconstruction of tsunami-stricken Aceh*, a pilot project of establishing a properly supervised system of Islamic cooperatives—to be backed up by Islamic cooperative rural banks—is in process. Donor support expires in 2009, the official end of the reconstruction period. The reconstruction agency BRR estimates that there is a potential for up to 1,000 Baitul Quirad in 335 sub-districts. Support is needed for (1) a self-sustaining structure of continued inputs beyond 2009; (2) expansion over all sub-districts with economic potential; (3) action research in support of the process of building a comprehensive and sustainable Islamic cooperative sector in Aceh as an example of decentralizing regulation and supervision of non-bank MFIs.

Comparative studies are proposed of conventional and Islamic microfinance systems in selected geographical areas (e.g., West Java, Lombok), with particular emphasis on the regulatory and supervisory framework as well as in-depth case studies of selected Islamic microfinance institutions within a microfinance system context of a given geographical area to serve as benchmarks.

Annex 1

Institutional variety in Indonesian microfinance: an overview

Indonesia is probably the country with the greatest diversity of conventional and Islamic microfinance, the former evolving over a period of over one hundred years (preceded by a history of informal finance of unknown depth), the latter, over a period of 15 years. Indonesia possesses one of the most differentiated microfinance infrastructures in the developing world, comprising some 6,000 formal and 48,000 semiformal registered microfinance units serving about 45 million depositors, 32 million borrowers and 800,000 channeling groups and millions of unreported informal financial institutions of indigenous origin. There is hardly an institutional type of microfinance that is not found in Indonesia, though there are wide regional disparities in diversity, depth and outreach, with Java and Bali at one extreme and the outer islands at the other. There is also great variety in institutional performance. Since 1998 there has been a new surge of special initiatives, among them poverty-lending programs with weak enforcement of loan repayment.

In Indonesia, Islamic microfinance is an emerging concept. The term microfinance is used in Indonesia in a wider and in a narrower sense. In this chapter the term microfinance is used, unless otherwise indicated, in a wider sense, referring on principle to small as well as large financial institutions that provide small-size financial services to the lower segments of the rural, peri-urban and urban population as well as larger-size financial services to successful micro and small enterprises or households. In this sense the term covers an immense variety of microfinance institutions (or institutions providing microfinance services), including indigenous SHGs functioning as financial intermediaries (*arisan, julo-julo* . . .), new types of SHGs established by governmental organizations and NGOs in large numbers, SHGs linked to commercial and rural banks, SHGs upgraded to semiformal or formal institutions, private deposit collectors and their self-organized associations, member-owned institutions, community- or sub-district-owned local financial institutions, savings and credit cooperatives, NGOs, regulated microbanks, national and provincial development banks, national and regional or provincial commercial banks with their local units. Such institutions may be owned by private shareholders, members with same or differing voting rights, communities, local or national government and NGOs. Both commercial banks and regulated microbanks may be under private, government or cooperative ownership. Some microbanks are de facto (not de jure) owned by NGOs. Depending on the applicable regulatory framework, financial institutions may belong to the formal, semiformal or informal financial sector; in Indonesia the latter two sectors also include institutions with financial services in kind (e.g., rice banks). All these types of institutions and ownership exist in Indonesia as part of the conventional financial sector.

In a narrower sense, the term microfinance is applied in Indonesia to a large number of mostly semiformal small local financial institutions, which also include associations of informal SHGs awaiting the passing of the draft microfinance law of 2001. This was formulated under the auspices of the central bank. Since authority over small financial institutions (Lembaga Keuangan Mikro, LKM) was passed to the Ministry of Finance, no further action has been taken. There is no information on how many of these adhere to Islamic principles.

To date only a limited number of these various types of financial institutions have generated known Islamic variants. Official statistics exist for Islamic commercial and microbanks; official statistics of limited reliability exist for Islamic financial cooperatives. There are no data on other types of Islamic financial institutions. As the emergence of Islamic finance has been an evolutionary process over a period of just 15 years, it is likely that the landscape of Islamic finance will become increasingly differentiated—hopefully guided by past experience. Some of the lessons (to be) learned will be presented in this chapter.

Overall Indonesia has acted as a *microfinance laboratory* of both conventional and Islamic financial institutions, demonstrating:

- the scope for institutional variety;
- the importance and the success of regulating and effectively supervising conventional and Islamic microbanking in the hands of two types of regulated institutions: commercial banks (among them BRI with its 4,000 microfinance units) and rural microbanks (BPR);
- the failure of effectively supervising vast networks of financial cooperatives and village funds/banks (BKD), most of them non-performing;
- the need of, and demand-from-below for, regulating and supervising small MFIs;
- the opportunities and future challenges of decentralizing regulation and supervision of non-bank MFIs.

During the past two decades, in an increasingly liberal policy environment, two types of regulated microfinance institutions under central bank supervision have gained prominence on the microfinance market: (1) the units of the Microbanking Division of BRI (the former agricultural development bank, until recently government-owned), reformed as of 1984 with technical assisstance from HIID; (2) rural banks (BPR), since 1988. In 2003, they accounted for 95 percent of recorded deposits and 75 percent of loans outstanding of recorded formal and semiformal MFIs. *Financial cooperatives*, about 40,000 in number, account for another 5 percent of deposits and 18 percent of loans; they have suffered, rather than benefited, from preferential government treatment and a general disregard for regulation and supervision. There has been no follow-up on the draft microfinance (LKM) law of 2001 for small local financial institutions.

Surplus liquidity and liquidity shortage are two core problems of the financial sector in Indonesia. Surplus liquidity has been a major problem of the commercial banking sector in Indonesia. As of November 2003, banks mobilized Rp 875.4tr (US$103bn) in deposits, but lent only Rp 475.7tr ($56bn), generating Rp 400tr ($47bn) in excess liquidity. Indonesia's problem is how to lend, not lack of funds. The LDR has been improving in recent years: from 26.2 percent in 1999 to 43.7 percent in 2003, but is still low. This problem also applies to the major rural and peri-urban microfinance provider, the BRI Microbanking Division. Since 1990, the BRI units have produced large amounts of excess liquidity from rural savings, consistently exceeding $1bn per year throughout and after the Asian financial crisis; as of December 2003, its LDR was 47.6 percent, close to the commercial banking average. There is thus little, if any, justification for donors to pour hard-currency liquidity into the national soft-currency intermediation circuit (Table 9.7).

A shortage of liquidity has been the problem of most small financial institutions, quite in contrast to commercial banks. Rural banks (BPR), the largest entities among the small financial institutions, with consolidated deposits of Rp 8.89tr and loans outstanding of Rp 9.12tr, had a slight liquidity shortage of Rp 0.23tr and an LDR of 103 percent as of Dec. 2003. Among the yet smaller non-bank financial institutions (NBFIs), with drastically lower average loan sizes, NBFI)comprising 4,482 BKD (*Badan Kredit Desa*, village credit funds, supervised by BRI) and 1,428 LDKP (*Lembaga Dana Kredit Pedesaan*, rural credit fund institutions, supervised by regional development banks), with total deposits of Rp 242bn and total loans outstanding of Rp 521bn, had a severe liquidity shortage of Rp 279 bn and an LDR of 215 percent. Similarly, the 40,527 financial cooperatives, with total consolidated deposits of Rp 1.66tr and loans outstanding of Rp 4.79tr, have a liquidity gap of Rp. 3.13tr and an LDR of 189 percent. The latter figures conceal major differences between the various types of cooperatives: the private credit unions and the Islamic cooperatives are quite balanced, with LDRs of 109 percent and 111 percent, respectively; while the government-pampered savings and credit cooperatives (*Kelompok Simpan Pinjam*, KSP) and savings and credit units (*Usaha Simpan Pinjam*, USP) have ratios of 469 percent and 314 percent, respectively (data approx. 2000). Two major issues and challenges in microfinance have remained: How to use the existing massive excess liquidity in the banking sector to extend financial services to those segments of the rural population without access; and whether,

Table 9.7 Liquidity surplus or deficit in US$ and LDRs of commercial banks and small financial institutions in Indonesia (BRI units 2003; others approx. 2000)

Type of institution	Deposits	Loans outstanding	Liquidity surplus*	LDR
Commercial banks	103bn	56bn	47bn	44%
BRI units	3.5bn	1.7bn	1.8bn	48%
Rural banks	923.6m	947.5m	(23.9m)	103%
NBFIs	25.1m	54.1m	(29.0m)	215%
Financial cooperatives	172.5m	497.7m	(325.2m)	189%

Note: * Liquidity deficit.
Source: Seibel (2005a: 20).

and how, to extend recognition, depositor protection, regulation and (delegated) supervision to large numbers of small financial institutions. These issues apply to both conventional and Islamic financial institutions in Indonesia.

Microfinance is no panacea but has contributed somehow to the reduction of poor from 60 percent in 1970 to 11.5 percent in 1996. The financial crisis of 1997/1998 interrupted this trend; poverty rates surged but then fell again below 20 percent. At the same time, the BRI units emerged strengthened, the rural banking sector restructured from the financial crisis, the latter responding positively to the enforcement of prudential regulation.

Below are some of the *highlights of the financial sector framework for Islamic banking and microfinance* in Indonesia:

1   A conducive policy environment for Islamic banking and regulated microbanking in Indonesia:

- a long history of banking and microfinance, dating back to 1895;
- a highly differentiated rural financial infrastructure,
- a deregulated policy and institutional framework since 1983;
- increasingly effective prudential regulation and supervision;
- an appropriate commercial and microbanking legal framework, with options for private, (local) government and cooperative ownership;
- effective supervision of commercial and microbanks by the central bank, greatly strengthened after the financial crisis of 1997/1998;
- a legal framework at provincial level for some types of non-bank MFIs;
- favorable regulation central bank for Islamic banks and microbanks;[6]
- establishment of an Islamic banking directorate in the central bank;
- BRI[7] units, a most successful network of microfinance sub-branches, as benchmark institutions;
- restructuring of the banking sector in response to the Asian financial crisis;
- a big emerging market for Islamic finance in the largest Muslim country of the world.

2   Lack of a conducive sectoral framework for Islamic cooperatives:

- lack of prudential regulation of financial cooperatives;
- lack of effective supervision of financial cooperatives;
- market distortions resulting from access to subsidized sources of finance;
- massive government interference in the past, but some recent relaxation and incipient reform efforts;
- cooperative sector in a generally undiagnosed state of ill-health;
- lack of coordination among organizations supporting Islamic cooperatives.

3   Core challenges to the overall financial sector:

- how to extend recognition, depositor protection, regulation and (delegated) supervision to large numbers of small financial institutions;

- how to use the existing massive excess liquidity in the banking sector to extend financial services to those segments of the rural population without access.

Annex 2

Institutional and regulatory framework: mainstreaming Islamic banking

BI (2002: 16) has provided the following vision and mission of *shari'a* banking development in Indonesia:

> A sound *shari'a* banking system that is competitive, efficient and compliant with prudential practices, and capable of supporting real economic sector through the implementation of share based financing and trades with real underlying transactions in the spirit of brotherhood and good deeds to promote well-being for all society.

The *strategic objectives* of *shari'a* banking development, according to BI (2002: 5), include:

- a high level of competitiveness while complying with *shari'a* principles;
- significant roles in sustaining national economy and public welfare;
- global competitiveness through compliance to international operational standards.

As of 1998 (Act No. 10), BI gave official recognition, as part of the new banking act, to the existence of a *dual banking system, conventional and shari'a-based*. The mainstreaming of Islamic banking was backed by Act No. 23 of 1999 concerning BI, which authorizes the central bank to also conduct its task according to *shari'a* principles (see chapter 2.1). Beyond this, the law does not specify any substantively different provisions for Islamic banking. In 1999 BI established a *shari'a* banking team, converted in 2001 into a bureau and in 2003 into a directorate, with the objective of monitoring the new segment of the banking sector. At national and institutional levels, Islamic finance is supervised by *shari'a* supervisory boards. On the whole, BI (2002: 11) states that there is a "lack of efficient institutional structure supporting efficient *shari'a* banking operations" and suggests to develop the following:

- *Shari'a auditor* to ensure the compliance of *shari'a* banks with *shari'a* principles.
- *Communication Board (FKPPS)* to enable an effective coordination of the effort to improve public awareness and education for *shari'a* banking.
- *Institution for Shari'a Financing Insurance* to provide financial protection to *shari'a* banks against fraudulent practices by recommended customers.
- *Shari'a Finance Information Center* as a linkage between the real and the *shari'a* finance sector.
- *Special Purpose Company* to facilitate asset securitization for Islamic banks.

Annex 3

Islamic microbanks (BPRS)

The *mission* of Islamic rural banks in Indonesia is helping the enterprising poor, particularly small traders and micro-entrepreneurs, in contrast to conventional BPR, which are oriented to profit-making. Two problems have resulted from the way the BPRS have defined their mission: On the demand side, many of the customers have a (mistaken) concept of low or no interest rates or profit margins in *shari'a* banking. On the supply side, BPRS focus on the micro-sector instead of starting with more profitable market segments such as salary earners and small entrepreneurs. It is this difference in mission that has significantly slowed the growth of BPRS. While both are (mostly) established by wealthy local people, the owners of BPR have a commercial orientation with the objective of increasing their wealth while the owners of BPRS have a social mission combined with the intention to cover their costs.

Ownership: Most BPRS are privately owned, usually by one majority shareholder and several minority shareholders. In some cases, Islamic foundations, companies and local government are shareholders. Some Islamic cooperatives, BMT, have initiated the establishment of a BPRS, but due to lack of capital are not shareholders. Most owners are absentee owners, living in Jakarta or a provincial capital. If there are many shareholders, their involvement in decision-making is small if not totally lacking. In contrast, many owners of conventional BPR also act as general managers or president-directors.

Board of directors: Every BPRS has three boards: a *shari'a* board that watches over Islamic principles, a management board and a supervisory board. Members of the *shari'a* board usually come from religious organizations such as the local Majlis Ulama, from mass organizations and Islamic universities. The supervisory board of commissioners (*komisaris*) comprises representatives of majority shareholders and financial experts. There are usually three members on the *shari'a* board and three on the supervisory board. It is rare that any one of them has a regular full-time or part-time position; most of them act perhaps one day a month or upon request—a significant factor in weak internal control.

Management, upon the insistence of BI as the regulator, is usually comprised of one or two directors with banking experience. Due to the recent history of Islamic banking and an overall shortage of trained bankers, very few BPRS managers have any experience in banking. Most are retirees from conventional banking, who have received some training in Islamic banking principles. This has resulted in a selection of older individuals frequently from state banks, lacking perhaps in drive and innovativeness as one might expect from younger individuals eager to experiment with fresh ideas in Islamic banking.

Control and supervision: Internal control is by absentee commissioners whose activities are limited to receiving monthly reports and monthly or quarterly visits: either the commissioners visiting the bank or the bank visiting the commissioners—sometimes in far-away places. External auditing by a public accountant is compulsory if assets exceed Rp 10bn, but most BPRS lack dynamic growth and remain below that limit. Supervision of BPRS as part of the banking system is compulsory and carried out by BI on an annual basis. Accounting and reporting standards, including the computation of standard performance ratios, are regulated and enforced by BI.

Market segment: The BPRS market segment covers the enterprising poor with existing enterprises, predominantly small traders. BPRS are open to all, irrespective of religion.

Islamic banking principles: Outside religious organizations, there seems to be little if any public debate over interest or profit-sharing rates and principles of conventional vs. Islamic banking. Reportedly Islamic banking is mostly a matter of access and effectiveness rather than religious conviction.

Financial products for the poor and non-poor: Under the *shari'a*, there are two models of client selection: (1) clients with existing businesses and successful operations for at least two years; (2) new entrepreneurs without preceding business experience. The vast majority of clients are those with existing business and a good track record; they can be financed through such financial products as *murabaha*, *musharaka* and *mudaraba*, which involve some form of profit-sharing. New clients without a track record are considered very risky and represent but a small minority; they can be financed through *qard hasan*, soft loans without any charge or profit-sharing. Islamic microbankers point out that not everyone is a born (micro-)entrepreneur; many of the poor lack the qualification to become entrepreneurs and should rather become workers in larger enterprises, which may in turn be financed through ICBs. Consumer loans and loans for speculative investments, which could be ruinous to the borrower, are excluded from the range of permissible purposes of financing.

Deposits: Remuneration of depositors is based on the *mudaraba* principle of partnership-based revenue-sharing between depositors and the bank. The ratios vary in the sample BPRS from 30:70 to 50:50. In some banks the revenue-sharing arrangements are negotiable. BPRS are less successful in deposit mobilisation than BPR. The deposit volume of an average BPRS is less than one-third of the sector average (Rp 1.31bn, or US$155,000, compared to Rp 4.17, or US$493,000). Among BPRS, deposits amount to 57.4 percent of total assets, among conventional BPR to 69.1 percent (BPR sector average: 68.9 percent). BPRS finance 79.4 percent of their loans outstanding from deposits, BPR 96.8 percent. In other terms, the LDR of BPRS is 1.26, the LDR of BPR is 1.03. We might conclude that revenue-sharing is not as attractive to depositors as a definite interest rate.

Financings (loans): The main loan product in BPRS is *murabaha* i.e., a sales contract between bank and customer with a fixed profit margin for the bank. Flexible profit-sharing, which is cumbersome to calculate, is of minor importance. *Qard hasan*, a financial product for the very poor for which the bank bears the full risk but receives no remuneration except an administrative fee of approx. 1 percent, exists only in theory. It is listed as one of the products in only one of the BPRS visited, but has no takers. Total financings (loans outstanding) of 84 BPRS as of Dec. 2003 amount to Rp 1.65bn (US$195,200) per BPRS, compared to Rp. 4.30bn (US$509,000) for the whole BPR sector and RP 4.41bn (US$522,000) per conventional BPR.

Case studies: Two of the five case studies of Islamic microbanks carried out in 2003, the smallest and the largest, are presented here.

Box 1: Two sample BPRS

BPRS Artha Fisabilillah in Cianjur, the smallest of the five sample BPRS, was established in 1994 by nine shareholders. By 1997, as a result of lack of management experience, it was technically bankrupt and was restructured. The new management was not very dynamic and was replaced in 2001 by a retired BRI credit officer. The bank, located next to a local market, has 1,150 savers and 163 borrowers. With a staff of 11, 6 of them loan officers, it offers doorstep collection services to about 200 clients a day. It also offers deposit services to school children and institutions. Total assets are Rp 1.40bn, deposits Rp 0.62bn and financings outstanding Rp 1.21bn. Its overall performance is not yet satisfactory. Its main problem is lack of funds, due to a shortage of deposits and capital from the owners. The bank is struggling with loan recovery and has improved considerably in 2003. Its non-performing facilities (NPF) ratios in 2001, 2002 and 2003 were 9.6 percent, 19.8 percent and 4.5 percent, respectively; its loan loss ratios were 8.9 percent, 18.7 percent and 6.25 percent. Yet the bank has been in the black for the past three years, with return on assets (ROAs) of 2.3 percent, 1.7 percent and 2.4 percent and return on equity of 7 percent, 4.3 percent and 8.75 percent, respectively. Its main future strategy to improve efficiency is staff upgrading through training.

BPRS Wakalumi in Ciputat, the biggest of the five sample BPRS, was established in 1990 by a foundation (Yayasan Wakalumi) as a conventional BPR and converted for religious reasons into a BPRS in 1994. It has 118 shareholders, among them Bank Muamalat Indonesia (BMI) (19 percent, down from 49 percent), the former Minister of Cooperatives (23.5 percent), a Citybank manager (26 percent), the founding foundation Yaysan Wakalumi (5.6 percent) and over a hundred individuals, mostly Muslims working at Citybank. The bank seems to have a successful staff promotion strategy: the president director, with a BA in agriculture, has been with the bank since 1994, learning on the job and promoted up the ranks; the director, a woman with a diploma in accounting, has been an employee since 1997 and was promoted to director in 2003. The bank has grown rapidly and now has five branches and a staff of 38, 13 among them loan officers. Its 2,000 borrowers are mostly small traders on traditional markets to whom it sells its financings as Islamic products. It has four financing products, with *murabaha* the dominant one. Through eight savings products and four term deposit products, it has attracted 5,000 savers. With ROAAs in 2001–2003 of 4.1 percent, 3.65 percent and 3.35 percent and return on average equity of 20.3 percent, 21.05 percent and 24.1 percent, respectively, it is highly profitable: apparently a showpiece that could serve as an exposure and apprenticeship training site for other banks.

Annex 4

Islamic cooperatives

Conventional and Islamic cooperatives: Indonesia has a differentiated sector of cooperatives, which has been historically dominated by the heavily subsidized KUD system: *Koperasi Unit Desa*, multi-purpose cooperatives at sub-district level with units at village level. By law all cooperatives had to be integrated into the KUD system. As government intervention in management and resource allocation stifled any spirit of autonomy and self-help, privately organized credit unions and large numbers of self-help groups resisted being incorporated, frequently with official sanctioning. Since the downfall of the Suharto regime, the cooperative sector has seen some liberalization but is still far from self-organization and autonomy. In fact, the very existence of a Ministry of Cooperatives, with unclear and perhaps counterproductive functions, stands in the way. In the framework of the new decentralization law, cooperatives are now being registered autonomously in the districts and provinces, which is likely to make the task of regulation and supervision more difficult.

According to statistics of the Ministry of Cooperatives, the total number of financial cooperatives (including single-purpose KSP and financial units, USP, of multipurpose cooperatives) amounted to 40,639 as of December 2003, which includes those credit unions and BMT which decided to register as cooperatives; they also include cooperatives which are inactive and have failed to report. The Ministry has financial information on 36,376 KSP/USP as of December 2003.

The KSP and USP are on principle registered with the Ministry of Cooperatives and are subject to a regulatory framework, with minimum capital requirements to become a cooperative, a soundness rating system (based on that for banks) and a loan classification system. However, deficiencies include the absence of legal lending limits, requirements for loan-loss provisioning (left up to individual cooperatives) and sanctions. There is no effective supervision, and whatever existing regulations are not enforced after registration. Also, there is no deposit protection system, and there are no associations of KSP/USP.

In addition there are 1,071 privately organized credit unions (Koperasi Kredit) as part of the world credit union movement, WOCCU. They are supervised by INKOPDIT, their national apex, which has rated 90 percent of them as sound. A small cooperative movement, Swamitra, has been organized and effectively supervised by the state cooperative bank, BUKOPIN.

Overview: Islamic cooperatives (BMT)[8] are a recent development, with rapid growth during the first part of the 1990s. Its 2,938 units (as of 2000) constitute 7.2 percent of all financial cooperatives, 2.8 percent of deposits and 1.1 percent of loans outstanding. Borrower outreach is reported as 73,000 accounts, which is less than 1 percent of total borrower outreach of the financial cooperative sector. There is no information on the number of deposit accounts (ADB 2003). The majority of them are registered with PINBUK, not with the Ministry of Cooperatives, which has no information on how many of them are registered as cooperatives. BI estimates the number of registered BMT at 500 out of a total of 3,000.

Islamic cooperatives suffer from the same benign regulatory neglect as conventional cooperatives. There is no overall supervision and no systematic recording of either conventional or Islamic cooperatives (BMT); most BMT (83 percent according to a BI estimate) are not even registered with the Ministry of Cooperatives. After a period of rapid growth after 1995 when PINBUK assumed their promotion, they are now in decline; the majority of the 3,000 BMT now are assumed to be dormant or technically bankrupt. PINBUK has no power to enforce reporting, much less prudential regulation. The Ministry has the power, but does not use it, and may in fact be an inappropriate organization to do so. All general information provided in this report on cooperatives is therefore of questionable validity. In recent years, efforts have been made to improve the quality of cooperatives, reportedly with initial success in some areas such as Central Java.

Regional distribution: The majority of the 2,900 BMT (60 percent in 2003) are located on Java but are spread far more equally over western, central and eastern Java. Twenty percent are on Sumatra, 12 percent on Sulawesi. BMT are underrepresented on Kalimantan and the smaller islands.

Mission, legal status, governance and supervision: The BMT in this sample see it as their mission to help the enterprising poor, particularly very small micro-entrepreneurs including food vendors. Only an estimated 500 out of 3,000 BMT are registered as financial cooperatives with the Ministry of Cooperatives. It is not expected that the draft microfinance law of 2001, which might have provided a legal framework, will be enacted within the foreseeable future. As cooperatives, BMT are owned by their members, but there is frequently a distinction between share-holding voting and associated members. Board size and composition are not standardized. Only about 50 percent report to PINBUK, which has no formal supervisory powers; a supervision project was short-lived as funds ran out. INKOPSYAH receives monthly reports from its members as a prerequisite of access to sources of refinancing. Officials from the Ministry of Cooperatives rarely go beyond attending annual meetings when invited. There is no external auditing. Supervisory arrangements, enforcement of standards, information and reporting are either absent or ineffective.

Delivery system, market and outreach: In four BMT visited in 2003, the average number of staff is close to four. The average service radius is about 14 km. BMT normally do not have branches. The majority of clients are small and itinerant traders and other micro-entrepreneurs. Total saver and borrower outreach is estimated at around 1.7m, but probably only about one-third of them are active.

Total assets and sources of funds: The median asset size per BMT is estimated by PINBUK at Rp 250 million (US$ 24,000) as of 2001. Two percent were listed with asset sizes above Rp 1 billion, 9.5 percent with asset sizes below 50 million. Deposits are the main source of funds, followed by capital. In contrast to conventional cooperatives, borrowings in BMT seem to be of minor importance; the mean loan portfolio is almost matched by deposits (LDR = 103 percent).

Islamic financial services: The question about differences between Islamic and comparable non-Islamic institutions evoked little response. Deposit products are mainly based on *mudaraba*, i.e., revenue-sharing between clients and BMT. The average ratio in the four sample BMT for savings accounts is 34:66, average annual returns are 8.8 percent; the respective values for term deposits are 42:58 and 13.6 percent—insignificantly higher than in the sample BPRS.

The average number of loan accounts in the four sample BMT, which are far above the national average in size, is 327. Loan sizes are less than half the volume of those in the sample BPRS. In the sample BMT, 61.5 percent of financings are *murabaha*, i.e., sales contracts between bank and client—less than in the BPRS. *Mudaraba*, based on profit-sharing, amount to 32 percent, and *qard hasan*, a free loan product for poor start-ups, to 3.5 percent. Requiring collateral is standard. In some cases there are compulsory savings around 5 percent. Effective annual gross mark-ups, or profit margins to the bank, are around 50 percent. It is common not to charge penalties on late payments. Given a sample size of 4 out of 2,900, these figures are at best indicative.

Economic performance: In the absence of effective regulation and supervision, the performance of BMT is very uneven; information is sporadic. A large number of BMT are dormant. PNM has identified 500 BMT, which are members of INKOPSYAH and registered with the Ministry of Cooperatives, as worth strengthening; this is less than one-fifth of the total number. In the four sample BMT, NPF ratios vary widely from 1.4 percent to 30 percent but are mostly estimates. All four BMT in our sample show positive returns on year-end assets, with ROAs ranging from 0.16 percent to 2.7 percent; but there may be sizeable bad debts, which are not shown as such.

Affiliations and support: The most important promoter of Islamic cooperatives is PINBUK, established in 1995. It provides a management information system to BMT and through regional offices, basic, intermediate and advanced training, plus training of trainers. INKOPSYAH, a commercially operating secondary-level cooperative, functions as a wholesaler of funds from other sources. Microfin has established a network of 109 BMT and channels project funds to a total of 673 BMT and KOPONTREN, plus 24 BPRS. It also tries to promote their institutional upgrading to MFIs (LKM) or BPRS. PNM, which has replaced BI's (the central bank) liquidity credit operations, has provided liquidity to 85 BMT. To step up its outreach and effectiveness, it will cooperate with PINBUK and ASBISINDO to provide supervision and training. Islamic banks provide additional financial resources. BMI, the first Islamic bank, channels funds through *Bayt al mal Muamalat* and technical assistance through the Muamalat Institute for Research, Training, Consulting & Publication. BMTs also receive donations from wealthy Muslims. The main constraints for BMT are management and supervision weaknesses, not funding.

Annex 5

Financial products in ICBs, microbanks and cooperatives in Indonesia

Islamic financial products do not seem to have any particular attraction to Islamic financial institutions and their customers in Indonesia. Revenue-sharing in deposits (*mudaraba*) is unduly complicated and little appreciated because of monthly fluctuations and annual ex-post calculations; remuneration-free *qard hasan* deposits, which are very important in Iran, are non-existent in Indonesia. Profit-sharing in lending (*mudaraba*), which should be the backbone of Islamic banking, constitutes but a small part of the portfolio as it does in Iran. *Qard hasan*, remuneration-free lending to the poor, is virtually non-existent in Indonesia. The largest part of the portfolio is trade finance at a fixed margin (*murabaha*), as is the case in Iran and among the *Sanadiq* (village funds) in Syria. But this again is complicated and increases transaction costs because it involves two contracts by the bank: one with the seller and one with the borrower. Simultaneously, it adds information, security and perhaps collateral in the form of the transacted commodity or equipment. Moreover, the art of Islamic banking is not fully mastered by many managers in Islamic institutions, many of them retired conventional bankers. The strength of Islamic finance lies in its conservative character: only real transactions, but no speculative investments, are financed. This reduces financings to micro-entrepreneurs without collateral to a minimum.

Financial products in ICBs

BMI, the first and largest ICB in Indonesia, reports the following yields to depositors of 6–7 percent p.a. on savings accounts and 7–9 percent on term deposits (Table 9.8).

Financings of BMI, with a loan portfolio of Rp. 2.25tr, are distributed product-wise as follows: *murabaha* 53.5 percent; *mudharaba* 34.6 percent; *musharaka* 1.6 percent, other 10.3 percent (Tables 9.9 and 9.10).

Table 9.8 Deposits in ICBs and ICBUs, Dec. 2003

Deposits	
Wadi'a current accounts	11.1%
Mudaraba savings accounts	28.1%
Mudaraba time deposits	60.7%
Total percent	99.9%
Total amount	Rp 5.72tr
Percent of total liabilities and equity	72.8%

Source: Seibel (2005a: 106).

Table 9.9 Financings by ICBs and ICBUs, Dec. 2003

Financings	
Musharaka financings	5.5%
Mudaraba financings	14.4%
Murabaha receivables	71.5%
Istinsa' receivables	5.4%
Other	3.2%
Total percent	100%
Total amount	Rp 5.53tr
Percent of total assets	70.4%

Source: Seibel (2005a: 106).

Table 9.10 Financial products of Islamic banks (commercial and rural), in percent, 2000 and 2005

	2000	2005
Financings		
Musharaka	2.6	12.5
Mudaraba	30.5	20.5
Murabaha	62.6	62.3
Istinsa'	6.0	1.8
Qard hasan	0.0	0.8
Other	0.8	2.1
Total financings in %	100.0	100.0
Amount in million rupiah	1,239,423	15,231,942
Deposits		
Wadi'a	21.5	13.1
Mudaraba savings	32.7	28.0
Mudaraba fixed deposits	45.8	58.8
Total deposits in %	100.0	100.0
Amount in million rupiah	1,028,923	15,582,329
FDR,%	123.5	97.8

Source: Seibel (2005a: 97).

Financial products in Islamic microbanks (BPRS)

Table 9.11 Deposit products in five sample BPRS

BPRS	Total amount (in million Rp)	Number of products	Savings accounts		Time deposits*	
			Revenue-sharing client–bank	Average return in % p.a.	Revenue-sharing client–bank	Return in % p.a.
1 Alwadi'ah	3,796	4	50:50	6%	70:30	10%
2 Artha Fis.	619	4	30:70	12%	40:60	18%
3 Harum Hik.	4,018	3	40:60	8.8%	65:35	14%
4 Wakalumi	6040	12	35:65	7.09	56:44 to 66:34	11.35 to 13.37
5 Bangka	5,622	n.a.	40:60	7.5%	55:45	11.5%
Mean	4,019	5.75	40:60	8.3%	60:50	13%

Source: Seibel (2005a: 110).

Table 9.12 Loan products in five sample BPRS

BPRS	Amount (in mn Rp)	No. of accounts	No. of products	Loan products in % of portfolio			
				Murabaha	Musharaka	Mudaraba	Other
1 Alwadi'ah	5,694.4	800	3	60	40		
2 Artha Fis.	1,208.0	163	4	85			15
3 Harum Hik.	4,312.7	800	1	100			
4 Wakalumi	9,652.8	2,000	4	93	5	0.5	1
5 Bangka	4,562.8	n.a.	2	90		10	
Unweighted mean	5,086.1	*941*	2,8	86	9	2	3

Source: Seibel (2005a: 111).

Financial products in Islamic cooperatives

Table 9.13 Deposit products in four BMT

BMT	Total amount (in million Rp)	Number of products	Savings accounts		Time deposit accounts	
			Revenue-sharing client–BMT	Average return in % p.a.	Revenue-sharing client–BMT	Return in % p.a.
At-Taqwa	1,957.9	5	35:65 40:60	9.0 9.6	45:55	13.2
Ibaadurrahman	199.3	4	25:75	5	35:65 40:60 45:55	Approx.12
Latanza	137.15	4	40:60	11	40:60	14–16%
Wira Mandiri	575.8	5		10		14
Mean	*717.5*	*4.5*	*34:66*	*8.8*	*42:58*	*13.6*

Source: Seibel (2005a: 119).

Table 9.14 Loan products in four BMT

BMT	Amount (in mn Rp)	No. of accounts	No. of products	Loan products in % of portfolio			
				Murabaha	Mudaraba	Qard hasan	Other
At-Taqwa	1,819.4	500	4	70	15	6	10
Ibaadurrahman	217.2	300	2	51	44	2	3
Latanza	345.8	200	2	33	61	6	
Wira Mandiri	587.3	308	4	92	8		0
Unweighted mean	742.4	327	3	61.5	32	3.5	3

Source: Seibel (2005a: 120).

Notes

1 This chapter was presented at "Financing the Poor: Towards an Islamic Microfinance," at a symposium held at Harvard Law School, Cambridge, MA, April 14, 2007
2 Professor emeritus, University of Cologne, Germany
3 Based on field research in Indonesia between May 24 and June 5, 2004, supported by GTZ. For a full report see Working Paper 2006–2, www.uni-koeln.de/ew-fak/aef.
4 This includes an ICBU of BRI with 17 branches, with *mudaraba* savings and fixed deposit products. The ICBU is expected to be transformed into a separate BRI Syariah Bank as of September 2007. The BRI village units do not offer Islamic financial products.
5 I gratefully acknowledge updating until 2006 by Dr. Michael Hamp, GTZ/BI, Jakarta.
6 No. 10/1998 on ICBs; 6/17/2004 on Islamic rural banks; 7/46/2005 on Islamic banking product standardization; 7/47/2005 on transparency of financial condition.
7 BRI is a previously government-owned agricultural development bank.
8 Mostly referred to as BMT, though there is also a small section of BTM and, in Aceh, of Baitul Qirad.

Table 9.15 Financing terms and conditions of BMT At-Taqwa

	Loan products			
	1: Murabaha	*2: Mudaraba*	*3: Qard hasan*	*4: Qard*
Portfolio	70%	15%	5%	10%
Number of borrowers	80%	4%	6%	10%
Minimum loan size in Rp million	1	5	0.1	0.5
Maximum loan size in Rp million	25	25	1	2
Profit-sharing margins:				
Nominal (flat)	18–24%	18–24%	0	0
Fees if any	1.5%	1.5	0	0
Effective p.a. (approx.)	38–50%	38–50%	0%	0%
Profit-sharing vs. interest rates	A fair system			
Admin. fee for late payment	0	0	0	0
Minimum loan period in months	3	12	3	3
Maximum loan period in months	36	24	12	12
Instalment schedule	M	M	M	M
Collateral/guarantee requirements	Yes	Yes	No	No
Loan size tied to savings?	10%	No	5–10%	5–10%

Source: Seibel (2005a: 121).

Note
M = Monthly.

10 Islamic microfinance in crisis countries

The unofficial developmental discourse

M. Siraj Sait[1]

Introduction

Islamic microfinance sectors emerging across the Muslim world exhibit considerable diversity owing to the context, the profile of the stakeholders, the manner of engagement with Islamic jurisprudence and the levels of institutionalization. There is growing consensus that Islamic banking to the poor could foster development "under the right application."[2] Yet, while the authenticity of specific Islamic microfinance products is often contested, the dynamics that create distinctive microfinance initiatives are mostly ignored. It is this interplay between the local, national and international microfinance actors that negotiates the Islamic design, content and delivery of microfinance services. Microfinance products are not always part of economic planning: they could well be generated by spaces or pragmatism within the development discourse. This chapter will focus on Afghanistan—and contrast with the Indonesian experience—to consider how particular political, economic and legal dynamics create opportunities for microfinance institutions (MFIs) to negotiate and play a significant role in the design and the delivery of microfinance products.

Microfinance in Afghanistan has been quite widely hailed as a success story, in terms of its rapid expansion and ability to encourage enterprise and alleviate poverty in a context of great need. For instance, Hilary Benn, the then UK Minister for International Development, told the British parliament that with its rapid development, effectiveness of outreach and a financially sustainable outlook, that the "design and implementation" of microfinance in Afghanistan could serve as "a good example for building microfinance sectors in conflict affected countries."[3] From a different perspective, Anand and Badawi, although again not making any specific reference to Islamic microfinance, drawing upon experience especially in Afghanistan, but also in Bosnia, Liberia and Iraq, state that microfinance has "helped to create a sense of community from the rubble." They further argue that "while money cannot heal all wounds, microfinance can help restore hope even for communities ravage by war."[4] While Afghanistan may be exceptional as a post-conflict country, its experience with Islamic microfinance could well influence developments elsewhere,[5] which is particularly important to initiatives such as the Global Land Tools Network (GLTN), which seek to systematically develop innovative, pro-poor and gendered Islamic tools that could assist the implementation of development policies.

Scope of this chapter

This chapter is not written as an evaluation of a microfinance project but as a narrative of how ground realities drive Islamic theoretical approaches into practical policies and programs. It explores the implications of the lack of Islamic microfinance tools in the back drop of a methodology and strategy developed by the GLTN, a network of 45 leading stakeholders serviced by UN-HABITAT. The GLTN Islamic mechanism was developed through a research carried out by University of East London, which produced a body of material and strategies through the book *Land, Law and Islam: Property and Human Rights in the Muslim World*,[6] of which Islamic microfinance is one of the main themes. In this research, Islamic microfinance was studied alongside other significant issues such as legal jurisprudence, human rights, women's rights, inheritance, *waqf* and land and property tenures and reform. The general findings of the research are that distinctive Islamic conceptions of land, property rights and finance exist, although they are varied in practice throughout the Muslim world. While Islamic law and human rights are often important factors, they intersect with state, customary and international norms in various ways. In doing so, they potentially offer opportunities for the development of "authentic" Islamic land tools that can support the campaign for the realization of fuller land rights for various sections of Muslim societies, including women. Islamic principles relating to land rights are therefore to be addressed as religious manifestations of cultural or traditional norms, but must also be constructively appraised in order to appreciate their relevance for Muslim societies in general. In clarifying Islamic principles and developing effective tools, injurious cultural practices carried out in the name of religion could be countered.

The GLTN,[7] brings together professionals, policy makers, experts and civil society to develop innovative, pro-poor and gendered tools aimed at creating steps for delivery of agreed objectives, particularly in the areas of land, property and housing rights. Tools for GLTN are the cogs in the wheel of planning implementation, monitoring and evaluation in relation to land. They are the means to convert objectives in legislation, policy or principles into implementation, through practical knowledge, skills and ability. A tools approach helps identify the what, who and how of implementation. Principles may guide, and policies reflect political will, but without tools they are abstract phrases and remain aspirations. From a GLTN perspective more attention needs to be given to knowledge transfer processes: an effective tool is a best practice that can be communicated, adapted and applied in various contexts. GLTN acknowledges that land tools are mostly predicated on the existence of functioning institutions, systems and processes, difficult to access and, at best, only partly effective. The introduction of conflict or displacement dramatically alters the conditions in which tools can operate to land rights. Thus, GLTN is focused on modified land tools, specific for post-conflict situations, which can work without the assumed agencies and guarantees.

In particular, GLTN has identified Islamic tools as a priority focus area. As such, the roles of and the relationship between Islamic microfinance practitioners and the international development community is one of the areas of attention in this discussion. At a key workshop, as part of a regional Arab ministerial conference in December 2005, the *Cairo Initiative on Islamic Land Tools*[8] called for further systematic development of Islamic tools to facilitate better policy implementation, identifying this UN-HABITAT research as a baseline study for further work, supported by *Al Azhar*. The objective of the GLTN Islamic Land Tools initiative is to facilitate the development of innovative, pro-poor, affordable and scalable gendered Islamic land tools that could be used appropriately in specific contexts. The "added value" of the GLTN approach is that it is a multi-stakeholder systematic initiative that aims to create replicable tools across countries. Islamic microfinance is one of the most challenging fields of tool development as it is both expanding as well as under-regulated without adequate study of its methodologies. There are complexities inherent in the subject matter that require the generation of Islamic tool expertise from cross-cultural and inter-disciplinary perspectives.

The Afghanistan context

Afghanistan's socio-political and economic profile is intriguing. In a country where an estimated 56 percent of the approximately 23 million Afghans live under the poverty line,[9] the post-conflict economy is still largely opium driven,[10] contingent on the security situation and based significantly on informal money transfers or *hawala*.[11] Microfinance was prioritized at the outset by the international community—the Afghanistan Reconstruction Trust Fund (ARTF)—as one of the core "reconstruction" projects. Since its initiation in 2003, the Microfinance Investment and Support Facility Afghanistan (MISFA) grew to approximately USD 75 million with ambition for 200,000 clients.[12] MISFA has several objectives that are common to microfinance sectors elsewhere, such as providing affordable financial services to poor people and integrating the financial sector. In addition, there are other objectives considered vital by the international community for Afghanistan. These include weaning away unemployed persons from participation in the conflict by providing opportunities,[13] increasing women's participation in the economy and creating alternative livelihoods in poppy-growing provinces.[14] Consider the gender focus of MISFA—74 percent of the microfinance clients are women and over two-thirds of those employed by this sector are women. Thus, Afghanistan's microfinance project is not merely about general poverty alleviation or sustainability, but also a targeted political and developmental endeavor.

Though the microfinance services in Afghanistan were to be "flexible and tailored to local priorities," despite the Islamic Republic of Afghanistan's overwhelmingly traditional and conservative Muslim profile, no conscious engagement with Islamic principles was intended. Of the 4 countries that contributed to the 24-member ARTF, only Saudi Arabia was a significant Muslim donor. Islamic transplantation could have materialized when the management committee of ARTF[15] (administered by the World Bank) included the Islamic Development Bank, which promotes and contributes to economic and social development in accordance with the principles of Islamic law, but it does not appear to have done so; rather, the modernization of post-Taliban Afghanistan was conceptualized through secularist approaches. Until recently, there was little evidence of interest in Islamic microfinance by the dozen or so Afghan MFIs. For example, the 2006 mid-term review of the microfinance sector and MISFA in Afghanistan only tangentially addresses Islamic microfinance.[16]

Islamic microfinance in Afghanistan

While Islamic microfinance was not part of the official development discourse or general microfinance planning, realities on the ground forced a rethink. The potential high demand for small loans was accompanied by end-user skepticism over their compatibility with Islam. For example, Ariana Financial Services Group (AFSG), established by Mercycorps, narrated its hard work to convince people that its services were not unIslamic. Making a virtue out of necessity, a number of MFIs in Afghanistan have since packaged themselves as Islamic. The Danish Microfinance Agency for Development and Rehabilitation of Afghan Communities (MADRAC) in November 2006 launched new Islamic credit services for needy people in rural areas. The US-based FINCA International also announced that as of September 2006 all FINCA Afghanistan credit products are now *shari'a*-compliant. Likewise, the French-based Oxus Development Network (ODN) now provides loans following the principles of Islamic banking.

While several MFIs such as MADRAC and FINCA explicitly identify the use of the Islamic *murabaha* model, in general there is an assortment in what is offered as Islamic. One MFI, PARWAZ, has argued that interest is not impermissible under the complex Islamic finance laws, while others use alternative descriptions of interest or strive to distinguish interest from usury. Some use color-coded forms for different types of loans that indicate the tariffs for services. The lending arrangement where loan fees are charged on the basis of profit-sharing or "cost plus mark-up" instead of a fixed interest rate invariably also includes overheads and running costs (including staff salaries, operating expenses, taxes, borrowing costs). This requires effective risk management and sustainable approaches.[17] However, Grace and Al-ZamZami,[18] in their report on microfinance in Yemen, are forthright in their assessment that the extent to which a microfinance product is altered to be Islamic depends on "how strongly these beliefs regarding interest are held." Therefore, where these beliefs are not as pervasive, institutions may make cosmetic changes to their operations and products, such as changing the term "interest" to "service charge." In other cases where these beliefs are fundamental and widespread, more extensive adaptations have had to take place, which affect the core of an institution's systems, operations and beliefs.

The expansion of microfinance in Afghanistan, Islamic microfinance in particular, is remarkable since it neither possesses a systematic Islamic banking infrastructure nor an established civil society. What is worrying though is that, given the post-Taliban environment, the religious sector has been largely excluded at a time of ad hoc growth of the microfinance industry. The casual sporting of the Islamic label raises questions over the integrity, transparency and accuracy of the information for a largely illiterate population—as well as its long-term sustainability. Neither MISFA nor the Central Bank of Afghanistan has addressed the need for concrete guidelines in a sector avoiding self-regulation. Islamic microfinance models in Afghanistan are being largely developed by its nascent civil society with individual MFIs—overtly or discreetly—in consultation with international donors, who are invariably Western partners. Therefore, the MFIs face the challenge of systematically developing innovative, pro-poor and gendered Islamic tools that could assist the implementation of development policies in Afghanistan almost on their own, with a little help from their international "secular" partners rather than a coordinated indigenous expert support.

Afghanistan and Indonesia

The development of Islamic microfinance in Afghanistan can be usefully explored further by drawing a contrast with Indonesia after the tsunami of December 2004.[19] First, there was no single coordinating microfinance agency in Indonesia like the MISFA in Afghanistan and microfinance initiatives were slower to start following the emergency relief efforts. Second, within Indonesia debates over the nature of Islamic financial services were already underway as, for example, between the influential Indonesian *Nahdlatul Ulama* (NU) and *Muhammadiyah* over the permissibility of interest. Yet, in the case of Afghanistan, microfinance was to a larger extent "introduced," and despite the relative autonomy of MFI had to be, curiously, ratified in its particular manifestations by the external partners. Third, the existence of credit institutions, including Islamic ones—*Baitul Quiradh* or BPRS (*Bank Perkreditan Rakyat Shariyah*)—meant that the focus was not on initiation but rather consolidation (or rectification), regulation and capacity building. The state and the Central Bank as well as the MFIs being better established entities[20] were able to negotiate more effectively with international players and draw in the support of the Asian Development Bank in a relatively more systematic way, focused on sustainability, capacity building and lobby for a viable and workable framework.[21]

In devising the appropriate Islamic microfinance models for Aceh, the various stakeholders have been aware of the region's distinctive concepts and terminologies. It was agreed that the principles of *shari'a* would govern Islamic microfinance in their legal and social framework.[22] Moreover, Indonesian legal pluralism[23] and autonomy for local determination of Islamic legal principles generated prospects for innovative and sustainable approaches.[24] Therefore, particularly with respect to Islamic cooperatives, the changes have come from within—with the external actors being arrayed as supporters.[25] This participative process of determining Islamic principles as applicable to microfinance in their particular context is in contrast to the Afghanistan experience where the designing have been largely externally mediated, though the MFIs have been localized in operations. Another vital difference is the direct role of commercial banking in Indonesia, unlike the

Afghan experience. This could be critical for sustainability of MFIs when international support runs out.

Both Afghanistan and Indonesia face opportunities for strengthening Islamic microfinance protocols—where the roles of stakeholders are generally fluid, negotiable and overlapping. The dynamics of creating an inclusive microfinance industry in post-conflict or post-disaster societies present particular challenges but they also offer stark choices not unlike in other "normal" situations.[26] The alternatives include pragmatic responses that are *shari'a*-conversant or justifiable,[27] on the one hand, and those rigorously conjured through Islamic jurisprudential inquiry as being *shari'a*-compatible, on the other hand.[28] Equally, there are attempts at adaptation and fusion of conventional and Islamic microfinance. Whether Islamic microfinance is being designed by the believer, agnostic or secular for faith, development or empowerment, legal methodologies matter as much as politics and economics. How can Islamic microfinance be gendered, made affordable and upscaled while upholding the fundamental Islamic principles? It appears that the approaches adopted in Afghanistan have not fully and holistically addressed this challenge.

Lessons learnt

Microfinance in Afghanistan has been considered a success in relative terms of post-conflict poverty alleviation. Funding proposals are currently developed by MFIs in close collaboration with MISFA staff, and then approved by a steering committee composed of the government of Afghanistan, the World Bank, and the Consultative Group to Assist the Poor as the representative of its participating member donors. Issues addressed include a clear understanding of client demand, strong management, capacity for outreach, cost-effectiveness, transparency and willingness to learn. In this context, whether and how the "Islamic" label is used may seem an academic question. Yet, it could have profound implications for its sustainability given its particular socio-cultural and political context. Afghanistan's microfinance experience flags several questions, which although not exclusive to this particular context, need to be addressed in particular from the context of determining whether it can indeed provide a model for other post-conflict situations. Moreover, does the Afghanistan experience provide the basis for the development of a replicable and sustainable framework here and elsewhere? Moreover, there is a need to consider the distinctiveness of post-conflict situations that create the particular power relations, dynamics, as well as opportunities.

Islamic microfinance by any other name?

Is it relevant that a substantial part of microfinance activities are being now promoted as "Islamic" even though they are part of a largely secularized policy discourse?[29] To what extent does the general lack of recognition of its Islamic character limit the fuller treatment of the issues at a policy level and the process of legitimization, authentication and ownership of microfinance at the end-user level?

These questions are related to the larger question of whether Islamic microfinance is about faith or empowerment or both. In this regard the skeptical view of Kuran that "the significance of the steps to give economics an Islamic character lies only partially in their economic content" is worth noting. He continues: "Much of their importance lies in their symbolism, in the present and future distribution of political power and their cultural meanings."[30] The debate over the nature and strategies of Islamic finance contribute to the larger issue of whether Islamic economics are merely a pragmatic strategy or a utopian ideal: the answer could, and should, be that Islamic microfinance is a practical vehicle of achieving both Islamic and universalist development goals.

Using Islamic principles of equal opportunity, entrepreneurship, risk sharing, charitable obligation and participation by the poor will strengthen microfinance principles.[31] As Dhumale and Sapcanin have argued, "many elements of microfinance could be considered consistent with the broader goals of Islamic banking. Both systems advocate entrepreneurship and risk sharing and believe that the poor should take part in such activities."[32] In its ideal form, an Islamic bank is much more than just an institution guided by Islamic principles and avoiding interest payments; it seeks to achieve a just and equitable society.[33] With their distinctive values, Islamic financial schemes can reach out to groups excluded by conventional banks and "catalyze economic development and reduce poverty."[34]

What is distinctive about the effect of Islamic microfinance?

There is a considerable amount of literature on the impact of microfinance on poverty alleviation generally, as well as its limitations. For example, it has been seen that it largely caters to the entrepreneurial poor and misses a range of services as well as constituencies amongst the poor. Ultimately, poor households should be able to use financial services to raise income, build their assets and cushion themselves against external shocks.[35] However, in practice, there is much more limited attention paid to the relationship between microfinance and access to land. Perhaps, in endeavoring to make Islamic microfinance like conventional microfinance, a simple mirror process is arising as is sometimes the case with Islamic financial products. Yet, Islamic finance has an important role to play in widening the provision of funds to enable the purchase of, or building of, homes for those without them, and in enabling their owners to use the property for further income generation.[36]

Since 1999 the outreach of the microfinance industry in the Arab world has more than quintupled in size going from over an estimated 129,000 active borrowers to over 710,000 at the end of 2003. A network of MFIs in Arab countries, known as SANABEL, was established in September 2002, drawing together institutional members from several countries including Egypt, Jordan, Lebanon, Morocco, Tunisia and the occupied Palestinian territories. It has produced regular surveys of the development of microfinance in the Arab states region, including the establishment of programs based on Islamic finance principles. In a survey published in October 2004,[37] SANABEL briefly recorded microfinance operations in Syria and

Yemen. However, microfinance services in the area, some compliant with Islamic law, are limited largely to credit for enterprise, not consumer credit, the building or purchase of homes, or home improvement. From Morocco[38] to the Grameen in Bangladesh, microfinance provision for land and housing has been shown to be possible but is not generally a priority area. However, one successful example in Afghanistan is the Aga Khan Agency for Microfinance (AKAM) where loans have allowed some farmers to repurchase land sold during civil strife to poppy-farming landlords and warlords, and enabled the replanting of the fields, with wheat and potatoes, as well as the purchase of livestock. Therefore, the challenge for Islamic microfinance is not merely to mirror conventional microfinance but to go beyond it and, true to the Islamic principles, address the broader issues of empowerment and poverty alleviation.

A methodology for Islamic microfinance?

It is agreed that there is at present no established model of Islamic microfinance, which has led to a patchwork of initiatives. Pragmatic and innovative approaches serve a short-term purpose of growth. But as the SANABEL reports shows, in many countries, while there has been a significant expansion, microfinance sectors have tended to stagnate. The lack of a coherent and reliable framework has implications for replicability, sustainability and ability for outreach, which are, of course, already issues for many MFIs. It is true that because of the relative infancy of Islamic financial institutions, in comparison to longer established conventional interest-based banking, these institutions face both "internal" and "external" problems,[39] but these will have to be addressed in order for them to work out. The challenge is not merely the absence of appropriate regulatory frameworks for Islamic microfinance, but the lack of necessary methodologies that reflect application of Islamic principles.

Here, the GLTN Islamic land tools initiative or its approaches may be considered as one of the strategies for the further systematic development of Islamic microfinance. Three broad challenges face tool development in the Muslim world. First, positive strategies from the Islamic discourse and best practices from the Muslim world need to be converted into the tool development process. This will require further country-specific study of tools. Second, there is a need to prioritize specific Islamic tools generation, which can be innovative, pro-poor, gendered, affordable and scalable. Third, interface between the various actors—tool developers, grass-roots, civil society, states, development partners and scholars—is needed to harmonize universal, Islamic and professional land principles. The ownership of the process by Muslims is important, but civil society and development partners must contribute to a process that is inclusive, objective, systematic and transparent.

Islamic tools, even in Muslim countries, cannot be seen in isolation. They are not a substitute for the continuing process of universal or generic land tool development because the complimentarily, role or appropriateness of Islamic tools depends on particular demands and contexts. The stakeholder consultations have indicated that the process must be representative, focused, constructive and non-ideological. The relationship between Islamic and other tools facilitates valuable cross-fertilization through best practices. Not unlike customary tools, the development of Islamic land tools is not an internal matter but a cross-cultural, inter-disciplinary and global effort. The relationship of Islamic systems with other models, such as formal and informal land tenure, needs further study. Harmonization of universal and Islamic principles, objectives and values enable systematic identification, upscaling, development and evaluation of Islamic tools. To facilitate this, GLTN envisages bringing together various stakeholders to constructively review the normative and methodological Islamic frameworks in line with established human rights and development approaches.

Islamic tool development is at an early stage of development and will require significant inputs and commitments. This raises several methodological questions related to the process of developing tools from Islamic best practices. Every Islamic professional tool undergoes the rigorous process and stages similar to development of other tools, adjusted to its distinctive sources, needs and sensitivities. The need for consultations between representative groups of professional tool developers, civil society, Islamic scholars, policy makers and development partners is acknowledged. However, there are no existing networks bringing together community groups including grass-roots women, tool developers, state officials and development partners, Islamic scholars, Muslim communities and institutions for the process of developing tools. In keeping with the Cairo Initiative, there is a need to follow up with activities aimed at stimulating a tools-based approach. The experience of Afghanistan with respect to its microfinance initiatives appears to demonstrate the need for methodologies that could enhance its effectiveness, consistency, legitimacy, sustainability and its ability to more fully address poverty alleviation.

Notes

1 Reader, in Law, University of East London, London, United Kingdom. The author wishes to acknowledge the contribution of his colleagues Dr. Hilary Lim and Dr. Clarissa Augustinus also from the University of East London.
2 R. Dhumale and A. Sapcanin, "An Application of Islamic Banking Principles to Microfinance: Technical Note," Washington, DC: UNDP/World Bank, 1999. See also Nimrah Karim, Michael Tarazi and Xavier Reille, *Islamic Microfinance: An Emerging Market Niche*. Washington, DC: CGAP, 2008.
3 See statement of Hilary Benn, then UK Minister for International Development, made to the British parliament, February 16, 2007.
4 M. Anand and S. Badawi, "Can Microfinance Heal Wounds of War?," Common Ground News Service (CGNews), December 12, 2006. http://www.commongroundnews.org/article.php?id=20192&lan=en&sp=1.
5 See note 3. He does not mention Islamic microfinance though.
6 S. Sait and H. Lim, *Land, Law and Islam: Property and Human Rights in the Muslim World*. London: Zed Books, 2006.
7 GLTN, www.gltn.net.
8 *Cairo Initiative on Islamic Land Tools*, reproduced at http://www.unhabitat.org/downloads/docs/3982_92780_CairoDeclaration.pdf.
9 International Monetary Fund (IMF), *Islamic Republic of Afghanistan: Statistical Appendix No. 6/114*. Washington, DC: IMF, 2006.

10 See Karri A. Goeldner, *Roles and Opportunities for Rural Credit Initiatives in Afghanistan's Opium Economy*. London: DfID, 2004.

11 S. Munzele Maimbo, *The Money Exchange Dealers of Kabul: A Study of the Hawala System in Afghanistan*. Washington, DC: World Bank, 2003.

12 Scanteam, *Assessment, Afghanistan Reconstruction Trust Fund (ARTF) Final Report*. Oslo: ARTF, 2005.

13 See note 4.

14 Gender was identified as one of the three cross-cutting themes in the 2002 National Development Framework (NDF). The others are "Governance, Financial Management and Administrative Reform" and "Human Rights, Security and Rule of Law."

15 Others members of the ARTF Management Committee are Asian Development Bank, United Nations Development Programme and the World Bank.

16 G. Nagarajan, H. Knight and T. Chandani, *Mid-Term Review of the Microfinance Sector and MISFA in Afghanistan*. Kabul: Government of Afghanistan and MISFA, 2006.

17 Some analysts argue that fee for services based on profit-sharing calculations would be higher than the interest rate, particularly in unstable or conflict societies.

18 L. Grace and A. Al-ZamZami, *Islamic Banking Principles Applied to Microfinance Case Study: Hodeidah Microfinance Program, Yemen*. Geneva: UNCDF, 2002.

19 Hans Dieter Seibel, *Reconstruction and Development of the Microfinance System in Nanggroe Aceh Darussalam (NAD), Indonesia*. Cologne: GTZ, 2005b.

20 See Cécile Lapenu, *The Role of the State in Promoting Microfinance Institutions Paper No. 89*. Washington, DC: International Food Policy Research Institute, 2000.

21 The German agency GTZ exceptionally undertook the laborious process of establishing partnerships between the Bank of Indonesia, reconstruction agencies, Islamic institutions and civil society while identifying pilots, strengthening structures and elaborating methodologies.

22 See note 19.

23 See note 6.

24 See John Bowen, *Islam, Law and Equality in Indonesia*. Cambridge: Cambridge University Press, 2003.

25 Iman Budi Utama, *Baitul Qiradh: Reconstructing Islamic Cooperatives in Aceh, Indonesia*. Jakarta: GTZ, 2005.

26 Marilyn S. Manalo, *Microfinance Institutions' Response in Conflict Environments – Africa Region Working Paper Series No. 54*. Washington, DC: World Bank, 2003; G. Nagarajan, *Microfinance in Post-Conflict Situations: Towards Guiding Principles for Action*. Geneva: ILO, 1999.

27 Muhammed Anwar, "Islamicity of Banking and Modes of Islamic Banking," *Arab Law Quarterly*, 2003, pp. 62–80.

28 See Kais Alirani, "Islamic Micro-finance—Yemen Experience," First Annual Conference of SANABEL, Micro-finance Network of Arab Countries, 2003.

29 Consider the Grameen experience. See S.M. Hashemi and S.R. Schuler, *Sustainable Banking with the Poor: A Case Study of Grameen*. Dhaka: Programme for Research on Poverty Alleviation, Grameen Trust, 2002.

30 T. Kuran, "Islamic Economics and the 'Clash of Civilisations'," 2 *Middle Eastern Lectures*. Tel Aviv: Tel Aviv University, 1977 at p. 37.

31 N. Ferro, *Value Through Diversity: Microfinance and Islamic Finance and Global Banking*. Milan: Fondazione Eni Enrioco Mattei, 2005.

32 See note 2, p. 1.

33 R.I. Molla, R.A. Moten, S.A. Gusau and A.A. Gwandu, *Frontiers and Mechanics of Islamic Economics*. Nigeria: University of Sokoto, 1988.

34 Asian Development Bank, *Technical Assistance for the Development of International Prudential Standards for Islamic Financial Services*. Asian Development Bank, 2004.

35 J. Brandsma and L. Hart, *Making Microfinance Work Better in the Middle East and North Africa*. Washington DC: World Bank, 2004.

36 A. Mirakhor, "Hopes for the Future of Islamic Finance," lecture at the Institute of Islamic Banking, London, 2002.
37 J. Brandsma and D. Burjorjee, *Microfinance in the Arab States: Building Inclusive Financial Sectors*. New York: UNCDP, 2004, pp. 29–30.
38 CHF International, *Practical Guide for Housing Microfinance in Morocco*. CHF International, 2005.
39 J.J. Donohue, *A Note on the Theory and Practice of Islamic Banking, Yearbook of Islamic and Middle Eastern Law*. London: Kluwer Law International, 2000.

11 Minority funds in India

Institutional mobilizing of micro savings

Shariq Nisar and Syed Mizanur Rahman

The role of savings in poverty alleviation has in many ways been overlooked by the priority given to creating channels of credit as a means of capital formation to spur economic growth. While the focus has now shifted from government-subsidized credit programs to non-governmental organizations (NGOs) and private players running microcredit programs to enable the weaker sections of society to diversify their income sources, some retrospection is needed to clarify the role of credit in economic development and the institutional designs that can make financial services available to the poor in the most efficient and client friendly manner.

The minority funds operating in northern India have charted their own path to bring the benefits of financial services to the sections of society that have no access to the formal sector due to a variety of reasons. These funds have grown and prospered on the concept of "*amana*"—where one party is entrusted with the property of the other for safekeeping and investments. The funds collect from their members the small amount of cash that they might be left with at the end of the day. The amounts are so trivial that in case they are not collected by the end of that day, they could be spent by the person in gratuitous, trifle and non-productive ways. The funds then manage the money they collect to meet the two fundamental goals of managing liquidity to provide members the facility of withdrawing their funds whenever they are confronted with a significant outflow and providing a lending facility to others who cannot completely finance their expenses from their savings. Some of the savings are also invested to generate returns that help the funds meet their operational expenses. Perhaps the most significant contribution of these funds has been their ability to harness the dormant savings potential among people of all income groups, particularly among Muslims, without holding out the allure of interest. As was to be only expected, they have been more successful in this with the lower and middle income strata. Another notable achievement of the funds has been the relative lower effective rate of interest they charge from their borrowers.

The modus operandi of most funds has been to employ deposit collectors or *muhassils* to collect small amounts of savings from the members at their residences or workplaces. Many funds also provide withdrawals in the field, at least in emergencies. This convenience aspect in their mode of operation as well as their ability to leverage the strong antipathy among Muslims to banking interest, has enabled them to demonstrate very convincingly that small savings-based operations can not only be initiated on a minor scale but also be successfully scaled up over time to the size of small to medium co-operative societies and co-operative banks (especially in rural, semi-rural areas and small towns).

On the lending side a fee is collected on the principal outstanding in contrast to the compound rates charged in the organized as well as the unorganized credit alternatives. The effective rates of interest charged are much lower compared to the other available options to the members of the community and the funds have been successful in running their loaning operations for over five decades now. This chapter attempts to study the reasons for the success of these funds and to place them in the overall context of the microfinance sector in the country from an operational and strategic angle.

Minority funds: an overview

The history of minority funds in India goes back to the pre-independence era when the first such fund—"The Muslim Fund Tanda Baoli"—was established in 1934 in Rampur estate. Due to partition of the country in 1947 the movement came to a temporary halt though there is a distinct possibility that some undocumented funds might have opereated during those tumultuous times. It was however the Muslim Fund Deoband that gave the much required impetus to the concept in 1961. Scores of such institutions have been started since then mostly in the northern part of the country, notably in the Bijnor district of the state of Uttar Pradesh (UP). Some studies claim there are more than a hundred funds operating in different parts of the country.[1] Among the many institutions, this study focuses on the four Muslim funds of Deoband, Najibabad, Nehtaur, Sherkot; the Awami Imdadi Society Kiratpur and the Islami Fund Najibabad. While all these funds operate on the same model and offer similar services, they are managed separately by local activists, social workers and entrepreneurs with some degree of social concern. All of these funds are started by members belonging to minorities. They provide services to members hailing from all communities living in their area of operations and employ people from all groups to maintain a relationship of trust with them.

The Muslim Fund Najibabad is the largest of these funds and controls more than $18,000,000 in deposits and is managed by Izfarul Haq Zaki who started the fund back in 1972. Zaki (popularly "Qaziji"), from the landed gentry of UP was then a fresh graduate with a BSc and an LLB degrees from the prestigious Aligarh Muslim University. He recounts the day he returned after his graduation to find his family being harassed by local moneylenders trying to force them to repay the loans they had taken to finance Zaki through college. Finding the terms of payment thoroughly unjust, Zaki decided that something had to be done to end the menace of the moneylenders once and for all. He started the fund a few years later and has been running it ever since. "My family had suffered badly at the hands of moneylenders. Since then I have promised myself never to let anyone from my community fall prey to them," said Zaki. Money has been a secondary motivation for this man, who even after four decades of relentless service draws a meager salary of $530 per month to manage the fund's assets and investments that could now be worth well over $22,000,000 (INR 1,000,000,000).

It is their drive that has kept Mr. Zaki and other minority fund promoters motivated to continue and expand their operations over these long years. Many other funds also have stories of commencement similar to the Muslim Fund Najibabad and have been started by socially inclined personalities who have dedicated their lives to enable the poor to become financially secure and less dependent on external sources of credit.

Fund structure

Most minority funds are named after the areas they operate in. The scope of operations of the funds is very limited geographically and they are run by groups of entrepreneurs and social workers working towards making the poor financially self-reliant. As these funds grow with time and reach a certain size and gain reputation in the society, then they begin to hire professionals to maintain their accounts, manage deposits and to provide security to the collateral the funds hold. However the deposit collection, which is the most labor intensive and critical aspect of the operations of the fund, is carried out by special handpicked personnel called Pigmy Deposit Agents (PDAs) or *muhassils*, whose antecedents are well-known in the localities they handle.

Deposit collection is carried out daily and involves the PDAs visiting groups of clients, collecting from them deposits as low as a few rupees and documenting the transaction on the spot. The money collected is then deposited with the fund by the PDAs who are often hired on a commission basis to maximize collections. The PDAs also have to visit borrowers with outstanding loans to help them make small repayments with whatever amount of money they have left at the end of the day. This doorstep collection service is so valuable to members that many of them prefer to have an account with these funds than operate a savings account at the local bank branch. This is in spite of the funds not paying any interest on the deposits or having any sovereign backing or security.

A few funds also provide a locker facility for people to store their valuables and levy a fee on customers that make use of this service. However Khan and Nisar's 2004 study raises concerns about the risks these funds face by concentrating valuables in places that could be potential targets at times of communal unrest.

The funds collected are put to use in one of the following ways:

1   Some 25–50 percent of the funds are forwarded in the form of loans to the poor against a collateral of jewelry (mostly gold and silver).
2   A fixed part of the savings deposited (10–33 percent) is maintained with the fund in its offices to act as liquidity for depositors who may wish to withdraw their savings. Some of the larger funds have more systematic liquidity management practices refined by the years of experience to hold money against vagaries of demand from depositors.
3   Most funds commit a significant part of the money (10–50 percent) they collect to their fixed deposit bank accounts. These accounts help the funds hold money in secure instruments and use the interest income they earn on the

deposits to meet their operational expenses and to finance the social undertakings of the funds.

4   Many funds hold investments in real estate and sometimes use their money in to build and maintain facilities such as marketplaces, lodges, hospitals etc. and earn profits and rents from these investments.

The interest income earned on the fixed deposits meets a significant portion of the costs that the funds incur in running their operations. Some funds report that they are able to meet their operating costs from the service charges they levy on the loans and the interest income earned is mainly used to finance the welfare activities that the funds undertake (Figure 11.1).

Loan disbursement

One of the primary goals of minority funds is to provide the poor loans at subsidized rates of interest. Loans are provided for the needy for expenses related to sickness in the family, social occasions such as marriages, repayment of other debts or small term loans to meet the expenses connected with the agricultural cycle, particularly in the sowing season.[2] More recently funds have started providing loans to people seeking employment in the Middle East to finance the travel and visa expenses incurred in the process. Some funds such the Muslim Fund Deoband also give out loans to help people set up businesses. However, most of the funds sampled limit their lending towards production-related activities. Loans are extended against collateral of jewelry and the amount loaned out is generally in the range of 60–80 percent of the value of the collateral pledged. The duration of a loan is commonly three months but often borrowers take advantage of the lax repayment regime to stretch the loan duration and often the

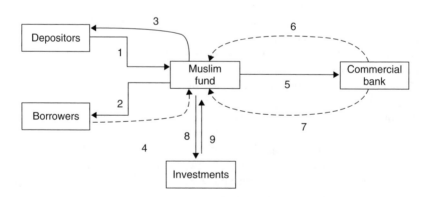

Figure 11.1 Fund management in minority institutions

1 Deposits collected; 2 Loans disbursed; 3 Withdrawals; 4 Repayment and service charges; 5 Fixed deposits (FDs); 6 Interest income on FDs; 7 Loans taken on FDs to meet emergency liquidity needs; 8 Investments made in fixed assets; 9 Rents/profits from assets.

loans are repaid only years later, as the funds have a policy of never selling the collateral to settle debts. Collateral plays an important role in the functioning of these funds and this aspect has been studied in depth in Khan and Nisar, 2004. They report the following:

- The collateral guarantees security of the loans outstanding. This increases the confidence that the depositors have in keeping their savings with the fund.
- The funds operate outside the banking framework of the country and therefore it is difficult for them to pursue legal methods to recover loans, so holding collateral provides a degree of safety to the funds.
- Functioning in an environment where most other lending options also require collateral (with the exception of the recently started microfinance institutions (MFIs)), relaxing this requirement might trigger the problem of adverse selection among borrowers.

Sometimes the fund loans out money to the poorest of the borrowers without any collateral as backing; however this is done only in extreme cases when families are faced with the most excruciating circumstances. It should be noted that such arrangements are made possible through the deep social bonding resulting from frequent interactions between the members and the managers of these funds in the context of community gatherings. The social bonding allows clients to in effect borrow against their reputation or the personal friendship they enjoy with the managers. While on the other hand, formal or organized credit sources are not at liberty to make such exemptions because of the lack of social mechanisms and incentives.[3]

Because a overwhelming number of the members of these funds belong to the Muslim community, the funds are careful in terming the charges levied on borrowing as the cost of various services bundled into the loan package such as "cost of loan form," "charges for (maintaining the) collateral" or "service charge(s)." Nevertheless there are significant differences in the application of charges levied by minority funds compared to interest charged by conventional banks. Primarily, the charges applied by the funds are calculated on the principal outstanding every quarter or every month at annualized rates ranging between 10 to 12 percent. Another standard that the funds apply is that the service charges are capped so as to never exceed the principal initially lent. This means that a borrower can extend the duration of the loan infinitely and will still only owe a maximum of twice the amount(s) initially borrowed. As will be seen later, this lax policy counter intuitively encourages people to repay their loans and collect their collateral in many cases. Most of the funds waive a significant part (30–40 percent) of the interest charges on the borrowers in case the borrower is going through a difficult situation such as loss in business or death in the family etc.

Management

Almost all the funds studied are started and are run by local, financially well-off activists and social workers with a strong sense of commitment towards the community. A great majority of the board members running these funds are either honorary or draw a very minimal salary. Reputation is paramount to these funds as a loss of confidence among the depositors could effectively close down the operations of the fund in a matter of days. In this regard the funds take a very cautious approach in most of their operational aspects including liquidity management, asset investments, collateral requirements etc. Revenue surpluses are often pumped into social initiatives such as running educational institutions, hospitals and other establishments for public welfare. Our study shows a strong relation between the size of the funds in terms of deposits and the contribution of the funds towards social causes. In fact, it is found that for every $1,000 managed by these funds, an annual contribution of approximately $4.3 is made to social programs. Exhibit 2 at the end of this chapter gives a list of the charitable institutions being run by the funds and the financial details of the welfare activities carried out.

Governance and auditing practices

Every fund has a "General Body" that is constituted at the time the fund is established. The General Body has 6–9 well known and influential people from the region as its members. Membership is generally for life and on the occasion of death of any of the members, the deceased is usually replaced by someone from the same family. The General Body elects the President of the fund who in turn selects a Management Committee to support the administration. The Management Committee consists of a few full-time employees of the fund and some honorary members and overlooks the functioning of the fund. The Committee also has a professional chartered accountant responsible for auditing the accounts and bringing discrepancies to the notice of the President. The audited reports of the functioning of the fund are circulated among the General Body and the Management Committee. Bigger funds are audited every six months while the rest audit their accounts once every year. It has to be noted that the financial results are generally not available in the public domain and the depositors rely on the faith, goodwill and the trust that the promoters of the funds enjoy within the community.

In the case of funds operating multiple branches, internal auditors from the head office visit the branches at regular intervals to tally the accounts and to verify proper functioning. There have been a few occasions of minor fraud committed by PDAs in reporting the deposits they collect at the end of the day. In case of fraud, an inquiry is set up and the people responsible for the misappropriation are suspended. No formal charges are pressed against the errant employees because in previous experience with law enforcement agencies, the funds have only had to deal with more complications without any resultant benefit. The employees risk a social boycott if they are suspended under such circumstances as the community has a strong sense of social ownership towards the fund. Any loss resulting from such frauds is taken as a cost and is met from the revenues the funds generate. As to date, the quantum of such scams has been quite minor.

Minority funds and micro savings

Micro savings has long been considered as the forgotten aspect of movements aiming to provide financial services to the underprivileged.[4,5] Some research has come to the conclusion that the demand for a "secure and convenient" savings service is much stronger than demand for credit services among the poor.[6] The concept of micro savings entails providing savings products to match the requirements of clientele that fall outside the formal financial system for a variety of reasons, including the minimum deposit requirements in banks, limit on the minimum transaction amount, intimidating procedures, product complexity, lack of legal documents, negative perception towards banks and an aversion to interest based institutions as in parts of the Muslim community. Micro savings is regarded as a possible way to bring these sections into the fold of the formal financial institutions or providing them with savings products to meet their requirements.

While a majority of the MFIs have neglected this aspect of financial intermediation or have required compulsory savings in some cases only to improve the repayment rates on loans withdrawn, micro savings are key to the running of minority funds as these funds depend solely on savings as their source of finance. Conventional MFIs on the other hand are driven by subsidized credit or capital from profit-driven financiers.[7]

The need for micro savings—financial exclusion

Despite the tremendous headway made by national banks in India towards expanding into rural areas and bringing larger sections of the rural population under the coverage of the banking sector, significant problems still exist. The Indian government nationalized banking in 1969 and by 1977 the Reserve Bank of India (RBI) rolled out policy initiatives to increase bank penetration in rural areas by mandating a minimum ratio for rolling out new branches in semi-rural and rural areas to the branches opened in urban areas. This policy was in place till 1991 after which the RBI discontinued it and the number of new branches opened in rural areas collapsed. While Panagariya[8] finds that the ratio of expansion actually exceeded the minimum requirement during the period the policy was in place, the effectiveness of the policy is a matter of debate. Some studies have found a relationship between patterns in opening of branches and some success in alleviation of poverty[9] while other studies dispute the findings and bring out the role of parallel policies such as the Integrated Rural Development Program (IRDP) in the reduction in poverty seen in parallel with the RBI policy of rural expansion (Kochar, 2005). It also needs to be pointed out that some government policy still remains in place to divert funds towards the rural sector including the 40 percent priority sector lending programs.[10]

The outcome of policy moves aimed at financial inclusion has been debated at length in the academic circles. The Hoff and Stiglitz (1993)[11] paper reports that government intervention has failed to achieve its intended results and rural expansion has in fact benefited the rich more than the poor for various reasons. In other places it is claimed that policy design and implementation issues have resulted in government subsidies being captured by sections other than those for whom the steps were intended.[12]

The failure of government efforts was followed by the microfinance movement that aimed to enable the poor access to financial credit. Microcredit institutions have largely taken to following the model developed by the Grameen Bank in Bangladesh and their operations have been categorized into four types in Sa Dhan (2005)[13] and Basu and Shrivastava (2005):[14]

1   Group models:

    a   Grameen model—Elaborate model, groups of five in which money is lent to two of the members while the other members act as chasers to help timely recovery.

    b   Self-help group (SHG) model—Flexible structure; credit given to a group of 15–20 "economically homogeneous" individuals.

    c   Joint liability model—Groups of four–six people mutually responsible for repayment of each other's loans.

2   Individual lending—Lender deals with the borrower on individual terms.

By this convention, minority funds can be categorized as individual lenders although they do differ from conventional microfinance institutions in their demand for collateral. However the demand for collateral has many advantages including reduction in the rate of interest charged and formalizing the "implicit" collateral characteristic of microfinance.

The advantages of micro savings

In a Consultative Group to Assist the Poor (CGAP) working paper, Hanning (1999) identifies three categories of MFIs according to their sources of funding:

1   formal banking institutions with a priority on "micro clients";
2   donor-sponsored or NGO-driven lending programs;
3   savings-driven "self-reliant" village savings and credit societies.

In a critical comparison of the different methods to raise funds, Wisniwski (1999) highlights the substantial benefits of micro savings-based MFIs over MFIs with other sources of funds such as external funding—subsidized or otherwise, compulsory savings or lopsided "large deposits" through which loans for other clients are funded. Micro savings have the crucial advantages of satisfying the demand for savings products from clients and mobilizing large amounts of funds at low financial costs. Low financial costs, which in turn reduces the rate of lending for borrowers can be viewed as a society subsidizing credit for needy members by demanding a low rate of returns on its capital. Combining operational costs of running the collection lending services simultaneously allows for the exploitation of synergies and the incentive structures for the management can be better geared towards efficiency and performance in these "self-reliant" savings and credit societies. All this is in contrast to the limitations placed on MFIs that rely on external sources or wholesale deposits that augur high financial costs, external dependence and conflicts between interests of different stakeholders. The complete comparison of the pros and cons of different sources of funds from the CGAP paper has been reproduced in Appendix 1 for reference.

Apart from the advantages of drawing micro savings as a source of funds, savings have strong macroeconomic implications. Savings strengthen the process of development in societies and for the poor savings act as an insurance substitute.[15] There are also other advantages of micro savings that make offering such services a rewarding proposition to the organizations as well as the clients themselves. Micro savings services with the right marketing can attract larger number of clients.[16] Savings also have significant advantages when compared to debt from the point of view of the poor, Adams and Pischke opine that debt is not an effective tool to enhance the economic condition of the poor.[17] Providing the option of savings reduces the incidences of borrowing and reduces the quantum of borrowing in cases where taking on debt becomes unavoidable. Encouraging savings also builds a culture of thrift and discipline that improves the credit worthiness of depositors eventually reducing their cost of debt.

Consumption and production loans—where conventional credit has failed

Studies on rural credit have given significant attention to the failure of massive government efforts in replacing the 'exploitative' informal lending sector. Hoff and Stiglitz's 1993[18] study looks into the issue of the dual credit markets that exist in developing countries and highlights the problems of imperfect information and difficulty in enforcement as the important reasons for the informal credit sector to have thrived despite unfavourable policy initiatives. One more important aspect of the story is the dichotomy that exists between consumption loans and production loans.

While the formality of government sector lending and the requirement of clear land titles has benefited mainly the larger farmers[19] and MFIs have aimed to finance productive income generating activity for the poor, the demand for consumption loans from the poor has been overlooked although their importance in their life cannot be underestimated. These sections of the society lack adequate savings and have no access to welfare or insurance and the people have no option but to borrow from moneylenders at very high rates of interest to finance their immediate needs or to borrow from MFIs and use the money for consumption purposes. In the sample MFI lending data studied in Banerjee, Duflo, Glennerster and Kinnan (2009), it is estimated that only one in every five additional loans provided under the study resulted in opening a new business underlining the significant use of MFI loans for the purpose of boosting immediate consumption.

An in-depth study in the dynamics of consumption loans has been reported in Jones (2006). People in the "backward" (Jones' category) tribal areas studied are forced to take on loans for a variety of reasons and social occasions. Consumption loans finance basic necessities such as food, medicine, housing, education and expenditures arising from social compulsions such as marriage ceremonies, occasions of death in the family and a range of other expenses that cannot be evaded. These expenses continue to channel clients to moneylenders while parallel efforts to supply credit to spur economic activity have received considerable interest from policymakers and failed to counter the exploitative practices in the informal credit sector.

Personal loans from banks are unavailable for most of sections living in rural settings and the daunting procedures necessary to avail these products frighten away potential clients looking to take loans against acceptable collateral. In addition much of what the families pledge as collateral happen to be precious heirlooms that people are not willing to surrender to faceless banks. Bridging this gap as a savings and credit intermediary and providing an appropriate face to its clients both in the terms of credit and the human element of interacting with clients has been one of the most important contributions of the minority funds towards a system that does justice to the credit requirements of the rural populace. It is perhaps because of this reason that many minority funds have succeeded in displacing moneylenders completely from the areas they operate in while formal banking and MFIs generally operate in parallel to moneylenders in the rural context.

How micro savings help

In the specific case of minority funds, micro deposits have shaped their operations in the following manner:

1 Micro deposits are the only source of funds, keeping the organization focused on its sole group of stakeholders—the community. This saves the funds from having to liaise with banks, NGOs, political organizations and capital providers for funds and having to restructure its priorities or compromise on its values.

2 Incidents in which the clients have to take on debt are reduced and people have increasingly started relying on their pooled savings to finance the schooling of their children and other expenses that can bring about an improvement in their living standards.

3 Cost of funds is lowered. No interest is paid on the deposits and this in turn reduces the rate of interest charged on loans. The depositors on their part subscribe to the services because of the convenience of having their savings collected from the doorstep and the security of keeping their money in deposits.

4 The savings operations help the funds have more efficient recovery methods. Loan repayment is done in tandem with deposit collection and there is no lower limit on the size of the installment in which the loan can be repaid.

5 The funds being run in the form of a society can offer unparalleled flexibility to their borrowers in the terms of repayment. Also the funds do not sell the collateral they hold and wait indefinitely for borrowers to close the loans. These factors have played their part in helping the funds boast of high repayment rates.

Comparison with credit-based microfinance

Hanning[20] outlines three major trends seen in MFIs that have shifted the focus of the industry from mobilizing savings. The trends highlighted in the working paper are:

- the view that microfinance is a "political movement aimed at eradicating poverty";
- an attempt at efficiently providing microfinance services;
- a profitable business opportunity.

The results of these trends are clearly visible in the context of the Indian microfinance industry. From the industry snapshot 2009 available in Srinivasan (2009), equity and debt are the most common sources of funds for a sector that has seen rapid growth with the loans outstanding becoming the most important metrics to measure the "success" of the movement illustrating the increasing interest in microfinance as a profitable business. MFIs in the country have shown a 7.9 percent profit margin in the year 2009 and are giving increasing priority to credit expansion. The MFIs in the country boast of over 22.6 million clients. Over the year 2009–10, the top five MFIs have increased their client base as well as the average loan quantum. While most of the top MFIs have shown profits, overall a third of the MFIs in the country have reported losses. These loss-making MFIs are especially common among the smaller institutions highlighting the role that subsidies have played in the growth of the industry. On the lending side, Srinivasan (2009) finds a significant correlation between the size of the non-banking finance company (NBFC) and the yield on its portfolio that indicated that larger MFIs would charge higher interest rates than the smaller players, which could explain for the higher incidences of reported losses among small MFIs.

In contrast, minority funds are wholly contained societies not dependent on external sources of funds or managerial expertise. The funds are geographically confined and prioritize on serving the needs of their client base completely rather than having an inclination of rapid expansion to appease capital providers. In this way being self-reliant in funding permits minority funds to remain dedicated to their social purpose while in contrast, there is growing discomfort that the pressure on MFIs to generate high returns on equity can be contrary to their "social orientation."[21] This profit-seeking motive has collided with the other view of microfinance being a political movement against poverty and has resulted in MFIs being accused of adopting coercive practices in their loan recovery strategies. These accusations have been reinforced with the state government of Andhra Pradesh taking a stand to rein in the lending institutions with legislated restrictions on recovery practices adopted by the MFIs operating in the state.[22, 23]

The social impact of MFIs has been a topic of great debate and is concisely summarized in Hanning (1999) as "it is evident that both microfinance institutions and donor agencies have vested interests in this debate." In fact some of the literature on the impact of MFIs also seems to follow political convictions rather than being based on hard facts. As an illustration, Morduch and Rutherford (2003) claim that micro lending has "allowed households to … export surplus labor to the cities or abroad" while Alam (2010) reports that among the borrowers "[m]any are thus forced to flee the village and try to find work in an urban area or abroad." Both the sources may be reporting the same phenomenon occurring in entirely different contexts; however it could be possible that the debate on the impact of micro lending on the lives of the poor has become sidelined by the profit vs. political debate on the topic. Similar contrasting research results have been documented in Banerjee, Duflo, Glennerster and Kinnan (2009).

We summarize the differences in the operations of MFIs and minority funds in Table 11.1.

Table 11.1 Operational differences between minority funds and MFIs

Parameter	Minority funds	MFIs
Source of funds	Small deposits collected from members on a daily basis that can be withdrawn as required	Capital, bank debt, subsidized funds from NGOs, large depositors, compulsory savings. In India private equity is also a significant source of capital (Chanchan, 2009)
Lending to	Predominantly consumption loans with some loans for production	Production loans to enable economic activity
Size of loan portfolio	The funds studied have loans outstanding varying between $13,000,000–$300,000	The top 50 MFIs covered in CRISIL (2009) have loans outstanding between $401,000,000–$2,750,000 on September 30th, 2008
Scale of operations	Geographically limited operations. Barring a few, most funds operate in rural and semi-rural areas	Vary considerably in size, some MFIs have operations across multiple states while others are smaller
Interest rates charged	Ten–12 percent simple rate charged on the principal outstanding. Interest amount capped and cannot exceed principal lent	Twenty-four–48 percent compounded. Effective rates charged could be much higher
Repayment	Considerable laxity in repayment with interest charge waivers quite common	Repayment schedules are enforced strictly and there is not much scope for waivers as very often groups have to make up for defaults from their members. Fresh loans are issued only to recover the same as payment for older loans
Collateral requirements	Money lent out against jewelry as collateral	Joint liability. Social pressure is the main deterrent against default
Managerial style	Operations are managed by social activists and philanthropists and local entrepreneurs who start the funds	Variety of organizational structures in place —SHGs, NBFCs, societies, Mutually Aided Cooperative Society etc.

Note
Conversion rate of 1 USD = 45.39 INR.

Impact of institutional structure on the operations

Cost of running the institutions

Mobilizing micro savings entail significant involvement from institutions. In general, it is important for the surpluses that the poor make to be collected at the end of the day otherwise the money could be spent on minor, avoidable involvements. A significant portion of the manpower at minority funds is dedicated to the task of collecting deposits. Other activities of the funds that add a significant cost to their operation include providing security to the collateral collected from borrowers, maintaining accounts, auditing and the maintenance of assets purchased from the excess funds.

Efficiency vs. size and scale

From the data collected by us, there seems to be a negative relation between the size of the fund in terms of deposits and the number of employees and the efficiency of operations in terms of the deposits managed per employee and the loans to deposit ratio. The "deposits managed per employee" metric is used as a proxy to measure the operational efficiency of the funds with respect to the costs incurred to manage the funds. The "loans to deposits ratio" metric has been used as a measure of the efficiency with which the fund has recycled its deposits to meet the credit requirements of the community members.

It must be noted here that these relations need to be adjusted for other parameters such as the level of automation in offices, the individual competence of local managers and the demand for credit in the community. All minority funds surveyed reported that much of the record keeping has been automated with all branches having computerized records, however we were unable to measure the level of automation in different funds at a deeper level and have hence assumed that the funds are running at the same level of automation in addition we also assume an infinite demand for credit from the community and that the amount loaned out by funds is limited only by their investment and liquidity management techniques. Making the above assumptions, we find that:

1   The loans to deposits ratio falls as the size of the fund increases, indicating that as the fund grows, it is forced to adopt more conservative loaning standards and keep a major portion of their deposits invested in safer options such as fixed deposits.
2   There are some diseconomies of scale from an operational standpoint that funds face as they grow larger. The deposits managed per employee falls dramatically with growth in deposits. However the Muslim Fund Najibabad, which is the largest fund in operations, shows a better ratio indicating that perhaps after a particular limit, there could be economies of scale that can be harnessed after the funds reach a critical size (see Figures 11.2–11.4).

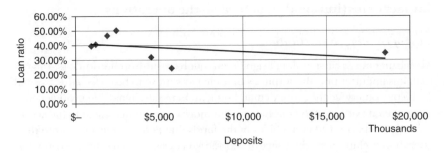

Figure 11.2 Loans to deposits ratio against deposits

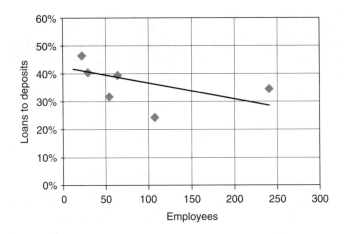

Figure 11.3 Loans to deposits ratio vs. no of employees

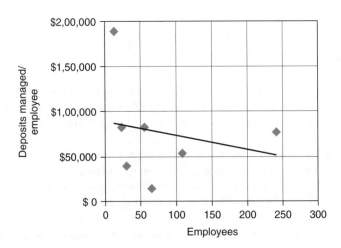

Figure 11.4 Deposits managed per employee vs. no of employees

Liquidity management

Micro deposits suffer from frequent deposit–withdrawal cycles—a problem that gets compounded by the seasonality of earnings and expenditures in semi-agrarian economies. To meet withdrawal requests from depositors, minority funds have to keep a significant portion of the deposits they collect in the form of cash that can be disbursed to the public on demand. Unlike banks, minority funds do not have access to money markets or the repo facility of the RBI. An inability to pay out cash can create panic among depositors that can result in insolvency as the minority funds cannot call in their loans from borrowers at will. To counter this problem, some minority funds are forced to keep around 30–40 percent of their assets in the form of cash with an exception of a few of the smaller funds such as the Muslim Fund Nehtaur and Islami Fund Najibabad that keep only around 10 percent of their deposits in cash or in current and savings accounts.

Some of the funds also manage the level of cash they hold keeping in mind the historic withdrawal patterns among their members. Members increase their withdrawals significantly during festivals and crop harvests and the funds need to make money available to meet this demand. Sometimes if the funds run low on cash, they take loans against the fixed deposits they hold in the bank to improve their liquidity. These loans are paid back when the deposits pick up again.

The study also finds some hesitation towards offering advanced savings products such as term deposits as the funds do not want to pay interest over the deposits they collect from their members. There also does not seem to be a perceivable need for such products from depositors who do not want their savings to be locked away in schemes that limit their flexibility in withdrawals.

Risk mitigation and loan portfolio

The loan portfolio of minority funds essentially comprises of a large number of small consumption loans with a few loans given out to start businesses or to enable other economic activity. In this way minority funds are protected from swings or losses seen in business sectors. The considerable laxity given to borrowers in repaying their loans and the policy of a capped interest expense act counterintuitively to decrease the default rate.

An important reason for the high rates of repayment could be because the total amount in arrears can never exceed twice the principal so in a way it is always beneficial for the borrower to close the loan and collect his collateral than to default and lose it. This reasoning is substantiated by the spurt in repayment of loans that is seen with appreciation in the price of gold. However in the downside, the lax repayment schedule and absence of penalties for delay in repayments does lead to loans being left overdue for long periods of time. Minority funds also prioritize on loan recovery and they often waive a sizable portion of the interest in consideration for difficulties the borrowers may be facing to incentivize loan closure. Since the funds almost never categorize loans as bad, unsettled loans are not taken as a cost and even in the rare case when a loan is classified as bad, the limited outstanding amount against that loan decreases the accounting loss the funds will have to incur and that would be covered by the value of the collateral sold. While this may seem to be an accounting trick, repayment rates on old loans seem to indicate that the incentives for repayment do work. All these reasons play a part in the low rates of default the funds boast, which in turn reduces the cost of funds and the rate of interest charged on all loans. As an illustration the Muslim Fund Deoband claims a recovery rate over 99 percent although the methodology followed to come to this figure is not disclosed. Figures from other funds are not available because the accounting seldom classifies loans as bad and true to this arrangement many loans are settled only years later, but the principal lent out is always recovered.

Regulatory aspects

Most minority funds are registered as charitable trusts.[24] To contrast this against the legal devices adopted by MFIs as listed in Ghosh (2005) and CRISIL (2009), MFIs can be divided into:

1   non-profit MFIs or NGO MFIs registered under the Societies Registration Act, 1860 and other related acts;
2   non-profit companies registered under Section 25 of the Companies Act, 1956;
3   for-profit MFIs registered under Indian Companies Act, 1956 and Reserve Bank of India Act, 1934.

Growth

All minority funds covered in the study have been showing impressive growth both in the deposits collected as well as in the loans outstanding over the period of our study. While the older funds such as the Muslim Funds Deoband and Najibabad are showing some signs of maturity and are growing at a comparatively slower pace of 11–13 percent compounded annual growth rate over the period 2007–10, the smaller funds are showing growth rates around 20 percent in the same period. It should be noted that four of the seven funds studied are showing higher growth rates on their loans outstanding compared to the growth in deposits, indicating that the funds are becoming less reliant on bank deposits and are converting an increasing portion of their assets into loans for the needy.

Shari'a aspect

While there has been no denying the role played by minority funds in improving the economic situation of a large number of people through the provision of saving and credit facilities and they are highly praised for their contribution to the cause of education and health, the one area where these funds are criticized is their non-adherence to *shari'a* principles. Two aspects of minority funds' functioning have received special attention in this regard, one is that they charge a principal based fee from the borrower and another they earn interest by keeping a substantial portion of their deposits in conventional banks. In fact a major portion of

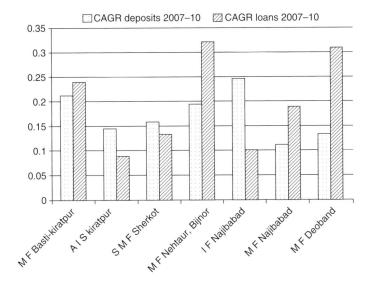

Figure 11.5 Growth of minority funds in terms of deposits and loans 2007–10

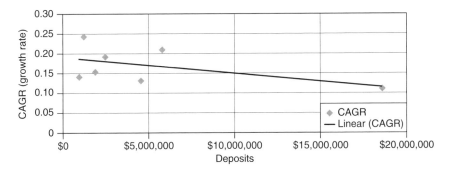

Figure 11.6 Growth of funds in 2007–08 to 2009–10 against their size

operating expenses of some of these funds is met through the interest received on their deposits. These aspects of minority funds' operations have been discussed by the scholars under the aegis of Islamic Fiqh Academy of India. The Academy has categorized these activities of minority funds as abhorred from the *shari'a* viewpoint. The Academy, in its Third Fiqhi Seminar, ruled that it is not permissible to charge anything other than the principal amount lent to the borrower in whatever forms it may be. Further the Academy ruled it unlawful (*haram*) to keep the depositor's money in commercial banks for the purpose of earning interest.[25]

While providing solutions, the Academy exhorted the affluent members of the community to bear the operational expenses of the funds. The Academy also suggests investments of the savings/capital into *shari'a*-compliant income-generating activities. Some of the *ulema* on the other hand supported the idea of service charges only in case the funds are not able to generate enough resources by themselves and contributions from the affluent class is insufficient to meet the entire expenses (Islamic Fiqh Academy).

Conclusions and suggestions

Minority funds have been doing a tremendous job in providing financial services to the lower strata of the society. While the funds are presently operating on a completely different paradigm from MFIs, some lessons can be shared. Minority funds are serving the much required need of encouraging and facilitating savings and while collateral-based lending has its limitations in lending to people with dire problems, it checks the problem of over indebtedness that is reported among scores of MFI borrowers. Minority funds reinforce and highlight the importance of leveraging the strong social fabric embedded in economically backward societies in developing financial and welfare services catering to them. Emphasis here should be placed on meaningfully utilizing social relationships to build a system that can benefit the people. Unlike microfinance where people are pitted against each other for loans and liable for each other's defaults, minority funds utilize social associations and bonds to generate resources, build trust and enable a system to function and serve the economic interests of the needy.

In their outlook towards the future, minority funds would have to expand their scope of lending to finance business enterprises among their clients to tackle the problem of poverty at its source. Another immediate task in front of the minority funds is the need to refine their audit mechanisms to make them more foolproof and transparent. The funds are presently critically dependent on social relationships and reputation in their functioning and this makes them vulnerable to management upheavals and the changing political dynamics within communities. It is suggested that the funds publish their accounts and make them available to the general public for review.

Exhibits

Exhibit 1: Comparison of minority funds operational in the country

Table 11.2 General and operational details of minority funds

Fund	Started in the year	Branches	Employees	Deposits in 2009–10	Asset Holding			Interest charged	Operating costs
					Loans	Fixed deposits and investments	Cash and current acc.		
Muslim Fund Basti-Kiratpur Awami Imdadi Society, Kiratpur	1977	8	108	$57,84,441	24%	50%	25%	12%	$220,000
	1997	4	65	$9,36,527	39%	<10%	50%	12%	$88,000
Sherkot Muslim Fund, Sherkot	1974	1	23	$18,97,660	47%	—	40–50%	12%	$48,000
Muslim Fund Nehtaur, Bijnor	1972	1	13	$24,58,254	50%	40–50%	10%	10%	$44,000
Islami Fund Najibabad	1984	4	30	$11,86,130	41%	40–50%	8–10%	12%	$55,000
Muslim Fund Najibabad	1971	33	241	$1,85,40,761	35%	35–45%	20–30%	12%	$930,000
Muslim Fund Deoband	1961	2	55	$45,43,351	30%	30%	40%	10%	$200,000

Source: Balance sheet and personal interviews.

Note
Conversion rate of 1 USD = 45.39 INR.

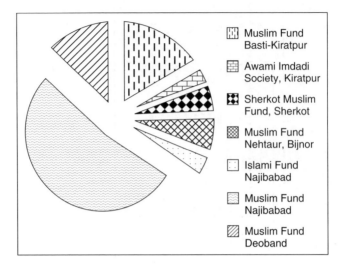

Figure 11.7 Relative sizes of the funds: deposits in 2009–10

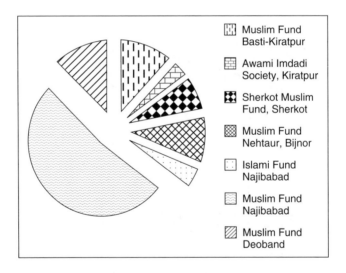

Figure 11.8 Relative sizes of the funds: deposits in 2009–10

Exhibit 2: Financial details of minority funds

Table 11.3 Financial details of the minority funds

	Deposits			Loan and advances			No. of Beneficiaries			Employees
	2007–08	2008–09	2009–10	2007–08	2008–09	2009–10	2007–08	2008–09	2009–10	2009–10
Muslim Fund Basti-Kiratpur	$39,37,032	$46,52,993	$57,84,441	$9,18,287	$11,57,519	$14,09,521	3219	4097	4825	108
Awami Imdadi Society, Kiratpur	$7,14,780	$8,22,675	$9,36,527	$3,12,177	$3,45,786	$3,69,782	2440	4570	6700	65
Sherkot Muslim Fund, Sherkot	$14,14,282	$17,08,365	$18,97,660	$6,87,120	$7,63,645	$8,82,662	1579	1737	1728	23
Muslim Fund Nehtaur, Bijnor	$17,23,049	$19,45,715	$24,58,254	$7,06,831	$9,36,614	$12,33,477	n/a	n/a	n/a	13
Islami Fund Najibabad	$7,63,518	$8,82,720	$11,86,130	$3,96,578	$4,26,309	$4,80,428	780	833	865	30
Muslim Fund Najibabad	$1,49,93,748	$1,59,89,132	$1,85,40,761	$45,39,366	$56,57,266	$64,17,860	n/a	n/a	241	
Muslim Fund Deoband	$35,36,659	$38,45,354	$45,43,351	$8,41,874	$9,47,758	$14,42,213	3083	3623	3860	55
Total	$2,70,83,069	$2,98,46,954	$3,53,47,125	$84,02,234	$1,02,34,897	$1,22,35,944	8018	11237	14118	535

Source: Balance sheet information.

Note
Conversion rate of 1 USD = 45.39 INR.

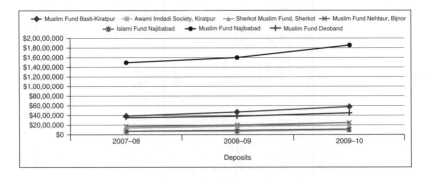

Figure 11.9 Growth of deposits held from 2007–08 to 2009–10 (all figures in INR)

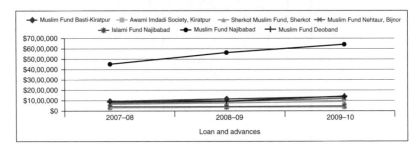

Figure 11.10 Growth of loans outstanding from 2007–08 to 2009–10 (all figures in INR)

Exhibit 3: Involvement of the funds in welfare activities

Table 11.4 Involvement of the funds in welfare activities

Parent fund	Institution supported	Contribution to welfare in 2009–10
Muslim Fund Basti-Kiratpur	Public Girls Junior High School Mushtaq Public Charitable Hospital	$25,125
Muslim Fund Nehtaur, Bijnor	Muslim Fund Girls High School	$11,975
Islami Fund Najibabad	Islamia Girls Jr High School	$1,146
Muslim Fund Najibabad	Aagosh Charitable Hospital Najibabad Aagosh Charitable Hospital Delhi Prposed LTI	$11,975
Muslim Fund Deoband	Public Girls Higher Secondary School Computer Training Center Motor Driving Training Center Madani Eye Hospital Madani Technical Institute	$8,231
Awami Imdadi Society, Kiratpur		$3,516
Sherkot Muslim Fund, Sherkot	Construction of Girls School	$58,371

Note
Conversion rate of 1 USD = 45.39 INR.

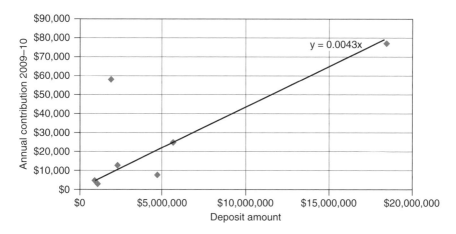

Figure 11.11 Contribution to welfare vs. deposits collected by the funds

Exhibit 4: Loan terms of the minority funds

Table 11.5 Loan terms of the minority funds

Fund	Effective interest rate (simple interest)	Maximum loan amount	Loan amount vs. collateral*	Duration of loan	Loans given for businesses	Interest charge waivers
Muslim Fund Basti-Kiratpur	12%	$419	44–56%	Open ended	No	Waivers for
Awami Imdadi Society, Kiratpur	12%	$441	44–50%	Open ended	No	widows, orphans
Sherkot Muslim Fund, Sherkot	12%	$430	44–50%	Open ended	3%	and farmers
Muslim Fund Nehtaur, Bijnor	10%	$1,102	56%	Open ended	Yes	facing crop
Islami Fund Najibabad	12%	$1,102	56%	Open ended	Yes	failure
Muslim Fund Najibabad	12%	$419	56%	Open ended	No	
Muslim Fund Deoband	10%	$1,102	44–50%	Open ended	Yes	

Note
* Gold price 10 grams = $396.56 and 1 USD = 45.39 INR.

Appendix 1

Table 11.6 Comparison of different sources of funds

Sources of funds	Advantages	Disadvantages
Grants, soft loans	• Facilitate lending institution start-ups: • Substitute for commercial funds that wholesale financial institutions will not or cannot provide; • Substitute for deposits that cannot be mobilized due to legal restrictions	• Lack of ownership: • Lack of market-based incentives to ensure sustainability; • Volatility and scarcity of funds does not allow for sustained institutional growth; • MFI more donor-oriented than client-oriented; • Clients' perception of the institutions as donor-driven.
Commercial loans	• Large amounts of funds can be mobilized on a permanent basis; • Low administrative costs; • Incentives for good governance and management.	• High financial costs; • High guarantee or collateral requirements.
Compulsory deposits	• Facilitate access to loans for the very poor; • Instill thriftiness and discipline.	• Inhibit future mobilization of voluntary savings; • Increase effective costs of borrowing; • Low volumes of funds mobilized; • Number of depositors restricted to number of potential borrowers.
Wholesale deposits Time deposits/ CDs	• Large amounts of funds can be mobilized; • Low administrative costs; • Incentives for good governance and management.	• High financial costs; • High liquidity risks (volatility) due to concentration; • Large depositors may require complementary financial services (overdrafts, credit cards etc.); • Large depositors may interfere in operations; • Eventually, costs due to external regulation and supervision and minimum reserve requirements.
Small and micro deposits Demand deposits and passbook accounts	• Satisfy an effective demand for savings facilities of microclients; • Large amounts of stable funds can be mobilized on a permanent basis; • Low financial costs; • Synergies between savings and lending reduces operating costs; • Even stronger incentives for good governance and management.	• Possibly higher administrative costs compared to other sources of funds; • Higher institutional requirements in treasury management, controls, etc.; • Eventually, costs due to external regulation and supervision and minimum reserve requirements.
Capital shares	• Risk-bearing funds; • Most stable funding source; • Leverage device for liabilities; • Owners generally interested in increasing profits through sound management.	• High capital costs due to risk premium required by owners; • High information costs; • Profit-orientation might reorient financial institutions towards better-off clients.

Source: Wisniwski, S. (1999). *Microsavings Compared to other Sources of Funds.* Eschborn: CGAP.

Notes

1 Khan, J.A. and Nisar, S. (2004). Collateral (*al-rahn*) as Practiced by Interest-free Credit Societies. *Journal of King Abdul Aziz University: Islamic Economics Jeddah*, 17–34.
2 Ibid.
3 Hoff, K. and Stiglitz, J.E. (1993). Imperfect Information and Rural Credit Markets: Puzzles and Policy Perspectives. In A.B. Klara Hoff, *The Economics of Rural Organization. Theory, Practices and Policy* (pp. 33–52). Oxford: Oxford University Press.
4 Hanning, D.A. (1999). Mobilizing Microsavings: The Millennium Challenge in Microfinance. *Sixth Consultative Group Meeting of CGAP*.
5 Vogel, R. (1984). Savings Mobilization: The Forgotten Half of Rural Finance. In D.G.D. Adams, *Undermining Rural Development with Cheap Credit* (pp. 248–265). Boulder, CO: Westview Press.
6 Wright, G. (1999). *A Critical Review of Savings Servicesin Africa and Elsewhere*. Nairobi: MicroSave.
7 Op. cit. Hanning, D.A., 1999.
8 Panagariya, A. (2006). *Bank Branch Expansion and Poverty Reduction: A Comment:* http://www.columbia.edu/~ap2231/technical%20papers/Bank%20Branch%20Expansion%20and%20Poverty.pdf.
9 Burgess, R., Pande, R. and Wong, G. (2005). Banking for the Poor: Evidence from India. *Journal of European Economic Association*, 268–78.
10 Op. cit. Panagariya, A., 2006.
11 Op. cit. Hoff, K. and Stiglitz, J.E., 1993.
12 Tsai, K.S. (2004). Imperfect Substitutes: The Local Political Economy of Informal Finance and Microfinance in Rural China and India. *World Development*, 32(9): 1487–1507.
13 Sa Dhan (2005). *Side by Side: A Slice of Microfinance Operations in India*. New Delhi: Sa Dhan.
14 Basu, P. and Srivastava, P. (2005). Scaling-up Microfinance for India's Rural Poor. World Bank Policy Research Working Paper 3646.
15 Morduch, J. (1999a). Between the State and the Market: Can Informal Insurance patch the Safety Net? *World Bank Research Observer*, 14(2): 187–207.
16 Feibig, M., Hanning, A. and Wisniwski, S. (1999). *Savings in the Context of Microfinance– State of Knowledge*. Eschborn: GTZ: CGAP Working Paper on Savings.
17 Adams, D.W. and Pischke, J.V. (1991). *Microenterprise Credit Programs: Deja Vu*. Columbus, OH: Agricultural Finance Program, The Ohio State University.
18 Ibid.
19 Op. cit. Burgess, R., Pande, R. and Wong, G., 2005.
20 Op. cit. Hanning, D.A., 1999.
21 Srinivasan, N. (2009). *Microfinance India State of the Sector Report 2009*. New Delhi: Sage Publications India Pvt Ltd.
22 Reddy, R. (2010, April 19). State for De-recognition of MFIs. Retrieved December 16, 2010, from *The Hindu* online edition of India's national newspaper: http://www.hindu.com/2010/04/19/21hdline.htm.
23 NDTV (2010, October 15). After 20 Suicides, Andhra Pradesh to Monitor Micro Finance. Retrieved December 15, 2010, from NDTV: http://www.ndtv.com/video/player/news/after-20-suicides-andhra-pradesh-to-monitor-micro-finance/169794.
24 Op. cit. Khan, J.A. and Nisar, S., 2004.
25 Mazhari, S.A. (1990). Banking Without Interest. *Proceedings of Third Fiqhi Seminar on Bay rights, Murabahah and Islamic Banking*, (pp. 602–07). Bangalore: Islamic Fiqh Academy, New Delhi, India.

12 Innovations in Islamic microfinance

Lessons from Muslim Aid's Sri Lankan experiment

Mohammed Obaidullah[1] *and*
Amjad Mohamed-Saleem[2]

Introduction

Microfinance for the poor has few similarities with banking. The well-known Grameen model according to its founder is exactly the opposite of the conventional banking methodology.[3] This model is characterized by the absence of any collateral, of any legal instrument between the lender and the borrower, and any provision to enforce a contract by external intervention, such as a court of law, or any transfer of liability to family members in case of the death of a borrower. While models of microfinance vary in terms of exact features, they are invariably characterized by an overwhelming concern for the welfare of their members and clients. Profit seeking is seen as a means to ensure sustainability and not an end in itself. While *shari'a* distinguishes between commercial and benevolent transactions and provides an elaborate framework for both kind of transactions that would ensure their freedom from *riba, gharar* and other prohibitions, some activities of microfinance institutions (MFIs) may not even involve contractual arrangements and stipulations and would call for a benevolence-driven framework rather than a prohibition-driven framework.

Where contracts form the basis of activities of MFIs, the distinction between microfinance and commercial banking should be clearly recognized in product development efforts. Many classical *shari'a*-nominate contracts have been modified by contemporary Islamic jurists to suit the needs of mainstream commercial banks. Arguably, these commercial banking products may not be appropriate for microfinance, given the points of difference between the two. Islamic microfinance product development albeit challenging would remain as a natural response to the needs of this sector.[4] A recent study by the World Bank's Consultative Group to Assist the Poor (CGAP)[5] indicates that the industry lacks a profound degree of product diversification and most firms offer only one or two *shari'a*-compliant products. Another recent study[6] on microfinance in three Islamic Development Bank member countries, Turkey, Bangladesh and Indonesia, notes that while there may be a multitude of *shari'a*-compliant modes of microfinance, it is important to take note of their comparative features to identify the ones that are practically and operationally more suitable than others. The present chapter captures these concerns, demonstrates the case of an innovative microfinance product being used successfully in Sri Lanka and highlights the richness of classical Islamic legal framework in providing such innovative solutions.

Bay' al-salam or *salam* sale is a deferred delivery mechanism. The classical *salam* has been used primarily as a financing mechanism for the agricultural sector under which farmers would receive the price of the produce in advance at the beginning of agricultural season against an obligation to deliver a defined quantity of the produce to the buyer after a definite time period in future (after harvest). The sale price received in advance is thus available to the farmer as a means of financing all farming-related needs. Another advantage is that the farmers do not have to sell their produce at a time when the market has an oversupply due to harvest, thus depressing the prices and bringing down the realized income of farmers. While the mechanism provides for much-needed financing, it is subject to abuse by unscrupulous middlemen and traders who seek to take advantage of low bargaining power of the poverty-ridden farmers and execute *salam* at unrealistically low prices. To counter this, mutuality-based models of microfinance have been suggested. Farmers' cooperative organizations can dramatically enhance the bargaining power of farmers and replace middlemen. In a *salam*-based framework, these cooperatives would provide funds in the form of advance price and would take delivery of the produce after harvest as above. The cooperative would also create appropriate warehousing facilities for storage of the produce and market the same in a manner that avoids depressed prices resulting in increased income for the members. It may be noted that an act of seeking to even out supply to counter exploitation should be clearly distinguished from the evil practice of hoarding or creating artificial scarcity in the market. Recent experiments of *salam*-based financing by Islamic banks have not been very successful however. El Zahi (2002)[7] documents the predicament of Sudanese Islamic banks extending *salam*-based financing to farmers in the form of advance sale prices only to witness large-scale diversion of funds away from intended use in farming and defaults at the time of delivery of the produce at harvest time. Another problem with classical *salam* for the financier arises out of its exposure to price risk or market risk. A financier who is not an astute player in the market for the concerned commodity and does not fully understand the economics of pricing in this market may be confronted with adverse prices and consequent losses when the financier seeks to sell the produce upon delivery by the farmer(s). This problem is taken care of in value-based *salam* as the case study highlights. The case study in this chapter is believed to be the first documented application of value-based *salam*, a creative variant of classical *salam* in the context of Islamic microfinance. The innovation enables a financier to hedge the risk of volatile agricultural prices associated with the classical *salam* sale.

Recent economic trends in Sri Lanka have discouraged paddy cultivation, paving the way for imports of rice, which is the main staple food of Sri Lankans. This chapter outlines a model developed and piloted by Muslim Aid Sri Lanka based on a combination of two *shari'a*-based modes—*salam* sale and *mudaraba* partnership—to empower poor paddy farmers from Sri Lanka. The model was developed to reduce the dependence of the poor farmers on financier-middlemen which resulted in the exploitation of the farmers through high-interest loans and artificially depressed market prices during harvesting season.

Project overview

The Sri Lankan agriculture sector has a long history of subsidies, government interventions and local food security measures. It is characterized by a decline in paddy cultivation over the last few decades. This is attributable to several reasons, such as lack of productivity, lack of sufficient income in the sector, increase of production cost and, above all, the ethnic conflict plaguing the country. These reasons may be interrelated. Therefore any rational response to this must involve a holistic approach. An average Sri Lankan farmer owns not more than two acres of paddy land. The only available financing option before him is to either pawn household assets, such as jewelry or mortgage the paddy fields with moneylenders (often the middlemen) with the hope of paying back the loan with interest after harvest and perhaps redeeming the mortgaged property. Therefore, should there be a crop failure, the mortgaged property would be lost. Indeed, there have been incidents of farmers resorting to suicide on being unable to pay the debts. Moreover most middlemen bargain to purchase the crop at a very low price and the farmer usually has no other option but to sell it to these middlemen. In addition mill owners also have to take loans from banks in order to purchase the paddy to process and sell on the market. This is normally given at a high interest rate. The farmer is, therefore, caught in a vicious cycle of poverty. While the government of Sri Lanka has initiated several programs in the past to enhance the paddy cultivation through fertilizer subsidies, renovating irrigation systems and even cheaper microfinance loans, these have repeatedly failed to have the desired impact. The suggested model emphasizes on "farmer participation" throughout the process as a "cooperative" or "association" to increase the bargaining power of the individual farmers and also to get a better value for their efforts.

Muslim Aid (MA) used a multi-stage model for provision of finance and other inputs to the farmers. The first stage involves a creative variant of the classical *bay' al-salam* or "deferred delivery" transaction. Under this mechanism, a farmer was provided funds in advance against a forward sale of his produce at the time of harvest. The funds were used by the farmer to finance purchase of the necessary inputs to start paddy cultivation. Unlike bank financings, no collateral was required from the farmer. Instead, a farmer needed to obtain a set of recommendations from the local mosque and community leaders who acted as guarantors.

The second stage began at harvest time once the agricultural produce was delivered to MA. It involved a partnership between MA and local miller(s) to take possession of the harvested paddy from the farmers, process it and sell the final product at the market with the profit being shared between MA and the miller(s) on the basis of a *mudaraba* partnership.

It was expected that the profit share of MA would cover the administration cost of the financing. In order to ensure that the overall model was on a not-for-profit basis and that it was also sustainable, any surplus profit share over administrative cost was to be used to create a revolving fund for the farmers (see Figure 12.1).

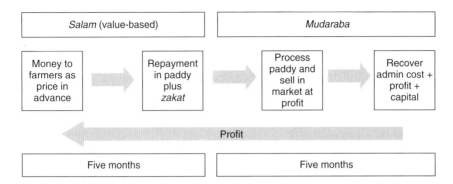

Figure 12.1 Overview of MA model

Farmers enjoying incremental income were also expected to make *zakat* contributions to this fund and therefore, adding to its size and ability to provide financing to greater numbers. This was the third stage of the model.

Application of the model

When the Asian tsunami swept across the Indian Ocean in 2004 it killed more than 200,000 people and washed away the livelihoods of hundreds of thousands of people in the region. After this devastation, very little progress was made in terms of constructive livelihood regeneration to elevate people's lives to the pre-tsunami period. In addition to this, the ethnic conflict in Sri Lanka has made reconstruction efforts extremely difficult. Muttur is one such area that was a victim to both the Tsunami and ethnic conflict. The Muttur division is based in the North east of Sri Lanka and is a part of Trincomalee district. Before the tsunami and at the time of the conflict there was a near absence of manufacturing industries, small trade and service sectors to cater to the basic needs of the local population. Economic activities were based more on fishing, livestock and agriculture with the agriculture and fishing sector being badly affected by the security issues. The people most severely affected by tsunami were those in the lowest income strata who had no stable assets or means of income generation.[8]

In August 2006 around 50,000 people were displaced from Muttur following a deterioration in security. For about six weeks these people were refugees. As the region regained normalcy with improvement in the security situation these people returned and tried to restart their lives. In addition to this, for the first time in about 20 years, much of Muttur and surrounding villages had been cleared of rebel activity and were being repopulated, thereby opening the door for economic activity. There arose an opportunity to re-cultivate land that had been previously abandoned due to the conflict. The returning refugees found themselves strapped for cash as they looked for ways to get back to normalcy. This model was devised in response to the need and tested with two associations: the Jaya Farmers' Association and the Knox Farmers' Association during the "Maha" season (October to February)

2006–07. While the model was experimented on cultivating paddy on irrigated as well as rain-fed lands, it may also be applied to other crops and vegetable cultivation. It is believed though that the capacity and the credibility of the farmers and/or their associations would play a major role in the success of the project.

The Jaya Farmers' Association cultivated 177 acres of paddy with 84 beneficiaries on irrigated lands, whilst the traditional method (rain-fed lands) was implemented with Knox Farmers' Association to cultivate 150 acres of paddy benefiting 83 farmers. Due to the differences in farming methods, cost differences arose between the processes.

Cost of inputs

Costs included preparation and crop maintenance costs. The calculations were per farmer/per acre. The preparation costs included cost of seed paddy, fertilizer and labor and tractor charges. The rain-fed lands (Knox farmers) were ploughed two week earlier than the irrigated lands. Hence they were disadvantaged in getting subsidies in fertilizer and seed paddy due to the delay in government distribution of subsidies. Therefore the average preparation cost of rain-fed land (Knox) was 33 percent higher than irrigated (Jaya) lands. However the maintenance cost of irrigated land was 30 percent higher than the rain-fed lands. Most of the maintenance costs were associated with the buying of additional fertilizer and supervision costs. Therefore the total cost of production did not indicate drastic differences between the two (see Table 12.1). Nevertheless it can be seen that the provision of financing to start the process is essential and productive.

As discussed above, the transactions were done in two stages. The first stage was a *salam* transaction which was in the form of provision of financing of about 3.9 million rupees (Rs) (US$39,000) to the two farmers' associations. These associations in turn provided loans in cash and kind to their members to help them purchase the necessary accessories to allow them to restart their farming. The money was used for hiring of the tractors, expenditure for fertilizer and agrochemicals, expenditure for seed paddy and labor charges (other than the farmer and his family). The work consisted of land preparation, distribution of fertilizers, the sowing of seeds and harvesting the paddy.

Table 12.1 Comparative cost of inputs

Cost of production per farmer/per acre in rupees	Jaya	Knox
Seed paddy	2,823	3,375
Fertilizer	3,390	3,700
Labor		4,500
Tractor charges	3,390	3,750
MA contribution	9,603	15,325
Farmer contribution	12,000	9,500
Total cost	21,603	24,825

Output and repayment

Both the associations claimed some crop failures. However Jaya farmers received a relatively better harvest and hence found it easier to fulfill their commitment regarding delivery of produce. The average yield per acre was 30 and 40 bags (each bag consists of 69kg of paddy) for Knox and Jaya farmers respectively. The Knox Farmers' Association was unable to deliver paddy due to the crop failure and management issues. While the Jaya Farmers' Association was able to do so. The total paddy production of Jaya farmers was estimated to be around 7,080 bags, MA recovered 1,351 bags or 19 percent of the yield. The farmers repayment also included a component of voluntary *zakat* payment (depending on the total harvest received), which was paid to the association, which subsequently was passed on to MA.

The second stage of this project entailed an arrangement between a miller and MA on the basis of a *mudaraba* partnership. The mill owner was recommended from the community and a legal agreement was entered into whereby he would proceed to mill the paddy (that MA had received) and sell the processed paddy at a higher rate (as the price had now increased since harvest time). The financial contribution of MA to the *mudaraba* enterprise was in the form of paddy as *mudaraba* capital plus the processing costs as a *qard* loan. Profits from the business (after repayment of *qard*) were to be shared between both MA as *rabb-al-maal* and the miller as the *mudarib* on an equal basis. Finally in the third stage, after taking back the equivalent of their financing and part of the operational costs, MA then voluntarily proceeded to donate its share of profits to the farmers' associations. All of this was done in a ten-month cycle. This can be explained further with a simple working example as follows.

An example

Farmer X wants to cultivate three acres of paddy. He needs money to prepare and till the land. He intends to take a loan for tilling, fertilizer and seed paddy. Likewise if there are other farmers within his association who would like to take a similar loan, the association will itself apply for the loan on behalf of the farmers. The association can approach banks or in this case it will apply to MA for financing. Assessing the capacity and need, MA will come to an agreement with the farmers' association. The amount of financing is agreed so as to pay for tractor charges, seed paddy and fertilizer whilst the farmer provides the labor costs. Some of the tractor charges are kept for expenses related to machine use during harvesting. MA gives the money to the association and the goods and services are procured by the association and disbursed in kind to the individual members.

Hence farmer X will get his share of Rs 8,470 worth of seed paddy, Rs 10,100 worth of tractor charges and another Rs 10,100 worth of fertilizer in kind as a loan from the association based on his need. Hence his loan from MA is Rs 28,670.

If the harvest is successful, a minimum of 40–60 bags of rice will be the output per acre. Therefore, a three-acre plot of land should yield a minimum of 120 bags

(40 × 3). If the value of each bag is Rs 900 (approximately $9), the total value of the yield (120 bags) will be Rs 108,000 ($1,080).

However with mutual agreement with the farmers, MA will receive as a loan repayment in kind, paddy at a value of Rs 1,000 ($10) per bag. Hence for farmer X, he will need to repay his loan of Rs 28,670, which is the equivalent of 28.67 bags.

This paddy is now given to the miller on a 50/50 profit-sharing basis.

Normally the milling cost will be about Rs 100 (approximately) per bag with the miller usually taking a loan (with interest) to purchase and process the paddy into rice, which he then proceeds to pay back after selling the rice. Hence for 28.67 bags it would cost approximately Rs 2,867 to process.

Processing/milling 28.67 bags of paddy will give on average 1,260 kg of rice. If it is sold at Rs 32 (price as of May 2007 against the current market price of Rs 65 per kg) the total turnover will be Rs 40,320.

The cost of production (investment from MA plus processing costs) is Rs 31,527. Therefore the profit (turnover minus cost of production) is Rs 8,800 (approx.). MA and the miller will share a profit of Rs 4,400 each. This is sufficient for MA to cover the operation cost of the project.

If all farmers have paid back the loan, a percentage of profit may go to them when MA passes on the surplus to the farmers' association to strengthen its funds position and which can be subsequently used to meet basic needs of its members.

Impact of the model

The experiment was conducted in a post-conflict/disaster situation. This is a common practice among development agencies in such a situation to give grants to farmers. Certainly the farmer needs capital to start cultivation and grants or loans from agencies would encourage the farmer to cultivate. However, MA believes that grants may increase "dependency syndrome" as the farmer will continue to seek subsides and grants to cultivate. But with the present model, a revolving fund can be established from where the farmers can continue seeking loans for cultivation with an assurance of repayment. This will empower the farmers' association to be self-reliant and also the farmer to engage and lobby collectively for a better outcome for his efforts.

Ideally, from an Islamic perspective, a farmer should use his own resources before he seeks a loan. This means the farmer should save for the upcoming season. In order to save he needs to get enough profit to reinvest. Hence a better price for his paddy is needed. A way to get a better price is to lobby as an association rather than as individuals. The proposed model facilitates the association to become a lobby in the long run to ensure a fair deal to the farmer. Moreover this model brings the middlemen (some of the millers) to a win–win situation too. Thus, the model encourages local millers to buy paddy, which not only increases local economic activities but also increase local food security.

The model does not intend to distort market prices. However the model expects to build the capacity of the farmers to have a better bargaining position. This may result in increase in market prices of paddy, which is in favor of the farmer. However as there is no fixed price for paddy the market demand and supply will determine the price. Moreover, unless the model is practiced by the majority it is unlikely bring a major impact on the price of paddy at macro level.

The model emphasizes on a cooperative structure of operation throughout the cultivation process. The decision making is done through the association with periodic meetings. This model has a potential to become a strong bargaining platform for subsidies, selling price and other services and facilities. Further, it is anticipated that farmers' associations could become self-reliant within five years or nine financing cycles.

Though in the experiment a component of *zakat* distribution was included, it was not very successful. However future projects can include a collective *zakat* component that will benefit the community at large.

Shari'a *issues*

As is clear from an analysis of the project, the composite model can be viewed as comprising three distinct components or stages. The first stage involves organizing the farmers into a cooperative/association and provision of financing to the cooperative on the basis of *bay' al-salam*. The association as a mutual entity in turn extends *qard* loans to its members to finance their farming related needs. The second stage involves a *mudaraba* partnership of the MFI with the miller under which the former provides *mudaraba* capital in the form of paddy and the miller performs the role of manager or *mudarib*. The MFI also provides funds for covering the processing cost through a *qard* loan that is recovered before profits are calculated and distributed between both parties as per pre-agreed ratio. Thus there is creation of additional value or wealth and its equitable sharing among both the parties. A for-profit mechanism is combined with not-for-profit financing to provide sustainability to the overall model. In the final stage the MFI donates the surplus if any, back to the farmers' cooperative to create a revolving fund to cater to basic needs and provide a safety net to members. The farmers themselves contribute *zakat* to the fund from their augmented income. The fund is expected to mature into a *takaful* fund that can provide micro-*takaful* to its members against unforeseen adversities on an ongoing basis.

Conditions for *shari'a* compliance

In a composite model as above, the first and foremost requirement for *shari'a* compliance is that the terms of the contracts must be clearly and objectively stated and understood by the parties and there must not be any element of interdependence between the contracts. It is important to move from verbal arrangements (that are quite common in a rural setting of a micro-economy) to written contracts. Each contract must be independent of the other in terms of rights and obligations of the parties. For example, if the MFI dons two hats—of a *rabb-al-maal* (capital provider) in the *mudaraba* partnership, and of a lender to the *mudaraba*—the rights of the

MFI being repaid the *qard* loan amount in full is independent of its share in profits or losses.

The cooperative organization is a voluntary association of farmers who become members by contributing a membership amount that should ideally be viewed as a *tabarru'/sadaqah* or a voluntary contribution to the fund and not charged as a fee against various services provided. This is important if the association plans to undertake *takaful* in future on a cooperative and not-for-profit basis to its members.

When the cooperative extends *qard* loans to its members, the contract must be free from any conditions, such as mandatory payment of *zakat* to the revolving fund or payment of any other benefit in kind along with their repayment.

A *shari'a*-compliant innovation

The MFI in the present case extends financing to the cooperative entity based on a value-based *salam* contract. Therefore, it is important here to highlight the difference between classical *salam* and the "value-based" *salam* and examine the *shari'a* basis of the latter. In a classical *salam*, the quantity of object of sale (agricultural produce), the price per unit of the object of sale are pre-determined at the time of contracting. If Q amount of paddy is sold on forward basis at price P on *salam* basis, then the financier (buyer) would pay the value of transaction PQ to the farmer (seller) at the time of contracting (before commencement of farming). After a defined and known time period (harvest time), the farmer would deliver Q amount of paddy to the financier. The financier in turn, would find a way to dispose of Q amount of paddy in the market at the prevailing market price P^*. If market price increases during the financing period, P^* would be higher than P. In other words, P^*Q would be higher than PQ and the financier would have positive profits (P^*Q-PQ). If however (and this is quite likely given the abundant supply of produce during harvesting season) the prevailing market price is depressed and P^* is lower than P, the financier would end up with losses. The value of P^*Q-PQ would be negative.

This market risk or price risk is mitigated in case of a value-based *salam*. In the latter type of *salam*, the MFI would pay an amount (say V) to the farmers' cooperative at the time of the contract against an obligation of the farmer to repay in physical quantities of its produce whose value at the time of delivery at a future date (after harvest) is pre-determined (say V^*). In other words, the farmer would deliver $V^*/P1$ quantity of paddy to the MFI if the future price at the time of delivery is $P1$; $V^*/P2$ quantity of paddy if the future price is $P2$ and V^*/P^* quantity of paddy if the future price is P^*. This settlement value (V^*) may indeed be in excess of the original value (V) received in advance by the farmer resulting in a known profit (V^*-V) to the financier. This form of contracting is not commonplace and is erroneously questioned on twin grounds of (1) violating the condition of pre-specifying quantity and object of sale as in classical *salam* and (2) suspicion of *riba* as the transaction appears dangerously close to cash-for-cash resulting in pre-determined profits.

Suweilem (2007)[9] advocates the use of value-based *salam* as a *shari'a*-compliant hedging device. While noting the approval of scholars such as Ibn Taymiah to value-based *salam*, Suweilem cites the following reasons why value-based *salam* should be accepted as a valid and *shari'a*-compliant product. First, the condition of pre-specifying quantity of produce to be delivered is essentially to avoid possibility of conflict between parties. In value-based *salam*, no such possibility exists. Second, the mechanism neither involves *riba* in form, nor in substance. The buyer in this case receives commodities and not money. Hence, this is not tantamount to cash-for-cash. Indeed the mechanism is exactly equivalent to *murabaha* where the MFI would buy spot and sell on a deferred basis for a mark-up. In value-based *salam* the MFI buys on a deferred basis and sells spot. The only difference is the sequence of steps.

It follows from the above that value-based *salam* would result in pre-determined profits for the MFI that could be further augmented through *mudaraba* in the subsequent phase. An MFI seeking profits as a means of achieving sustainability may opt for this model. The case of MA is however different as it seeks moderate profits only through *mudaraba* with the millers in stage two and not through *salam* with farmers in stage one. MA in the present case ensures that *salam* is undertaken without any element of profits. In other words, for MA, $V = V^*$. The farmers collectively would deliver PQ/P^* quantity of paddy to the MFI. By ensuring equality between funds that MFI originally provided to farmer and what it received later, value-based *salam* enables the MFI to hedge the price risk associated with classical *salam*. The MFI essentially receives back the same amount of funds it provided to the farmers in the beginning and it is easy to see the similarity of this mechanism with a simple *qard* loan that is repayable at par on maturity without any increment. However, they are not same. A merit with *salam* involving physical produce as compared to a *riba*-free financial loan is its effect on market prices that tend to be depressed during harvest. As the case demonstrates, MA in the process of settlement of the transaction is able to intervene in the market with a settlement price that is more equitable to the farmers.

Summary and conclusion

Islamic microfinance, as the case of MA financing for paddy cultivation in Sri Lanka demonstrates, is often a composite mechanism that involves benevolent intervention. Such intervention by an Islamic MFI may use a complex web of contracts that may be based on donations, loans, trade and partnership. However, it is extremely important that all contracts—not-for-profit and for-profit—are independent of each other with the rights and obligations clearly understood by stakeholders. Models of microfinance may vary in terms of exact features, but they are invariably characterized by an overwhelming concern for the welfare of their members and clients. Profit seeking is seen as a means to ensure sustainability and not an end in itself. It follows from the case study that some activities of MFIs may not involve contractual obligations, as exemplified by the overwhelming concern of MA to take care of the safety needs of the poor farmers, to build a sustainable source of funds for them as a cooperative organization and to free them from exploitation by trader-middlemen by intervention through the market mechanism. MA also seeks to create a win–win situation for the trader-middlemen by forming a partnership with them. Needless to say, the ultimate objective of an Islamic MFI is benevolence and benevolence alone. Profits are a means to achieve benevolence that sustains itself and are not an end in themselves.

The study also highlights the need to move beyond the "popular" Islamic banking instruments, such as *murabaha*, and to search for innovative and appropriate solutions. This study on financing paddy cultivation for impoverished and displaced farmers is demonstrative of one such *shari'a*-compliant innovative solution that involves the use of value-based *salam* and *mudaraba* in a benevolence-driven framework as distinct from a prohibition-driven framework. Of course, the framework remains free from *shari'a* prohibitions relating to *riba* and *gharar*. The study also highlights the need to develop the institutions of *zakat* and perhaps cash *waqf* and integrate them with microfinance initiatives.

Islamic MFIs should practice inclusive microfinance. The beauty of the MA model is that it addresses the needs of all stakeholders—the farmers as well as the millers—and therefore should encourage an interest in agriculture contributing to food security. A mutuality-based cooperative model of organizing the farmers is seen as the preferred alternative to improve their bargaining power on the one hand and to ensure proper end use of funds on the other. Of no less importance is the need to do away with farmers' dependence. Dependence, whether on government grants or on *zakat*, is incompatible with true empowerment. A holistic approach to livelihood development that includes the use of market mechanisms as the tool of intervention as demonstrated in the present study should lead to desired outcomes.

Notes

1 Senior Economist, Islamic Research and Training Centre, Islamic Development Bank, Jeddah, Saudi Arabia.
2 Country Director, Muslim Aid, Sri Lanka.
3 Yunus, M. "Each of You Has the Power to Change the World." Boston: Lecture at MIT, June 6, 2008.
4 Obaidullah, M. and Khan, T. "Islamic Microfinance Development: Challenges and Initiatives." Islamic Research and Training Institute, Islamic Development Bank, Policy Dialogue Paper No. 2, 2008.
5 Nimrah, K. et al. "Islamic Microfinance: An Emerging Market Niche." CGAP: Focus Notes, No. 49, 2008.
6 Obaidullah, M. "Role of Microfinance in Poverty Alleviation: Lessons from Selected IDB Member Countries." Islamic Research and Training Institute, Islamic Development Bank, 2008.
7 El-Zahi, A. "The X-Efficiency of Sudanese Islamic Banks (1989–98)." International Islamic University, Malaysia, unpublished PhD thesis, 2002.
8 DLDP (District Livelihood Development Programme) report, prepared by University of Colombo, facilitated by RADA (Reconstruction and Development Agency), Livelihood Development Unit and Ministry of Labour Relations and Foreign Employment, Technical Advisory Support: ILO-IRTAP, 2006.
9 Suweilem, Sami. "Hedging in Islamic Finance." Islamic Development Bank, Islamic Research and Training Institute, 2007, pp. 131–35.

Part IV

Resources on Islamic microfinance

13 Information sources on Islamic microfinance

A critical literature review

Islamic Finance Project Staff[1]

Introduction

With the potential of microfinance to reach out to a plethora of low-income societal groups, and provide them with financial access, and the vision of Islamic economics which is to restructure society on the basis of socio-economic justice and equality, it is astonishing to note that there are still three billion people in the world who do not have access to basic financial services. Despite the willingness of the poor populations of most economies to start up their own projects, they lack the necessary means to finance these projects. Is the union of microfinance and Islamic finance a solution to this unsatisfied demand? Is Islamic microfinance a sustainable solution to the problems currently facing the microfinance sector? Is Islamic microfinance the new poverty-alleviation accelerator that the world needs?

The primary motive of every government and every country's finance minister is to account for a sound and stable financial system in the economy, and try to alleviate poverty. However, it appears that there is no evidence of a system that has succeeded in the above-mentioned attempts. With the emergence, instant success and exponential growth of the microfinance sector, it has been claimed that microfinance has the potential to eradicate global poverty. This claim obviously comes with its share of criticism and debate; how does microfinance aim to defeat poverty, if it charges its high-risk, poor customers, excessive rates of interest? The sector is getting carried away by its potential to generate profits; there is an increasing number of microfinance institutions (MFIs) that have started operating under the business objectives of the commercial world, with profits and expansion being their main aim. MFIs have started to go *public*, when the only beneficiaries of this sector, as stated by Muhammad Yunus, should be the poor population it was initially created for. Of course, other social goals such as justice and equality, and a proper distribution of income and wealth, remain just as unattainable and distant as the sector is moving farther away from its actual goals.

The Harvard Islamic Finance Project (IFP), part of the Islamic Legal Studies Program at Harvard Law School, is a program that explores new opportunities in the research and development of the field of Islamic finance. In support of this mission, a commendable effort has been made by the IFP in the form of a compilation of a specialized annotated bibliography of Islamic microfinance sources.

This compilation is a significant platform, bringing together a vast array of Islamic microfinance sources, which looks at the burgeoning sector through a microscopic eye. The bibliography features a total of 128 items, inclusive of published and unpublished articles, reports and presentations. Many of the papers in this compilation are a consequence of the growing number of Islamic microfinance meetings and conferences around the globe. The Islamic Development Bank's Islamic Research Training Institute (IRTI), particularly, has been sponsoring such conferences to generate interest, research and development in the field. Also worth mentioning are the Islamic microfinance project proposals that are included in this bibliography; these are an evidence of the new models of Islamic microfinance being researched, developed and proposed by experts in the field. These diverse projects range from an alternative development project in Northern Lebanon to a housing microfinance model to a Chicago-based *shari'a*-compliant investment financing project to *Al-Taawun*, a cash savings reserve model built on community cooperation and trust.

The bibliography brings together sources that shed light on the strengths and weaknesses of conventional MFIs, talk about Islamic microfinance being the more effective counterpart to microfinance and, most importantly, establish the Islamic microfinance sector as a feasible and viable contributor to poverty alleviation.

Islamic microfinance emerging as a stronger counterpart to conventional microfinance

Islamic microfinance overcomes the problem of exorbitant interest rates that conventional microfinance comes with, besides being an acceptable means of finance to the estimated 72 percent of people living in Muslim-majority countries that do not resort to conventional financial services (Honohon 2007) due to religious or cultural reasons. Replacing the traditional interest-based financing technique with mostly profit and loss sharing techniques, the exponential growth of the Islamic microfinance sector, considering its humble beginnings, is now being acknowledged by international governments and organizations as a new paradigm to poverty alleviation: "Islamic Microfinance has the potential to expand access to finance to unprecedented levels throughout the Muslim World," as quoted in the Consultative Group to Assist the Poor (CGAP) Focus Note, "Islamic Microfinance: An Emerging Market Niche." CGAP, in collaboration with Deutsche Bank, Islamic Development Bank and Grameen–Jameel, announced the Islamic Microfinance Challenge in early 2010 in an effort to canvass the industry for new ideas for sustainable, scalable and authentic Islamic microfinance business models to meet the financial needs of the Muslim poor. Organizing sponsors will grant the finalist US$100,000 in prize funds to be used to implement a pilot project of the finalist's proposed business model.

In his paper "Financing Microenterprises: An Analytical Study of Islamic Microfinance Institutions", Habib Ahmed (2002) talks about financing microenterprises as a "new paradigm." Ahmed talks about the success of MFIs in providing credit to millions of people worldwide; however, most of this financing is "interest-based," with the MFIs' social development programs being mostly secular in nature. Ahmed also points out that the Islamic microfinance sector has been modeled upon the strength of the conventional microfinance sector, with the scope to correct some of the inherent problems that exist within the conventional system.

Muhammad Taqi Usmani's *An Introduction to Islamic Finance* (2000b) remains an invaluable resource for Islamic microfinance developers, containing important guidelines to be followed in developing any Islamic microfinance products as it deals with the fundamental issues of *shari'a*-compliant finance, which also includes Islamic microfinance.

The rationale behind the prohibition of interest (*riba*) in the Islamic *shari'a* is related to the promotion of the Islamic idea of an ethical, moral, fair and just society. Therefore, alternate means of finance to interest-based means, prescribed by Islamic finance, adhere to these Islamic principles. Asad Kamran Ghalib talks about how Islamic modes of finance "can be employed by Microfinance Institutions to enable poor micro-entrepreneurs to gain access to the use of assets which otherwise have been unattainable" in his (2008) paper, "Re-thinking Leasing from an Islamic Perspective: The Prospects of Islamic Micro-leasing for Poverty Alleviation."

Unlocking the door to global poverty alleviation

It is interesting that even though microfinance was initially identified to be a poverty-alleviating mechanism, there has been a general concern that it increases the disparity between the rich and the poor sectors of the economy; the high interest rates on the micro-loans that are lent to the poor being what widens this gap. The Islamic microfinance model provides for an interest-free start-up of micro-enterprises, hence overcoming this problem. Even so, if Islamic finance does have the potential to reach out to the segment of society that conventional microfinance fails to cater for, what is its current role in global poverty alleviation? The findings of a global survey on Islamic microfinance carried out by CGAP in 2007 show that "Islamic microfinance has a total estimated global outreach of only 380,000 customers," this figure being representative of a meager estimate of one-half of 1 percent of total microfinance outreach. What does the Islamic microfinance sector need to do to unlock its great potential to serve as a catalyst towards global poverty alleviation?

The key lies in diversifying the array of Islamic microfinance products, and a systematic supply of these products to satisfy demand. Since Islamic microfinance is a relatively new and upcoming field, with scope for research and development of more diverse products, Islamic microfinance products such as *mudaraba* and *musharaka* are being employed, for the most part, by MFIs to provide financing to micro-businesses and to allow micro-entrepreneurs to save. Whether these financing techniques sustain effectiveness and institutional viability, however, is a question that has been addressed by many sources in the annotated bibliography.

Evaluating Islamic microfinance's financing techniques and opening doors to a diverse number of products

As with conventional microfinance, the problems that exist with the profit-sharing *mudaraba* and *musharaka* models include asymmetric information and adverse selection; while the MFI lacks the ability to fully monitor the client, the client has an incentive to not repay the loan and underreport profits. A *group lending* approach has been identified as a solution to these problems by Gaffar Abdalla Ahmed in his (2008) paper, "Islamic Microfinance Practices with a Particular Reference to Financing Entrepreneurs through Equity Participation Contracts in Sudanese Banks," and by Habib Ahmed in his (2007) paper, "*Waqf*-based Microfinance: Realizing the Social Role of Islamic Finance." The idea of "social collateral" entails forming a group, with every member monitoring other group members; this model of peer monitoring partially addresses the problem of asymmetric information, and reduces transaction costs involved in monitoring for the MFI, as noted by Habib Ahmed in his paper.

Alternate solutions to manage the risk involved in financing the poor include the possibility of financing through a Special Purpose Vehicle/Entity (SPV/E), as well as resorting to *zakat* and *awqaf* as a means of financing. While minimizing the credit risk, these financing techniques also have an expansive scope for research and development, which if exploited, would help diversify the Islamic microfinance sector. Asyraf Wajdi Dusuki analyzes the implementation of SPVs in his (2008) paper, "Banking for the Poor: The Role of Islamic Banking in Microfinance Initiatives." SPVs, being tax-exempt legal entities created to undertake specific activities of the sponsoring firm, are characterized to serve as effective vessels to carry the microfinance agenda. Dusuki talks about the "bankruptcy remote" nature of SPVs, which prevents creditors from seizing its assets, as one of these essential characteristics; being bankruptcy-remote would also prevent the sponsoring Islamic bank from any adverse effect of the microfinance activities. Hence, the institutional viability and sustainability of the sponsoring firm would always be maintained.

The ideas of *zakat* and *awqaf* are key in the development of the Islamic microfinance sector; these Islamic principles that have been followed and practiced for centuries. An institution governed by these principles can have multiplier effects in the economy such as poverty-reduction and income and wealth equalization. The benefits of such a model have been explored by Habib Ahmed in his aforementioned paper, "*Waqf*-based Microfinance: Realizing the Social Role of Islamic Finance," where he talks about *waqf, qard hasan, zakat* and *sadaqah* as means to "effectively alleviate absolute poverty" if integrated into microfinancing programs. In his theoretical framework of an alternative *waqf*-based Islamic MFI, Ahmed identifies group-lending and weekly repayments of loans as an effective moderator of the credit risk problem, and the use of *waqf* as a financing means to sustain the financial/institutional viability of these institutions. The Islamic Financial Services Board and IRTI also identify the integration of *zakat* and *awqaf* in financial sector reforms as significant factors in shaping the microfinance sector, in their (2007) paper, "Islamic Microfinance Development: Challenges and Initiatives." The paper interestingly notes findings of a recent CGAP survey that concludes that the member donors, the

World Bank, the Asian Development Bank, the Inter-American Development Bank and the European Commission are among the largest public funders of microfinance. In the field of Islamic microfinance, however, the Islamic Development Bank is perceived to be the most prominent contributor. The need for financing means, such as *awqaf*, to fund the Islamic microfinance sector can hence be extrapolated. The importance of these Islamic financing techniques has been highlighted by many writers and authors in this bibliography. In his (2007) paper, "Applications of *Awqaf* and Islamic Microfinance in a Post-Soviet Secular State: A Hypothetical Model of *Awqaf*-based Credit Unions," Fuad Aliyev argues that the revival of the institution of *awqaf* is necessary; its development and potential role in poverty reduction through introduction of the "community capitalism" model is still undiscovered.

Finally, another model worth mentioning is Anas Zarka's monetary *waqf* for microfinance. In his paper (2007, and also see Chapter 6), Zarka talks about the "great reserve of goodwill towards the poor and needy" that most human beings possess and that is nurtured by Islam and all other religions. His monetary *waqf* model employs "philanthropic resources" to allow people of "average means" to be a part of poverty alleviation through microfinance.

However, even though many of the esteemed sources in this bibliography envision the *awqaf* mechanism to play a great role in furthering Islamic microfinance's great mission, it can be argued that the *waqf* is not a truly infallible solution to the sector's current failures. The *waqf* might be resistant to market forces, but it does not have the resources to be completely non-adaptive, owing to its rigid and specific nature. Some *waqf* property could be more efficiently allocated if it were isolated from the entirety of the *waqf*.

Conclusion

Any business that is a part of an Islamic economic system is built upon a foundation of Islamic values; it ensures that all basic needs of the economy are met; it is geared towards eliminating poverty in society and addressing every individual's basic needs. With the idea that an Islamic society is built upon mutual cooperation and trust, the Islamic microfinance sector's application of Islamic finance instruments together with other mechanisms such as *zakat* and *waqf* are bound to accelerate the income equality and poverty-alleviation motto that the sector was founded on. Besides, the increasing awareness of the potential of the Islamic microfinance sector is attracting attention from an increasing number of international organizations, such as Deutsche Bank, as well as encouraging academics, scholars and researchers to enter the field. The line-up of new research techniques and product development that this increasing awareness has in store for the sector is a great sign of hope, and something for the entire financial sector to look forward to.

Note

1 A number of Islamic Finance Project (Harvard Law School) researchers have participated in the compilation of the bibliography since 2007; the Project is especially grateful to Neha Tahir in preparing the critical review.

Annotated bibliography

Abdalla, Mustafa Gamal-Eldin. "Partnership (*Musharaka*): A New Option for Financing Small Enterprises?" *Arab Law Quarterly*, Vol. 14, No. 3, 1999, pp. 257–267.

Abstract: The importance and magnitude of small and micro-enterprises at a national as well as a multi-national level are discussed. It touches on the financing problems of this sector and proceeds to provide examples of micro-enterprises in Sudan that have dealt with this issue. Furthermore, the main Islamic financing methods that have been adopted in Sudan, such as *murabaha, mudaraba* and *musharaka* are highlighted. The article discusses the suitability of each method of financing for small enterprises and goes into further detail with regards to *musharaka* as it outlines the pros and cons of this method. It concludes by suggesting modifications to overcome *musharaka*'s shortcomings.

Abdul Rahman, Abdul Rahim. "Microfinance: An Ethical Alternative to Poverty Alleviation." Paper presented at the *Pre-Forum Workshop on Microfinance: Towards a Sustainable Islamic Finance Model* (Eighth Harvard University Forum on Islamic Finance), at Harvard Law School, Cambridge, MA, April 18, 2008.

Abstract: The primary mission of microfinance is to help the poor in assisting themselves to become economically independent. This paper assesses the potential of Islamic financing schemes for microfinancing purposes. Islamic finance plays an important role in furthering the socio-economic development of poor and small (micro) entrepreneurs by charging interest (read: *riba*). Islamic financing schemes also have moral and ethical attributes that can effectively motivate micro-entrepreneurs to thrive. Islamic finance offers various schemes and instruments that can be advanced and adapted for the purpose of microfinance. Comparatively, *qard hasan, murabaha* and *ijara* schemes are relatively easy to manage and will ensure the capital needs (*qard hasan*), equipments (*murabaha*) and leased equipments (*ijara*) of potential micro-entrepreneurs and the poor. Participatory schemes such as *mudaraba* and *musharaka*, on the other hand, have great potentials for microfinance purposes as these schemes can satisfy the risk sharing needs of micro-entrepreneurs. However, the latter require specialized skills in managing risks inherent in the structure of the contracts. In theory, different schemes can be used for different purposes depending on the risk profile of the micro-entrepreneurs.

Abdul Rahman, Abdul Rahim. "The Islamic Microfinance Potential." *New Horizon*, Issue No. 162, November/December 2006, pp. 9–12.

Abstract: An introduction and brief history of microfinance, including Muhammad Yunus's Grameen Bank is provided. The strengths and weaknesses of several Islamic microfinance schemes are examined such as *mudaraba, musharaka, murabaha, ijara*, and *qard hasan*. Thus far, Islamic microfinancing schemes have not been adopted by Muslim nations. However, Islamic microfinancial schemes will require specialized skills to manage properly in order to place them into effect to directly meet the needs of Muslim micro-entrepreneurs.

Ahmad, Abu Umar Faruq and Ahmad, Rafique A.B. "Islamic Micro and Medium Sized Enterprises Finance: The Case Study of Australia." In *Islamic Finance for Micro and Medium Enterprises* by Mohammed Obaidullah and Hajah Salma Haji Abdul Latiff, Islamic Research Training Institute, Islamic Development Bank and Centre for Islamic Banking, Finance and Management, University of Brunei Darussalam, Jeddah/Brunei, 2008, pp. 233–258.
Abstract: An overview of Islamic finance and the laws that govern it, as well as a background on general microfinance and Islamic microfinance are provided. Microfinance tools can be adapted to meet the financial and economic needs of every local environment. The Islamic microfinance enterprises in Australia that rely on the savings of the shareholders have been very successful in delivering microfinance to their clients. The emergence and development of Islamic MMEs (micro and medium-sized enterprises) finance in Australia is also explored. These MMEs serve to meet the need of financing a large and growing Muslim community while following Islamic tenets. The current realities of the Islamic financial system in Australia in the light of the theories of modern financial intermediation as well as Islamic microfinance contracting are also analyzed. The Islamic microfinance techniques used by the Islamic Financial Services Providers of Australia are also evaluated.

Ahmad, Moid and Mahmood, Athar. "Islamic Venture Capital—a Tool for Social and Economic Development." Paper presented at the *Pre-Forum Workshop on Microfinance: Towards a Sustainable Islamic Finance Model* (Eighth Harvard University Forum on Islamic Finance), at Harvard Law School, Cambridge, MA, April 18, 2008.
Abstract: Venture capital is a source of funding for entrepreneurs. Any entrepreneurial activity is directly proportional to the economic growth of a country. Venture capital encourages entrepreneurs in a country, but the traditional objective of venture capital is to invest in an entrepreneurship venture, breed it, grow it and sell it at a huge profit. This fundamental concept of venture capital is carried forward in Islamic venture capital but follows the basic tenets of Islam and *shari'a*. The first half of the paper redefines the concept of Islamic venture capital and underlines its role in the social and economic development of a country. By encouraging Islamic venture capital, entrepreneurial activity can be exploited to its fullest potential. This would result in economic development coupled by social development, resulting in the removal of social evils such as poverty and unemployment. The latter half of the paper suggests a working model for Islamic venture capital. There exist a number of variants of Islamic venture capital in the existing financial system. There is a lacuna in the system: it is profit oriented. In this model, effort has been made to study the system in totality and suggest a model considering the given constraints in the system and the objective of both social and economic development. The underlying belief behind the concept is that any system that follows the fundamental tenets of Islam is workable, profitable and acceptable to all and benefits all related entities.

Ahmed, Gaffar Abdalla. "Islamic Microfinance Practices with a Particular Reference to Financing Entrepreneurs through Equity Participation Contracts in Sudanese Banks." In *Islamic Finance for Micro and Medium Enterprises* by Mohammed Obaidullah and Hajah Salma Haji Abdul Latiff, Islamic Research Training Institute, Islamic Development Bank and Centre for Islamic Banking, Finance and Management, University of Brunei Darussalam, Jeddah/Brunei, 2008, pp. 75–106.

Abstract: There are many obstacles and factors that influence the decision-making of small and medium enterprises (SMEs) and the performance of the Islamic entrepreneurship projects financed through the banking system in Sudan. Sudanese Islamic banks face the major dilemma of long-term financing of SMEs. For socio-economic development, especially in rural areas, it is important that banking facilities are fairly distributed. The use of the group lending concept in financing *musharaka* to SMEs is recommended. This reduces the administrative work of the bank staff and also increases the security in the case of default. The share of the management in the profit should be fair and indicative of the role of the management in the generation of the profit. The banks should not be allowed to interfere with the management affairs of the SME nor should they be allowed to disclose information about the business without prior consent of the business.

Ahmed, Habib. "Financing Microenterprises: An Analytical Study of Islamic Microfinance Institutions." *Islamic Economic Studies*, Vol. 9, No. 2, March 2002, pp. 27–69.
Abstract: The paper gives a general outline and an implementation plan for the establishment of Islamic microfinance institutions (MFIs). An evaluation of conventional MFIs is followed by the delineation of an Islamic alternative. There is great potential in Islamic MFIs that can cater to the needs of the poor. It is evident from case studies in Bangladesh, that although Islamic MFIs have not used the variety of apparatuses at their hands, nor tapped into all of their potential sources of funding, Islamic MFIs have certain inherent characteristics that could lend themselves to helping the poor.

Ahmed, Habib. "Frontiers of Islamic Banks: A Synthesis of the Social Role and Microfinance." *European Journal of Management and Public Policy*, Vol. 3, No. 1, 2004, pp. 120–140.
Abstract: Islamic MFIs have seen slow progress due to their lack of funds and dearth of trained employees. There is no doubt that the workings of these institutions must be modified to pave the way for economic success among the poor. There is evidence that Islamic banks can provide microfinance services more efficiently and easily due to their broad scale of operations. Results and examples are provided from the experience of the Rural Development Scheme, an MFI based in the Islamic Bank Bangladesh Limited as well as the Islamic Development Bank.

Ahmed, Habib. "Islamic Alternatives to Finance Poverty Focused Group-based Microfinancing." Paper presented at *the Annual Meeting of the IDB with NDFIs*, Tehran, Iran, September 13, 2004.
Abstract: A theoretical framework for MFIs to provide microfinance according to Islamic principles is provided in this paper. The strengths and weaknesses of conventional MFIs are delineated with typical group-based lending named as a positive and moral questionability as a negatives. Because the transactions only involve the transfer of real assets and goods, the problem of the diversion of funds to non-productive uses is alleviated. Currently however, Islamic MFIs are dealing with very high costs of operations. Islamic banks can provide micro-financial services more efficiently and effectively. The varied institutional structures of contemporary Islamic banks can be used to finance poor microenterprises.

Ahmed, Habib. "Role of Zakah and Awqaf in Poverty Alleviation." IDB/IRTI Occasional Paper No. 8. Jeddah: Islamic Development Bank Group, Islamic Research Training Institute, 2004, 150pp.

Abstract: This paper attempts to identify some of the causes and dimensions of poverty and discusses how *zakat* and *awqaf* can be structured in a way that will mitigate poverty. The potentials of *zakat* and *awqaf* are considered. Recommendations and policies are outlined in the paper, based on theoretical discussions and empirical findings.

Ahmed, Habib. "*Waqf*-based Microfinance Realizing the Social Role of Islamic Finance." Paper presented at the *International Seminar on Integrating Awqaf in the Islamic Financial Sector*, Singapore, March 6–7, 2007.
Abstract: The creation of *waqf*-based Islamic MFIs that can provide microfinancing services to the poor may alleviate poverty in the world through Islamically-permissible methods. It identifies the strengths and weaknesses of traditional MFIs; in short, traditional MFIs solve the credit risk problem by institutionalizing group lending and the collection of weekly installments, but do not align with Islamic law due to their collection of interest. Islamic MFIs can use the effective methods of conventional institutions as well as utilize *waqf* to finance their operations, thus reducing financing costs. There risks inherent in a *waqf*-based MFI, including various withdrawal risks. However, these may be mitigated by the use of *takaful* and profit-equalization reserves.

Ahmed, Habib. "Zakah, Macroeconomic Policies and Poverty Alleviation: Lessons from Simulations on Bangladesh." *Journal of Islamic Economics, Banking and Finance*, Vol. 4, No. 2, May–August 2008.
Abstract: The paper studies the role of *zakah* and macroeconomic policies aimed at growth of income and providing opportunities to the poor in eliminating poverty. Simulation of various macro-regimes and *zakah* schemes for Bangladesh indicate that while macroeconomic policies play an important role in reducing poverty, poverty cannot be eliminated without using *zakah* in an effective way. The paper also suggests that there are certain conditions under which *zakah* will be able to make an impact on poverty. First, *zakah* has to be complimented by robust macroeconomic policies that enhance growth and also redistribute income to eliminate poverty. Second, while more *zakah* has to be collected and disbursed, the impact on poverty will only be significant when a larger percentage of *zakah* proceeds are used for productive purposes. Given the important role of *zakah* in poverty alleviation, there is a need for countries to integrate this vital faith-based institution in the development strategy and programs of Muslim countries, including Bangladesh.

Ahmed, Mahmood. "Impact of Rural Development Scheme on Poverty Alleviation: A Case Study." Paper presented at the *International Seminar on Islamic Alternatives to Poverty Alleviation: Zakat, Awqaf and Microfinance*, Dhaka, Bangladesh, April 21–23, 2007.
Abstract: A spectacular growth of micro-credit did not contribute much to poverty alleviation in Bangladesh. In order to address the problem properly, an Islamic microfinance model Rural Development Scheme (RDS) was implemented since 1995 by the Islamic Bank Bangladesh Limited (IBBL). The main objective of RDS has been the implementation of an integrated program of income generation, education and sanitation for fulfillment of basic needs and the overall betterment of targeted poor households. This paper questions the assumption that the success of microfinance programs depends on their impact in raising the income of their members and ultimately on improving the living standard of the poor. The aim of this paper is to assess the extent to which this objective has been achieved by RDS of IBBL. Identification of the contributory factors of RDS in poverty alleviation shall pave the way for diversification of RDS activities and development plans.

Ahmed, Mahmood. "The Role of RDS in the Development of Women Entrepreneurship under Islamic Microfinance: A Case Study of Bangladesh." In *Islamic Finance for Micro and Medium Enterprises* by Mohammed Obaidullah and Hajah Salma Haji Abdul Latiff, Islamic Research Training Institute, Islamic Development Bank and Centre for Islamic Banking, Finance and Management, University of Brunei Darussalam, Jeddah/Brunei, 2008, pp. 211–232.

Abstract: The RDS, a *shari'a*-based model of poverty alleviation program, is used by the IBBL to provide microfinance services, mainly to poor women of the rural areas of Bangladesh. By using a survey, the basic characteristics of women entrepreneurs in an Islamic perspective are identified those characteristics of the women entrepreneurs associated with RDS are verified. Regarding the development of women entrepreneurship, some grass-roots-level experiences from the RDS are presented along with policy prescriptions for renewing the role of the RDS in the development of woman entrepreneurship in Bangladesh.

Ahmed, Mahmood. "Scope for Micro Enterprise Development in Bangladesh under Islamic Finance." *Journal of Islamic Banking and Finance*, Vol. 15, No. 1, 1998, pp. 19–22.

Abstract: Non-governmental organizations (NGOs) in Bangladesh are of varied character—ranging from large to local, secular to religious, interest-charging and *shari'a*-compliant. Most garner funding from foreign donors. Furthermore, Christian and secular NGOs (CARE, CARITAS, World Vision, BRAC, ASA, Grameen Bank etc.) play a dominant role. Grameen Bank, for example, covers 36,843 villages whereas RDS (and project of IBBL) covers only 71. However, the Bangladeshi public is distrustful of interest-based financial transactions and, as such, welcomes Islamic microfinancing schemes. Examples include: (1) the Association of Muslim Welfare Agencies in Bangladesh (with 12–15 percent effective rate of return); (2) the RDS, arranged from the IBBL's general investment fund (12 percent rate of return); and (3) the Islamic Bank Foundation, arranged from IBBL's *zakat* and charity donation funds.

Ahmed, Salih Gibriel Hamid and Ibrahim, Ali Hussein. "Micro-Finance as a Mechanism for Poverty Alleviation in the Sudan." Paper presented at the *Pre-Forum Workshop on Microfinance: Towards a Sustainable Islamic Finance Model*, at Harvard Law School, Cambridge, MA, April 18, 2008.

Abstract: Microfinance/micro-credit has been practiced informally in Sudan and elsewhere for a long time through conventional relations in rural agricultural communities. But the steady increase in population and competition for the meager resources has spurred interest in other methods. The main obstacle for a family to meet its basic needs is income poverty. Before the twentieth century, formal financial institutions were not involved in microfinance delivery (i.e., lending, savings, money transfer, insurance, etc.). NGOs served as efficient means for practicing credit delivery to the needy people. Unfortunately, the efforts of NGOs have diminished due to the scarcity of resources. Donors have curbed giving as a result of economic, political, social and strategic causes. This paper presents the findings of a field survey in the Sudan; the author has conducted two random samples. The first survey covered four sectors: agriculture, livestock, small-industries and service. The second survey is intended to trace the performance of microfinance in tea vending as a new initiative dealing specifically with women. This survey strengthened the outcome of the first survey, and assured the possible success of microfinance as a poverty-alleviation intervention mechanism. In spite of the great progress that has been achieved, the recommendations of the paper dealt with the major elements that affect the performance of the Savings and Social Development Bank in microfinance at both the governmental and banking levels.

Ahmed, Sami and Karim, Nimrah. "A Socio-Economic Solution to Poverty," unpublished paper, Washington, DC, 2007.
Abstract: Street Bank's vision is to create a venture capital—and non-profit hybrid, providing—mass delivery of microfinance and social services to the impoverished all over the world. The unique features of the model allow the bank to quickly develop into a premier institution in the effort to alleviate poverty, and in the process act as a catalyst in the transformation of the social finance services industry. This would all be made possible by harnessing the economic power within the micro-enterprise to generate profits, and the networking power of the internet to include the masses in this all-important initiative.

Akhter Waheed, Akhter, Nadeem and Jaffri, Syed Khurram Ali. "Islamic Microfinance and Poverty Alleviation: A Case Study of Pakistan". Proceedings 2nd CBRC, Lahore, Pakistan, November 2009.
Abstract: This research paper recognizes Islamic microfinance as an important component in poverty-alleviation strategies. While conventional microfinance products have been successful in Muslim majority countries, these products do not fulfill the needs of all Muslim clients. While taking an overview of Islamic microfinance in Muslim countries, this research paper undertakes a case study of Akhuwat, an Islamic microfinance organization operating in Pakistan. Critical financial analysis of Akhuwat indicates that it is providing its services to all those living below the poverty line including the "extreme poor" and that interest-free loans can be used as a powerful tool against poverty. It recommends that integrating Islamic microfinance with NGOs, non-profit organizations, *zakat*, *awqaf* and with *takaful* as well as with professional training and capacity building institutions will enhance the financial stability of Islamic microfinance institutions and will be helpful to achieving their aim of providing micro financial services to the poorest of the poor under one roof.

Akkas, S.M. Ali. "An Islamic Alternative to Poverty Alleviation: The 'PARSHI' (Neighborhood) Model." Paper presented at the *International Seminar on Islamic Alternatives to Poverty Alleviation: Zakat, Awqaf and Microfinance*, Dhaka, Bangladesh, April 21–23, 2007.
Abstract: The inadequacies of the market mechanism, as well as the current interventions at governmental and non-governmental levels under its tools of poverty alleviation are analyzed. There is a need for introducing a continuous basic minimum initial asset/capital transfer mechanism, like *zakat*, as follows: government safety net programs are often seasonal, poorly covered, and aptly regarded as the least organized, thereby having a very marginal impact on poverty. The important government safety net programs are Food for Works (FFW), Food for Education (FFE), Vulnerable Group Development (VGD) Program for Disadvantaged Women, and Test Relief (TR). It should be noted that the safety net programs are based on donors' humanitarian grants which have a high degree of fluctuation. At the same time, it is hardly a net transfer mechanism since FFW, the major component of the safety net programs, is given as wage to construct and repair rural infrastructure. On the other hand, the government transfer mechanism, another out of the market intervention, works heavily against the poor, favoring those who are in a higher income bracket. While NGOs provide alternative models of poverty alleviation, sustainability becomes increasingly threatened by inclusion of the ultra-poor. Alternatively, MFIs, which are mostly based on donors' funds, are not sustainable by their very nature. With the above mentioned three sustainability grounds, the endorsement of "entitlement to a basic minimum initial asset/capital" seems to be the sine qua non of any approach to poverty alleviation. One can find here the real implication of introducing *zakat* in the economy as the most effective tool to

eradicate poverty. Only after *zakat* creates this initial asset base can one expect the smooth functioning of a financing scheme, regardless of loan size.

Alam, Mohammad N. "Micro Credit through *Bai-Muajjal* Mode of Islamic Financing System." Paper presented at the *First Annual Conference of SANABEL, Microfinance Network of Arab Countries*, Dead Sea, Jordan, December 15–17, 2003.
Abstract: Micro-credit given by Islamic banks through the *"Bai-Muajjal"* model of Islamic financing is a proven method of developing saving habits among the rural poor. The article highlights the methodological and theoretical aspects used for the research, outlines the differing financing modes of Islamic banks, and finally analyzes the research results showing exactly how the *"Bai-Muajjal"* model is currently working among the pastoral poor.

Alam, Nafis. "Islamic Venture Philanthropy: A Tool for Sustainable Community Development." Paper presented at the *Pre-Forum Workshop on Microfinance: Towards a Sustainable Islamic Finance Model*, at Harvard Law School, Cambridge, MA, April 18, 2008.
Abstract: The magnitude of philanthropic giving in Muslim communities is estimated to total between USD 250 billion and USD 1 trillion annually. In spite of being such a huge philanthropic wealth base, in most countries it is being either mismanaged or misappropriated. The current research proposes that this Islamic philanthropy can be interpreted using conventional models of venture philanthropy. This can be done by applying tailored financing. For example, it can be used for professional financial advice and assistance to build strong communities. Philanthropic wealth can be invested in *shari'a*-compliant activities and the returns can be further used for larger community development. This model will encourage networking of local business people and Islamic investors; a true partnership based on shared risk and profit and with clear development objectives. This model measures both social and financial impact of Islamic venture philanthropy for Muslim communities at large.

Alhabshi, Syed Othman. "Poverty Eradication from Islamic Perspective." *E-Source*, 1996.
Abstract: The paper begins by laying out the socio-economic definitions of different types of poverty, along with the various methods to alleviate "absolute" and "relative" poverty. Poverty is then analyzed through the lens of Islam and traditional Islamic methodologies for ameliorating its dire effects. The Amanah Ikhtiar Malaysia (AIM) in Malaysia is an example of a modern Islamic response to poverty, which has provided loans to many impoverished Malaysians, particularly women. As a result of its successes, the Malaysian government is providing the organization with more money in order to carry on their financial goals.

Ali, Mohammad I. "Islamic Microfinance: Innovation for Freedom," unpublished paper, United Arab Emirates, 2008.
Abstract: The paper seeks to develop two models of Islamic microfinance based on *shari'a*. The need-based *tabarru'* model provides a kind of financial security to the underprivileged and distressed in the time of immediate financial needs. The enterprise *mudaraba* model is developed for individuals with entrepreneurial capabilities lacking financial strength to enhance their income levels. This model provides comfort and security both to the fund provider and to the entrepreneur. The paper details the summary of transaction flow and highlights the special features of each model.

Ali, S. Nazim. "Financing the Poor: Towards Islamic Microfinance." *New Horizon*, Issue No. 165, July–September 2007, pp. 18–20.

Abstract: The Islamic Finance Project (IFP), under the auspices of the Islamic Legal Studies Program at Harvard Law School, seeks to foster cooperation between academic and applied knowledge experts in order to confront the most pressing issues that the Islamic finance industry faces today. To that end, IFP has held numerous conferences, workshops and other events on a broad range of pertinent issues. The symposium entitled "Financing the Poor: Towards an Islamic Microfinance" brought together a diverse and international group of speakers from both the microfinance and Islamic finance sectors. Chaired by Professor Baber Johansen, it provided a great opportunity for a distinguished panel of speakers such as Robert Annabelle, Shaykh Nizam Yaquby, Michael Ainley, Samuel Hayes and others to share their experiences and offer their expert opinions on potential collaborative moves. The symposium, attended by over 120 scholars, professionals and students, was praised by many attendees as a landmark event. The session was characterized by a healthy exchange of ideas between both sectors with marked interaction between the audience and the panels.

Ali, S. Nazim. "Islamic Principles and Pro-Poor Financing." Paper presented at the *UN-HABITAT Expert Group Meeting on the Cross-Fertilization of Universal and Islamic Land Approaches*, at the University of East London, London, May 17–18, 2007.

Abstract: Islam has a strong connection with commerce, but it also provides clear guidelines for charity, equity, partnership as well as social and economic justice. Islamic finance is a market-driven community banking proposition, enabling a wider base of society to participate in the financial market consistent with their beliefs. It can also be used as a medium for economic and social development, using tools such as *musharaka*, *mudaraba*, *murabaha*, *zakat* and *waqf*. The case of Islamic microfinance is particularly interesting. Several questions need to be addressed in order to predict its success. Will existing microfinance institutions be ready to eliminate interest in order to tap into Islamic funding sources? Can the Islamic finance industry initiate microfinance windows? And can it develop the right tools to promote pro-poor financing?

Alirani, Kais. "Islamic Microfinance—Yemen Experience." Paper presented at the *First Annual Conference of SANABEL, Microfinance Network of Arab Countries*, Dead Sea, Jordan, December 15–17, 2003.

Abstract: The important features of the *murabaha*, *mudaraba* and *musharaka* models of Islamic lending as applicable to microfinance are presented. *Mudaraba/musharaka* models have limited application and work best when the return on investment for a particular loan can be accurately predicted. Microfinance is constrained in the Arab world because of cultural barriers and problems of accessibility. The paper recommends promoting experiential learning in developing more tools for administering microfinance in order to promote the activity in the region.

Aliyev, Fuad. "Applications of *Awqaf* and Islamic Microfinance in a Post-Soviet Secular State: A Hypothetical Model of *Awqaf*-Based Credit Unions." Paper presented at the *International Seminar on Islamic Alternatives to Poverty Alleviation: Zakat, Awqaf and Microfinance*, Dhaka, Bangladesh, April 21–23, 2007.

Abstract: This paper examines the applications of Islamic finance in Azerbaijan, a secular post-Soviet state in which Islamic financial institutions (including microfinance) have emerged and developed, and in which the *waqf* institution has been revived. The potential of these institutions has not been utilized and conventional Western mechanisms are taking the lead. Despite huge oil revenues, there is still a problem of access to financing and credit for poor and rural communities. Lack of financing contributes significantly to the level of poverty and the gap between the wealthy and poor. Interest-based microfinance and even informal usury result in exploitation of the poor, while credit unions lack enough financial resources for addressing existing challenges. This paper argues that the revival of the institution of *awqaf*, its development and role in poverty reduction through introduction of the "community capitalism" model is yet to be undertaken. In this paper the author proposes and thoroughly analyzes a hypothetical model of *awqaf*-based credit unions, their development opportunities and possible contribution to reducing poverty in Azerbaijan.

Allen & Overy. "Islamic Microfinance Report," for the International Development Law Organization. February 25, 2009.
Abstract: This report has been prepared to assist the International Development Law Organisation in understanding the basic Islamic law (*shari'a* law) principles governing the provision of Islamic finance products and services, the processes typically involved in obtaining *shari'a* approval for *shari'a*-compliant financing transactions and products and the relationship between *shari'a* law and secular law in certain jurisdictions. This report also summarizes the results of our research into the state of Islamic microfinance in certain Middle Eastern, South Asian and Southeast Asian countries.

Anon. "Benchmarking Arab Microfinance." *Microfinance Islamic Exchange (sponsor). First Annual Conference of SANABEL, Microfinance Network of Arab Countries*, Dead Sea, Jordan, December 15–17, 2003. http://www.sanabelnetwork.org/pastconferences/conference/pdf/Arab-Benchmarking-Final%20 Version.pdf.
Abstract: The report addresses the performance of the microfinance sector within the Arab world by identifying its strengths and its progress in juxtaposition with its status in the wider world. Performance variance within the Arab world is given a thorough analysis. Arab microfinance is growing at a pace that is much faster than in other regions and is exceeding global averages. In short, Arab microfinance has crossed the "threshold of sustainability."

Ansari, Javed Akbar. "A Proposal for Establishing a Micro-Enterprise Islamic Bank (MIB)." *Journal of Islamic Banking and Finance*, Vol. 13, No. 3, 1996, pp. 53–64.
Abstract: Increasing Islamic financing through the establishment of a Micro-enterprise Islamic Bank (MIB) would provide a means for developing Islamic community work and government. Such an *ulema*-sponsored bank would link depositors, small traders, manufacturers, service sector owners and shopkeepers seeking *halal* investment. The MIB would have paid equity of R 500 million, of which 25 percent would be provided by each of the following groups: (1) a "strategic investor" consortium of religious groups, *ulema*, etc.; (2) the non-financial corporate sector; (3) Islamic banks in Pakistan and the Gulf region. An additional 20 percent and 4 percent would be paid by the Islamic Banking Division and the Muslim community, respectively (the latter through sale of MIB membership certificates). The bank would facilitate deposit mobilization, checking and saving accounts for the general public, *shari'a*-compliant financing, as well as support a regional clustering strategy for enterprises.

Al Asaad, Mahmoud. "Village Funds: The Experience of Rural Community Development at Jabal al Hoss, Syria." In *Islamic Finance for Micro and Medium Enterprises* by Mohammed Obaidullah and Hajah Salma Haji Abdul Latiff, Islamic Research Training Institute, Islamic Development Bank and Centre for Islamic Banking, Finance and Management, University of Brunei Darussalam, Jeddah/Brunei, 2008, pp. 197–210.

Abstract: The Jabal al Hoss project in Syria uses an innovative model of Islamic microfinance based on *sanadiq* or village funds. Community partnership, participation and risk sharing form the basis of the model. Given the preferences of the community, the model has been found to be sound and culturally appropriate. The project pays dividends to its shareholders using a profit-sharing scheme and is the only membership-based model in the region that does so. The objectives of the project are institutional and financial sustainability by using a strategy that ensures implementation. The project is located in one of the most economically disadvantaged areas of the country and is thus benefiting the poorest Syrians.

Ashraf, Ali. "Incorporating *Zakat, Awqaf,* and Microfinance into a Single Model: An Islamic Alternative to Poverty Alleviation." Paper presented at the *International Seminar on Islamic Alternatives to Poverty Alleviation: Zakat, Awqaf and Microfinance,* Dhaka, Bangladesh, April 21–23, 2007.

Abstract: This paper presents a single model integrating *"zakat, awqaf* and Microfinancing" on Islamic principles and concepts that could work as an Islamic alternative to poverty alleviation. The paper analyzes three separate models of *zakat, awqaf* and microfinancing as if they were managed separately and discovers problems relating to separate models. The paper looks into developing a single model and discusses how such a model could work from organizational, operational and financial management points of view. The concluding chapter analyzes whether such a model complies with benchmark questions on Islamic principles and its impact on economic welfare.

Badawi, Samer and Wafik Grais. "Challenges of Microfinance and Potential of Islamic Microfinance." Paper presented at *Financing the Poor: Towards an Islamic Micro-Finance,* at Harvard Law School, Cambridge, MA, April 14, 2007.

Abstract: Though Islamic finance has grown and continues to grow rapidly, it has yet to reach the vast majority of Muslims, many of whom live in the poorest countries on earth. The scale of this untapped "market" is already drawing mega-banks into microfinance, but whether these players can attract Muslim clients may largely depend on their ability to incorporate products that are at once affordable and *shari'a*-compliant, while managing political risk and instituting transparency measures. This paper examines these prerequisites from the perspective of practitioners, looking first at the challenges faced by conventional microfinance providers and, second, at how Islamic financial providers might address these challenges using the materiality and risk-sharing principles underlying Islamic financial services.

Calò, Cecilia, De Nardi, Sabrina, Faussone, Luigi Galimberti, Genisio, Benedetta and Pallotto, Paola. "Islamic Microfinance: Alternative Development in Northern Lebanon - Project Proposal," Istituto per gli Studi di Politica Internazionale, Milan, June 2008.

Abstract: The financial instruments *murabaha, mudaraba, musharaka, ijara* and *ijarah wa iqtina'* and *takaful* may be used to increase the per-capita gross domestic product by 30 percent in 203 villages in Akkar, Lebanon within a period of 24 to 30 months by creating new employment opportunities. The target of this effort would be the 14,250 economically active poor in the region of the district. Partners in this action would be the Al-Baraka Bank Lebanon (BBL) and Al Manar University of Tripoli. The timeline for such a plan would be as follows: (1) the signature of an agreement with BBL within one week; (2) one-month training in Tripoli for the BBL clerks who will work in the microfinance section; (3) the opening of a BBL microfinance branch (headquarters and field office) in Akkar within one month; (4) the opening of four BBL field offices in the villages of Bire, Qoubayer, Halba, Mechmech within one month; (5) one-month advertisement of new microfinance products offered in the district of Akkar; (6) employment of four national experts in accounting, remittances management, environmental impact of human activities and biodiversity, each for three months a year; and (7) once every six months advertisement of the seminars organized in the district of Akkar. Personal income and level of consumption are key indicators related to the overall success of the project.

CGAP, Deutsche Bank, Islamic Development Bank and Grameen–Jameel (sponsors). *Islamic Microfinance Challenge 2010: Innovating Sustainable, Scalable, and Market-driven Models,* May 2010.
Abstract: The contest was a joint initiative to promote the innovative design of *shari'a*-compliant products for Islamic microfinance clients. Finalists of this competition were awarded USD 100,000 in grant funds as well as need-based technical support to launch a pilot project of their proposed business idea.

Cheston, Susy and Kuhn, Lisa. *Empowering Women through Microfinance.* Micro credit Summit Campaign, Washington, DC, 2002. http://www.microcreditsummit.org/papers/empowerintro.htm.
Abstract: Microfinance has had a positive impact on the status of women globally. What does it mean for women to be "empowered" and why should MFIs care? The examination of a case study of the Sinapi Aba Trust in Ghana makes clear that though microfinance does not always empower women, more often than not it can aid their situation.

CHF International (sponsor). *Practical Guide for Housing Microfinance in Morocco.* CHF International, 2005. 40pp. www.mftf.org/resources/index.cfm?fuseaction=throwpub&ID =166.
Abstract: Progressive building is well suited to Morocco and should include the following practices: (1) the use of physical collateral to minimize default for larger and long-term loans; (2) technical assistance to be carefully assessed by each MFI; (3) price lists to be prepared by each institution; (4) pilot tests to be performed on all new products; and (5) housing loans to be used to allow MFIs to reduce their risk from incurring high delinquency rates. If MFIs commit to providing housing finance, then such loans can be used to improve the lives of many Moroccan families.

Choudhury, Masudul Alam. "Micro-Enterprise Development Using Islamic Financing and Organizational Instruments: Modality and Practicum." *International Journal of Social Economics,* Issue 1/2, January 2002, pp. 119–134.
Abstract: The paper proposes a micro-enterprise modeled on Islamic law. The case study is specifically for Bangladesh, with the intent that the reader will infer the solutions as answers to current global microfinance problems. Various organizational features of this micro-enterprise model are explained in detail, with an emphasis on the human resource component. The author develops the various features of a grass-roots development program, focusing on its financial, organizational and socio-economic elements. The first part lays out the philosophies of microfinance and Islam and establishes the fact that the two are compatible. The second posits a micro-enterprise development project. The paper concludes with planning for the implementation of such a project.

Chowdhry, Sajjad. "Creating an Islamic Microfinance Model—The Missing Dimension." *Dinar Standard,* November 2006. http://www.dinarstandard.com/finance/MicroFinance111806.htm.

Abstract: Microfinance has followed economics in its use of Islamic debt-based apparatuses for limiting risk. While it may seem counterintuitive, microfinance is already more structurally aligned to applying Islamic equity economic structures. This calls for the inclusion of a *musharaka*-based model. In short, MFIs can find Islamic finance a natural fit in their agendas—for both debt and equity models.

Chowdhury, M. Abdul Mannan. "The Role of Islamic Financial Institutions in Resource Mobilization and Poverty Alleviation in Bangladesh: An Empirical Study of Rural Development Scheme (RDS) of Islamic Bank Bangladesh Ltd. (IBBL)." Paper presented at the *International Seminar on Islamic Alternatives to Poverty Alleviation: Zakat, Awqaf and Microfinance*, Dhaka, Bangladesh, April 21–23, 2007.

Abstract: Agriculture, or more specifically, the rural sector, occupies an important place in the economy of Bangladesh. Unfortunately, the majority of rural people live below the poverty line. Due to the dearth of employment opportunities, a bulk of the labor force is either unemployed or without work. Of the most effective measures to alleviate this economic gap, provision of credit to the needy and the hardcore poverty group is considered as the most significant since it allows the poor to break away from their dependence on traditional moneylenders and mobilize their own resources for income and employment-generating activities. After analyzing several studies evaluating the achievement of NGOs and microfinance organizations, including the Grameen Bank, it becomes clear that models such as the Grameen Bank are most successful in empowering the rural poor and bettering the general economy of rural areas.

Chowdhury, Nurul Ahad. "The Impact of *Qard Hassan* at Higher Education of Muslim Students: A Sample Case Study." Paper presented at the *International Seminar on Islamic Alternatives to Poverty Alleviation: Zakat, Awqaf and Microfinance*, Dhaka, Bangladesh, April 21–23, 2007.

Abstract: *Qard hasan* is one of the most powerful benevolent sectors and tools for alleviating poverty in Islamic economics. Unlike *zakat*, there is no specific calculation for *qard hasan* that certain amount of money will have to be spent during a year. Such a practice can improve the situation of the neediest segments of society. *Qard hasan* can directly impact and the lives of Muslim students and thereby allow them to contribute positively towards their communities, nations and the *umma* as a whole. This empirical study collects data from a number of recipients of *qard hasan* (Muslim students) and payees of *qard hasan* (donors). Data were collected using the questionnaires, and face-to-face, online and telephone interviews. The outcome of the data is to be analyzed in terms of the attitude, intention, motivation and dedication of the people involved in the study.

Cokro, Widiyanto B. Mislan and Ismail, Abdul Ghafar B. "Sustainability of BMT Financing for Developing Micro-enterprises." Paper presented at the *International Seminar on Islamic Alternatives to Poverty Alleviation: Zakat, Awqaf and Microfinance*, Dhaka, Bangladesh, April 21–23, 2007.

Abstract: The aim of this study is to analyze the sustainability of Islamic microfinancing for developing micro-enterprises by examining Baitul-Mal Wat Tamwil (BMT), an Islamic MFI in Indonesia. Two approaches will be used to explore sustainability: data envelopment analysis and level of outreach. The efficiency of BMTs is relatively low. Scale efficiency also indicates that BMTs operate far from optimally. The results suggest that there is a gap in efficiency scores obtained from the Charnes–Cooper–Rhodes (CCR) and the Banker–Charnes–Cooper (BCC) models. This shows that BMTs still face managerial problems. But it must be noted that Islamic microfinancing is useful for developing micro-enterprises and is greatly beneficial to society. Although the profitability efficiency of BMTs is relatively low, since BMTs have generally profited and been of social benefit, Islamic financing can be predicted to be sustainable.

Conroy, John D. *Microfinance in Malaysia: Time to Rebuild.* The Foundation for Development Cooperation, Brisbane, 2002, 5pp. http://www.fdc.org.au/Files/Microfinance/MF%20in%20Malaysia.pdf.
Abstract: The paper is a short summary of the recent developments in AIM, the major MFI in Malaysia. Citing the organization's handling of Islamic law, the paper lays out certain contemporary problems AIM faces. These problems may shed a cynical light on the Grameen model as a whole, and how it could be adapted in the future in an Islamic context.

Dadgar, Y. and Saadat, M. "Possibility of '*Waqf* in Money' (as a New Productive Instrument in Islamic Economics)." Paper presented in *International Seminar on Islamic Alternative to Poverty Alleviation: Zakat, Awqaf and Microfinance*, Dhaka, Bangladesh, 21–23 April 2007.
Abstract: Waqf has always been a productive instrument in alleviating poverty and enhancing welfare. However, a novel (and challengeable) subject is the "possibility or impossibility of *waqf* in money." Could we use money or monetary assets (instead of real assets) as *waqf*? There is a difference in opinion amongst Muslim scholars regarding this issue. The authors use analytical and Islamic reasoning methods to investigate it. Meanwhile, the Arabic equivalent terms of some *fiqh* rules, verses of the *Qur'an* and *ahadith* are used in the footnotes. The first section is devoted to the methodological considerations and conceptual framework. Opposing viewpoints concerning *waqf* in money, along with its feasibility are analyzed in the second and third sections. The paper ends with some concluding remarks and some policy implications.

Dhumale, Rahul and Sapcanin, Amela. "An Application of Islamic Banking Principles to Microfinance." A study by the Region Bureau for Arab States, World Bank Group, Washington, DC, December 1999, 14pp. http://www.ruralfinance.org/servlet/BinaryDownloaderServlet/2637_Technical_Note.pdf?filename=1114499916629_WB_Islamic_MF_edited.pdf&refID=2637.
Abstract: The author gives a brief summary on Islamic banking's objections to conventional banking and provides a detailed analysis of various contracts within the scope of Islamic banking, as well as the different kinds of transactions. Microfinance is a powerful tool for reaching the poor by raising their living standards, creating jobs and contributing to economic growth. More needs to be done to reach the 4.5 million entrepreneurial poor in the Middle East and North Africa. As of today, only Egypt's National Bank is an active participant in the microfinance industry. Within the field of Islamic banking, the three basic instruments of trustee financing, equity participation and cost plus mark-up could have a successful microfinance program built into them. Borrower feedback implies that the profit-sharing mechanism is the most widespread methodology as well as the one most people are comfortable with. If such a program were to be created, it would have to account for the administrative costs and risks to itself and to borrowers. Islamic banking's emphasis on risk sharing and collateral free loans make it compatible with the endeavors of some micro-entrepreneurs. While allowing room for financial innovation, Islamic banking allows the poor to foster economic development.

Djojosugito, Reza Adirahman. "Legal Framework to Induce Paradigm Shift in Islamic Alternatives to Poverty Alleviation." Paper presented at the *International Seminar on Islamic Alternatives to Poverty Alleviation: Zakat, Awqaf and Microfinance*, Dhaka, Bangladesh, April 21–23, 2007.

Abstract: The Islamic approach to poverty alleviation is mainly done through the redistribution of wealth to fulfill the basic needs of the poorer strata of the society. However, even though this approach has been successful in mitigating absolute poverty, the emphasis of the system is simply the fulfillment of basic needs and not towards the creation of viable financial systems. While the redistribution of wealth can sometimes lead to a system of providing subsidized credit to the poor, there is no viable Islamic compatible system of creating sustainable financial intermediation among the poor. Albeit lacking Islamic elements, microfinance has been successful in creating a sustainable financial intermediation among the poor and is considered the "new paradigm" in the fight against poverty. This paper argues that this approach can potentially help to shift the paradigm of an Islamic charitable model of poverty eradication. By combining the microfinance model with existing Islamic wealth redistribution models, an Islamic microfinance model can be devised. However, in order to work, this model necessitates a proper legal framework. This paper highlights issues that need to be addressed by a greater legal framework, such as the difficulties in finding a legal vehicle which would enable MFIs to mobilize *zakat* or to receive *awqaf* property. Such a legal framework can induce the paradigm shift toward creation of sustainable financial intermediation among the poor by creating microfinance system combined with the traditional Islamic wealth redistribution system.

Dusuki, Asyraf Wajdi. "Banking for the Poor: The Role of Islamic Banking in Microfinance Initiatives." *Humanomics*, Vol. 24, No. 1, 2008, pp. 49–66.

Abstract: The main purpose of this paper is to review the microfinance scheme and discuss how Islamic banks can participate in such an endeavor without actually compromising the issue of institutional viability and sustainability. The paper is based on an extensive review of microfinance with the objective of building a case for Islamic banking to participate in a microfinance initiative. Microfinance requires innovative approaches beyond the traditional financial intermediary role. Among others, building human capacity through social intermediation and designing group-based lending programs are proven to be effective tools to reduce transaction costs and lower exposure to numerous financial risks in relation to providing credit to the rural poor. The use of a special purpose vehicle (SPV) is one possible alternative for Islamic banks channeling funds to the poor. Islamic banks may benefit from the spectrum of *shari'a*-compliant sources of funds and offer a wide array of financing instruments catering for different needs and demands of their clients. Furthermore, the use of a bankruptcy-remote entity such as SPV can protect Islamic banks from any adverse effect of microfinance activities. These conclusions may alert Islamic banking practitioners to the fact that they can actually practice microfinance without undermining their institutional viability, competitiveness and sustainability. This is evident from the proposed model to incorporate SPV into their microfinance initiatives.

Dusuki, Asyraf Wajdi. "Lifting Barriers in Financing the Small and Poor Entrepreneurs: Lessons from Group-based Lending Scheme and Ibn Khaldun's Social Solidarity." In *Islamic Finance for Micro and Medium Enterprises* by Mohammed Obaidullah and Hajah Salma Haji Abdul Latiff, Islamic Research Training Institute, Islamic Development Bank and Centre for Islamic Banking, Finance and Management, University of Brunei Darussalam, Jeddah/Brunei, 2008, pp. 15–36.

Abstract: Asabiyah or social solidarity is the core of Ibn Khaldun's thought concerning the rise and decline of a civilization. In the *Muqaddimah*, Ibn Khaldun emphasizes the importance of having a sense of solidarity or "espirit de corp," the state of mind that makes individuals identifies with a group and subordinates their own personal interests to that of group interest. The implication of Ibn Khaldun's social solidarity concept to the present world is imperative. The concept of social solidarity can be enforced through formation of group-based lending among small entrepreneurs and rural poor communities who are normally denied access to credit by mainstream financial institution and market. Group-based lending approach is not a subject alien to Islam, as it is deeply inscribed in Ibn Khaldun's concept of "*Asabiyah*" or social solidarity. By adopting group-based lending approach, banks may offer various financial products and services without compromising on the issue of institutional viability and sustainability.

El-Hawary, Dahlia and Grais, Wafik. "Islamic Financial Services and Microfinance." *E-Source,* June 2005. http://siteresources.worldbank.org/EXTISLAMF/Resources/Islami cFinancialServicesandMicrofinanceJune20b.pdf.
Abstract: Islamic Financial Services is unique in the sector of microfinance. As such, it is plagued by limited availability and faces many challenges, including the role of public policy in its inclusion. Although the diffusion of financial services often leads to economic growth and poverty reduction, this has not been the case with Muslim communities. The legal and regulatory framework that governs the Micro Islamic Financial Services needs to conduct research to incorporate mainstream conventional finance into itself.

Farook, Sayd. "A Standard of Corporate Social Responsibility for Islamic Financial Institutions: A Preliminary Study." In *Islamic Finance for Micro and Medium Enterprises* by Mohammed Obaidullah and Hajah Salma Haji Abdul Latiff, Islamic Research Training Institute, Islamic Development Bank and Centre for Islamic Banking, Finance and Management, University of Brunei Darussalam, Jeddah/Brunei, 2008, pp. 37–52.
Abstract: There is a difference of opinion in academic and practitioner circles regarding the social role of Islamic finance institutions (IFIs). This study presents a structured definition of the function of IFIs based on Islamic principles of social equity and justice as it relates to redistribution of wealth. It also provides a practical framework with which IFIs can fulfill a collective religious obligation and make use of their position as financial intermediaries. Guidelines for the social responsibilities of financial corporations ought to be similar to guidelines of personal responsibility and be based on the contradictions between permissible and impermissible actions.

Farook, Sayd. "Social Responsibility." *Islamic Banking & Finance,* December/January 2009, pp. 17–20.
Abstract: There is much that Islamic finance can do to change the world in a manner profitable to its shareholders. Islamic law requires some sort of re-distribution of wealth and opportunity. This is most evident in contracts such as *mudaraba* and *musharaka* but institutions, infrastructure and controlling mechanisms for the likes of credit bureaus to reduce moral hazard must first be developed along with a strong culture of strong governance to be able to implement *mudaraba* and *musharaka* in their true form. Yet the truly Islamic objective of wealth and opportunity redistribution does not necessarily require Islamic finance: conventional financial institutions rose to the challenge of helping the poor in the form of microfinance. Other non-Islamic innovations have evolved to serve public interest, such as public–private residential ownership, while Islamic finance and its rationalizing masses

delve deep into legal semantics. Scholars and academics are saying that too little is being done to achieve the ends while too much concentration is being placed in ensuring the means are compliant. Some of the tried and tested initiatives, such as microfinance and restricted investment funds, in the Islamic finance market space that can bridge this long-standing gap between means and ends are reviewed to see how they can fit in with the overall architecture of a socially responsible industry.

Feroz, Ehsan H. "A Proposal for Making Grameen Bank Sharia Compliant," unpublished papter, Tacoma, WA. (Contact author for full paper at ehf2@u.washington.edu.)
Abstract: The study explores the advantages of the proposed LaRiba Bank (GLB) over the extant Grameen Bank. GLB retains many of the positive features of the Grameen Bank such as zero tangible collateral and portfolio approach and at the same time avoids the pernicious dysfunctional effects of *riba*. GLB may provide higher motivational incentives for repaying the loan since it will significantly reduce the cost of the capital by avoiding compound interest. (Compound interest could make the cost of a machine twice or more as high depending on the rate of discount and time to maturity.) It concludes by describing in detail GLB's socially responsible "*lariba*" approach in order to promote a noble social agenda.

Feroz, Ehsan H. "The Halal Way to Social Change." *Islamic Horizons*, Vol. 36, No. 1, January/February 2007, 42pp.
Abstract: The article explores methods through which Muhammad Yunus' ingenious concept of Grameen Bank can be combined with the Islamic principle of non-interest. Money could be garnered through a "profit/loss regime" in which the borrower's share increases as s/he pays off the loan until s/he is in full possession of the financial asset. Such an idea would incorporate Yunus' original portfolio scheme of assessing his borrowers along with the feature of zero tangible collateral.

Feroz, Ehsan H., Goud, Blake and Rahman, Mohammad. "The Development and Implementation of a Shariah Based Microfinance Using the Grameen Group Financing Methodology." Paper presented at the *Pre-Forum Workshop on Microfinance: Towards a Sustainable Islamic Finance Model*, at Harvard Law School. Cambridge, MA, April 18, 2008.
Abstract: The objective of this project is to develop and implement an Islamic microfinance model using the Grameen group financing approach initially to *murabaha* and *mudaraba* contracts. The authors' model begins with providing clients in carefully self-selected groups with *murabaha* contracts before providing *mudaraba* finance. The *murabaha* financing agreement includes fixed payments each period of repayment and therefore is easier to administer and can be used to screen out potentially problematic clients who are most likely to default. Those clients who are in groups with successful repayment of the *murabaha* finance will have a choice between *murabaha* and *mudaraba* financing in the future. Finally, some preliminary results from the authors' pilot study in Colombo and Bibile, Sri Lanka are reported.

Ferro, Nicoletta. "Value through Diversity: Microfinance and Islamic Finance and Global Banking." *Feem Working Paper*, No. 87, June 2005. http://ssrn.com/abstract=755447.
Abstract: The paper sketches many elements of microfinance that could be considered consistent with the general goals of Islamic banking. By addressing new markets and embracing alternative financial proposals, the global banking sector can be a factor in the search for diversity-oriented policies posed by an increasingly globalized scenario. The consequences this new trend is likely to have on inner banking structures are still unknown and are likely to interest the issue of wealth distribution. The banking sector can play a

potential role in disseminating awareness on specific cultural and religious issues, resulting in increased integration of Muslim communities and low income investors in the long run while supporting commercial banks in the standard relationship between economy and culture.

Frasca, Alexandra. "A Further Niche Market: Islamic Microfinance in the Middle East and North Africa," Center for Middle Eastern Studies & McCombs School of Business University of Texas, Austin, November 2008.
Abstract: This paper examines whether there is potential synergy between microfinance and Islamic finance. It also explores the possibility of expanding microfinance facilities in the Middle East and North Africa (MENA) region by offering Islamic financial instruments to those reluctant to try conventional financial instruments. The paper presents case studies of two Islamic finance projects, namely, the *Sanduq* project in Syria and the *Hodeidah* micro-finance program in Yemen, to demonstrate that Islamic MFIs can compete with conventional MFIs in the MENA region.

Ghalib, Asad Kamran. "Re-Thinking Leasing from an Islamic Perspective: The Prospects of Islamic Micro-leasing for Poverty Alleviation." Paper presented at the *Pre-Forum Workshop on Microfinance: Towards a Sustainable Islamic Finance Model*, at Harvard Law School, Cambridge, MA, April 18, 2008.
Abstract: Islam prohibits *riba* and prescribes alternative mechanisms for financing that are free from interest, the underlying rationale of this being the emphasis of the *shari'a* on business practices that are ethical, moral, fair and promote equality in society. The paper opens with a brief discussion of the basic modes of Islamic financing and subsequently carries out an appraisal of the basic principles and concept of leasing from an Islamic perspective. It contemplates how this mode of financing can be employed by MFIs to enable poor micro-entrepreneurs to gain access to the use of assets which otherwise have been unattainable. The paper examines the critical and vital nexus between the principles of Islamic financing, a micro-leasing model and the basic theory of microfinance whereby collateral-free facilities are provided to the destitute. It aims to establish how this model facilitates borrowers to start up micro-enterprises of their own and eventually help themselves out of poverty, ultimately leading towards alleviating poverty and achieving equity in society.

Grace, Lorna and Al ZamZami, Ahmed. *Islamic Banking Principles Applied to Microfinance Case Study*. Hodeidah Microfinance Program, Yemen, UNCDF, 2002.
Abstract: Using the Hodeidah Microfinance Program (HMFP) in Yemen as a case study, this paper looks at the ways in which Islamic banking principles can be applied to microfinance. Countries in which conservative Islamic practices hold sway often discourage the practice of charging interest; however, respective to how strongly these beliefs are held, MFIs have adapted in a variety of ways. The paper concludes that Islamic banking principles pose several operational and financial challenges to an MFI and outlines some of the similarities and differences between ideal practices of a traditional MFI and those of an MFI practicing relatively strict Islamic banking practices as in the case of HMFP. HMFP focuses on providing a good service or product to the client by providing a culturally and religiously acceptable financial product in a timely manner with little or no collateral.

Hamzé, Imad A. *The Role of Micro-credit in Poverty Alleviation: Profile of the Micro-credit Sector in Lebanon*. New York: United Nations, 2001,102pp. http://www.escwa.org.lb /information/ publications/edit/ upload/sd-00-2-e.pdf.

Abstract: The study includes an analysis of micro-lending in Lebanon, beginning with an introduction of the major global micro-lending schemes and a detailed explanation of Islamic banking. The criteria used to determine the extent of a program's success is laid out, followed by a list of the different micro-lending programs in Lebanon with some recommendations for enhancing the effectiveness of each program.

Al-Harran, Saad Abdul Sattar. "Islamic Finance Needs a New Paradigm." *Alternative Finance*, ITDG Publishing, February 1996. http://www.alternative-finance.org.uk/cgi-bin/summary.pl?id=287&view=html&la.

Abstract: Islamic finance may well be the solution to the fiscal situation in South East Asia, which is becoming more akin to the current situation of Western societies. In the case of America, 50 percent of stocks are owned by 1 percent of families. Certain actions of multinational corporations place the assumption of "free trade" in question. After outlining current practices of Islamic finance, such as *mudaraba* and *musharaka* contracts, the author writes about the possibilities for micro-credit from a grass-roots level.

Harper, Malcolm. "Musharakah Partnership Financing—An Approach to Venture Capital for Micro-Enterprises." *Small Enterprise Development*, Vol. 5, No. 4, 1994, pp. 27–36.

Abstract: *Musharaka*, or partnership credit, provides a unique solution to the two issues that most plague micro-enterprise programs: inflation and individual failure. While the latter discourages the poor from accessing financial services, it also deters financial institutions from lending to such groups. The brunt of the former is borne by banks whose funds are severely diminished by high inflation. Money recovered by partners in *musharaka* is based on a proportion of the profits actually earned—not fixed in monetary terms at the time of the initial agreement. Thus, it is automatically adjusted for inflation. Furthermore, if risks are properly assessed by the lender, his losses from failures will be met by his share of the profits earned by successful enterprises Similarly, the application of *musharaka*, which utilizes the qualities of venture capital for the benefit of small-enterprise, may resolve the individual failure issue by mitigating risk to the entrepreneur through recognition of his or her management role. As *musharaka* has been practiced by the Prophet Muhammed himself and is fully *shari'a*-compliant, it is an attractive option for financing communities that are reluctant to borrow money or to deposit their savings in interest-based accounts. Such has been the case with the Sudanese Islamic Bank which began employing more partnership credit (in lieu of *murabaha*, or hire purchase) as a result of high inflation rates. This led to the creation of the specialist "Productive Families" branch which serves approximately 400 clients who are engaged in small-scale non-farm enterprises. Its partners are generally depositors engaged in a variety of small urban enterprises, including: tailoring, food production, small-scale manufacturing and animal husbandry. Notably, the Bank has made the decision to donate the profits of the branch to the community in which it operates to foster mutual trust between its staff and clients. As *musharaka* necessitates that a bank lucidly appraise the earning capacity of an entrepreneur and his or her proposed investment, as well as regular monitoring, such an environment of cooperation ought to be more widely cultivated.

Harper, Malcolm. *Partnership Financing for Small Enterprise: Some Lessons from Islamic Credit Systems*. London: ITDG Publication, 1997, 70pp.

Abstract: The author describes the experiences of a wide range of enterprises, banks and other agencies with partnership finance. Partnership financing is a relatively little-known approach to enterprise finance that appears to have the potential to overcome potential problems. In addition, it has been practiced for the benefit of small businesses and micro-enterprises with some success.

Hashemi, Syed M. and Schuler, Sidney Ruth. *Sustainable Banking with the Poor: A Case Study of Grameen.* PRPA, Grameen Trust, Dhaka, Bangladesh, 2007.
Abstract: This report presents the recent findings of a wide ranging study on Grameen Bank and its operations, success factors and most importantly provides explanations to some of the criticisms. Using multivariate analysis, it examines and discusses the access to loans among the poor, women in particular, and addresses the economic and social impact of access to loans, as well as women's control over their enterprises and income. Finally, it investigates the exclusion of the poorest in micro-credit schemes.

Hassan, Abul and Baha, Roslee. "The Challenge in Poverty Alleviation: Role of Islamic Microfinance and Social Capital." Paper presented at the *International Seminar on Islamic Alternatives to Poverty Alleviation: Zakat, Awqaf and Microfinance,* Dhaka, Bangladesh, April 21–23, 2006.
Abstract: Islamic microfinance is an intervention-based social intermediation in which poor people can mobilize their savings, which are linked with Islamic investment, and ideally become self-employed. It results in building social capital. This study attempts to understand the growth of Islamic microfinance and how the Islamic microfinance sector and social capital can contribute to the challenge of poverty alleviation. Collective action actually provides the means to adopt and benefit from agricultural innovations, generate economic and human capital, and make the development process sustainable. A non-random survey, including Islamic microfinance group members, suggests increased environmental awareness, economic uplift of members and the potential for local common resource management through Islamic microfinance.

Hassan, Kabir M. "A Case Study of Islamic Microfinance by Islamic Bank: The Case of Rural Development Scheme (RDS) in Bangladesh. 2010," unpublished paper. (Contact author for full paper: Kabir_Hassan@comcast.net; mhassan@uno.edu.)
Abstract: The paper assesses the extent to which the objective of using microfinance to improve the income and living standard of poor objective has been achieved by RDS of IBBL. Since 1995, the Islamic microfinance model RDS has been implemented by IBBL. The main objective of RDS is to implement an integrated program of income generation, education and sanitation for the fulfillment of basic needs and the uplifting of targeted poor households. It concludes that identification of the contributory factors of RDS in poverty alleviation will pave the way for the diversification of RDS activities and a development plan.

Hassan, Kabir M. and Ashraf, Ali. "An Integrated Poverty Alleviation Model Combining Zakat, Awqaf and Micro-finance," unpublished paper, 2007. (Contact author for full paper: Kabir_Hassan@comcast.net; mhassan@uno.edu.)
Abstract: This paper presents a single model integrating *"Zakat, Awqaf* and Micro-Financing" based on Islamic principles and concepts aimed to work as an Islamic alternative to poverty alleviation. The paper analyzes models in which *zakat, awqaf* and microfinancing were managed separately and discovers problems of each individual model. Later, the paper looks into developing a single model and discusses how such a model could work from organizational, operational and financial management points of view. The concluding chapter analyzes whether such a model complies with benchmark questions on Islamic principles and examines the possible impact of such a business on economic welfare.

Hossain, Monowar. "An Islamic Non-Banking Financial Institution for Accelerated Poverty Eradication." Paper presented at the *Pre-Forum Workshop on Microfinance: Towards a Sustainable Islamic Finance Model*, at Harvard Law School, Cambridge, MA, April 18, 2008.

Abstract: Poverty eradication, acknowledged since World War II as a global responsibility, received increasing attention during 1980s and 1990s, culminating in United Nation's adoption of the Millennium Development Goals in 2002. Although microcredit's success in alleviating poverty has now been recognized worldwide, it has two main weaknesses— high interest rates and, for Muslim clients, *shari'a* non-compliance. Of several approaches evolved through a search for Islamic alternatives, two are controversial—reinterpreting microcredit's interest as *shari'a*-compliant and using *zakat/waqf* to subsidize MFI's overheads for reducing interest rates. A third approach, using *murabaha* or *bay' al-mu'ajjal*, seems uncomfortably close to conventional interest-based products. This article suggests a fourth approach, drawing upon universal teachings of Prophet Mohammad, by combining *zakat* and *musharaka* investments on a non-banking financial institution platform—and using these for selected projects, ensuring a steady stream of dividends and employment income to the poor. It is contended with some empirical data from Bangladesh that the proposed model would greatly accelerate poverty eradication.

Hossain, Monawar. "*Zakat*-based poverty eradication in Bangladesh: The Millennium Development Goal is Exceedable." Paper presented at the *International Seminar on Islamic Alternatives to Poverty Alleviation: Zakat, Awqaf and Microfinance*, Dhaka, Bangladesh, April 21–23, 2006.

Abstract: Poverty alleviation has been a priority in Bangladesh's development plans and programs since 1972. In 2005, the Institute of Hazrat Mohammad in Dhaka proposed a new methodology of *zakat* payment and utilization to achieve optimal success in poverty eradication, This paper shows, on the basis of simulation analysis using household income and expenditure data, that following the proposed methodology of converting *zakat* from a temporary consumption item to investable wealth, utilizing it in both micro projects such as pisciculture in a village and macro projects such as an information technology software company in Dhaka, through a dedicated and professional Islamic institution, poverty can be eradicated in Bangladesh in 10–12 years. It could also pave the way for existing interest-based micro-credit programs to make a transition to interest-free Islamic microfinance as well as macro-finance.

Huq, Begum Ismat Ara. "Poverty Alleviation thorough Islamic Mircofinancing—A case study of Bangladesh." Paper presented at the *International Seminar on Islamic Alternatives to Poverty Alleviation: Zakat, Awqaf and Microfinance*, Dhaka, Bangladesh, April 21–23, 2006.

Abstract: In most developing countries of the world, financing micro-enterprises (microfinancing) is considered a "new paradigm" for bringing about development and alleviating poverty. Bangladesh is one of the biggest Muslim countries in the world. This paper is an effort to examine the existing role of Islamic microfinance institutions in alleviating poverty in Bangladesh. The existing role of such institutions can be strengthened by combining their role with that of traditional Islamic institutions and NGOs, on one hand, and traditional MFIs, on the other. The main sources of Islamic microfinancing are Islamic banks, Islamic insurance companies, Islamic NGOs and traditional Islamic institutions such as *zakat, awqaf, qard hasan, al-maniha* (gifts) etc. On the other hand, the major sources of traditional microfinancing are commercial banks, both public and private, insurance companies and NGOs such as ASA, PROSHIKA, BRACK, GB, BRDP, etc. This paper sheds light on how to make their roles consistent with Islamic principles and also suggests some recommendations to alleviate poverty through financing microenterprises according to the principles of Islam.

Hussein, Mohamed Abdikadir. "Islamic Finance as a Tool of Microenterprise Development in Sub-Saharan Africa." LL.M. thesis, Cambridge, MA: Harvard Law School, 2001, 103pp.
Abstract: An LL.M. thesis accepted at Harvard Law School and supervised by Professor Frank Vogel, this work examines aspects of Islamic microfinance in Sub-Saharan Africa by an overview of the environment in Kenya with emphasis on recent developments such as financial deepening and outlining infrastructural and other shortfalls requiring attention for the establishment and nurturing of an Islamic microfinance industry.

Ibrahim, Ali Adnan. "Incentivizing Microfinance for Islamic Finance Institutions." Paper presented at the *Pre-Forum Workshop on Microfinance: Towards a Sustainable Islamic Finance Model*, at Harvard Law School, Cambridge, MA, April 18, 2008.
Abstract: IFIs operate within a special incentive structure, as briefly discussed below. While operating within the incentive structure, the IFIs cannot invest in microfinance initiatives beyond a certain limit, which is often criticized to be nominal or unsatisfactory. Therefore, in order for the IFIs to play the desired microfinance role, microfinance needs to be incentivized for the IFIs in a manner that is consistent with the existing structure. As for the existing incentive structure, the IFIs not only compete with their conventional counterparts but are also striving to integrate Islamic finance with the international financial markets. Both competition and the pressure for integration create a special legal, regulatory and financial environment for IFIs. On the legal and regulatory side, IFIs must conform to the conventional corporate form, which introduces a first tier of constrains on the IFIs activities. The need to be financially competitive introduces a second tier of constrains. A third tier of constrains comes from the obligation to remain *shari'a*-compliant. Put differently, all these considerations force the IFIs to (1) keep maximizing the shareholders' value within the applicable legal and regulatory framework; (2) stay profitable; and (3) remain *shari'a*-compliant. As a result, the market forces and the relevant constituencies punish a tendency for deviant behavior. The incentive structure is developed on a hybrid model that seeks to encourage partnership between the IFIs and the philanthropic organizations, as generally preferred by some scholars. The hybrid model appears quite attractive, but is susceptible to a number of challenges unless structured in a manner that is consistent with the above incentive structure. These considerations include retaining the IFIs' profit motives, compliance with international legal and regulatory framework, and, importantly, compliance with *shari'a*. The paper, accordingly, proposes a unique microfinance model that will not only be attractive for the IFIs but also for their conventional counterparts. Consequently, there would be more financial resources available for microfinance.

Imady, O. and Seibel, H. *Sanduq: A Microfinance Innovation in Jabal Al-Hoos, Syria.* September 2003.
Abstract: The establishment of 22 *"sanadiq"* in one of Syria's poorest neighborhoods saw extremely positive growth in its first year of existence. The article deals with how these 22 organizations were developed and how their programs, many of which that catered to illiterate women, developed. Future challenges are also delineated, with the conclusion that future problems will be rectified through close cooperation between government agencies, donors and private organizations.

Islam, M. Shahidul and Hashmi, M.S.J. "Zakah Investment and its Role in Poverty Alleviation in Contemporary Muslim Countries." Paper presented at the *International Seminar on Islamic Alternatives to Poverty Alleviation: Zakat, Awqaf and Microfinance*, Dhaka, Bangladesh, April 21–23, 2006.

Abstract: This study focused on the entrepreneurial characteristics of the marginal poor of Bangladesh. Of the target group, 21 families have been taken as samples and three potential inputs have been supplied to the sample families in order to carry out the study. The inputs were small business capital, indigenous technology and training to build up moral capacity. Over five years, the impact of inputs on the growth of the economy of the marginal poor was observed. Business capital alone cannot create a sustainable environment. Indeed, indigenous technology produced sustainable growth by producing higher value-added products. Moreover, the results indicated that for ultimate success, training to build up moral capacity is essential. A sustainable growth model has been developed for in-depth study in order to establish a general model to be followed.

Islamic Financial Services Board and Islamic Research Training Institute. *Islamic Microfinance Development: Challenges and Initiatives.* Working Paper for Islamic Financial Services Board Forum Framework and Strategies for Development of Islamic Microfinance Services, Dakar, Senegal, May 27, 2007, 81pp.

Abstract: While the Islamic financial services industry has made great strides in recent years, it has not adequately addressed poverty alleviation. This must be remedied, as diverse approaches are needed to provide poor Muslims with access to financial services. A charity program based both in *zakat* and *awqaf* for the "unbankable" as well as a microfinance program of wealth creation would be one such example. A variety of Islamic contracts are available for deposit mobilization, financing and risk management in a *shari'a*-compliant framework. Challenges facing Islamic microfinance occur at three levels: micro, meso and macro. Similarly, solutions to such issues must also be implemented at various levels. At the micro level, the challenge is that of diverse organizational structures, issues relating to *shari'a*-compliance, lack of product diversification and poor linkages with banks and capital markets. An example initiative would be to create *qard hasan*-specific funds to support various *qard hasan*-based MFIs across the globe. At the meso level the following reforms are necessary: (1) provision of education and training; (2) better coordination and networking, technical assistance through *awqaf* and *zakat* funds; (3) provision of rating services specific to Islamic MFIs in view of their unique risks through creation of a rating fund. At the macro level a major concern is the lack of an enabling regulatory and policy environment. The integration of *zakat* and *awqaf* in financial sector reforms would facilitate the development of such an environment. Donor institutions with a social mission to alleviate poverty have played and continue to play a significant role in shaping the microfinance industry through their policy, technical and financial support at macro, meso and micro levels. According to a recent survey of Consultative Group to Assist the Poor member donors, the World Bank, the Asian Development Bank, the Inter-American Development Bank and the European Commission are among the largest public funders of microfinance. In the domain of Islamic microfinance, the Islamic Development Bank is perceived to be the most important player. Furthermore, Islamic microfinance has the potential to make great contributions to poverty alleviation and socio-economic development in Muslim societies.

Islamic Religious Council of Singapore. Singapore International *Waqf* Conference 2007: Integration of *Awqaf* (Islamic Endowment) in the Islamic Financial Sector. Singapore, March 6–7, 2007.

Abstract: This two-day conference in 2007 focused on the role of *awqaf* in Islamic finance and as a tool for enhancing public welfare and public utility. The keynote address was given by Goh Chok Tong, the Senior Minister of the Republic of Singapore and the following papers were presented: Attributes of Twenty-First-Century Muslims to Ensure the Success of *Awqaf* in Social and Economic Development; The Role of *Waqf* in Developing the Socio-Economy of a Country; Revitalizing the Institution of *Awqaf* in Developing the Community; Legal and Regulatory Framework on *Waqf* Management; The Role of Islamic Finance in Developing *Waqf*; Islamic Investment Strategy in Developing *Waqf*; I-REITs in Waqf Properties; *Waqf* and Islamic Property Management; and Structuring Islamic Financing for the Development of *Waqf*. Authors for the preceding papers were not available.

Ismail, Abdul Ghafar, Cokro, W. Mislam and Maamor, Selamah. "A Comparative Study of the Relative Efficiency of Conventional and Islamic Pawnshop." In *Islamic Finance for Micro and Medium Enterprises* by Mohammed Obaidullah and Hajah Salma Haji Abdul Latiff, Islamic Research Training Institute, Islamic Development Bank and Centre for Islamic Banking, Finance and Management, University of Brunei Darussalam, Jeddah/Brunei, 2008, pp. 185–196.

Abstract: The productive efficiency of pawnshops concerning their ability to provide and distribute funds to the society (marketability efficiency) is investigated in the study. Data envelopment analysis using the Charnes–Cooper–Rhodes (CCR) model and the Banker–Charnes–Cooper (BCC) model is used to perform efficiency analysis of conventional and Islamic pawnshops. The most productive scale size for pawnshops is also investigated as well as a comparison of the mean efficiency of conventional and Islamic pawnshops is made using independent tests. The CCR and BCC efficiency score analyses shows that 5 and 11 pawnshops respectively out of 39 pawnshops in the study are relatively efficient. Of these 39 pawnshops, 30 (76.90 percent) showed increasing returns-to-scale, 5 (12.90 percent) showed constant returns-to-scale and 4 (10.20 percent) showed decreasing returns-to-scale. These results suggest that to increase the efficiency of pawnshops in providing and distributing funds to society, the managers' capability to utilize pawnshops' given resources needs to be enhanced. The independent statistical tests showed that the efficiency of conventional pawnshops is similar to the efficiency of Islamic pawnshops (*ar-rahnu*).

Jayashankar, Priyanka and Goedegebuure, Robert. "Islamic Microfinance—An Idea Whose Time Has Come in India?" *Microfinance Focus,* July 16, 2010.

Abstract: As a plethora of financial inclusion models emerge across India, vast segments of the Muslim community still remain under-banked. In recent years, a handful of leading financial players have developed *shari'a*-compliant funds for the Indian market. However, full-fledged Islamic banks are yet to make inroads into the microfinance sector. Many Muslims hail from low income groups across India and typically lack access to bank credit, as documented in the Sachar Committee report (2006). In such a scenario, can Islamic microfinance be the tipping point for bringing an end to the financial exclusion of the Muslim community?

Kahf, Monzer. "Role of *Zakah* and *Awqaf* in Reducing Poverty: A Case for *Zakah–Awqaf*-based Institutional Setting of Micro-finance." Paper presented at the *International Seminar on Islamic Alternatives to Poverty Alleviation: Zakat, Awqaf and Microfinance,* Dhaka, Bangladesh, April 21–23, 2007.

Abstract: The provision of microfinance is a high-cost operation because of its target clients. They are in need, not only of financing, but of education, training and direct guidance for preparing their first investment plans/steps, healthcare, childcare, psychological rehabilitation and immediate provision of essential consumer goods. Despite the often-quoted experience of microfinance with the Grameen Bank, whose main sources of funds are grants and whose rate of interest charged to the poor reaches up to 56 percent, very little is usually mentioned about intuitive spontaneous multi-dimensional experiences of local charities in the Muslim communities, especially in rural areas and in old, predominantly Muslim inner cities. The objective of this paper is to propose an institutional structure for microfinance that simultaneously deals with the many facets of poverty and depends on combining the *waqf* and the *zakat* principles together. It does not quarrel with the basic premise of microfinance: that enabling the poor to increase the amount of income generated is better than giving hand-outs. The focus is on the theoretical structure of new institutional forms and analyzes the experience of the *Zakat* Corp. of Sudan. The paper is divided in two sections: section I briefly reviews the relevant *shari'a* rulings of *zakat* and *awqaf*; it is mainly based on the author's earlier paper on "*Zakah* and *Awqaf* in *Shari'a* and History." Section II outlines the proposed institution and its functions.

Kaleem, Ahmed. "Application of Islamic Banking Instrument (*Bay' al-Salam*) for Agriculture Financing in Pakistan" In: *Islamic Finance for Micro and Medium Enterprises* by Mohammed Obaidullah and Hajah Salma Haji Abdul Latiff, Islamic Research Training Institute, Islamic Development Bank and Centre for Islamic Banking, Finance and Management, University of Brunei Darussalam, Jeddah/Brunei,, 2008, pp. 131–148.

Abstract: The possibilities of applying *bay' al-salam* contracts in the agriculture sector of Pakistan are investigated in this article. Information regarding crop inputs, output and credit requirements was gathered from farmers in four districts of Punjab province by using a specifically designed survey. The survey revealed that 60 percent of the income of an average farm household came from agriculture. Seventy percent of the farmers use the credit market for purchasing crops, paying labor and hiring rental machinery. Farmers believe that by purchasing crop inputs on cash, they can reduce their cost by 25 percent. In the rural economy, the survey revealed, middlemen are the major financers and purchasers of crops. Two possible models for introducing Islamic banking in the agriculture sector and some policy recommendations are also suggested in the article.

Karim, Nimrah, Tarazi, Michael and Reille, Xavier. "Islamic Microfinance: An Emerging Market Niche." *Focus Note 49.* Washington, DC: CGAP, August, 2008, pp. 1–15.

Abstract: The outreach of Islamic finance is very limited, with only 380,000 customers worldwide. Similarly, Islamic microfinance accounts for a very small portion of total microfinance outreach. NGOs serve the greatest number of clients. If Indonesia is any indication, *shari'a*-compliant rural banks exhibit the following characteristics: (1) higher costs than conventional microfinance; (2) elevated portfolio delinquency that improves over time; and (3) lower return on assets. And while Islamic microfinance has the potential to greatly expand access to financial services among Muslims, possible challenges are manifold. Areas of operational efficiency and risk management must be addressed if the sector is to develop sustainable business models. Capacity building is also needed. The Islamic Development Bank and Islamic financial standard setters (such as IFSB or AAOIFI) should consider developing global financial reporting standards adapted to microfinance to build the infrastructure for transparency in the global sector. International donor agencies can assist existing institutions to reach scale and fund pilot projects testing various business models. Product diversity ought to be cultivated through reduced reliance on *mubaraha* and innovative design of *shari'a*-compliant products and services. Similarly, dependency on *zakat* for the development of a large and sustainable sector may not be the most viable model and other commercial motivated streams of funding should be explored. Finally, although there is great demand for Islamic microfinance products in low-income communities, clients need to be satisfied that the products being used are authentically Islamic. To this end, greater efforts should be made to increase education, exchange and co-operation between financial and *shari'a* experts, local religious leaders with ground knowledge of *shari'a* compliance in products and low-income populations.

Kessey, Charles. "Empowering Muslim Women through Micro-credit Scheme: The Case of the Sunyani Gonja Muslim Women's Group." *Working Papers on Ghana (WOPAG): Historical and Contemporary Studies*, No. 7, October 2005. http://www.helsinki.fi/project/wopag/WoPaG7Kessey.pdf.
Abstract: Study of the Muslim community in Sunyani, the capital of Brong Ahafo, reveals that women can be empowered through micro-credit by having greater access to resources and thus more power to monitor their own earnings. The government should implement a number of policy changes, as follows: (1) embark on a comprehensive program of re-capitalizing the rural banks, credit unions, and other financial institutions; (2) make the cost recovery and financial criteria for Enhancing Opportunity for Women in Development membership flexible and reasonable but not so harsh as to frighten off potential members; and (3) induce donors and development co-operation actors to opt for the Gender and Development instead of the Women in Developement paradigm to forestall any cultural backlash and expand the scope of participation.

Khan, Ajaz Ahmed. *Islamic Microfinance: Theory, Policy and Practice.* Islamic Relief Worldwide, Birmingham, United Kingdom. February 2008. 74pp.
Abstract: This document relies heavily on the accumulated experience of Islamic Relief's microfinance programs in four countries: Bosnia and Herzegovina, Kosovo, Pakistan and Sudan. The examples that are provided are drawn almost exclusively from these countries. Chapters 1 and 2 are introductory, with the latter providing a brief introduction to Islamic financing principles and lending methodologies that need to be considered when designing and operating an Islamic microfinance program. Chapter 3 examines the importance of microfinance program objectives and mission statements. It is essential that each microfinance program has a clear organizational structure with clearly defined staff roles and responsibilities. Chapter 4 explores these issues with examples from Islamic Relief's microfinance program in the aforementioned countries. Chapter 5 discusses which types of lending methodology are most suitable to extending microfinance to relatively poor people, once again with examples. Chapter 6 provides practical advice that should be considered when selecting borrowers and assessing loan applications, while Chapter 7 describes procedures for disbursing loans as well as collecting repayments. The issue of monitoring and evaluating the performance of microfinance programs, with respect to both the service provider itself as well as on the lives of the borrowers is explored in Chapter 8.

Khan, Atif R. "Poverty to Profit." *Islamica Magazine*, Issue 12, Summer 2005, pp. 6–10. http://www.islamicamagazine.com/issue-12/poverty-to-profit-9.html.
Abstract: Conventional microfinance's exorbitant interest rates range from 22 percent at Grameen and as high as 50 percent elsewhere; Islamic microfinance provides an alternative under the *mudaraba* contract. However, banks undertaking such financing should not interfere with business transactions, although they should be permitted to give advice. The

amount banks collect from profit should not be fixed but rather be percentage-based and agreed upon before the business opens.

Khan, Javed Ahmed and Nisar, Shariq. "Collateral (*Al-Rahn*) as Practiced by Muslim Funds of North India." *Journal of King Abdulaziz University: Islamic Economics*, Vol. 17, No. 1, 2004, pp. 17–34.
Abstract: This study aims at highlighting the issues related to collateral as practiced by the five leading representative Muslim MFIs of Northern India, which is a densely Muslim populated area. The study, examines the need for collateral, its composition, safety and costs involved, modus operandi, socio-economic impacts and its legal status in the context of India. There is great potential for the expansion of collateral funds in the area of equity and venture finance.

Kholis, Nur. "*Murabahah* Mode of Financing for Micro and Medium-sized Enterprises: A Case Study of Baitul Mal Wattamwil (BMT), Yogyakarta, Indonesia." In *Islamic Finance for Micro and Medium Enterprises* by Mohammed Obaidullah and Hajah Salma Haji Abdul Latiff, Islamic Research Training Institute, Islamic Development Bank and Centre for Islamic Banking, Finance and Management, University of Brunei Darussalam, Jeddah/Brunei, 2008, pp. 161–184.
Abstract: The *murabahah* mode of financing as an Islamic instrument and contract for MMEs in the working of a unique Islamic microfinance institution BMT, Yogyakarta, Indonesia is investigated in this study. The practice of *murabaha* financing products, its procedures and its applications in the BMTs is examined with regard to *shari'a* rules. The study compares the method of marking up price in *murabaha* financing products to the way interest rates are determined in conventional banks. The policies and actions of BMTs' management in case of defaults are also evaluated.

Laila, Tanim. "Innovations in Islamic Philanthropy and Monetization of Islamic Philanthropic Instruments." Paper presented at the *Pre-Forum Workshop on Microfinance: Towards a Sustainable Islamic Finance Model*, at Harvard Law School, Cambridge, MA, April 18, 2008.
Abstract: The world today is plagued by hunger, health epidemics, global warming and human rights violations. While several Western civil organizations are actively dealing with these challenges, Muslims have yet to be identified as global partners associated with peace building. To meet these challenges and to bring the world's poor out of poverty; the author finds a strong demand for carefully monetized Islamic philanthropic instruments. Thus the introduction of specifically designed Islamic philanthropic instruments for the two major sectors of Islamic endowments, *zakat* and *waqf*. Specialized financial institutions can be used to deal with long-mismanaged charitable funds, introduce new scopes for participation in charities, enhance opportunities for participation, provide efficient and improved management of endowments, ensure selective investments to maximize the socio-economic benefit, and most importantly, invest funds for productive usage as opposed to the current practice of consumerism.

Lim, Hilary and Sait, M. Siraj. "Islamic Micro-finance in Crisis Situations: The Unofficial Development Discourse." Paper presented at *Financing the Poor: Towards an Islamic Micro-Finance*, at Harvard Law School, Cambridge, MA, April 14, 2007.
Abstract: While the authenticity, effectiveness and sustainability of specific Islamic micro-finance products are often contested, the dynamics that create distinctive microfinance

models are mostly ignored. Comparative study of two countries—Afghanistan and Indonesia—sheds light on how the interplay of particular political, legal and economic factors creates opportunities for MFIs to use their relative autonomy to negotiate the design and the delivery of microfinance products. The invisibility of Islamic microfinance in the 2006 mid-term review of microfinance in Afghanistan as well in the donor development discourse in Indonesia is in contrast to the increasing demand for Islamic microfinance in both the countries. This has resulted in roles of various stakeholders driving the Islamic microfinance movement and creating new microfinance models being improvised. However, the translation of Islamic principles into innovative, pro-poor, gendered and sustainable Islamic tools—through lessons learnt and best practices—will require appropriate and rigorous methodologies, with inputs from multi-stakeholder initiatives such as the Global Land Tool Network's Islamic Tools Initiative.

Linari-Pierron, Vincent and Flatter, Elie. "Islamic Microfinance in Luxembourg." Luxembourg: Ernst and Young, April 2009, 6pp.
Abstract: Investment law and financial organizations present in Luxembourg have been constructed to accommodate the needs of foreign investors, including those engaged in Islamic microfinance. The flexibility incorporated into the structure of Luxembourg's investment legislation simplifies the set-up of microfinance vehicles. Examples of such efforts include: (1) the undertakings for collective investment law; (2) the specialized investment fund law; and (3) the law on investment company in risk capital. The country actively maintains security in its financial sector through the supervisory body Commission de Surveillance du Secteur Financier. Two institutions have been assembled to provide financial expertise to microfinance organizations, the Luxembourg Micro-banking Intermediary Scheme and the Luxembourg Fund Labeling Agency.

Madawela, Roshan and Amjad, Mohamed-Saleem. "Tackling Urban Poverty in Sri Lanka—A Case Study for Viable Shariah Compliant Microfinance Practice." Paper presented at the International Islamic Finance Forum, Dubai, United Arab Emirates, 2008, 33pp.
Abstract: Important work is being done by Muslim Aid in collaboration with Amana Investments Ltd to provide opportunities for the economic regeneration of the urban poor community in Colombo, Sri Lanka, through the provision of ethical microfinance (based on *shari'a*-compliant finance mechanisms), entrepreneurship development and training. This study is purely intended to share experiences, the results of which have been twofold: (1) profit and non-profit organizations for the same cause have indeed been tested; (2) *shari'a*-compliant microfinance is a workable and viable contribution towards poverty alleviation.

Manjoo, Faizal Ahmad. "Tax Engineering Pertaining to *Zakat* and *Waqf* for Poverty Alleviation and Micro-financing on South Africa." In *Islamic Finance for Micro and Medium Enterprises* by Mohammed Obaidullah and Hajah Salma Haji Abdul Latiff, Islamic Research Training Institute, Islamic Development Bank and Centre for Islamic Banking, Finance and Management, University of Brunei Darussalam, Jeddah/Brunei, 2008, pp. 259–288.
Abstract: Even though the majority of the Muslims in South Africa do not live below the poverty line, they still have a duty to help the poor. *Zakat* and *waqf* are two financial instruments that can help to reduce poverty. The conversion of *zakat* into an economic stimulus for reducing poverty due to a proper application of the Income Tax Act 1962 (as amended) is argued in the paper. By assessing the amount of cash that requires payment of *zakat*, one can make an analysis of the manifestation of poverty in South Africa. By using the present

tax system to optimize poverty alleviation, there is a possibility that a proper National Zakat Fund can be developed. The National Zakat Fund can be established as a Public Benefit Organization, thus creating room for tax engineering to generate more funds for poverty reduction.

Mirakhor, Abbas and Iqbal, Zamir. "*Qard Hasan* Microfinance (QHMF)." *New Horizon*, April/June 2007, pp 18–20.
Abstract: MFIs have been successful in conventional markets but there are a few cases of such institutions operating on Islamic finance principles. In an Islamic system, instruments such as *qard hasan*, *sadaqah* and *zakat* can play a vital role in serving the poor and the function each instrument can serve needs to be reviewed. The article focuses on how *qard hasan* can play an effective role within successful microfinance activities in empowering the poor in Muslim countries.

Mohamed, Nafisah, Ismail, Abdul Ghafar and Maamor, Selamah. "The Effects of Competition on the Outreach Level of the Pawnshop Industry in Malaysia." Paper presented at the *International Seminar on Islamic Alternatives to Poverty Alleviation: Zakat, Awqaf and Microfinance*, Dhaka, Bangladesh, April 21–23, 2007.
Abstract: The question of whether competition is a good or bad model for microfinance markets is as of yet unsolved. However, by empirically analyzing how the degree of competition affects the achievement of development projects promoting micro-credit, one can shed new light on this topic. Projects usually provide subsidies to MFIs for capacity and institution building with a dual objective: MFIs should be enabled to extend their loan supply for MSE (outreach to the target group) while at the same time aim at cost coverage and profitability (financial sustainability). Specifically, one must measure how competition influences the outreach and the financial situation of MFIs. Due to the authors' unique set of micro-data on the credit portfolio as well as on cost and revenues of competing microfinance operators in Malaysia, such analysis has been made feasible. This particular microfinance program directly focuses on poverty reduction by offering financial services to the very poor, often in the form of small credit. Islamic pawnshops have been designed to develop the non-bank market. Additionally, the financial institutions in Malaysia also support the expansion of Islamic pawnshops to build up the knowledge and infrastructure needed to hand out individual credit to micro and small entrepreneurs who have no access to formal sector finance.

Mohammad, Faiz. "Prospects of Poverty Eradication through the Existing *Zakat* System in Pakistan." *The Pakistan Development Review*, Vol. 30, No. 4, 1991, pp. 1119–1129.
Abstract: In 1980, the Islamic Republic of Pakistan implemented a *zakat* tax on non-agricultural assets—an unprecedented step in light of its history. This additional revenue was intended for use in poverty alleviation, especially in the countryside. The paper has three main components: first the data, then the analysis of the data, and finally the potential of such a system in the future. Its conclusion provides a positive outlook on the future of Pakistan's *zakat* system.

Mohammed, Aliyu Dahiru and Hasan, Zubair. "Microfinance in Nigeria and the Prospects of Introducing its Islamic Version There in the Light of Selected Muslim Countries' Experiences." *MPRA Paper* No. 8287, April 2008. http://mpra.ub.uni-muenchen.de/8127/1/MPRA_paper_8127.pdf.
Abstract: In recent years, microfinance has emerged as an important instrument to relieve poverty in the developing countries. Today there are more than 7,000 micro-lending

institutions providing loans to more than 25 million poor individuals across the world, the vast majority of them being women. The existing microfinance in Nigeria serves less than 1 million people out of the 40 million living in a state of poverty. Also, the aggregate micro-credit facilities in Nigeria account for about 0.2 percent of the gross domestic product and are less than 1 percent of the total credit in the economy. Addressing this situation inade-quately would further accentuate the problem and slow down the growth and development of the country. Certain microfinance institutions charge interest rates as high as 100 percent for lending and pay as low as 5 percent on savings. This aggravates existing inequality in the distribution of wealth and income in Nigeria. Under these circumstances, Islamic microfi-nancing may potentially serve the country better.

Mojtahed, Ahmad and Hassanzadeh, Ali. "Evaluation of *Qard al Hassan* as a Microfinance Approach in Poverty Alleviation Programs." Paper presented at the *International Seminar on Islamic Alternatives to Poverty Alleviation: Zakat, Awqaf and Microfinance*, Dhaka, Bangladesh, November 24–27, 2006.
Abstract: Different countries have implemented various methods in their poverty elimina-tion programs such as redistribution policies, financing low income groups, subsidizing and enhancing the capabilities of the poor. The study of poverty alleviation is one of the most important considerations in Islamic thought. *Ihsan, zakat, waqf* and *qard hasan* are elements of the principles and economic behaviors of Muslims that have considerable positive effects on poverty elimination. By emphasizing *qard hasan* as a means of microfinance in the banking system and Islamic *shari'a* in order to finance the poor in accordance with modern financing tools, one may evaluate the effects and results of the application of interest-free loans in pov-erty elimination programs in Iran. Accordingly, by compiling data of 28 provinces of the country during 1996–2003, the effects of providing interest-free loans on per-capita income as a proxy variable for poverty elimination indicator are analyzed and evaluated.

Moussa, Magdy M. "Islam and Microfinance." Paper presented at the *First Annual Conference of SANABEL; Microfinance Network of Arab Countries*, Dead Sea, Jordan, December 15–17, 2003.
Abstract: The paper makes comparisons between Islamic microfinance and traditional lend-ing on parameters such as business risks, repayments, administrative costs and growth in three methods of financing—*musharaka, mudaraba* and *murabaha*—and discusses challenges and opportunities faced in customizing these three methods in order to address microfi-nance's demands.

Muhammad, Adnan Akhyar Muhamad. "Agency Problems in *Mudarabah* Financing: The Case of Shari'ah (Rural) Banks, Indonesia." In *Islamic Finance for Micro and Medium Enterprises* by Mohammed Obaidullah and Hajah Salma Haji Abdul Latiff, Islamic Research Training Institute, Islamic Development Bank and Centre for Islamic Banking, Finance and Management, University of Brunei Darussalam, Jeddah/Brunei, 2008, pp. 107–130.
Abstract: Mudaraba financing in Indonesian rural *shari'a* banks gives rise to many agency problems. The attributes of the project and those of the *mudaribs* are financed by the banks under consideration are investigated in the study. The *mudaraba* project's point of view considers six attributes. They are: (1) the prospect of project; (2) availability of collateral; (3) healthiness of the project; (4) the project's financial statements; (5) clarity of contract conditions; and (6) conformity of time period. There are five *mudarib* attributes that are con-sidered important: business capacity, (personal) collateral, *mudarib*'s reputation and family background, and their business commitments. These attributes can be further analyzed into

five most important factors. They include the skill, reputation and commitment in business of the *mudarib*, the financial report and the length of contact of the project.

Muhtada, Dani. "The Role of *Zakat* Organization in Empowering the Peasantry: A Case Study of the Rumah Zakat Yogyakarta, Indonesia." In *Islamic Finance for Micro and Medium Enterprises* by Mohammed Obaidullah and Hajah Salma Haji Abdul Latiff, Islamic Research Training Institute, Islamic Development Bank and Centre for Islamic Banking, Finance and Management, University of Brunei Darussalam, Jeddah/Brunei, 2008, pp. 289–310.
Abstract: Discussing the economic condition of peasants in Indonesia and their eligibility for *zakat* in detail, the paper investigates the economic benefits of the Rumah Zakat Yogyakarta by studying five peasants that received *zakat* funds from this organization. Although the Rumah Zakat had alleviated some of the peasantry's problems, namely limited income and urbanization, it was unsuccessful in dealing with the fundamental problems of the peasantry. The paper evaluates the reasons as to why this failure occurred.

Murdhatillah, Amy and Rulindo, Ronald. "Building Capacity of Micro and Medium Enterprises through Spirituality Training." In *Islamic Finance for Micro and Medium Enterprises* by Mohammed Obaidullah and Hajah Salma Haji Abdul Latiff, Islamic Research Training Institute, Islamic Development Bank and Centre for Islamic Banking, Finance and Management, University of Brunei Darussalam, Jeddah/Brunei, 2008, pp. 323–338.
Abstract: A survey of micro-enterprises in Malaysia managed by Muslim women is used to examine the correlation between spirituality and business success. Two models of spirituality are used in the survey: Daily Spirituality Experience Scale (a spirituality scale that uses Western values) and ESQ Asma'ul Husna Model (a scale based on Islamic spirituality). A qualitative analysis of the influence of spiritual training on business performance is also made in the survey. Research reveals that there exists a high correlation between spirituality and performance of Muslim entrepreneurs. Entrepreneurs who attended the ESQ spirituality training became more satisfied with their businesses as they were able to better manage stress, become more persistent in striving for success and increase their business performance after attendance.

Nadeem, Azhar. "Islamic Business Contracts and Microfinance. A Case of *Mudaraba*," Dec 2010. http://www.microfinancegateway.org/p/site/m/template.rc/1.9.48077/.
Abstract: This article presents the *mudaraba* partnership as an example of financial products compatible with the norms of Islamic finance. The article explains the assumptions and terms and conditions of the *mudaraba* model and lists challenges involved. The article concludes that patronage of Islamic financial institutions will enable Islamic microfinance to develop *shari'a*-compliant products that can contribute to poverty reduction.

Nisar, Shariq "Microfinance in Muslim Community: A Panacea for Poverty Alleviation." *Muslim India*, Vol. 22, No. 11–12, New Delhi, India, 2004.
Abstract: Original empirical research is employed in this paper to capture poverty alleviation efforts in Muslim community of North India. Legal structure, resource mobilization and utilization and the problems associated with it are highlighted. Over 200 Islamic micro-financial institutions are working in India under the Trust Act, most prominent among them are the Muslim funds functioning successfully in almost all the Muslim-dominant areas of the country. These financial institutions have not faced many problems in resource mobilization, which points towards a remarkable aspect of their functionality. However,

resource utilization stands as a major cause of concern for these institutions. Their problems are further compounded due to the non-recognition of Islamic modes of financing in the country. Because of this, a number of Muslim funds are forced to suspend their expansion plans, which in turn, has other side effects, like lower efficiency, lower competitiveness and lower public welfare activities. Based on the primary as well as secondary data, attempts may be made to identify the problems of resource utilization of selected Muslim MFIs in Northern India.

Nisar, Shariq. "Problems in Resource Utilization by Islamic Micro Financial Institutions in India." Paper presented at the *International Seminar on Islamic Alternatives to Poverty Alleviation: Zakat, Awqaf and Microfinance*, Dhaka, Bangladesh, April 21–23, 2006.
Abstract: While the problems of resource mobilization within Islamic financial institutions are few, their difficulties with resource utilization, specifically among selected Muslim funds of Northern India, stands as major cause for concern. By Islamic micro-credit institutions suspending their expansion plans, such organizations thereby reduce their efficiency, competitiveness and public welfare activities.

Obaidullah, Mohammed. "Islam, Poverty and Microfinance: Best Practices." *Islamic Finance Today: The Pulse of Ethical Business*, 2007, 8pp. http://instituteofhalalinvesting.org/content/Islam_and_poverty.pdf
Abstract: The fundamental features that a successful microfinance program should have are described in the light of *ahadith* and they include several layers of intervention and features such as ensuring the program is accessible to the poorest, careful assessment of the financial health of the borrowers and involvement of the larger community in the process. A charity-based intervention inherent in the institutions of *zakat* and *sadaqah* is recommended to take care of consumption needs of the destitute and to create a social safety net. *Awqaf* is ideal for creating and preserving assets that can build capacity and provide technical assistance for skill improvement and human resources development. The social safety net and technical assistance may then be linked to financial assistance which should aim at wealth-creation using *shari'a*-compliant for-profit modes with free pricing. The Islamic approach to alleviating poverty is more inclusive than the conventional approach, providing for basic conditions of sustainable and successful microfinance and combining wealth creation with empathy for the poor. Furthermore, transparency in all financial transactions, group-based financing and mutual guarantee within the group are amongst the strong aspects of the Islamic approach.

Obaidullah, Mohammed. "Role of Microfinance in Poverty Alleviation: Lessons from Experiences in Selected IDB Member Countries." Islamic Research and Training Institute, Islamic Development Bank, Jeddah, 2010, 92pp.
Abstract: There is a need for a two-pronged strategy for poverty alleviation through micro-enterprise development in membership countries of the Islamic Development Bank (ISDB) basing their strategy on the dichotomy between livelihood and growth enterprises. The focus of the study is on provision of *shari'a*-compliant financial services and enterprises. It reviews thematic issues in light of case studies from three ISDB member countries— Bangladesh, Indonesia and Turkey—and draws valuable lessons from the case studies in terms of the two complimentary approaches to micro-enterprises development contributing to poverty alleviation.

Obaidullah, Mohammed and Abdul Latiff, Haji Salma Haji. *Islamic Finance for Micro and Medium Enterprises*. In *Islamic Finance for Micro and Medium Enterprises* by Mohammed

Obaidullah and Hajah Salma Haji Abdul Latiff, Islamic Research Training Institute, Islamic Development Bank and Centre for Islamic Banking, Finance and Management, University of Brunei Darussalam, Jeddah/Brunei, 372pp.
Abstract: This book provides the reader with a collection of articles with extensive background information on various aspects of microfinance. Chapters discuss the effect of group-based lending schemes on barriers to financing, social responsibility and accountability among IFIs, the role played by the Indonesia government in facilitating microfinance, Islamic contracts and products, financing through decreased partnership as well as equity participation. Various models (from village funds to Islam micro- and medium-sized enterprises in Australia) are examined along with methods of intergrading *zakat* and *awqaf* into microfinance, as well as the need for education and training in Muslim enterprises.

Obaidullah, Mohammed and Khan, Tariqullah. *Islamic Microfinance Development: Challenges and Initiatives.* Islamic Research Training Institute, Islamic Development Bank. Policy Dialogue Paper No. 2, Jeddah, 2008.
Abstract: The document highlights the importance of microfinance as a tool to fight poverty. It presents the "best practices" models of microfinance and the consensus principles of the microfinance industry. The document examines Islamic microfinance at three levels— micro level (microfinance institutions, contracts/products and resources), meso level (financial infrastructures) and macro level (policy and regulatory framework). The landscape is analyzed, followed by discussing the major challenges and offering strategic solutions to the challenges. The document envisages that multilateral institutions such as the ISDB can play a major role in micro-, meso- as well as macro-level initiatives to strengthen the Islamic microfinance industry.

Patel, Sabbir. "Tak{abar}ful and Poverty Alleviation." International Cooperative and Mutual Insurance Corporation (ICMIF), London, 2004.
Abstract: This PowerPoint presentation discusses the role of insurance in poverty alleviation in Muslim countries through *takaful*. It delineates the challenges in providing insurance to the poor, and the advantages of the cooperative structure. It lends insight into lessons from the micro-insurance experience, and advises on how to establish micro-*takaful* products.

Permatasari, Soraya. "Microfinance Dominates Indonesian Shariah Loans: Islamic Finance," *Bloomberg*, November 2010. http://www.bloomberg.com/news/2010-11-24/microfinance-dominates-indonesian-shariah-loans-islamic-finance.html.
Abstract: Islamic loans targeting Indonesian small businesses have grown to dominate *shari'a*-compliant credit in the world's most-populous Muslim nation, prompting the country's biggest banks to expand.

Rahmatullah, Muhammad. "*Zakat* and Poverty Alleviation among Indian Muslims." Paper presented at the *International Seminar on Islamic Alternatives to Poverty Alleviation: Zakat, Awqaf and Microfinance*, Dhaka, Bangladesh, April 21–23, 2006.
Abstract: Approximately 40 percent of Muslims in India, i.e., 60 million out of 150 million individuals, live below the poverty line. This raises the debate about the effectiveness of the prevailing *zakat* practice in reducing poverty. Muslims in India suffer from a lack of systemic and planned use of *zakat* funds. The purpose of this study is to identify the major uses of *zakat* funds, the percentage of *zakat* that is being used to alleviate poverty, and whether there is an alternative plan or model for a more effective use of *zakat* to eradicate poverty.

Rahmatullah, Dr. Zaki Kirmani. "Report of the First Conference on Networking of NGOs in India." 12pp.
Abstract: A one-day conference on "Networking of NGOs of India" was organized under the aegis of the All India Council of Muslim Economic Upliftment Ltd; more than 60 active NGOs hailing from all over India participated in the conference, although the majority was from the state of Maharashtra. The primary objective of the conference was to explore the possibility of networking among NGOs working toward similar objectives. The conference was addressed by experts at the international level, as well as those with rich experience in the field of welfare and developmental programs.

Rehman, Aamir A. "*Shari'a* Compliant Endowments in the United States: Commercial and Legal Challenges." Paper presented at the *Sixth Harvard University Forum on Islamic Finance*, at Harvard Law School, Cambridge, MA, 2004.
Abstract: A limited set of investment options challenge *shari'a*-compliant endowments (the traditional supporters of US Islamic non-profit institutions), however equity investments are available which would provide endowment clients greater diversification, stable income and capital appreciation. Furthermore, the market for Islamic endowments is estimated to surpass $200 million by 2010 and several types of revenue opportunities are foreseen in the sector. The study explores the implications of these findings for firms seeking to serve the Islamic endowment market and suggest strategies for serving endowment clients profitably.

Sabur, Aqil A. "Islamic Microfinance, *Zakat* and *Waqf*: Proven Structure for Wealth Creation," unpublished paper, 2010. (Contact author for full paper: Aqil610@aol.com.)
Abstract: While the standard global micro-entrepreneurs originate from the lowest socio-economic levels of society, this characterization does not hold true for American Muslims. Within an institutional context, Islamic microfinance coupled with the traditional institutions of *zakat* and *waqf* can facilitate significant business opportunities and wealth creation for low to moderate income individuals in the United States.

Sadique, Muhammad Abdurrehman. "Financing Micro and Medium Sized Enterprises through Decreasing Partnership (*Musharakah Mutanaqisah*): Refining *Shari'ah* and Banking Aspects for Enhanced Applicability." In *Islamic Finance for Micro and Medium Enterprises* by Mohammed Obaidullah and Hajah Salma Haji Abdul Latiff, Islamic Research Training Institute, Islamic Development Bank and Centre for Islamic Banking, Finance and Management, University of Brunei Darussalam, Jeddah/Brunei, 2008, pp. 53–74.
Abstract: MMEs can decrease partnership when acquiring assets and financing complete ventures as suggested by contemporary scholars. Increasing emphasis on equity participation will allow ancillary contracts of *ijara* and sale to function independently. Instead of focusing on the calculation of the profit from the capital outlay, the realistic pricing of *ijara* rentals and the units should be emphasized as the reality of the underlying contracts. Expenses of the business should be proportionally shared in businesses that are financed on decreasing partnership. This way, the bank's stake in the business will dictate the profit share of the bank and the unit price of the bank's share could be fixed after professional evaluation or could be negotiated at the time. Unfortunately, conditions that should be met for full *shari'a* compliance are often violated in practice.

Sadr, Kazem. "*Gharzul-hasaneh* Financing and Institutions." In *Islamic Finance for Micro and Medium Enterprises* by Mohammed Obaidullah and Hajah Salma Haji Abdul Latiff, Islamic

Research Training Institute, Islamic Development Bank and Centre for Islamic Banking, Finance and Management, University of Brunei Darussalam, Jeddah/Brunei, 2008, pp. 149–160.

Abstract: The allocation of incomes into consumption and savings by consumers is analyzed in the context of *qard hasan*. Alternative methods of saving are then discussed including: *qard-hasan* savings; charity donations; and long-term investments. The functioning and performance of *qard hasan* funds in the urban and rural sectors of Iran is explored. It follows that in the Islamic financial markets, *qard hasan* financing and *qard hasan* organizations can possibly have unique role.

Sait, M. Siraj and Lim, Hilary. "Paper Eight: Islamic Credit and Microfinance." *Land, Law & Islam: Property & Human Rights in the Muslim World*. London: UN-Habitat and Zed Books, 2006, pp. 174–201.

Abstract: The paper is divided into seven distinct sections: Contextualizing Islamic Finance; Distinguishing Features of Islamic Finance; Application of Islamic Banking to Microfinance; Islamic Financial Objectives and Products; Islamic Microfinance in Practice; Strategies for Empowerment through Islamic Finance; and Mainstream Islamic Microfinance. Islamic financial systems are located within the larger context of Islamic religious, ethical and economic systems. A short introduction of the key terms of Islamic banking is provided. Microfinance in Muslim countries offers a choice of conventional, informal and Islamic financial products, but an Islamic financial system will try to ensure that its business activities avoid prohibited activities and that its financial products permit the financing of individuals or commercial enterprises through the profit-and-loss-sharing principle. The author proceeds to cite case studies of Islamic banking within the Arab world, recommending that analysts authenticate Islamic finance products, regulate Islamic microfinance, diversify Islamic microfinance products, ensure the stability of MFIs and endeavor to make Islamic microfinance more mainstream.

Samsudin, Anna Maria. "Microfinancing: New Door of Innovation?" *Islamic Finance Asia*, December/January 2009, pp. 37–39.

Abstract: Islamic banks have lagged behind in their participation in microfinancing. Though some argue that the banks lack the "capacity or capability" to engage in the activity, the projection that Islamic banks will hold assets worth $3 trillion (USD) contradicts this claim. Others say that unfamiliarity prevents the banks from making small loans on a large scale, however, Islamic banks could very well make efforts to *develop* expertise in *shari'a*-compliant microfinance products, according to Saad al-Harran. While Islamic banks were initially intent to prove themselves in relation to conventional institutions through asset size, rather than providing services to all client levels, they are increasingly engaging in microfinance, according to Isaac Fokuo of the BOTHO Advisory Group. In addition, established Islamic banks with the capacity to offer microfinance are relatively distant from areas in India, Pakistan, Africa and Indonesia where such services are particularly needed. Over time, the banks may be able to provide *shari'a*-compliant products in distant locales, according to Mohamed Ismail Shariff of Skrine. There is a consensus among experts in the field that microfinancing can be profitable when monitored regularly and correctly managed.

Segrado, Chiara. *Islamic Microfinance and Socially Responsible Investments: Case Study*, University of Toronto, August 2005. http://www.saa.unito.it/meda/pdf/Islamic%20microfinance.pdf.

Abstract: Examination of the study conducted by Dhumale and Sapcanin (1999), reveals that Islamic banking and micro-credit programs may complement one another through, for example, the disbursement of collateral-free loans. In addition, Islamic finance and micro-finance both started from a marginal position and grew with their increasing popularity. A general summary of Islamic finance is juxtaposed to a similar analysis of microfinance.

Seibel, Hans D. *Islamic Microfinance in Indonesia.* Easchborn: Sector Project Financial Systems Development, Deutsche Gesellschaft für Technische Zusammenarbeit (GTZ). 2005, 110pp. http://www.gtz.de/de/dokumente/en-islamic-mf-indonesia.pdf.pdf.
Abstract: Islamic microfinance is an emerging field in Indonesia and many the key stakeholders include actors such as Islamic commercial banks, rural banks and financial co-operatives. A few ways to encourage the development of a healthy Islamic financial sector in Indonesia include establishing of branch networks of Islamic MFIs on the part of Islamic commercial banks, revamping Islamic rural banks and adopting prudential regulation with mandatory auditing. Full finance from the equity and savings of members from Islamic co-operatives may further promote the development of the Islamic financial sector. For example, in the Indonesian province of Aceh, the incorporation of strong Islamic financial institutions may lead to effective reconstruction and development after the 2004 tsunami.

Seibel, Hans D. "Islamic Microfinance in Indonesia: The Challenge of Institutional Diversity, Regulation, and Supervision." *Sojourn: Journal of Social Issues in Southeast Asia*, Vol. 1, Issue 23, 2008, pp. 86–103. http://findarticles.com/p/articles/mi_hb3413/is_1_23/ai_n29444200/.
Abstract: Forays into Islamic microfinance have been few, scattered and of limited scale, but in Indonesia, the world's largest Muslim country, several strands of Islamic microfinance, formal and semi-formal, have evolved in tandem since 1990. Despite its diversified portfolio, Islamic finance has performed poorly in Indonesia. A number of factors can explain this trend, including a lack of popular demand for Islamic finance, a lack of regulation as well as basic knowledge of Islamic banking, and the dominance of the informal sector in the Indonesian economy. The province of Aceh has become an important site of microfinance efforts related to development, especially after the 2004 tsunami and the end of secessionist violence.

Seibel, Hans D. *Islamic Republic of Iran: Bank Keshavarzi, the Agricultural Bank.* Teheran: Near East North Africa Regional Agricultural Credit Association (NENARACA), October 28, 2008, 57pp.
Abstract: Sustainable MFIs in Iran have been poorly developed, mainly due to overregulation and subsidization on the part of the government. Bank Keshavarzi (BK) is a government-owned agricultural bank acting as both a development and a commercial entity. BK undertook a period of structural reform between 1998 and 2004 that involved resource mobilization, e-banking initiatives, credit and investment services, finance strategies and human resources strategies. BK has been a profitable bank since 2001–2002 and has become gradually more self-reliant. BK's success in agricultural development and rural diversification as well as its presence in urban areas is remarkable considering the macro-economic climate of financial repression in Iran. A major unbanked category is the young educated men and women who could add up to 2.5 million new borrowers to the market.

Seibel, Hans D. "Rural Microfinance Support Project (RMFSP)." A joint project in cooperation with Bank Keshavarzi of the Islamic Republic of Iran. Rome: The International Fund for Agricultural Development, 2004, 37pp. http://www.microfinancegateway.org/p/site/m/template.rc/1.9.28098/.

Abstract: The Rural Microfinance Support Project aims to expand microfinance services to poor areas of Iran, especially targeting rural women and young adults. The current policy environment in Iran has not been able to support the Rural Microfinance Support Project and has been hampered a lack of experience in sustainable microfinance in both the governmental and non-governmental sectors. In spite of this, the Rural Microfinance Support Project has proven capable and willing to expand financial services to new market segments through "mutual guarantee groups," which would consist largely of young adults.

Shah Mohammad, Saif I. "Islamic Finance and Microfinance: An Insurmountable Gap?" Paper presented at *Financing the Poor: Towards an Islamic Microfinance*, at Harvard Law School, Cambridge, MA, April 14, 2007.
Abstract: Observations and interviews with microfinance practitioners in Bangladesh are used to explore problematic perceptions of traditional scholars of Islamic law and the Islamic finance sector that may obstruct co-operation with MFIs. Unfortunately, suspicion and misunderstanding may be mutual as microfinance is poorly understood by the Islamic finance sector, and arguments against the activities of microfinance institutions are often based upon misconceptions that overlook ground realities. The gap between Islamic finance and microfinance is not insurmountable—but given trends in the microfinance industry, may become so if not acted upon quickly.

Shehata, Ismail Shawki. "Limitation on the Use of *Zakah* Funds in Financing Socioeconomic Infrastructure." *Islamic Economic Studies*, Vol. 1, No. 2, June 1994, pp. 63–78.
Abstract: This paper draws its conclusions about the role of *zakat* in poverty alleviation in light of the *shari'a* and assesses the criteria for eligibility, going on to propose various ways and means of wider utilization of *zakat* proceeds for the community at large, including a five-year plan for an annual *zakat* budget and many social services.

Siswantoro, Dodik. "The Role of Indonesian Government in Enhancing Islamic Financing for Small and Medium Enterprises (SMEs)." In *Islamic Finance for Micro and Medium Enterprises* by Mohammed Obaidullah and Hajah Salma Haji Abdul Latiff, Islamic Research Training Institute, Islamic Development Bank and Centre for Islamic Banking, Finance and Management, University of Brunei Darussalam, Jeddah/Brunei, 2008, pp. 355–370.
Abstract: During the economic adversities in Indonesia in late 1997, the SMEs proved to be more resilient than larger companies which were tied to foreign debts and imported materials. Due to their resilience, SMEs have the potential to improve the economic landscape of Indonesia provided that they are developed well. The continued running of the SMEs depends in many ways on value chains in the business environment. Strong financial institutions or banks are needed to finance the SMEs. In Indonesia, Islamic banking is a new and promising alternative for financing SMEs. The government's intervention strategies and efforts to support such financing are analyzed in the paper.

State Bank of Pakistan. "Special Section 2: Role of Microcredit in Poverty Alleviation." *The State of Pakistan Economy: First Quarterly Report for FY05*, February 16–19, 2004, pp. 105–116.
Abstract: In recent years, microfinance has gained a global reputation as an effective method of promoting poverty alleviation. Pakistan is no exception. The increased use of Rural Support Programs (RSPs) has given the poor alternatives to familial loans (or complete lack of access to financing) by providing small loans for enterprise, aiming to make poverty

alleviation the focus of all development activity. RSPs foster self-reliance via community organizations managing rural development. Participating groups include: (1) The Aga Khan Rural Support Program (AKRSP), which was established to provide access to financial and technical support for farmers in Northern Pakistan living at the subsistence level. The program has an impressive pay back rate of approximately 98 percent; (2) Sarhad Rural Support Program (SRSP), akin to AKRSP, the program seeks to improve the quality of life of the poor through micro-finance; (3) National Rural Support Program (NRSP), which provides social guidance and technical assistance in rural credit, enterprise development and urban poverty alleviation project as well as social organization, human resource development, development of physical infrastructure and technology, accounts and finance, etc.; (4) Punjab Rural Support Program (PRSP), whose operations are generally related to microcredit along with assistance in the areas of business development, health and education. Comparisons of these programs yield interesting results. For instance, NRSP has the widest coverage (in terms of active borrowers and loans) among the support programs, whereas SRSP has the best operational efficiency—though its number of borrowers is the smallest of the three RSPs. Analysis of the two specialized MFIs operating in Pakistan, First Microfinance Bank Limited (FMFBL) and Khushali Bank (KB), reveals that KB has a greater number of female borrowers and the market share of MFI activity. KB's loan portfolio is skewed toward livestock, while micro-enterprise dominates that of FMFBL.

State Bank of Pakistan, Islamic Banking Department. *Guidelines for Islamic Microfinance Business by Financial Institutions.* Karachi: State Bank of Pakistan, Islamic Banking Department, 2008, 9pp. http://www.sbp.org.pk/ibd/2007/Annex-c5.pdf.
Abstract: This paper delineates guidelines related to Islamic banking and microfinance by financial institutions in Pakistan. It gives an overview of Islamic microfinance services by conventional banks, by conventional microfinance banks, and by full-fledged Islamic banks, briefly discussing the establishment of full-fledged Islamic microfinance banks in Pakistan.

Tahir, Neha. "*Al-Taawun*—Creating a Reserve on the Basis of Justice and Cooperation," unpublished paper, Islamic Finance Project, Harvard Law School, Cambridge, MA, 2010.
Abstract: A model as an alternative to the problems faced by conventional microfinance is proposed. *Al-taawun*, built on the foundation of the idea of *qard hasan*, creates a network of individuals that works collectively to allow each member of the network to reap the benefits of group savings. The principle focus of *al-taawun* is to create awareness about the concept of saving versus the concept of credit, encouraging people to create their own cash-based reserve rather than resorting to credit-interest-based means of finance. The religion of Islam promotes the idea of *adl* or justice; the practice of interest-based forms of finance creates injustice in society, widening the income and wealth inequality between the rich and poor. There has to be an alternative for the common man, in need of immediate cash, but unqualified to get this loan from banks. This common man will resort to pawnshops, despite their high rate of interest, to satisfy his urgent cash needs. The model tries to conquer this problem, and create a fair system of finance, which caters to every individual man's needs. In the Islamic finance industry, there is still scope for research and development of new products and services that target the consumer banking sector; *al-taawun* is an attempt to serve this unattended audience.

Usmani, Muhammad Taqi. *An Introduction to Islamic Finance.* Karachi: Idaratul Ma'arif Karachi, 1998.

Abstract: Although the principles of *shari'a* require banks and financial institutions to be structured on an interest-free basis, this does not mean that such institutions are charitable concerns. As long as a person advancing money expects to share in the profits earned (or losses incurred) by the other party, a stipulated proportion of profit is legitimate. The philosophy is enshrined in the traditional Islamic concepts of *musharaka* and *mudaraba*, along with their specialized modern variants *murabaha*, *ijarah*, *salam* and *istisna'*. This guide to Islamic finance clearly delineates the all-important distinctions between Islamic practices and conventional procedures based on interest. Justice Usmani of Pakistan, who chairs several *shari'a* supervisory boards for Islamic banks, clearly explains the various modes of financing used by Islamic banks and non-banking financial institutions, emphasizing the necessary requirements for their acceptability from the *shari'a* standpoint and the correct method for their application. He deals with practical problems as they arise in the course of his presentation, and offers possible solutions in each instance. Investors and others doing business (or intending to do so) in Islamic countries have in this book a clear, well-informed and practical guide to a crucial factor in the success of their endeavors.

Wahyuni, Ersa Tri. "The Accountability of Islamic Microfinance Institutions: Evidence from Indonesia." In *Islamic Finance for Micro and Medium Enterprises* by Mohammed Obaidullah and Hajah Salma Haji Abdul Latiff, Islamic Research Training Institute, Islamic Development Bank and Centre for Islamic Banking, Finance and Management, University of Brunei Darussalam, Jeddah/Brunei, 2008, pp. 339–354.
Abstract: Islamic saving and loan cooperatives, or BMTs, in Indonesia have undergone exceptional development. However, the accountability of BMTs in Indonesia in the development of reporting regulation and accounting standards has not followed the rapid development of BMTs. Due to a lack of a supervisory board and a low demand for audited financial statements, there is little incentive for BMT managers to have independent auditors audit their financial statements. Only 7–20 percent of BMTs, statistics reveal, are audited by independent auditors, raising questions about BMT managers' decisions not to opt for a process of audit and transparent reporting services.

Waspodo, Agung Aws. "The Need to Educate Muslims on Islamic Financial Principles and Practices: A Step Towards fertilizing MMEs in the Islamic World." In *Islamic Finance for Micro and Medium Enterprises* by Mohammed Obaidullah and Hajah Salma Haji Abdul Latiff, Islamic Research Training Institute, Islamic Development Bank and Centre for Islamic Banking, Finance and Management, University of Brunei Darussalam, Jeddah/Brunei, 2008, pp. 311–321.
Abstract: The growth of Islamic financial institutions and banking in Muslim-majority countries may be indicative of increasing adherence of Muslims toward Islamic principles in their countries. Islamic financial institutions and banking are becoming widespread even in Muslim-minority countries. Whether the increasing popularity of Islamic financial practices is consistent with the increase in adherence of Muslims towards Islamic principles or not remains a question. Two closely connected issues concerning the challenges and consequences of educating Muslims dependent on MMEs in Islamic financial practices and principles are addressed.

Wilson, Rodney. "Making Development Assistance Sustainable Through Islamic Microfinance." IIUM *International Conference on Islamic Banking & Finance*, Kuala Lumpur, Malaysia, April 2007.

Abstract: This paper explores how microfinance can be provided on a *shari'a*-compliant basis and what instruments and structures might be used. The paper explores whether Islamic microfinance would be best provided by specialist *shari'a*-compliant financial institutions or by existing Islamic and conventional banks, and also whether credit unions organized through co-operatives are preferable to commercial institutions (such as banks or investment companies).

Vaziri, Mo. "Islamic Finance, Rural Cooperative Financial Institutions (Credit Unions) and Micro Financing Strategies." *Investment Management and Financial Innovations*, Vol. 3, No. 2, 2006, pp. 18–33. http://scholar.google.com/scholar?q=islamic+microfinance&hl=en&lr=&start=20&sa=N.
Abstract: The paper analyzes Islamic finance within several countries, focusing on rural co-operative financial institutions and microfinancing strategies. Main organizations and high-stake operators are identified, along with the roots and causes of the "underground economy." The "underground economy" of an Islamic country depends on its tax system, its penal code and the enforceability of its financial regulations. The paper addresses the traditional Islamic injunction against interest, the rise in total liquidity within these nations, and how microfinancing strategies can easily comply with Islamic law.

Yusoff, Asry and Kechik, Mohd Nor Awang. "Mobilizing *Zakah* Funds through Microcredit Programs to Expedite Poverty Alleviation in Muslim Societies: A Special Reference to the Malaysian Structure of *Zakah* Funds and Microfinance Institutions." Paper presented at the *International Seminar on Islamic Alternatives to Poverty Alleviation: Zakat, Awqaf and Microfinance*, Dhaka, Bangladesh, November 24–27, 2006.
Abstract: The microcredit approach has proven to be a versatile, effective and efficient alternative for poverty alleviation. While the cost of running such programs is high, *zakat* funds under *asnaf faqir, miskin* and *fi-sabilillah* may be used to support MFIs' operating costs. Under such a system, MFIs would extend the benefit of subsidies to its recipients through reduction in the lending rate. The poor would, therefore, earn a wider profit margin from their micro-enterprise activities, and thus leave low-income circles sooner than expected. Exploratory research, involving fourteen Amanah Ikhtiar Malaysia Kelantan Region senior personnel and two Muslim scholars, was carried out to verify the feasibility of the proposed model. The overall response is highly positive with general concern for reaffirming the structure governing the interactive link between *zakat* institutions and MFIs.

Zafor, Mohammad. "Islamic Alternative to Poverty Alleviation, *Zakah, Awqaf* and Microfinance: Bangladesh Perspective." Paper presented at the *International Seminar on Islamic Alternatives to Poverty Alleviation: Zakat, Awqaf and Microfinance*, Dhaka, Bangladesh, November 24–27, 2006.
Abstract: Poverty alleviation is a much talked-about issue in contemporary politico-economic discourse across the globe. Many NGOs and other types of organizations are striving to address this issue but their progress is not as encouraging as one might hope. Fundamental to their limitation is the fact that they are using secular and value-neutral methods to achieve their goals. In recent days, microfinance has emerged as a dominant mechanism for poverty alleviation. However contemporary perspectives on microfinance are flawed because they do not adequately acknowledge that the concept of poverty alleviation is an ethical and moral one. Islam provides a viable alternative for alleviating poverty by offering a mechanism that is integrated with social and financial systems. Islamic institutions of *zakat, waqf,* and *qard hasan* can be used as mechanisms for direct poverty alleviation, as well as being as

sources of microfinance capital. The analysis focuses on Bangladesh—a pioneering country in the area of microfinance.

Zarka, Muhammad Anas. "Leveraging Philanthropy: Monetary *Waqf* for Microfinance." Paper presented at *Financing the Poor: Towards an Islamic Microfinance*, at Harvard Law School, Cambridge, MA, April 14, 2007.

Abstract: Monetary *waqf* (MW) of a variable size, whose major assets are monetary, may be employed to provide microfinance to the productive poor. MW depends, as in any *waqf*, on initial permanent donations whose expected income covers the administrative and maintenance needs of the MW. A novel feature in the proposed waqf is the mobilization of temporary funds extended to MW as interest-free loans, on call or for a fixed term. MW guarantees repayment to providers of funds, and uses the funds to provide microfinance to the productive poor in various *shari'a*-compliant modes, at terms that sustain the *waqf* but are most favorable to recipients. To strengthen its guarantee, MW must have two tiers of philanthropic guarantors: guarantors of liquidity and guarantors of losses. Guarantors of losses help insulate fund providers from risk of default by microfinance recipients. This helps to attract to MW temporary funds many times larger than the guarantee commitments. Payments to make up the losses can be counted by these guarantors towards their annual *zakat* obligations.

Al-Zoubi, Haitham, Hassan, Kabir, Al-Zubi, Bashir and Maghyereh, Aktham. "Debt, *Zakah* and Optimal Taxation in Islamic Economy." Paper presented at the *International Seminar on Islamic Alternatives to Poverty Alleviation: Zakat, Awqaf and Microfinance*, Dhaka, Bangladesh, November 24–27, 2006.

Abstract: The role of *zakat* in income re-distribution in Islamic economics lends itself to theoretical examination. While governments in capitalist societies issue debt such as T-bills and government bonds in the financial markets to make trades among generations possible, constructing *zakat* funds in a certain manner may take the role of issuing debt in the market economy. The model also sets the functional form of the optimal tax rate that the government must set in order to achieve Pareto optimality. Islamic economics can converge to Pareto optimality by its nature without government debt in the financial market, while providing the optimal tax rate for that economy.

Appendix 1

Financing the Poor: Towards an Islamic Microfinance—A Short Report

Harvard University, Cambridge, MA, April 2007

This April, the Islamic Finance Project (IFP) of the Islamic Legal Studies Program (ILSP) at Harvard Law School hosted a symposium on "Financing the Poor: Towards an Islamic Microfinance." The symposium brought together a diverse, international group of speakers from the microfinance and Islamic finance sectors who shared their experiences and offered their opinions on potential collaboration between the two sectors.

Nazim Ali, the Director of IFP, opened the symposium and noted the inspiration behind this conference: that microfinance has repeatedly arisen as a topic of interest for Islamic finance as a means to reach the average person and help alleviate poverty. Baber Johansen, Acting Director of ILSP and Affiliated Professor at Harvard Law School, commented upon the burgeoning interest in financing the poor, and Islamic finance's longstanding interest in promoting equitable economic development, as reflected in the ample attendance at this symposium. The keynote speakers then opened the symposium with discussions on the synthesis of Islamic finance and microfinance.

The first keynote speaker was Robert A. Annibale, Global Director of Microfinance at Citigroup, who shared his insights about Islamic finance and microfinance, especially since the two have not been integrated in many discussions. In his experience, microfinance institutions, "bankers to the poor," originally took root in domestic, local markets, but now have expanded to larger markets with a broader range of services. He noted that these microfinance institutions tend to have high operating costs that are offset by charging high interest rates, which are hard for the poor to afford. Therefore, Annibale urged institutions to make their methods more efficient, because the customer pays for the inefficiencies.

It is here that Annibale sees potential for Islamic finance to make a difference. Under conventional microfinance, risk is borne by the borrowers, and rarely by the institutions. Non-governmental organizations and other institutions offer efficient services to supplement their lending—but these services add to the cost base. Islamic finance stresses interest-free methods of providing capital, including joint venture methods where risk and reward are shared by the institution and the borrower. In terms of the overall market picture, Annibale discussed the Microfinance Information Exchange and its transparent analysis of microfinance groups. He has found that there are only small-scale offerings across the North African region and

Pakistan, areas where more competition would be beneficial. On the other hand, Indonesia and Bangladesh have developed microfinance markets. In Bangladesh, microfinance institutions have penetrated the population more than traditional banks. According to Annibale, microfinance is also growing in India, especially south India, although restrictions have been placed in some areas because people had to pay very high interest rates, and religious leaders spoke out against this usury and exploitation by telling people they did not have to pay these rates. Annibale stressed that microfinance is most successful when there is competition and, therefore, innovation, as consumers benefit the most from such circumstances.

Aamir Rehman, former Global Head of Strategy at HSBC Amanah, presented the second keynote on behalf of Iqbal Khan, HSBC Amanah's founding CEO. Rehman discussed how the ethos of Islamic finance is highly compatible with the spirit of microfinance. Islamic finance is *shari'a*-based, focusing on ethics and values that are, at root, universal. It also offers a community-based, alternative program to promote genuine economic activity. Islamic finance has many challenges, as it is a young industry that still has to work to establish credibility. Rehman argued that the industry has not focused on poverty alleviation because it needed to meet both world-class banking standards and *shari'a* requirements to serve its customers, in addition to providing profits to investors. While the social goals of the *shari'a* are noble, Islamic finance has been working to meet commercial standards first as a sign of the sector's viability before trying to meet its social responsibilities, according to Rehman.

Rehman noted that microfinance aligns well with Islamic finance because both share the same social goals and finance-related goals, such as fair access to capital and reaching an under-served population. He said that Islamic finance must work to move from a consumer-debt industry to a savings industry, which dovetails with microfinance because it assists in business development and savings. If integrated, Islamic finance and microfinance could reach a three-billion-person market. Rehman reminded the audience that in the past, trade played an integral role in the spread of Islam, so Islam has a history of valuing trade and entrepreneurship.

According to Rehman, traditional banks often seek growth through increasing the debts of consumers, but Islamic banking seeks to depart from this debt-based approach. The instruments for this shift from a "*shari'a*-compliant" to a "*shari'a*-based" mindset exist, but they must be enhanced and used appropriately for success. There must also be a change in measurements of success. To do this, Rehman thinks that Islamic finance must partner with microfinance as a philanthropic endeavor. Microfinance institutions have access to rural and poor communities, and Islamic finance offers *shari'a*-based commercial services to create a strong partnership.

It was in the context of these two keynote speeches that proposals for and case studies of Islamic microfinance were presented in the symposium's first panel, which was moderated by Asim I. Khwaja, Associate Professor of Public Policy at the John F. Kennedy School of Government, Harvard University.

Opening with an alternative view of microfinance, Samer Badawi of the Consultative Group to Assist the Poor, Washington, DC, opined that although there is evidence supporting the value of microfinance, there is also enough evidence to the contrary to cause alarm. Microfinance is not reaching the poorest of the poor, even though this was its purpose, and loans are going to activities unrelated to entrepreneurship. Islamic finance can in principle and practice correct these defects.

Hans Dieter Seibel, Professor at the University of Cologne, Germany, discussed the case study of Indonesia, the largest Muslim country in the world with a mixed history of Islamic microfinance. Seibel noted that Islamic microfinance banks statistically have not done well compared to their conventional counterparts. Part of the reason for the decline is absentee ownership and little competence in Islamic finance, but *mudaraba* savings and fixed deposits have proved to be successful. Seibel emphasized that a proper legal framework and regulation of interest rates are important for the success of Islamic microfinance, which faces many challenges as a developing industry.

Contrasting Afghanistan with Indonesia, Siraj Sait, a Senior Lecturer in Law at the University of East London, UK, introduced the Global Land Tool Network, which uses Islamic land instruments as a priority to empower the poor. Sait argued that the poor do not consist of the "end line," but are part of the entire process. The challenges of Islamic microfinance include an end-user skepticism about Islamic compatibility and a lack of state regulation. The goals are to create pro-poor, scalable and replicable tools; cross-fertilize between generic and Islamic tools; and define stakeholders.

Then Taha Abdul Basser, a Ph.D. candidate at Harvard University, presented a paper by Dr. Muhammad Anas Zarka, advisor to The International Investor, suggesting that a monetary *waqf* (cash trust) be used as an Islamic vehicle to help the productive poor. He explained that the Islamic finance industry has not focused as much on these tools for social justice because the industry was new. In order for Islamic finance to succeed in the social justice aspect of its mission, it must convince its clients and develop managerial talent.

Saif I. Shah Mohammed, a J.D. candidate at the Columbia University School of Law, New York agreed with Badawi that microfinance has been over-hyped and that a partnership between Islamic finance and microfinance may be the best approach, focusing on Bangladesh in particular. However, Islamic microfinance institutions must overcome distrust from the microfinance sector of the Islamic finance industry, especially since there is a confusion of terms. To heal some of these wounds, Mohammed proposed that the *ulema* need to explain terms, and provide practical solutions to the problem.

The speakers also contended, however, that these issues can be resolved if people from the Islamic finance and microfinance sectors work together. Aamir Rehman and Robert Annibale reiterated that a hybrid model integrating philanthropic and commercial goals or a non-profit model using charitable sources such as *zakat* offer a relationship between the Islamic finance and microfinance industries.

Michael Ainley of the UK Financial Services Authority connected the current development of microfinance to Europe's past transition from credit unions and community banks to its contemporary economic system. Ainley also noted the importance of effective government regulation and supervision of the industries. Aqil Abdus Sabur, interim President of the Philadelphia Commercial Development Corporation, linked the discussion to microfinance as practiced by the Prophet Muhammad's companions over a thousand years ago.

The panelists offered closing remarks, reminding the audience of Islam's history in finance and the great potential future of Islamic microfinance. This is a project that is growing in the United States, the United Kingdom, continental Europe, the Middle East and Asia. However, it is important to keep the purpose in mind, as Shaykh Nizam Yaquby insisted during his conclusion: the goal is to eliminate poverty, not to cloak goals to exploit people.

The symposium, attended by over 120 scholars, professionals and students, was praised by many attendees as a landmark event. The session was characterized by a genuine exchange of ideas between two sectors—Islamic finance and microfinance—that share core ideals but have not cooperated meaningfully before.

Appendix 2
Microfinance: Towards a Sustainable Islamic Finance Model—A Short Report

Harvard University, Cambridge, MA, April 2008

A workshop entitled "Microfinance: Toward a Sustainable Islamic Finance Model" was held on April 18, 2008, at Harvard Law School before the Eighth Harvard University Forum on Islamic Finance, entitled "Innovation and Authenticity." Despite the fact that Islamic finance is inherently social justice-oriented, Islamic financial institutions have not yet made significant forays into the area of microfinance. This workshop focused on how we could change this model and bring forth ideas that foster a more organic connection between Islamic finance and microfinance initiatives to alleviate poverty and stimulate economic growth.

Hosted by the Islamic Finance Project (IFP), a program sponsored by the Islamic Legal Studies Program (ILSP) at Harvard Law School, the workshop attracted leading international academics, *shari'a* scholars and practitioners in the field of microfinance and Islamic finance generally. In his opening remarks Nazim Ali, the director of the IFP, reminded the audience that IFP is an academic project that encourages discussion and debate without endorsing any specific opinions or viewpoints. This workshop, he noted, was a departure from past initiatives because we would learn from practitioners who are building their own innovative pathways to development throughout the Muslim world. Mahmoud el-Gamal, Professor of Islamic Economics, Finance and Management at Rice University, opened the workshop by remarking on its timeliness, as microfinance is an emerging field with the potential to make a tremendous impact on developing and developed countries. The issue becomes how to balance the social benefits of microfinance with Islamic finance and its requisite structures.

Microfinance as a key to poverty alleviation

This year's workshop marked a union of social and legal debates surrounding Islamic finance with an economic analysis of its future. Sameera Fazili, a lecturer at Yale Law School, began the first session, entitled "Microfinance as a Key to Poverty Alleviation," noting that economists have begun to seek innovative ways to help poorer elements in societies through alternative banking mechanisms. In the United States this is seen with community development banks, and in Muslim countries we see promising uses of micro-credit and micro-loans. Salih Gibriel Hamid Ahmed, the manager of research and planning for the Savings and Social Development Bank based in Khartoum, Sudan, then examined issues surrounding the use of micro-credit in four key industries: agriculture, livestock, small industries and services. Few conventional banks lend to poor customers, and local and traditional moneylending mechanisms are often detrimental to the borrower, who is subject to high interest rates. Ahmed contended that the install-ment-payment plans that are commonly featured as part of *murabaha* financing may provide a means for social development banks to lend to poorer clientele in a commercially viable manner that is beneficial to the customer as well. He gave examples of small textile companies that were able to open through *murabaha*-structured micro-loans and sheep-rearing projects that came to fruition with the aid of restricted *mudaraba* lending.

Nafis Alam, a lecturer and Ph.D. candidate at Monash University in Malaysia, delivered his paper, entitled "Islamic Venture Philanthropy: A Tool for Sustainable Community Development." Alam's paper asked whether using a *zakat* model for charitable philanthropic giving could prove a useful alternative to traditional bank-centered modes of financing. In his model, a network of Muslim investors and local business efforts would create an environment of shared risk and profits compliant with the principles of Islamic financing. Providing another alternative financing model, Tanim Laila, from the Institute of Hazrat Mohammad (SAW) in Bangladesh, proposed a *zakat* and *waqf*-based lending structure that uses these two traditional Islamic charitable endowments as income sources. Introducing new scope for participation in charities, she contended that there is a great deal of money that goes mismanaged in traditional *awqaf* and that it is imperative to dis-tribute charitable monies to the poor more efficiently.

Kim Wilson, a lecturer at the Fletcher School at Tufts University, described microfinance projects in several Muslim countries that had met with varying degrees of success. She used examples of micro-credit and micro-insurance from Syria, Pakistan and Indonesia. The challenge, she remarked, lies not so much in starting these programs as in scaling them up and building them from small projects to ones with greater reach.

Lastly, we aired a series of short video clips presenting the opinions of *shari'a* scholars regarding microfinance; these included Anas Zarka, Duad Bakar, H. Hassan, Nizam Yaqubi and Essam Haq. Most of the scholars agreed that *shari'a* welcomes innovations in Islamic finance that keep with the spirit of *shari'a*, and that microfinance is a good example of a financing methodology that shares the goals of Islamic finance's altruistic nature. The tension lies not in theory, but in managing the high interest rates that often accompany microfinance ventures.

The panels were followed by a lively question and answer session. Several attendees wondered what exactly was Islamic about Islamic finance in a micro-finance model. Were the efforts described simply applying conventional microfi-nance models and giving them Islamic names or stretching the manner in which certain Islamic financing tools can be used? Other audience members responded to the tensions created by microfinancing's high interest rates by noting that per-haps it is best to look to the spirit of *shari'a* and the Qur'an rather than the black letter law of Islamic finance because the goals of microfinance are most important. These issues carried into the second session as well.

Models of Islamic microfinance

The second session, "Models of Islamic Microfinance," was moderated by Mahmoud el-Gamal. Ali Adnan Ibrahim, adjunct professor of law and an S.J.D. Candidate at Georgetown University, began with a speech on "Incentivizing Microfinance for Islamic Financial Institutions." Ibrahim examined the tension within the Islamic finance field in which the development of Islamic microfinance is highly desirable but Islamic finance models are forced away from microfinance. While doctrinal injunctions for fighting poverty encourage Islamic finance institutions to move toward Islamic microfinance, the pressures of doing Islamic finance in the international markets discourage such expansion. Ibrahim sought to resolve this tension by proposing a new model for the Islamic finance industry to profitably conduct Islamic microfinance. His model separates for-profit and non-profit activities by introducing an incentivized actor that assumes the non-profit side to enhance the economic efficiency of microfinance transactions; this new hybrid model encourages a partnership between Islamic finance institutions and philanthropic organizations.

Providing a different Islamic model of microfinance, Moid Uddin Ahmad presented a paper he co-wrote with Athat Mahmood, both of whom are lecturers at Northern Indian Engineering College in Lucknow. Ahmad asserted that venture capital initiatives modeled with Islamic financing may provide a useful tool for social and economic development. Providing a model that also looked at ways to re-appropriate existing financing methods for Islamic ends, Asad Kamran Ghalib, a doctoral research fellow at the University of Manchester, presented a paper entitled "Re-thinking Leasing from an Islamic Perspective: The Prospects of Islamic Micro-Leasing for Poverty Alleviation." According to Ghalib, basic principles of leasing from an Islamic perspective can be applied by microfinance institutions to enable poor micro-entrepreneurs to gain access to the use of assets that would otherwise be too costly and therefore unattainable. In this manner, we can provide collateral-free facilities to the destitute to encourage micro-enterprises and ideally to alleviate poverty.

Turning to more traditional microfinance models Ehsan Feroz, Blake Goud and Mohammad Rahman, of the Institute of Halal Investing in Portland, Oregon, presented a paper entitled "The Development and Implementation of a *Shari'a*-based Microfinance Model Using the Grameen Group Financing Methodology." Echoing concerns voiced by earlier panelists, they asked how we can move productive models forward by expanding their scope and impact. Using *murabaha* and *mudaraba* contracts akin to the Grameen model in Bangladesh they presented the initial findings of a pilot study in Sri Lanka. Putting forth a universalist perspective, they argued that Islamic finance models have the potential to benefit the Muslim and non-Muslim world. They see greater room for synergy between Islamic finance models of microfinance and more traditional models because non-interest-based microfinance is based on Islamic principles, and both Islamic finance and microfinance are business ventures guided by concerns for ethics, morals and social outcomes. Outlining future challenges in the field of Islamic microfinance,

Goud noted it is important to expand product offerings to include consumer and education financing, to develop *salam* financing for agricultural production, to provide *takaful* options to protect clients against business failure and to use charitable grants and training to expand a client base for microfinance ventures.

The final paper of the day, "An Islamic Non-Banking Financial Institution for Accelerated Poverty Eradication," was delivered by Hossain Monowar, director of the Institute of Hazrat Mohammad (SAW) in Bangladesh where he is developing a project on accelerated poverty eradication using *zakat, waqf* and *musharaka* investments. Monowar began with two criticisms of microfinance: first, it charges excessively high interest rates; second, for Muslim clients it is not *shariʿa*-compliant. He then examined two controversial alternatives. One involves reinterpreting the microcredit interest rates as *shariʿa*-compliant and using *zakat* or *awqaf* to subsidize microfinance institutions' overheads so as to reduce interest rates. Another approach, using *murabaha* or *bayʾ-al-muʾajjal*, seems too close to conventional interest-based products. Monowar explored another methodology that draws from the *sunnah* by combining *zakat* and *musharaka* investments on a non-banking platform. He asserts that this methodology provides a way to ensure a steady stream of dividends and employment income to the poor.

The remarks of the workshop's final speaker, Ibrahim Ali Hussein, a manager at the London-based Muslim Aid, provided a perfect complement to Monowar. Hussein used examples from Muslim Aid's initiatives to illustrate the successes and limitations of Islamic finance models in the Muslim world. Hussein explained that the goal of Muslim Aid is to reduce poverty and make the beneficiaries self-reliant by building the capacity of the poorest communities and providing them interest-free capital support on soft terms and other support services. Although micro-loans have significantly improved the lives of recipients, he stressed that we must develop stronger monitoring mechanisms to determine who the client-base is, what exactly is done with loan money and how, in real and quantifiable ways, the loan money changes their lives.

Upon the conclusion of another lively question and answer session, Baber Johansen, the director of ILSP and Affiliated Professor of Law at Harvard Law School, thanked the presenters and organizers of the conference. He remarked on the relevance of this discussion to global trends as we explore the possibilities of making Islamic finance a model for growth and development that works with the world's poor to alleviate poverty through microfinance models.

Glossary

adl   Justice especially distributive justice: social, economic, political, environmental.

amana   Where one party is entrusted with the property of the other for safekeeping and investments.

asabiyah   Group feeling, group (as in tribal or ethnic) chauvinism or partisanship.

asnaf faqir   One who has no material possessions or means of livelihood.

awqaf   (Sing. *waqf.*) See entry for "*waqf.*"

bay'-al-mu'ajjal   Deferred-payment sale; credit sale; a sale where delivery of the contracted goods is immediate and payment is delayed.

bay' al-salam   Purchase with deferred delivery.

bayt al-mal (baitul-maal)   The treasury of the Muslim community (*umma*); historically, the *bayt al-mal* as an institution was developed by the early caliphs that soon fell into disrepair. The *bayt al-mal* contained funds meant to be spent on the needs of the *umma*, e.g., supporting the needy.

dirham   Principal monetary unit of a number of Muslim countries in the past and present.

fiqh   Islamic jurisprudence.

fi-sabilillah   In the way of God.

gharar   Lit. peril, risk, uncertainty.

gharim   (Pl. *gharimun.*) One burdened with debt.

hadith   (Pl. *ahadith.*) Lit. report; historical account of a saying, act or omission of the Prophet or, secondarily, of an esteemed figure among his companions and early Muslim generations.

halal   Allowed; lawful.

haram   Impermissible, unlawful. Opp. *halal.*

hawala   informal money transfers

ihsan   Perfection in worship, such that Muslims try to worship God as if they see Him, and although they cannot see Him, they undoubtedly believe He is constantly watching over them.

ijara   Operating lease.

ijara wa iqtina'   Financial lease.

imam   Lit. leader; e.g., a man who *leads* a community or *leads* the prayer; the *shi'a* sect use the term only as a title for one of the 12 God-appointed successors of Prophet Muhammad.

istinsa' Contract providing for the manufacture and purchase of a specified item.

ji'ala Service charges/wage.

kafalah Assumption of the responsibility for debt repayment; a standard Islamic financial transaction where X (the *kafil*) agrees to assume responsibility for the debts of Y (the *makful 'anhu*). Similar to *hawala*.

khalifah Man's trusteeship and stewardship of earth; most basic theory of the caliphate; flora and fauna as sacred trust; accountability to God for harms to nature, failure to actively care and maintain. Three specific ways in which *khalifa* is manifested in Muslim practice are the creation of *haram* to protect water, *hima* to protect other species (including those useful to man), and by resisting infidel domination over Muslim lands, in *jihad*.

maqasid Objectives of the *shari'a*.

minah (Sing. *minhah*.) Grants, gifts, awards.

miskin A poor, indigent person. The *miskin* is mentioned in the *Qur'an* as one of the recipients of *zakat*.

mu'awadat Type as of transactions such as sales, leases in which there is compensation (e.g., money) form one party and the object of the sale from the other.

mudaraba (Also called *qirad*.) A form of partnership to which some of the partners contribute only capital and the other partners only labor (some schools do not treat it as a partnership but as a contract *sui generis*).

mudarba sukuk A bond whose underlying activity is based on *mudaraba*.

mudarib A partner contributing labor in a *mudaraba*.

muqaddimah Introduction, preface.

murabaha Sale at a percentage mark-up; one of the sales *(bay')* in which the price is stated in terms of the sale object's cost to the seller, the others being sale at cost *(tawliya)* and sale at discount *(wadi'a)*.

mutamainna Satisfaction.

musharaka Equity participation contract.

muzara'a Share-cropping; an agreement between two parties according to which one agrees to allow a portion of one's land to be used by the other in return for a part of the produce from the land.

qard hasan Goodwill short-term loans with no compensation whatsoever.

qirad (Also called *mudaraba*.) A form of partnership to which some of the partners contribute only capital and the other partners only labor (some schools do not treat it as a partnership but as a contract *sui generis*).

rabb-al-mal Lit. the owner of the property; a partner who contributes capital.

al-rahn Collateral; a pledge or the transaction that governs a pledge.

riba (Adj. *ribawi*.)Usury as forbidden in the *Qur'an*; interpreted in classical *fiqh* as including interest and various other forms of gain in contract.

sadaqah (Pl. *sadaqat*.) Charitable giving.

salam Sale with deferred delivery of the sales item.

sanadiq "Funds" as in "investment funds." (*Sanadiq istithmariyya*; plural of *sunduq* = fund.)

shari'a The divine law known from the *Qur'an* and *Sunna*.

sharika   (Also called *musharaka*.) Any contract between two or more persons who agree to jointly enter a financial enterprise whose profits will be divided between them.

sukuk   (Sing, *sakk*.) Islamic bonds; certificates.

sunnah   The Prophet Muhammad's normative example, as known from the *ahadith*; one of the four roots (*usul*) of *fiqh*.

surah   Chapter; the *Qur'an* is composed of 114 *surahs*.

al-taawun   Co-operation, mutual assistance.

tabarru'   Contribution, donation (voluntary contribution).

takaful   Islamic insurance; based on the concept of mutual financial support, an Islamically acceptable alternative to conventional commercial insurance.

tawarruq   A practice in which a person buys something on credit and at once sells it for cash to a third party in a separate transaction.

ulema   Muslim religious scholars.

umma   The Muslim community.

wadi'a   Lit. safekeeping deposit. In the standard Islamic financial transaction where X entrusts property to Y for safekeeping, *wadi'a* refers to the deposited property.

wakala   Agency; a standard Islamic practice wherein X (the *wakil*) acts as the agent of Y. In this capacity X may execute the affairs of Y. A widely applicable phenomena in Islamic practice, *wakala* is often used in financial transactions. Whenever a party cannot personally supervise a given affair, it deputizes another party to execute it on its behalf.

waqf   A standard Islamic transaction where one "freezes" one's property such that it is considered to have been arrested in perpetuity and can neither be sold, inherited, nor donated. The term *waqf* frequently refers to the property itself. The use of a *waqf* (e.g., a park) is often reserved for the relief of the poor, for the public at large, or for other charitable ends.

zakat   The third pillar of Islam; obligatory alms-giving that every well-off Muslim is required to relinquish to the Islamic authority for distribution to the poor and needy.

Bibliography

2009 Arab Microfinance Report. "2009 Arab Microfinance Analysis & Benchmarking Report," a report by Microfinance Information Exchange (MIX), Sanabel and CGAP (May 2010). http://www.themix.org/sites/default/files/2009%20Arab%20 Microfinance%20Analysis%20and%20Benchmarking%20Report_0.pdf.

Adams, D.W. and Pischke, J.V. *Microenterprise Credit Programs: Deja Vu*. Columbus, OH: Agricultural Finance Program, The Ohio State University, 1991.

ADB (Asian Development Bank). *Draft Report Rural Microfinance Indonesia*. Manila: ADB, March 2003.

Ahmad, Aka Firowz. "The Management System of NGOs Micro-Credit Program for Poverty Alleviation in Bangladesh," paper presented at the First International Conference on Islamic Development Management, Penang, December 1998.

Ahmad, Ausaf. *Contemporary Practice of Islamic Financing Techniques*. Islamic Research and Training Institute research paper, Jeddah, 1993, 20pp.

Ahmed, Gaffar Abdalla. "Islamic Microfinance Practices with a Particular Reference to Financing Entrepreneurs through Equity Participation Contracts in Sudanese Banks," in Mohammed Obaidullah and Hajah Salma Haji Abdul Latiff *Islamic Finance for Micro and Medium Enterprises*. Islamic Research Training Institute, Islamic Development Bank and Centre for Islamic Banking, Finance and Management, University of Brunei Darussalam, Jeddah/Brunei, 2008, pp. 75–106.

Ahmed, Habib. "Financing Microenterprises: An Analytical Study of Islamic Microfinance Institutions," *Islamic Economic Studies*, 2002, 9(2), pp. 27–64.

Ahmed, Habib. "Frontiers of Islamic Banking: A Synthesis of Social Role and Microfinance," *The European Journal of Management and Public Policy*, 2004, 3, pp. 120–140.

Ahmed, Habib. "*Waqf*-based Microfinance: Realizing the Social Role of Islamic Finance," paper presented at International Seminar on Integrating *Awqaf* in the Islamic Financial Sector, Singapore, March 6–7, 2007.

Akhter, N. *BRAC's Experience in Flood Disaster Management*. BRAC Working Paper (BRAC RED: September 2004).

Alam, K. "Grameen Bank and 'Microcredit': The 'Wonderful Story' that Never Happened—Reputation and Reality," October 21, 2001. From LINKS *International Journal of Socialist Renewal*. http://links.org.au/node/1955.

Ali, Abbas J. *Islamic Perspectives on Management and Organisation*. Cheltenham: Edward Elgar, 2005.

Ali, S. Nazim. "Financing the Poor: Toward an Islamic Microfinance," Cambridge, MA: Islamic Finance Project, Harvard Law School, 2007. http://ifp.law.harvard.edu/login/ view_pdf/?file=Financing%20the%20poor.pdf&type=seminars.

Alirani, Kais. "Islamic Micro-finance—Yemen Experience," First Annual Conference of SANABEL, Micro-finance Network of Arab Countries, 2003.

Aliyev, Fuad. "Applications of *Awqaf* and Islamic Microfinance in a Post-Soviet Secular State: A Hypothetical Model of *Awqaf*-based Credit Unions," paper presented at the *International Seminar on Islamic Alternatives to Poverty Alleviation: Zakat, Awqaf and Microfinance*, Dhaka, Bangladesh, April 21–23, 2007.

Alvi, I.A. "Need for a global unified Sukuk [i.e., Islamic bonds] market: Key challenges & role of Islamic Financial Institutions." *International Islamic Financial Market*, 2007.

Anand, M. and Badawi, S. "Can Microfinance Heal Wounds of War?," Common Ground News Service (CGNews), December 12, 2006. http://www.commongroundnews.org/article.php?id=20192&lan=en&sp=1.

Anwar, Muhammed. "Islamicity of Banking and Modes of Islamic Banking," *Arab Law Quarterly*, 2003, 18(I), pp. 62–80.

Al Asaad, Mahmoud. "Village Funds: The Experience of Rural Community Development at Jabal Al Hoss, Syria," in Mohammed Obaidullah and Hajah Salma Haji Abdul Latiff *Islamic Finance for Micro and Medium Enterprises*. Islamic Research Training Institute, Islamic Development Bank and Centre for Islamic Banking, Finance and Management, University of Brunei Darussalam, Jeddah/Brunei, 2008, pp. 197–210.

El-Ashker, Ahmed Abdel-Fattah and Sirajul Haq, Muhammad. *Institutional Framework of Zakah: Dimensions and Implications*, Islamic Research and Training Institute, Jeddah, Seminar Proceedings 1995, No. 23.

Ashraf, Muhammad. "*Shariah*-compliant Financial Products." *Accountancy*, 2007. http://www.accountancy.com.pk/articles.asp?id=174.

Asian Development Bank. *Technical Assistance for the Development of International Prudential Standards for Islamic Financial Services*. Asian Development Bank, 2004.

Badwi, Samer and Grais, Wafij. "Meeting the Demand for Sustainable, *Shari'a*-Compliant Microfinance." Paper presented at Financing the Poor: Toward an Islamic Microfinance." Cambridge, MA: Finance Project, Islamic Legal Studies Program, Harvard Law School, 2007.

Banerjee, A. and Duflo, E. *Do Firms Want to Borrow More? Testing Credit Constraints Using a Directed Lending Program*. MIT Working Paper, 2004. http://econ-www.mit.edu/files/791.

Banerjee, A., Duflo, E., Glennerster, R. and Kinnan, C. *The Miracle of Microfinance? Evidence from a Randomized Evaluation*. Chennai: IFMR Research Center for Micro Finance, 2009.

BI (Bank Indonesia). *The Blueprint of Islamic Banking Development in Indonesia*. Jakarta: BI, 2002.

BI (Bank Indonesia). *Economic Report on Indonesia*. Jakarta: BI, 2003.

BI (Bank Indonesia). *Compilation of Indonesian Islamic Banking Regulations*. Jakarta: BI, February 2000–May 2003.

BI (Bank Indonesia), Direktorat Perbankan Syariah. *Statistik Perbankan Syariah*. Jakarta: BI, January 2004.

BI (Bank Indonesia) and Research Center on Development Studies. *Research on Potency, Preference and Society Behavior Toward Shariah Banking System in Central Java and Yogyakarta Provinces*—Executive Summary. Semarang, Diponegoro University. Jakarta: BI, 2000.

Basar, Hasmet (Editor). "Management and Development of *Awqaf* Properties," Islamic Research and Training Institute, Research–Seminar–Workshop Proceedings, 1987, No. 1.

Basu, P. and Srivastava, P. "Scaling up Microfinance for India's Rural Poor," World Bank Policy Research Working Paper Series No. 3646 (2005).

Baue, W. "First and Largest International Microfinance Bond Issued," *Sustainability Investment News*, August 18, 2004.

Bennett, Lynn. "Combining Social and Financial Intermediation to Reach the Poor: The Necessity and the Dangers", in Mwangi S. Kimenyi, Robert C. Wieland and J.D.V. Pischke (Editors), *Strategic Issues in Microfinance*. Aldershot: Ashgate Publishing Ltd, 1998.

Bonvin, J. and Al-Sultan, F. "Preface," in Hartmut Schneider (Editor), *Microfinance for the Poor?* Paris: OECD, 1997.

Bornstein, David. *The Price of a Dream: The Story of Grameen Bank and the Idea that is Helping the Poor to Change their Lives*. Dhaka: University Press, 1996.

Bowen, John. *Islam, Law and Equality in Indonesia*. Cambridge: Cambridge University Press, 2003.

Brandsma, J. and Burjorjee, D. *Microfinance in the Arab States: Building Inclusive Financial Sectors*. New York: UNCDP, 2004.

Brandsma, J. and Chaouali, R. *Making Microfinance Work in the Middle East and North Africa*. Washington, DC: The World Bank, Middle East and North Africa Region, Private and Financial Sector Development Group and Human Development Group, 1998.

Brandsma, J. and Hart, L. *Making Microfinance Work Better in the Middle East and North Africa*. Washington DC: World Bank, 2004.

Brennan, Margaret. "Sequoia Invests $11.5 Million in Microfinance Fund," CNBC.com. March 27, 2007. http://www.cnbc.com/id/17844093.

Bruck, C. "Millions for Millions," *The New Yorker*. http://www.newyorker.com/archive/2006/10/30/061030fa_fact1.

Buckley, Graeme. "Rural and Agricultural Credit in Malawi, A Study of the Malawi Muzdi Fund and the Smallholder Agricultural Credit Administration," in David Hulme and Paul Mosley, *Finance Against Poverty*, Volume 2, London: Routledge, 1996, pp. 333–407.

Burgess, R., Pande, R. and Wong, G. "Banking for the Poor: Evidence from India," *Journal of European Economic Association*, 3(2–3), 2005, pp. 268–278.

CGAP (Consultative Group to Assist the Poor). "Core Performance Indicators for Microfinance," April 2006, 12pp.

http://www.uncdf.org/english/microfinance/uploads/evaluations/Core%20Indicators--UNDP%20version.pdf.

CGAP (Consultative Group to Assist the Poor). "Financial Institutions with a Double Bottom Line: Implications for the Future of Microfinance," Occasional Papers No. 8. July 2004, 20pp. http://www.cgap.org/gm/document-1.9.2701/OP8.pdf.

CGAP (Consultative Group to Assist the Poor). "Graduating the Poorest into Microfinance: Linking Safety Nets and Financial Services," *Focus Notes*, No. 34, February 2006, 8pp. http://www.cgap.org/gm/document-1.9.2586/FN34.pdf.

CGAP (Consultative Group to Assist the Poor). "Using Technology to Build Inclusive Financial Systems." *Focus Notes*, No. 32, January 2006, 16pp. www.ictregulationtoolkit.org/en/Document.3436.pdf.

CGAP (Consultative Group to Assist the Poor). "Islamic Microfinance: Emerging Market Niche," CGAP *Focus Notes*, No. 49, August 2008. http://www.cgap.org/gm/document-1.9.5029/FN49.pdf.

CGAP (Consultative Group to Assist the Poor). "Glossary of Financial Terms." http://www.cgap.org/p/site/c/template.rc/1.26.3803/#par.

Chanchan, M.A. "Microfinance's Small-town Success Attracts Venture Investors," from livemint.com & *The Wall Street Journal*, July 13, 2009. http://www.livemint.com/2009/07/13221413/Microfinance8217s-smalltow.html.

Chapra, M.U. "The Islamic Vision of Development in the Light of Maqasid Al-Shariah," *International Institute of Islamic Thoughts*, 2008.

Chapra, M.U. *Towards a Just Monetary System*. Leicester: Islamic Foundation, 1985.

Chaudhuri, S.H. "Downscaling Institutions and Competitive Microfinance Markets: Reflections and Case Studies from Latin America," August 2004. http://india.micro-save.org/research_paper/downscaling-institutions-and-competitive-microfinance-markets-reflections-and-case-st.

Chen, Greg et al. "Growth and Vulnerabilities in Microfinance," Focus Note 61, Washington, DC: CGAP, February 2010.

CHF International. *Practical Guide for Housing Microfinance in Morocco*. CHF International, 2005.

Chowdhry, Sajjad. "Creating an Islamic Microfinance Model—The Missing Dimension," *Dinar Standard*, November 2006. http://www.dinarstandard.com/finance/Micro Finance111806.htm.

Christensen, R.P. "Commercialization and Mission Drift: The Transformation of Microfinance in Latin America." CGAP Occasional Paper, January 2001.

Cizakca, Murat. "The Relevance of the Ottoman Cash *Waqfs* (*Awqaf al Nuqud*) for Modern Islamic Economics," in M.A. Mannan (Editor), *Financing Development is Islam*. Jeddah: Islamic Research and Training Institute, Seminar Proceedings Series, 1996, No. 30.

Cizakca, Murat. "*Awqaf* in History and Implications for Modern Islamic Economics," paper presented at International Seminar on Awqaf and Economic Development, Kuala Lumpur, 1998.

Cizakca, Murat. "Latest Developments in the Western Non-Profit Sector and the Implications for Islamic *Awqaf*," in M. Iqbal (Editor), *Islamic Economic Institutions and the Elimination of Poverty*. Leicester: Islamic Foundation, 2002, pp. 263–292.

Cizakca, Murat. "Cash Waqf as Alternative to NBFIs Bank," paper presented in the International Seminar on Nonbank Financial Institutions: Islamic Alternatives, Kuala Lumpur, jointly organized by Islamic Research and Training Institute, Islamic Development Bank and Islamic Banking and Finance Institute Malaysia, March 1–3, 2004.

Clark, Heather. "Islamic Banking Principles Applied to Microfinance: Case Study—Hodeidah Microfinance Programme, Yemen," United Nations Capital Development Fund, New York, January 2002.

Crimm, N.J. "Post-September 11 Fortified Anti-Terrorism Measures Compel Heightened Due Diligence." *Pace Law Review*, (25), 2005, p. 23.

CRISIL. *India Top 50 Microfinance Institutions*. Mumbai: CRISIL, 2009.

Cull, R., Demirguc-Kunt, A. and Morduch, J. "Financial Performance and Outreach: A Global Analysis of Leading Microbanks," *Economic Journal*, 117, February 2007.

Delgado, E. *Group Lending: Learning from the International Experience. Urban & Regional Planning Economic Development Handbook*. Ann Arbor, MI: Taubman College of Architecture and Urban Planning. University of Michigan, 2005.

Development Unit and Ministry of Labour Relations and Foreign Employment, Technical Advisory Support. ILO-IRTAP, 2006.

Dhumale, Rahul and Sapcanin, Amela. "An Application of Islamic Banking Principles to Microfinance," a study by the Region Bureau for Arab States, World Bank Group, Washington, DC, December 1999, 14pp. http://www.ruralfinance.org/fileadmin/templates/rflc/documents/1114499916629_WB_Islamic_MF_edited.pdf.

Djojosugito, Reza Adirahman. "Legal Framework to Induce Paradigm Shift in Islamic Alternatives to Poverty Alleviation," paper presented at the *International Seminar on Islamic*

Alternatives to Poverty Alleviation: Zakat, Awqaf and Microfinance, Dhaka, Bangladesh, April 21–23, 2007.

Donohue, J.J. *A Note on the Theory and Practice of Islamic Banking, Yearbook of Islamic and Middle Eastern Law*. London: Kluwer Law International, 2000.

Dow Jones. *Guide to the Dow Jones Islamic Market Index*. New York, June 2005.

Dowla, A. *Micro Leasing: The Grameen Bank Experience*. St. Mary's City, MD: St. Mary's College of Maryland, 1998.

Dusuki, Asyraf Wajdi. "Banking for the Poor: The Role of Islamic Banking in Microfinance Initiatives," *Humanomics*, 24(1), 2008, pp. 49–66.

Eagle, L. "Banking on *Sharia* Principles: Islamic Banking and the Financial Industry," 2009. http://www.bankersacademy.com/pdf/Islamic_Banking.pdf.

Edwardes, W. "Islamic Banking," *Princeton Economics Journal*. Princeton Economics International, Princeton, NJ, 1999.

Feibig, M., Hanning, A. and Wisniwski, S. *Savings in the Context of Microfinance —State of Knowledge*. Eschborn: GTZ: CGAP Working Paper on Savings, 1999.

Ferro, N. *Value Through Diversity: Microfinance and Islamic Finance and Global Banking*. Milan: Fondazione Eni Enrioco Mattei, 2005.

Fischer, S. "Wall Street Meets Microfinance," WWWB/FWA Lenore Albom Lecture Series, 2003.

http://www.citigroup.com/citigroup/citizen/microfinance/data/031103a.pdf.

Fuglesang, Andreas and Chandler, Dale. *Participation as Process – Process as Growth: What We Can Learn from Grameen Bank*. Dhaka: Grameen Trust, 1993.

Gafoor, A.L.M.A. *Interest-free Commercial Banking*. Groningen: APPTEC Publications, 1995.

Gallardo, J. "Leasing to Support Micro and Small Enterprises," Policy Research Working Paper, Washington, DC: The World Bank, 1857, 2003.

El-Gamal, M.A. *Islamic Finance: Law Economics, and Practice*. Cambridge: Cambridge University Press, 2006.

El-Gari, Mohamed A., "The *Qard Hassan* Bank," paper presented in the *International Seminar on Nonbank Financial Institutions: Islamic Alternatives*, March 1–3, 2004, Kuala Lumpur, jointly organized by Islamic Research and Training Institute, Islamic Development Bank and Islamic Banking and Finance Institute Malaysia, 2004.

Gaudiosi, M. "The Influence of the Islamic Law of *Waqf* on the Development of the Trust in England: The Case of Merton College, Oxford," *University of Pennsylvania Law Review*, 136(1231), 1988.

Ghalib, Asad Kamran. "Re-thinking Leasing from an Islamic Perspective: The Prospects of Islamic Micro-leasing for Poverty Alleviation," paper presented at the *Pre-Forum Workshop on Microfinance: Towards a Sustainable Islamic Microfinance Model*, Harvard Law School, Cambridge, MA, April 18, 2008.

Ghosh, R. "Microfinance in India: A Critique," *Independent*, 2005.

Goeldner, Karri A. *Roles and Opportunities for Rural Credit Initiatives in Afghanistan's Opium Economy*. London: DfID, 2004.

Goetz, A. Marie and Gupta, Rina S. "Who Takes the Credit? Gender, Power, and Control over Loan Use in Rural Credit Programmes in Bangladesh," *World Development*, 24, 1996, pp. 45–63.

Goldberg, N. *Measuring the Impact of Microfinance: Taking Stock of What We Know*. Grameen Foundation USA, December 2005.

Grace, L. and Al-ZamZami, A. *Islamic Banking Principles Applied to Microfinance Case Study: Hodeidah Microfinance Program, Yemen*. Geneva: UNCDF, 2002.

Grameen Foundation. "Grameen–Jameel Initiative Engineers $2.5 Million Investment to Boost Microfinance in Egypt," September 9, 2006. http://www.syminvest.com/market/news/microfinance/grameenjameel-initiative-engineers-25-million-investment-in-dbacd/2006/9/27/119.

Grameen Foundation. "Grameen Foundation Engineers More Than $100 Million in Local Currency Financing," December 12, 2007a. http://www.syminvest.com/market/news/microfinance/grameen-foundation-engineers-more-than-100-million-in-local-currency-financing/2007/12/12/751.

Grameen Foundation. "Grameen Foundation Supports Landmark Deal for Kashf Foundation in Pakistan," May 31, 2007b.

Grameen Foundation. *Growth Guarantees: Fact Sheet*. Washington, DC: Grameen Foundation, February 26, 2008a.

Grameen Foundation. "Grameen–Jameel Guarantee for the Arab World: A Guarantee Financing Program for Poverty-Focused Microfinance Institutions in the Arab World," February 26, 2008b.

The *Halal Journal*. "Malaysian Islamic Banks Profits Lag behind Gulf Counterparts," TodayOnline July 7, 2006, 11:44. http://www.halaljournal.com/artman/publish/article_832.shtml#top.

Hanning, D.A. "Mobilizing Microsavings: The Millennium Challenge in Microfinance," *Sixth Consultative Group Meeting of CGAP*, 1999.

Al-Harran, Saad. "Islamic Finance Needs a New Paradigm," 1996. http://www.kantakji.com/fiqh/Files/Finance/ISLAMIC%20FINANCE%20NEEDS%20A%20NEW%20PARADIGM.htm.

Al-Harran, Saad. "The Musharakah Financing Model," n.d. http://www.iefpedia.com/english/?p=819.

Hashemi, Syed M. "Building up Capacity for Banking with the Poor: The Grameen Bank in Bangladesh," in Hartmut Schneider (Editor), *Microfinance for the Poor?* Paris: OECD, 1997, pp. 635–653.

Hashemi, Syed M. and Schuler, S.R. *Sustainable Banking with the Poor: A Case Study of Grameen*. Dhaka: Programme for Research on Poverty Alleviation, Grameen Trust, 2002.

Hashemi, Syed M., Schuler, Sidney R. and Riley, Ann P. "Rural Credit Programs and Women's Empowerment in Bangladesh," *World Development*, 24, 1996, pp. 635–653.

Havers, M. "Microenterprise and Small Business Leasing-Lessons from Pakistan," *Small Enterprise Development Journal*, 10(3), 1999.

El-Hawary, D.A. and Grais, W. "Islamic Financial Services and Microfinance," June 2005a.

El-Hawary, D.A. and Grais, W. "The Compatibility of Islamic Financial Services and Microfinance: A Little-Explored Avenue for Expanding Outreach. Microfinance Matters," United Nations Capital Development Fund, 2005b.

Hoff, K. and Stiglitz, J.E. "Imperfect Information and Rural Credit Markets: Puzzles and Policy Perspectives," in A.B. Klara Hoff, *The Economics of Rural Organization. Theory, Practices and Policy*. Oxford: Oxford University Press, 1993, pp. 33–52.

Holloh, D. *Microfinance Institutions Study*. Jakarta: Ministry of Finance, 2001.

Holloh, D. and Seibel, Hans Dieter. "Member-based Microfinance Institutions in Syria: The Example of the Sanduq Programme," *Proceedings of Finance for Small-Scale Commodity Processing: From Micro to Meso Finance—An International Workshop*. Amsterdam: Common Fund for Commodities, 2004, pp. 149–159.

Honohon, Patrick. "Cross-Country Variations in Household Access to Financial Services," presented at the World Bank Conference on Access to Finance, Washington, D.C., March 15, 2007.

Hossain, M. *Credit Programme for the Landless: The Experience of Grameen Bank Project*. Dhaka: Bangladesh Institute of Development Studies, 1983.

Hossain, M. "Employment Generation through Cottage Industries—Potentials and Constraints: The Case of Bangladesh," in Rizwanul Islam (Editor) *Rural Industrialisation and Employment in Asia*. New Delhi: ILO, Asian Employment Programme, 1987.

Hulme, David and Mosley, Paul. *Finance Against Poverty*, Volume 1, Routledge, London, 1996a.

Hulme, David and Mosley, Paul. *Finance Against Poverty*, Volume 2, Routledge, London, 1996b.

Hulme, D. and Moore, K. "Why Has Microfinance Been a Policy Success in Bangladesh (and Beyond)?," Manchester: Institute for Development Policy and Management, University of Manchester, 2006.

Huppi, M. and Feder, Gershon. "The Role of Groups and Credit Co-operatives in Rural Lending," *World Bank Research Observer*, 5, 1990, pp. 187–204.

Ibrahim, Ali Adnan. "Convergence of Corporate Governance and Islamic Financial Services Industry: Toward Islamic Financial Services Securities Market," Cambridge, MA: Harvard Law School, 2007.

Ibrahim, Ali Adnan. "The Rise of Customary Businesses in International Financial Markets: An Introduction to Islamic Finance and the Islamic Financial Services Industry," *American University International Law Review*, 2008.

IFLR. "Islamic Finance: Sovereign *Sukuk* for UK," *International Financial Law Review*, January 2008a.

IFLR. "Islamic Finance: Hong Kong Bids for *Shariah*," *International Financial Law Review*, January 2008b.

IFLR. "Islamic Finance: Projects to Grow," *International Financial Law Review*, January 2008c.

Ifthikar, H. and Saleem, A.M. "Challenges for Practical *Shari'ah*: Experiences from Muslim Aid," Sri Lanka Field Office, August 2008.

IIFM. "A Series of Studies on *Sukuk* Issuances from different Jurisdictions Series: A Study on *Sukuk* Issuances in Indonesia," 2010, online, IIFM. http://www.iifm.net/customer/MailDocument.aspx?DocID=33.

Imady, Omar and Seibel, Hans Dieter. "Sanduq: A Microfinance Innovation in Jabal Al-Hoss, Syria," *NENARACA Newsletter*, Amman, September 2003, pp. 1–12.

Imady, Omar and Seibel, Hans Dieter. *Principles and Products of Islamic Finance*. Cologne: University of Cologne, Development Research Center. 2006. http://www.uni-koeln.de/ew-fak/aef/06-2006/2006-1%20Principles%20and%20products%20of%20Islamic%20finance.pdf.

International Monetary Fund (IMF). *Islamic Republic of Afghanistan: Statistical Appendix No. 6/114*. Washington, DC: IMF, 2006.

Iqbal, Munawar (Editor). *Islamic Economic Institutions and the Elimination of Poverty*. Leicester: Islamic Foundation, 2002.

Iqbal, Zamir and Mirakhor, Abbas. "Islamic Banking," IMF Occasional Paper 49. Washington, DC: International Monetary Fund, 1987.

"Islam, Poverty and Microfinance: Best Practices," *Islamic Finance Today: The Pulse of Ethical Business*, Colombo, Sri Lanka, 2007, 8pp.

Islamic Financial Services Board and Islamic Research and Training Institute. "Islamic Microfinance Development: Challenges and Initiatives," working paper for Islamic

Financial Services Board Forum Framework and Strategies for Development of Islamic Microfinance Services, Dakar, Senegal, May 27, 2007, 81pp.

Islamic Fiqh Academy. *Proceedings of Third Fiqhi Seminar on Bay Rights, Murabahah and Islamic Banking.* New Delhi: Islamic Fiqh Academy, n.d., pp. 547–549.

Ivatury, Gautam and Pickens, Mark. "Mobile Phone Banking and Low-Income Customers: Evidence from South Africa," 2006, 14pp. http://www.globalproblems-globalsolutions-files.org/unf_website/PDF/mobile_phone_bank_low_income_customers.pdf.

Jannson, T. "Microfinance: From Village to Wall Street," IADB Sustainable Development Department Best Practices Series 1, November 2001.

Jones, J. H. "Some Issues in Informal Finance: Perspectives from a Rajasthan Village," in *Towards a Sustainable Microfinance Outreach in India.* New Delhi: Microcredit Innovations Department, NABARD, 2006, pp. 137–149.

Kahf, Monzer. "*Shari'ah* and Historical Aspects of *Zakat* and *Awqaf*," background paper prepared for Islamic Research and Training Institute and Islamic Development Bank, 2004.

Kahf, Monzer and Khan, Tariqullah. *Principles of Islamic Financing, A Survey.* Jeddah: Islamic Research and Training Institute, Research Paper No. 16, 1992.

Kamoche, K. "Kenya's Naked Constitution," 2005. http://generator21.net/g21archive/africa108.html.

Karim, Nimrah, Tarazi, Michael and Reille, Xavier. *Islamic Microfinance: An Emerging Market Niche.* Washington, DC: CGAP, 2008.

Karlan, D.S. and Goldberg, N. "The Impact of Microfinance: A Review of Methodological Issues," World Bank Doing Impact Evaluation Series, 2006.

Kazarian, E. *Islamic versus Traditional Banking. Financial Innovations in Egypt.* Boulder, CO: Westview Press, 1993.

Keyes, D. "Protecting the Peace While Profiting the Poor: Microfinance Terrorist Financing Regulation," *Law and Business Review of the Americas,* 12, 2006, p. 545.

Khan, Atif R. "Poverty to Profit," *Islamica Magazine,* Issue 12, Summer 2005, pp. 6–10.

Khan, J.A. and Nisar, S. "Collateral (*al-rahn*) as Practiced by Interest-free Credit Societies," *Journal of King Abdul Aziz University: Islamic Economics Jeddah,* 2004, pp. 17–34.

Khan, M. Fahim. "Social Dimensions of Islamic Banks in Theory and Practice," Islamic Research and Training Institute, Islamic Development Bank, manuscript, 1997.

Khandker, Shahidur R., Khalily, Baqui and Khan, Zahed. *Grameen Bank: Performance and Sustainability,* World Bank Discussion Papers, No. 306, The World Bank, Washington, DC, 1995.

Kimenyi, Mwangi S., Wieland, Robert C. and Pischke, J.D.V. (Editors). *Strategic Issues in Microfinance.* Aldershot: Ashgate Publishing Ltd, 1998.

Kochar, A. *Social Banking and Poverty: A Micro-empirical Analysis of the Indian Experience.* Stanford Center for International Development, Stanford University, 2005.

Krause, N. and Walter, I. "Can Microfinance Reduce Portfolio Volatility?" *Economic Development and Cultural Change,* 58(85) (October 2009).

Kuran, T. "Islamic Economics and the 'Clash of Civilisations'," 2 *Middle Eastern Lectures.* Tel Aviv: Tel Aviv University, 1977.

Kwok, V.W. "Hong Kong Developing Islamic Bond Market," *Forbes* (Market Scan), September 11, 2007. http://www.forbes.com/2007/09/11/hk-islamic-finance-markets-econ-cx_vk_0911markets2.html.

Lapenu, Cécile. *The Role of the State in Promoting Microfinance Institutions Paper No. 89.* Washington, DC: International Food Policy Research Institute, 2000.

Latortue, A. "Tackling Aid Effectiveness from the Top: Donor Peer Reviews Synthesis Report. CGAP III Strategy, 2003–2008." Washington, DC: CGAP, January.

Lewis, Mervyn K. "Wealth Creation through *Takaful*," in Munnawar Iqbal and Rodney Wilson (Editors), *Islamic Perspectives on Wealth Creation*. Edinburgh: Edinburgh University Press, 2005, 187pp.

McGuire, P.B. and Conroy, J.D. "Bank–NGO Linkages and the Transaction Costs of Lending to the Poor through Groups: Evidence from India and Philippines," in Hartmut Schneider (Editor) *Microfinance for the Poor?* Paris: OECD, 1997.

MacLean, A. "Islamic Banking: Is It Really Kosher?" *The American*, 2007.

Manalo, Marilyn S. *Microfinance Institutions' Response in Conflict Environments – Africa Region Working Paper Series No. 54*. Washington, DC: World Bank, 2003.

Mandela, N. "Make Poverty History," 2005. http://www.makepovertyhistory.org/extras/mandela.shtml.

Al-Mawsu'a al-fiqhiyyah (*The Encyclopedia of Islamic Fiqh*). The Ministry of Awqaf, Kuwait, Vol. 44, pp. 123–124, 166–167.

Mayer, A.E. "Islamic Banking and Credit Policies in the Sadat Era: The Social Origins of Islamic Banking in Egypt." *Arab Law Quarterly*, 1, 1985, 50pp.

Mazhari, S.A. "Banking Without Interest." *Proceedings of Third Fiqhi Seminar on Bay rights, Murabahah and Islamic Banking*. Bangalore: Islamic Fiqh Academy, New Delhi, India, 1990, pp. 602–607.

Meehan, J. "Tapping the Financial Markets for Microfinance: Grameen Foundations Promotion of this Emerging Trend," Grameen Foundation USA Working Paper Series (October 2004).

Micro-Credit Coverage Maps 2006. http://www.pksf-bd.org/index.php?option=com_mapping&Itemid=284.

Mirakhor, A. "Hopes for the Future of Islamic Finance," lecture at the Institute of Islamic Banking, London, 2002.

Mirakhor, Abbas and Iqbal, Zamir. "*Qard Hasan* Microfinance (QHMF)." *New Horizon*, April/June 2007, pp. 18–20.

Molla, R.I., Moten, R.A., Gusau, S.A. and Gwandu, A.A. *Frontiers and Mechanics of Islamic Economics*. Nigeria: University of Sokoto, 1988.

Morduch, Jonathan. "The Microfinance Schism." *World Development*, 28, 1998.

Morduch, Jonathan. "Between the State and the Market: Can Informal Insurance Patch the Safety Net?" *World Bank Research Observer*, 14(2), 1999a, pp. 187–207.

Morduch, Jonathan, "The Microfinance Promise," *Journal of Economic Literature*, 1999b, No. 37, pp. 1569–1614.

Morduch, Jonathan and Rutherford, S. "Microfinance: Analytical Issues for India," World Bank, South Asia Region—Finance and Private Sector Development, 2003.

Munzele Maimbo, S. *The Money Exchange Dealers of Kabul: A Study of the Hawala System in Afghanistan*. Washington, DC: World Bank, 2003.

Nagarajan, G. *Microfinance in Post-Conflict Situations: Towards Guiding Principles for Action*. Geneva: ILO, 1999.

Nagarajan, G., Knight, H. and Chandani, T. *Mid-Term Review of the Microfinance Sector and MISFA in Afghanistan*. Kabul: Government of Afghanistan and MISFA, 2006.

National SME Development Council Secretariat. "Strengthening Enabling Infrastructure to Support SME Development," *Bank Negara Press Release*, Kuala Lumpur, August 8, 2006.

NDTV. "After 20 Suicides, Andhra Pradesh to Monitor Micro Finance." http://www.ndtv.com/video/player/news/after-20-suicides-andhra-pradesh-to-monitor-micro-finance/169794.

Nelson, Stephanie. "Microfinance: The Opportunity for Islamic Banks." *Islamic Finance News*, Kuala Lumpur, 3(43), December 1, 2006, 19pp.

Nimrah, K. et al. "Islamic Microfinance: An Emerging Market Niche," CGAP: *Focus Notes*, No. 49, 2008, 8pp.

Obaidullah, M. "Islam, Poverty and Microfinance 'Best Practices'," 2007. http://instituteofhalalinvesting.org/content/Islam_and_poverty.pdf.

Obaidullah, M. and Khan, T. "Islamic Microfinance Development: Challenges and Initiatives," Islamic Research and Training Institute, Islamic Development Bank: Policy Dialogue Paper No. 2, 33pp.

Otero, Maria and Elisabeth Rhyne (Editors). *The New World of Microenterprise Finance.* West Hartford, CT: Kumarian Press, 1994.

Panagariya, A. *Bank Branch Expansion and Poverty Reduction: A Comment.* 2006. http://www.columbia.edu/~ap2231/technical%20papers/Bank%20Branch%20Expansion%20and%20Poverty.pdf.

Patten, R.H., Rosengard, J.K. and Johnston, Jr., D.E. "Microfinance Success Amidst Macroeconomic Failure: The Experience of Bank Rakyat Indonesia During the East Asian Crisis," *World Development*, 29, 2001.

Pilling, D. et al. "JBIC in talks on Islamic bond issue in Tokyo," *Financial Times*, August 17, 2006.

Pischke, J.D. et al. "Introductory Overview: Principles and Perspectives," in Hartmut Schneider (Editor), *Microfinance for the Poor?* Paris: OECD, 1997.

Porteous, D. and Helms, B. "Protecting Microfinance Borrowers," CGAP *Focus Note* No. 27, 2005.

Pronyk, P.M., Hargreaves, J.R. and Morduch, J. "Microfinance Programs and Better Health Prospects for Sub-Saharan Africa." *Journal of the American Medical Associations*, 298(16), October 2007.

PT Permodalan Nasional Madani (PNM), Melangkah Bersama. *Step Forward with PNM.* Jakarta: PNM, 1999–2004.

Rahman, Aminur. "Micro-credit Initiatives for Equitable and Sustainable Development: Who Pays?" *World Development*, 27(1), 1999, pp. 67–82.

Rahman, R. and Shah Mohammed, S.I. "Securitization and Micro-Credit Backed Securities," in S. Sundaresan (Editor), *Microfinance: Emerging Trends and Challenges.* Cheltenham: Edward Elgar, 2008.

Reddy, R. "State for De-recognition of MFIs." From *The Hindu* online edition of India's national newspaper. http://www.hindu.com/2010/04/19/21hdline.htm.

Reed, Larry R. and Befus, David R. "Transformation Lending: Helping Microenterprises Become Small Businesses," in Maria Otero and Elisabeth Rhyne (Editors), *The New World of Microenterprise Finance.* West Hartford, CT: Kumarian Press, 1994, pp. 185–204.

Reille, X. and Foster, S. "Foreign Capital Investment in Microfinance," CGAP *Focus Note* No. 44, January 2008.

Roberts, R. *The Social Laws of the Qoran.* London: Williams and Norgate Ltd, 1925.

Rhyne, E. and Busch, B. "The Growth of Commercial Microfinance: 2004–2006," Council of Microfinance Equity Funds, September 2006.

Rutherford, S. "Raising the Curtain on the Microfinancial Services Era." CGAP *Focus Notes*, No. 49. May 2000. http://www.cgap.org/p/site/c/template.rc/1.9.2560/.

Sa Dhan. *Side by Side: A Slice of Microfinance Operations in India.* New Delhi: Sa Dhan, 2005.

Said, Pervez, Shafqat, Mahmood and Ur-Rehman, Zahid. *Draft Guidelines for Provision of Islamic Microfinance Services and Products by Financial Institutions.* Karachi: State Bank of Pakistan, 2006.

Sait, Siraj and Lim, Hilary. *Land, Law and Islam: Property and Human Rights in the Muslim World.* London: Zed Books, 2006.

Sait, Siraj and Lim, Hilary. "Islamic Microfinance in Crisis Situations: The Unofficial Development Discourse," paper presented at *Financing the Poor: Toward an Islamic Microfinance.* Cambridge, MA: Islamic Finance Project, Harvard Law School, 2007.

Segrado, C. "Islamic Microfinance and Socially Responsible Investments," MEDA Project. Microfinance at the University, Torino: University of Torino, 2005.

Scanteam. *Assessment, Afghanistan Reconstruction Trust Fund (ARTF) Final Report.* Oslo: ARTF, 2005.

Schneider, Hartmut (Editor). *Microfinance for the Poor? Development Centre of the Organization for Economic Cooperation and Development.* Paris: OECD, 1997.

Seibel, Hans D. "Finance with the Poor, by the Poor, for the Poor: Financial Technologies for the Informal Sector, With Case Studies from Indonesia," *Social Strategies* (Basel), 3(2), 1989, pp. 3–47.

Seibel, Hans D. *Indonesia, IFAD Country Programme Evaluation.* Working Paper Rural Finance. Rome: IFAD, 2003.

Seibel, Hans D. *Islamic Microfinance in Indonesia.* Sector Project Financial Systems Development, Deutsche Gesellschaft für TechnischeZusammenarbeit (GTZ), Easchborn & Jakarta, January 2005a, 124pp. www.gtz.de/de/dokumente/en-islamic-mf-indonesia.pdf.pdf.

Seibel, Hans D. *Reconstruction and Development of the Microfinance System in Nanggroe Aceh Darussalam (NAD), Indonesia.* Cologne: GTZ, 2005b.

Seibel, Hans D. "Islamic Microfinance: The Challenge of Institutional Diversity," ICMIF Takaful, No. 12, October 2007. http://www.kantakji.com/fiqh/Files/Insurance/D315.pdf.

Seibel, Hans D. "Islamic Microfinance in Indonesia: The Challenge of Institutional Diversity, Regulation, and Supervision," *Journal of Social Issues in Southeast Asia*, 23(1), April 2008, pp. 86–103.

Seibel, Hans D. *Restructuring of State-owned Financial Institutions: Lessons from Bank Rakyat Indonesia.* Manila: Asia Development Bank, 2009. http://www.adb.org/Documents/Books/Restructuring-Financial-Institutions/.

Seibel, Hans D. and Agung, W.D. "Islamic Microfinance in Indonesia." Cologne: University of Cologne, Development Research Center, 2006.

Shah, A. "Poverty Facts and Causes: Causes of Poverty," 2006. http://www.globalissues.org/TradeRelated/Facts.asp#fact1.

Shehabuddin, Elora. "Contesting the Illicit: Gender and Politics of Fatwas in Bangladesh," *Signs*, Summer 1999.

Srinivasan, N. *Microfinance India State of the Sector Report 2009.* New Delhi: Sage Publications India Pvt Ltd, 2009.

Steinwand, D. *The Alchemy of Microfinance.* Berlin: FWF, 2001.

Stiglitz, Joseph E. "Peer Monitoring and Credit Market," *World Bank Economic Review*, 4(3), 1999, pp. 351–366.

Sullivan, N. *You Can Hear Me Now: How Microloans and Cell Phones Are Connecting the Poor to the Global Economy.* San Francisco: Jossey-Bass, 2007.

Suwailem, Sami. "Hedging in Islamic Finance," Islamic Development Bank: Islamic Research and Training Institute, 2007, pp. 131–135.

Tarek, Z.S. and Kabir, H.M. "A Comparative Literature Survey of Islamic Finance and Banking," *Financial Markets, Institutions & Instruments. New York University Salomon Center*, 10(4), 2001, p. 155.

Timberg, Thomas A. *Islamic Banking in Indonesia.* Jakarta: USAID, 1999.

Timberg, Thomas A. *Islamic Banking and its Potential Impact. Paving the Way Forward for Rural Finance: An International Conference.* Jakarta: USAID and WOCCU, 2003.

Townsend, R.M. "Microcredit and Mechanism Design," *Journal of the European Economic Association,* 1(2–3), April 2003, pp. 468–477.

Trofimov, Y. "Malaysia Transforms Rules for Finance under Islam: In a Lesson to Arabs, Asian Bankers Mix Religion, Modernity." *The Wall Street Journal,* April 4, 2007.

Tsai, K.S. Imperfect Substitutes: The Local Political Economy of Informal Finance and Microfinance in Rural China and India," *World Development,* 32(9), 2004, pp. 1487–1507.

Usmani, M.T. *An Introduction to Islamic Finance.* The Hague: Kluwer Law International, 2000a, 248pp.

Usmani, M.T. *An Introduction to Islamic Finance.* Karachi: Idaratul Ma'arifa, 2000b, 246pp.

Usmani, M.T. *An Introduction to Islamic Finance.* Washington, DC: CQ Press. http://www.muftitaqiusmani.com/images/stories/downloads/pdf/an%20introduction%20to%20islamic%20finance.pdf.

Usmani, M. T. "Musharakah & Mudarabah." *Islamic Finance,* 2004. http://www.muftitaqiusmani.com/images/stories/downloads/pdf/an%20introduction%20to%20islamic%20finance.pdf.

Utama, Iman Budi. *Baitul Qiradh: Reconstructing Islamic Cooperatives in Aceh, Indonesia.* Jakarta: GTZ, 2005.

Vogel, R. "Savings Mobilization: The Forgotten Half of Rural Finance," in D.G.D. Adams, *Undermining Rural Development with Cheap Credit.* Boulder, CO: Westview Press, 1984, pp. 248–265.

Wilson, Rodney. "Screening Criteria for Islamic Equity Funds," in Sohail Jaffer (Editor), *Islamic Asset Management: Forming the Future for Shariah Compliant Investment Strategies.* London: Euromoney Books, 2004, 45pp.

Wilson, Rodney. "Making Development Assistance Sustainable Through Islamic Microfinance." IIUM *International Conference on Islamic Banking & Finance,* Kuala Lumpur, Malaysia, April 2007.

Wisniwski, S. *Microsavings Compared to Other Sources of Funds.* Eschborn: CGAP, 1999.

World Bank. Access Finance Newsletter Issue No. 8 (November 2005). http://siteresources.worldbank.org/INTACCESSFINANCE/64187549-1131655269330/20737909/Mahajan.pdf.

World Bank. *Employment and Development of Small Enterprises.* Sector Policy Paper, World Bank, Washington, DC, 1978.

World Bank/IFC Report. *The Next 4 Billion: Market Size and Business Strategy at the Base of the Pyramid.* http://rru.worldbank.org/features/thenext4billion.aspx.

Worth, R.F. "Rising Inflation Prompts Unease in Middle East." The *New York Times,* February 25, 2008.

Wright, G. *A Critical Review of Savings Services in Africa and Elsewhere.* Nairobi: MicroSave, 1999.

Yaron, Jacob. "Performance of Development Finance Institutions: How to Access It?" in Hartmut Schneider (Editor), *Microfinance for the Poor?* Paris: OECD, 1997.

Yasni, M.G. and Winarni, E.S. "The Role of *Kafalah* in Improving the Safety of Micro and Medium Sized Enterprises Financing," *The First International Conference on Inclusive Islamic Financial Sector Development: Enhancing Islamic Financial Services For Micro and Medium Sized Enterprises (MMEs),* Darussalam, 2008.

Yunus, M. Nobel Lecture at the Oslo City Hall, Norway, December 10, 2006a. Transcript available at http://nobelprize.org/nobel_prizes/peace/laureates/2006/yunus-lecture-en.html.

Yunus, M. "What is Microcredit?," 2006b.

Yunus, M. "Creating a World Without Poverty: Social Business and the Future of Capitalism," 2007.

Yunus, M. "Each of You Has the Power to Change the World," Boston: Lecture at MIT, June 6, 2008.

Zaheer, K. "A Critical Look at the Alternatives to the Popular Models of Interest Free (IF) Banking," *Renaissance*, May–June 1996.

Zaheer, K. "Condemnation of Concentration of Wealth," *Renaissance*, October 2001.

El-Zahi, A. "The X-Efficiency of Sudanese Islamic Banks (1989–98)," International Islamic University, Malaysia, unpublished Ph.D. thesis, 2002.

Zaman, H. *Assessing the Impact of Micro-Credit on Poverty and Vulnerability in Bangladesh*, World Bank Working Paper, 1999. http://ideas.repec.org/p/wbk/wbrwps/2145.html.

Zander, R. "Integrating the Poor into the Rural Financial Mainstream: Issues and Options," in Hartmut Schneider (Editor), *Microfinance for the Poor?* Paris: OECD, 1997.

Zarka, M.A. "Leveraging Philanthropy: Monetary *Waqf* for Microfinance," paper presented at *Financing the Poor: Toward an Islamic Microfinance*. Cambridge, MA: Islamic Finance Project, Harvard Law School, 2007.

Zawya Sukuk Monitor. *Sukuk Quarterly Bulletin: Issue 7 – 3Q10*. Online, Zawya, 2010. http://ae.zawya.com/researchreports/zr/20101001_zr_102240.pdf.

Index

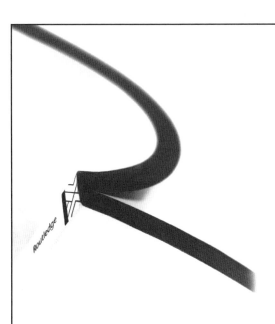